*Ph. Schuyler*

THE

# LIFE AND TIMES

OF

# PHILIP SCHUYLER

BY

BENSON J. LOSSING, LL.D.

VOL. I.

NEW YORK:
SHELDON & COMPANY, 677 BROADWAY,
AND 214 & 216 MERCER ST.

Stereotyped by Smith & McDougal, 82 Beekman St., N. Y.

TO

GEORGE LEE SCHUYLER, Esq.,

A GRANDSON OF GENERAL SCHUYLER,

THESE VOLUMES ARE DEDICATED

IN TOKEN OF GRATEFUL APPRECIATION OF HIS GENEROUS

AID IN THE PRESENTATION OF THEM

TO THE PUBLIC, BY

THE AUTHOR.

# PREFACE.

Of all the prominent men in public life in America during the last half of the eighteenth century, not one so really distinguished for important services as General Schuyler has received so little attention from the essayist, the historian, or the biographer, as he. His name is familiar to all who possess even a superficial knowledge of his country's annals, and yet, to all, the details of his career in civil and military life are unknown. His figure, as drawn by the historian's pen, is seen in bold relief, in detached pictures illustrative of his country's history from the dawn of the birth-day of the Republic until the firm establishment of government under the federal constitution; but the really more important phases of his useful life are hidden or but imperfectly apprehended.

General Schuyler's career was not brilliant but eminently useful. He was one of those men who often work noiselessly but efficiently; whose labors form the bases of great performances; who lay the foundations and modestly assist in building the structures of law, government, morals, and philosophy, which give true glory to a state, and who rest contented, when the labor is over, with the reward of conscious merit as benefactors of mankind, indifferent to that popular applause which follows the enunciation of startling opinions, or the performance of brilliant services.

No man was ever more keenly alive to the influence of just censure or praise than General Schuyler; and yet no man ever felt less concern than he about the verdict of the popular feeling of the hour. Conscious of unswerving rectitude and fidelity, he was ever perfectly willing to submit his character and motives to the analysis of dispassionate posterity.

General Schuyler did not leave behind him any autobiography, in the form of a diary or a narrative of his career. Of his early life we have very little knowledge, except such as is preserved in family traditions and passages in the public records. Hitherto no biography of him has been written. Many years ago the late Chancellor Kent wrote a brief memoir of him, which occupies a few pages in the American Portrait Gallery. It is general and necessarily meager. More recently the late Mr. Irving, and also the author of this work, in their respective elaborate biographies of Washington, have given many new and interesting details of General Schuyler's military life; and his grandson, John C. Hamilton, Esq., in his work entitled "History of the Republic of the United States of America, as traced in the Writings of Alexander Hamilton and his Cotemporaries," has given much more information concerning Schuyler's civil life than had ever before been published. With these exceptions, very little has hitherto been written concerning the subject of these volumes.

This biography of General Schuyler has been constructed with much labor and care, from family traditions and records, the public documents and records of the country, printed and in manuscript, authentic histories of his times, and his own correspondence. The latter, evidently somewhat imperfect, but still voluminous, commences with the period when the old War for Independence was kindling, and extends to the day of his death, in 1804. It is in the form of manuscript letter books on his part, and autograph letters on the part of his correspondents. The former are contained in several large volumes; the latter comprise several thousand loose sheets of paper, all carefully filed and endorsed by Schuyler. These, for many years after his death, were neglected, and became somewhat scattered. Many letters have been lost, and some have been given away as autographs.

To Mr. and Mrs. George L. Schuyler, of Dobbs' Ferry, New York (the former a grandson of General Schuyler), the world is indebted for the collection and preservation of all that are left of the papers of General Schuyler. Having, a few years ago, expressed to them a desire to prepare a biography of their illustrious ancestor, they readily offered me the free use of the materials in their possession. I have examined every paper carefully, and have endeavored to make judicious use of the matter placed in my hands, in the preparation of a history of the "Life and Times of Philip Schuyler," in two moderate sized volumes, adapted to popular use.

With these few prefatory remarks, the work is submitted to the public.

B. J. L.

THE RIDGE, September, 1872.

# CONTENTS.

## CHAPTER I.

PAGE

Beverwyck, or Ancient Albany.—The Patroons of Rensselaerwyck.—Their Agent and Governor Stuyvesant.—A Row in Albany.—Philip Pietersen Schuyler in the Affray.—He marries the Daughter of Van Rensselaer's Agent.—Her Character.—Their Son Peter becomes first Mayor of Albany.—Their Son John the Grandfather of General Schuyler.—His Expeditions against the French.—Peter takes Indian Chiefs to England.—John sent on a Mission to Canada.—Influence of the Schuyler Family over the Indians.—Philip Schuyler's Family.—His Birth........................ 17

## CHAPTER II.

Social and Political Aspect of New York, at the Time of Philip Schuyler's Birth.—Prevalence of Democratic Ideas.—Birth of Representative Government in New York.—Toleration of the Dutch.—The Iroquois Confederacy.—Their Intercourse with the Dutch, and its Results.—Charter of Liberties.—Jacob Leisler.—The Liberty of the Press asserted and vindicated in the Person of John Peter Zenger.—Growth of Albany.—Society there.—Peculiarities of Social and Domestic Life.—Hunting and Trading Excursions... 27

## CHAPTER III.

Young Schuyler left in the Care of his Mother.—Her Firmness illustrated.—Expected War with the French.—Frontiers of New York and New England exposed.—Albany included in every Scheme of Invasion.—Effect of current Excitement on young Schuyler's Mind.—Siege and Capture of Louisburg.—Effects of British Injustice on the Colonists.—Providential Dispersion of a French Fleet.—Upper Valley of the Hudson desolated.—Saratoga Destroyed.—Murder of Colonel Schuyler.—Excitement throughout the Colony.—Political Affairs.—William Johnson made Indian Commissioner.—Preparations for War.—Council with Indians at Albany.—Peace of Aix-la-Chapelle.—The War a School for American Patriots...... 47

## CHAPTER IV.

Young Schuler's earlier Instructors.—Neglect of Education.—List of University Graduates in the Province.—Young Schuyler at a Huguenot School in New Rochelle.—His Sufferings from Hereditary Gout.—On a Hunting and Trading Excursion in the Wilderness.—His Defense of the Indians from Fraud.—Their Reverence for Him and his Family exhibited.—Character of the People of New York City.—Young Schuyler's Letter respecting his first Evening at a Theater.—Schools, Newspapers, and Libraries in New York City.—Religious Divisions and Churches.—Religious Controversies.—The Independent Reflector.—Excitement in the Colonies.—Material Aspects of New York.................................. 62

## CHAPTER V.

PAGE

Schuyler's Marriage to Catherine Van Rensselaer. — Her Character.—Schuyler's Personal Appearance at that Time.—Mrs. Grant's Description of the Household and Domestic arrangements of "Aunt Schuyler."—Charming Life-Pictures of Society.—Schuyler's Estate.—His noble Generosity.—War with the French and Indians .................................. 82

## CHAPTER VI.

The Treaty of Aix-la-Chapelle only a Truce.—Disagreement about Boundaries.—French Ambition.—The Ohio Company and their Land Grant.—The French in the Ohio Valley.—Forts built in the Wilderness.—Young Washington sent on a Mission to French Officers.—Its Result.—Preparations for Hostilities.—Virginians in the Field.—Other Colonies Tardy.—Troops march from Alexandria for the Ohio.—Fort Du Quesne.—Washington's Encounter with his Enemy at Fort Necessity.—His Defeat.—Colonial Convention at Albany.—Its Action and Results.—Proposed Plan of Union rejected.—Arrival of General Braddock.—Plan of the Campaign of 1755.—New York Politics.—Preparations for defending the Northern Frontiers. — Schuyler Authorized to raise a Company, and Commissioned a Captain ........................................ 93

## CHAPTER VII.

Troops at Albany.–Expedition against Ticonderoga, under General Johnson.—Schuyler in the Field.—General Lyman builds Fort Edward.—Troops March for Lake George.—Desolation of Acadie by the New Englanders.—Braddock's unfortunate Expedition.—Failure of Expedition against Niagara.—The Provincial Army at Lake George.—Approach of French and Indians under Dieskau.—Defeat of Colonel Williams.—Death of Williams and King Hendrick.—Attack upon Johnson's Camp.—The French Repulsed.—Dieskau badly Wounded.— Pursuit not Allowed.— Johnson builds Fort William Henry.—Is Knighted.—His Meanness.—Captain Schuyler's Nuptials.—Dieskau in Albany.—Hospitably treated by Schuyler's Family.—Dieskau's Letter to Schuyler .................................... 111

## CHAPTER VIII.

Shirley's Plan for the Campaign of 1756.—Loudoun a weak and indolent Man succeeds Shirley as Commander-in-chief.— England declares War against France.—Abercrombie, Loudoun's Lieutenant, at Albany.—Bradstreet's Expedition to Oswego.—Encounter with and Repulse of the French on the Oswego river.—Generous Conduct of Captain Schuyler.—Montcalm at Ticonderoga.—His Expedition against Oswego.—Captures and demolishes the Forts.—Loudoun's Irritating conduct in New York.—Indians Smitten at Kittanning.—Captain Schuyler leaves the Service.—Is frequently Consulted.—Loudoun's Plans condemned and his Inefficiency deplored.—Weakness of the British Cabinet.—Expedition against Louisburg defeated by Loudoun's Tardiness.—Montcalm captures Fort William Henry.—Bad Conduct of General Webb.—Pitt called to the Head of Public Affairs.—His Efficiency and Popularity.—Plans a vigorous Campaign.—His Liberality Responded to.—Abercrombie in Chief Command.—Capture of Louisburg.—Expedition against Quebec abandoned ....................... 127

## CHAPTER IX.

PAGE

Captain Schuyler and Lord Howe.—Schuyler promoted to Major and joins the Army.—Lord Howe's Character and Services.—Expedition against Ticonderoga.—Passage of the Army over Lake George.—The French Outposts Surprised.—Skirmish in the Forest.—Lord Howe Killed.—Attack on Ticonderoga.—The British repulsed with great Loss, and Retreat to the Head of Lake George.—Captain Schuyler conveys Lord Howe to Albany for Interment.—Curious Phenomenon.—Bradstreet's Expedition against Fort Frontenac.—Schuyler at Oswego.—Capture of Frontenac.—Fort Stanwix.—Expedition against Fort Du Quesne.—Incidents of the Expedition.—The Fort abandoned.—French Pride humbled .... .............. 145

## CHAPTER X.

Final Struggle between the French and English for the Mastery in America.—Pitt's Scheme for conquering all Canada.—Amherst in chief Command.—Campaign of 1759.—Advance upon Ticonderoga.—Capture of Fort Niagara by the British.—Schuyler forwards Supplies to the Army under Amherst.—The French flee from Lake Champlain.—Wolfe before Quebec.—The City Taken.—Death of Wolfe and Montcalm.—Unsuccessful Attempt to recover Quebec.—Montreal taken by the British.—Capture of Detroit. 162

## CHAPTER XI.

Colonel Bradstreet commits his Private Affairs to Schuyler.—Schuyler goes to England to settle Bradstreet's public Accounts.—Stirring Incidents of his Voyage.—Performs his Duties and Returns.—Affairs in England.—Lord Stirling.—Commercial Restrictions.—Unaided Struggles of the Colonies.—Political Affairs in England.—Writs of Assistance and their Fruits.—James Otis on the Subject.—Political Affairs in New York.—Question of Church and State revived.—Schuyler on the Side of the People.—Affairs in the West Indies.—The British Arms successful.—Financial Condition of France.—Treaty of Paris.—Indian War in the Southwest.—Pontiac's Conspiracy and Defeat.................................... 179

## CHAPTER XII.

Schuyler in Civil Employment.—Proprietor of large Tracts of Land.—Correspondence with Professor Brande of London.—Land Schemes.—Obstacles in the Way of Emigration.—Boundary Disputes.—Schuyler a Commissioner to settle them.—Stirring Scenes in the New Hampshire Grants.—Hostile Collisions.—Schuyler an active Participant in the Disputes.—The Stamp Act.—Violent Opposition to it.—Stamp Act congress in New York.—Riots.—Repeal of the Act.—Rejoicings.—Statues voted to the King and Pitt.—The Declaratory Act and its Effect on the Americans.—The New York Assembly and the Governor at Variance.—Offensive Parliamentary Acts.—Letters of a Pennsylvania Farmer.......................................... 196

## CHAPTER XIII.

PAGE

Schuyler an Active but Conservative Politician.—A welcome Guest in New York.—Participates in the Rejoicings there on the Repeal of the Stamp Act.—Is intimate with Governor Sir Henry Moore.—Their Families visit each other.—Is engaged in the Commissary Department.—Raises a Regiment and is Commissioned a Colonel.—Aids the Boundary Commissioners.—His Country-seat at Saratoga.—Correspondence with Professor Brande.—Establishes a Flax-mill at Saratoga.—Elected a Member of the Colonial Assembly.—Embassy of Southern Indians to Sir William Johnson.—Colonel Schuyler a leading Republican in the new Assembly.—Blow aimed at Free Discussion.—Action of Massachusetts and New York Assemblies.—Troops in Boston.—Non-importation Leagues.......................................... 214

## CHAPTER XIV.

Schuyler a Leader in the assembly.—Riots in New York.—Address to the Governor written by Schuyler.—Its Loyalty and Independence.—Translation of the Dutch Records of Albany.—The Governor officially offended by bold Resolutions of the Assembly.—He Dissolves the Assembly.—Troubles in New York.—Schuyler's Relations with Sir William Johnson and Governor Moore.—His Vigilance and Activity as a Legislator.—His Immigration Scheme.—The Indian Trade.—Schuyler's Attempt to purify Legislation.—Events in Massachusetts, Virginia, and other Provinces.—The British Ministry baffled.—Effects of Non-importation Leagues....... 230

## CHAPTER XV.

Death of Governor Moore.—Colden his Successor.—Schuyler banquets with the Sons of Liberty in New York. — Coalition between Colden and De Lancey.—A Deceptive Financial Scheme.—Public Alarm.—Great Meeting in the Open Air.—An offensive Placard pronounced a Libel by the Assembly.—Schuyler alone, in that Body, stands by the People.—He nominates Edward Burke for the Agency of New York.—McDougal Imprisoned as the Author of the Libelous Placard. — Popular Enthusiasm in his Favor.—Loyalist Party gain Ascendency in the Assembly.—Affrays in New York.– The "Boston Massacre."—Political Changes in New York.—Lord Dunmore Governor.—Abject Address of the Assembly deplored by Schuyler and his Friends.—Schuyler disabled by Gout.—New Hampshire Grants.—Ethan Allen and his Movements.—Schuyler in the Disaffected Assembly of 1772.—Difficulty between Him and Henry Van Schaack.—Governor Tryon and his Land Speculations.—Schuyler's Scheme for preventing Counterfeiting.—He submits a Statement of "The just Rights of New York," in the Matter in Dispute with the New Hampshire Grants.—It offends the New England People........................................... 245

## CHAPTER XVI.

Schuyler proposed for a Judge in Charlotte County.—Lord North's Scheme in Relation to Tea.—East India Company send Tea to America.—The Tea sent back or destroyed.—"Boston Tea Party."—Firmness of the Sons of Liberty in New York.—Schuyler confined with the Gout.—Parties in New York.—Committee of Correspondence appointed by the Assembly.—Depar-

PAGE

TURE OF GOVERNOR TRYON FOR ENGLAND.—RETALIATORY MEASURES OF PARLIAMENT.—GREAT EXCITEMENT IN AMERICA.—THE REVOLUTION KINDLING.—MINUTE MEN.—THE BOSTON PORT BILL, AND ITS RESULTS.—EXCITEMENT IN NEW YORK.—PUBLIC PROCEEDINGS THERE. — CONTINENTAL CONGRESS PROPOSED. — "GREAT MEETING IN THE FIELDS."—ALEXANDER HAMILTON.—EFFECT OF HIS ORATORY.—SCHUYLER'S HEALTH COMPELS HIM TO DECLINE A SEAT IN THE CONTINENTAL CONGRESS........ 266

## CHAPTER XVII.

THE FIRST CONTINENTAL CONGRESS.—ITS MEASURES.—ADJOURNS CONDITIONALLY.—THE COLONIES IN A BLAZE OF EXCITEMENT.—POLITICAL CORRESPONDENCE BETWEEN COUNCILOR SMITH AND SCHUYLER.—EFFORTS OF LOYALISTS AGAINST THE REPUBLICANS. — SCHUYLER IN NEW YORK. — DEATH OF GENERAL BRADSTREET. — SCHUYLER'S FRIENDLY SERVICES IN BEHALF OF HIS FAMILY.—SCHUYLER THE ACKNOWLEDGED LEADER IN THE ASSEMBLY.—TESTS OF THE POLITICAL CHARACTER OF THE ASSEMBLY.—REJOICINGS OF LOYALISTS.—EFFORTS OF SCHUYLER AND HIS FRIENDS TO PROCURE A VOTE OF THE ASSEMBLY, APPROVING THE ACTION OF THE CONGRESS.—HIS AMENDMENTS TO OBSEQUIOUS RESOLUTIONS OF THE ASSEMBLY.—FINAL ADJOURNMENT OF THE ASSEMBLY.—REVOLUTIONARY MOVEMENTS IN NEW YORK AND BOSTON.— BLINDNESS OF THE BRITISH PARLIAMENT.— GAGE SENDS TROOPS FROM BOSTON TO SEIZE ARMS AND STORES.—SKIRMISHES AT LEXINGTON AND CONCORD.—THE WAR FOR INDEPENDENCE BEGUN........ 285

## CHAPTER XVIII.

THE PEOPLE IN CONVENTION, IN NEW YORK, APPOINT DELEGATES TO THE CONTINENTAL CONGRESS.—COLONEL SCHUYLER IN THE CONVENTION.—HE IS CHOSEN A REPRESENTATIVE IN THE CONGRESS.—AT SARATOGA WHEN THE NEWS OF THE AFFAIR AT LEXINGTON AND CONCORD REACHED HIM.—HIS LETTER TO JOHN CRUGER.—THE AFFECTION AND CONFIDENCE OF HIS NEIGHBORS.—NEW YORK PROVINCIAL CONGRESS.—REVOLUTIONARY MOVEMENTS IN ALL THE COLONIES.—SEIZURE OF TICONDEROGA AND CROWN POINT BY THE REPUBLICANS.—THE GREEN MOUNTAIN BOYS.—BAD CONDUCT OF BENEDICT ARNOLD.—THE SECOND CONTINENTAL CONGRESS.—COLONEL SCHUYLER IN THAT BODY.—ACTION OF THE CONGRESS.—CAUTIOUS PROCEEDINGS RELATIVE TO THE LAKE CHAMPLAIN FORTS.—POLITICAL ASPECT OF NEW YORK.—ALLIANCE OF CANADA DESIRED.—SCHUYLER RECOMMENDED BY THE NEW YORK PROVINCIAL CONGRESS AS MAJOR-GENERAL. — PLANS FOR AN AMERICAN GOVERNMENT........ 304

## CHAPTER XIX.

LORD NORTH'S CONCILIATORY BILL REJECTED AS DECEPTIVE.—WAR SPIRIT IN THE GENERAL CONGRESS, AND AMONG THE PEOPLE.—A REPUBLICAN ARMY AT BOSTON.—CONFIDENCE OF THE BRITISH OFFICERS.—BATTLE OF BUNKER'S HILL.—WASHINGTON APPOINTED COMMANDER-IN-CHIEF OF THE CONTINENTAL ARMY.—SCHUYLER CHOSEN THE SECOND MAJOR-GENERAL.—EMISSION OF PAPER MONEY.—SCHUYLER ACCOMPANIES WASHINGTON TO NEW YORK.—RECEPTION OF THE COMMANDER-IN-CHIEF THERE. — A DILEMMA.—WASHINGTON'S INSTRUCTIONS TO SCHUYLER.—SCHUYLER LEAVES HIS GENERAL AT NEW ROCHELLE —HE ENTERS UPON HIS DUTIES AS COMMANDER-IN-CHIEF OF THE NORTHERN DEPARTMENT.—THE CANADIANS APPEALED TO.—PROPOSITION TO INVADE CANADA REJECTED.—OPERATIONS ON LAKE CHAMPLAIN.—CONNECTICUT TROOPS SENT TO LAKE CHAMPLAIN.—OPERATIONS OF BENEDICT ARNOLD.—ALLEN IN THE NEW YORK ASSEMBLY.—PREPARATIONS TO INVADE CANADA........ 323

## CHAPTER XX.

PAGE

Schuyler leaves New York for the North.—His Letter to General Wooster on that Occasion.—Schuyler's Public Reception at Albany.—The Future Dark and Unpromising.—Bad Influence of the Johnson Family over the Indians.—The Indians Uneasy.—Unhappy State of Affairs at Ticonderoga.—The quarrelsome Benedict Arnold the chief Cause of Trouble there.—He leaves the Lake in Anger.—Startling Intelligence from the Mohawk Valley.—Guy Johnson among the Indians.—His Letter to the New York Provincial Congress.—Commissioners for Indian Affairs appointed by the Continental Congress.—Schuyler at the Head of it.—Indians employed by the British.—Schuyler's Labors and Responsibilities.—Washington Sympathizes with Him.—Organization of the Green Mountain Boys.—Allen Repudiated by them, and Acts as a Volunteer.—Major Brown employed as a Scout in Canada.......................................................... 345

## CHAPTER XXI.

Scarcity of Provisions in the Northern Army.—Schuyler's Efforts to produce Supplies.—Jealousies among the Troops.—Schuyler's trouble with the Commissaries.—He Rebukes them Severely.—Schuyler as a Military Commander.—Cause of Ill-will toward Him.—Intelligence from Canada makes Schuyler Impatient to move forward.—Difficulty in raising Men for the Service.—New York Troops.—Dr. Franklin sends Powder to Schuyler.—Arnold proposed as Adjutant-General of the Nothern Army.—Letters of Duer and Deane on the Subject.—Deane's Appeal in Behalf of Arnold.... 369

## CHAPTER XXII.

Schuyler at a Council with the Indians at Albany.—General Montgomery left in Command of the Northern Army.—Movements of the Indians.—The Conference.—Address of the Continental Congress to the Indians.—Results of the Council.—Troubles in the Mohawk Valley.—Sir John Johnson and his Influence.—Sheriff White.—Schuyler hastens to Ticonderoga.—Montgomery moves down the Lake with a Part of the Army.—Character of Montgomery.—Schuyler is taken Sick.—Difficulty with the Indians settled.—He overtakes the Army at Isle la Motte.—Schuyler's Address to the Canadians.—Allen and Brown sent among the Canadians with it................ 386

## CHAPTER XXIII.

The Army at Isle aux Noix.—Preparations to attack St. John's.—The Troops move forward.—A Skirmish.—False Information given to Schuyler.—The Army withdraws to Isle aux Noix.—Anxiety of the Continental Congress for the Invasion of Canada.—Public and Private Letters to Schuyler.—The Troops again sent forward to Attack St. John's.—Schuyler extremely Ill.—Bad Conduct of some of the Troops.—Return to Isle aux Noix.—Schuyler compelled to Return to Ticonderoga.—His timely Services there save the Army.—Montgomery besieges St. John's.—Insubordination of the Troops.......................................................................... 408

## CHAPTER XXIV.

PAGE

Attempt to Capture Montreal.—Colonel Allen made a Prisoner and sent to England.—His Boldness before his Captors.—Inhumanly treated by the British.—His Imprudence caused Difficulties.—Montgomery Distressed by the Bad Conduct of his Troops.—His generous Loyalty to his Country.—Schuyler seriously Ill at Ticonderoga.—He is Distressed by the Conduct of the Troops there.—The Fidelity of Schuyler and Montgomery.—A Deceptive Treaty.—Capture of Chamblee.—First Colors taken in the War, sent to the Continental Congress, by Schuyler.... 417

## CHAPTER XXV.

The Seige of St. John's pressed Vigorously.—Schuyler has unpleasant Experiences with Wooster.—He is Warned of coming Trouble.—The Congress aware of it, take Measures accordingly.—Letter of Mr. Bedford.—Bad Conduct of some of Wooster's Troops at Ticonderoga.—Wooster courteously received by Schuyler. — His satisfactory Declarations to Schuyler.—Wooster's Conduct not in accordance with his Professions.—Correspondence.—Action of the Connecticut Assembly.—Schuyler tortured by Disease and Disappointment.—An Injudicious Letter.—Wooster joins Montgomery.—The British repulsed at two Points on the St. Lawrence.—St. John's Surrenders to Montgomery.—The Spoils of Victory.... 433

## CHAPTER XXVI.

Arnold's Expedition to Quebec through the Wilderness.—His Ambition gratified by his Appointment to the Command of it.—His Instructions from Washington.—Incidents of the Expedition.— Arrival at the French Settlements.—The Expedition opposite Quebec.—Alarm of the Town and Garrison.—Montgomery marches upon Montreal.—Reluctance of his Troops to go.—Carleton Abandons the Town and flees to Quebec.—Montgomery takes Possession of Montreal.—His Welcome Reception.—Carleton's Flotilla Captured.—Escape of Carleton.—Montgomery anxiously desires to proceed to Quebec.... 448

## CHAPTER XXVII.

New England Troops refuse to go to Quebec.—Great Homesickness among them.—Large Numbers Discharged by Schuyler at Ticonderoga.—Washington's Trouble with his Troops at Boston.—Schuyler's Rebuke of Inhumanity.—Montgomery distressed by Insubordination.—A Turbulent and Mutinous Spirit in the Army.—Dilatoriousness of the Congress.—Montgomery resolves to Leave the Army at the Close of the Campaign.—Schuyler's continued Ill Health.—He Returns to Albany.—Conference with some Indians there.—A Glance at Schuyler's Services.—His Justice and Truthfulness.—General Wooster's Inefficency suspected.—Schuyler desires to Retire from the Service.—Congress and Washington Appeal to Him.—He Consents to Remain.... 465

## CHAPTER XXVIII.

PAGE

JOY BECAUSE OF MONTGOMERY'S SUCCESSES.—HIS NEED AND LACK OF SUPPLIES.—HE ASSUMES RESPONSIBILITIES FOR THE GOOD OF THE SERVICE.—ARNOLD CROSSES THE ST. LAWRENCE AND APPEARS BEFORE QUEBEC.—HIS OPERATIONS BEFORE THE CITY.—DEMAND FOR SURRENDER, TREATED WITH CONTEMPT.—HE WITHDRAWS TO POINT AUX TREMBLES.—MONTGOMERY LEAVES MONTREAL FOR QUEBEC.—HIS PLANS FOR CONQUEST.—HE JOINS ARNOLD AT POINT AUX TREMBLES, AND CLOTHES AND ADDRESSES HIS TROOPS.—THE COMBINED FORCES BEFORE QUEBEC.—MONTGOMERY'S FLAG OF TRUCE, FIRED UPON.—HIS INDIGNATION.—PREPARES FOR AN ASSAULT.—CARLETON WOULD HOLD NO COMMUNICATION WITH HIM.—AN ICE BATTERY CONSTRUCTED AND DEMOLISHED.—TROUBLE AMONG ARNOLD'S OFFICERS.—SUCCESS OF THE EXPEDITION THEREBY PERILLED.—HARD MONEY NEEDED.—FUTILE EFFORTS IN THE RECRUITING SERVICE.......................................................... 478

## CHAPTER XXIX.

MONTGOMERY SURROUNDED WITH DIFFICULTIES.—LAYS A PLAN OF ATTACK BEFORE A COUNCIL OF OFFICERS.—DIFFICULTIES WITH SOME OF ARNOLD'S OFFICERS.—MONTGOMERY'S LAST LETTER TO SCHUYLER.—PLAN OF ATTACK AGREED UPON.—ATTEMPTS TO CARRY IT INTO EFFECT.—THE ARMY IN TWO DIVISIONS.—MONTGOMERY LEADS ONE ALONG THE ST. LAWRENCE.—HIS HOPEFULNESS AND BRAVERY.—HIS DEATH AND REPULSE OF HIS TROOPS.—MCPHERSON AND CHEESMAN.—ARNOLD LEADS THE OTHER DIVISION.—HE IS WOUNDED.—MORGAN IN COMMAND.—DESPERATE ENCOUNTER.—CAPTURE OF DEARBORN.—THE AMERICANS MADE PRISONERS.—DISPOSITION OF THE TROOPS.—EFFECTS OF MONTGOMERY'S DEATH.—PROCEEDINGS IN RELATION TO IT.—SCENE IN THE BRITISH PARLIAMENT.................................. 493

# LIFE AND TIMES

OF

# PHILIP SCHUYLER.

---

## CHAPTER I.

About thirty years after Albany, the capital of the State of New York, was founded by the erection of Fort Orange upon its site, and half that length of time before the English conquest gave new masters to the province and new names to the principal settlements, a serious disturbance occurred in the little village that had grown up along the bank of the Hudson, near that earliest regular fortification erected by the Dutch in America. At that time, Beverwyck,* as the village around Fort Orange was called, contained about one hundred houses, seated along a single street in regular line, with gardens between, and here and there a stray one upon the slope whereon broad State street now reposes. Around these, in a figure of septangular form, were palisades for defense against the savages or other foes; and in due time several minor fortifications, holding allegiance to Fort Orange, were interlinked by these defenses.

* The Mohegan name of Albany was *Pem-po-ta-wuth-ut*, or "place of fire"—a council ground.

North of Albany was the seat of the *Patroon* of Rensselaerwyck, called the *Colonie*, where the representatives of the lord of that superb manor that stretched along the Mauritius, as the Hudson river was then called, north and south, east and west from Fort Orange, over an area of almost a thousand square miles, assumed an independence of the servants of the Dutch West India Company, by whom the purchase of this large domain from the Indians had been confirmed.* That assumed independence, and the petty tyranny of the *Commissary*, as the commander of Fort Orange was called, became, in the course of time, productive of bitter blood.

Killian Van Rensselaer, the first Patroon, and lord of this manor, never came to America. Johannes, his son and heir, likewise never saw the noble domain of which he was proprietor. The management of the great estate was entrusted to agents. When Killian died, Johannes was a minor, and his uncle, Van Wyley, and Wouter Van Twiller, who had been to America previously to examine the lands in the neighborhood of Fort Orange, became his guardians. Brant Arent Van Slechtenhorst, of Niewkerke, in Guilderland, was commissioned Director of the *Colonie*, President of the Court of Justice, and immediate manager of the whole estate of the *Patroon*. He came over with his family in 1647, the same year when Peter Stuyvesant arrived at New Amsterdam as governor or director-general of the province. Being an energetic man, full of loyalty

* For the purpose of encouraging emigration to New Netherland, the Dutch West India Company offered, in 1620, large tracts of land and certain privileges to those persons who should lead or send a given number of emigrants to occupy and till the soil. The land was to be fairly purchased of the Indians, and the title was to be confirmed by the Company. The proprietors were called *patroons*, (patrons,) and held a high political and social station in the New World.

to his young master, and inspired with that Dutch spirit of independence that was born centuries before among the Batavian marshes, he became a practical rival in authority, not only of the *Commissary* at Fort Orange, but of Stuyvesant himself.

From the first attempt to plant patroon colonies in New Netherland, the directors of the Amsterdam chamber of the West India Company had been jealous of them, and Stuyvesant, and his immediate predecessors in office, used every fair means to wipe out those already in existence. Two of them were purchased of the grantees, but neither money, threats, nor persuasions could induce the proprietors of Rensselaerwyck to relinquish that princely estate. The company therefore determined to weaken a power which they could not suppress by purchase, and Governor Stuyvesant and Commissioner Van Slechtenhorst became obstinate champions of rival interests. The former claimed general jurisdiction over the whole province; the latter acknowledged no authority within the domains of Rensselaerwyck outside of Fort Orange, except that of the *Patroon* himself.

For three years the quarrel went on, when a call for a subsidy from Rensselaerwyck, made by Governor Stuyvesant, produced a crisis. Commissioner Van Slechtenhorst went to New Amsterdam to remonstrate with the governor. Both were equally unyielding, and high words ensued at their separation. As it was the custom of Peter the Headstrong to use the logic of physical force against an opponent when oral argument failed, he caused Van Slechtenhorst to be visited that day, before he had finished his dinner, by an officer charged to bring him before the director-general and council. By these he was immediately condemned as an unruly subject, and when he asked

"Can a man be condemned unheard?" he was answered by an arrest. He was detained four months on Manhattan Island, when he escaped in a sloop and returned to the *Colonie.* At about that time Jean Baptiste Van Rensselaer, the first of that name who came to America, appeared at Beverwyck, and was elected one of the magistrates. Very soon after this, an order was issued, requiring all the freemen and other inhabitants to take the oath of allegiance to the *Patroon* and his representative.

The disturbance alluded to now occurred. On New Year's night, 1652, some soldiers, armed with match-locks, issued from the fort and fired several shots at the *Patroon's* house. The reed-covered roof was ignited by the burning gun-wads, and for a while the mansion was in imminent peril. Hard words passed between the soldiers and the friends of the *Patroon;* and on the following day a son of Commissioner Van Slechtenhorst was assailed in the street by some of the former, badly beaten, and dragged through the mud, while Johannes Dyckman, the West India Company's commissary at Fort Orange, stood by and encouraged them, saying, "Let him have it now, and the devil take him!" Young Van Slechtenhorst found a champion in Philip Pietersen Schuyler, a spirited young gentleman from Amsterdam, who, a little more than a year before had married the victim's sister Margaret. Young Schuyler endeavored to save his brother-in-law, when Dyckman drew his sword and threatened to run him through. A general fracas ensued, but ended without serious bloodshed.

Here we will leave the actors in this quarrel, the events and results of which are recorded in history. Nor will we further display the chronicles of the manor and of the province. The curtain has been thus slightly lifted from the interesting picture of the past, that a glimpse might be had of the first of the Schuyler family who appeared in America, the lineal ancestor of the one whose character and services will be portrayed in the pages that follow.

Of the antecedents of Philip Pietersen Schuyler, who first appears in history in the famous quarrel at Beverwyck, we have no positive knowledge. We only know that he came to the New World from Amsterdam, in Holland, in the year 1650. Tradition says that his family were merchants in that old city, were connected with the West India Company, and had a country seat near Dordrecht. Ancient pieces of silver plate, with the family arms* and year marks engraved on them, yet in possession of some of the descendants of Van Slechtenhorst's son-in-law, attest the opulence of the family previous to the appearance of Philip Pietersen in America.

The marriage of young Schuyler and Margaret Van Slechtenhorst was celebrated at Rensselaerwyck on the 12th of December, 1650. The nuptial rites were performed by Anthony de Hooges, the Secretary of the *Colonie*, in the presence of the officers of Fort Orange, the magnates of Rensselaerwyck, and of some of the principal inhabitants. These were the ancestors of the Schuyler family in America.

* The arms of the Schuyler family are as follows: ESCUTCHEON *argent*, a falcon *sable*, hooded *gules*, beaked and membered *or*, perched upon the sinister hand of the falconer, issued from the dexter side of the shield. The arm clothed *azure*, surmounted by a helmet of steel, standing in profile, open-faced, three bars *or*, lined *gules*, bordered, flowered and studded *or*, and ornamented with its lambrequins *argent* lined *sable*. CREST—out of a wreath, *argent* and *sable*, a falcon of the shield.

In the original genealogical record of the family in the Dutch language, the name of the first emigrant, who arrived in 1650, is written Philip Pietersen Von Schuyler, which may be translated Philip, son of Peter, from Schuyler. No doubt the latter was the name of the place where the family resided, and had been recently adopted as a surname, as it is not found as such in the records of Holland at that time.

Margaret Van Slechtenhorst was two-and-twenty years of age when she married young Schuyler, and ten children were the fruitful results of their union.* She lived sixty years after her nuptials, and survived her husband more than a quarter of a century. She possessed great energy of character and independence of spirit, like her father ; and after her husband's death her wealth and position enabled her to exercise a controlling influence in public affairs at Albany. In 1689 she advanced funds to pay troops at Albany; and it is asserted that toward the close of that year she made a personal assault upon Milborne, the son-in-law of Jacob Leisler, (the usurper, as he was called, of political power at New York,) when he came to Albany to assume command of the fort, then under charge of her second son Peter, the eminent mayor of that city, and commander of the militia in the northern department of the province.

Peter inherited the talents and virtues of his parents, and for many years was one of the most prominent men in the province. He was mayor of Albany from 1686 until 1694, and was the first chosen chief magistrate of that city after its incorporation in 1683, the year before his father died.† In 1688 he was commissioned major of the militia, and toward the close of the following year he was placed in command of the fort at Albany. It was about that time that Milborne went up with some armed men to take Schuyler's place, but the latter, aided by some Mohawk

* These were Guysbert, Gertrude, (who married Stephanus Van Cortlandt,) Alida, (who married, first, Reverend Nicholas Van Rensselaer, and second, Robert Livingston, the first lord of the manor of Livingston, on the Hudson,) Pieter, Brant, Arent, Sybilla, Philip, Johannes, and Margretta.—*From Dutch Genealogical Manuscript, translated by S. Alofsen, Esq.*

† Philip Pietersen Schuyler died on the 9th of March, 1684, and was buried, on the 11th of the same month, in the ancient Dutch Church at Albany, that stood in the center of State street at the intersection of Broadway. His will bears date "Tuesday evening, May 1, 1683."—*Dutch Manuscript.*

Indians who were in the neighborhood, successfully resisted his pretensions. Over the Mohawks, the most noble of the nations of the Iroquois confederation, Peter Schuyler then had almost unbounded control ; and until that league was broken, and the nations had dwindled to a few hundreds in the State of New York, at the close of the last century, the Schuyler family had no competitors in influence and friendship with those sons of the forest except Sir William Johnson. They always treated the Indian as a brother and friend, dealt honorably with him, and never deceived him in word or deed.

John, the youngest brother of Major Schuyler, was an active young man at this time ; athletic, brave, and full of military aspirations. He was the paternal grandfather of General Philip Schuyler. When, in February, 1690, a party of French and Indians came from the north, and at midnight set fire to Schenectada, and butchered the unsuspecting inhabitants, the vengeance of this young man was powerfully stirred, and he sought and obtained the command of a small force of white people and Indians, with which to penetrate the country of the enemy on the borders of the St. Lawrence. He was then only twenty-two years of age. He received a captain's commission, and in August he set out "with twenty-nine Christians, and one hundred and twenty savages," whom he recruited at the foot of Lake Champlain "to go to Canada to fight the enemy." They went down the Lake in canoes, penetrated to Laprairie, destroyed considerable property, took quite a number of prisoners, and returned with little loss, after an absence of seventeen days. The journal of this expedition, kept by Captain Schuyler, reveals the fact that the elk deer were very abundant in northern New York at that time. They have now entirely disappeared.

In June, the following year, Major Peter Schuyler led a small force into Canada. It consisted of "Christians, 120; Mohawques, 80; R. (River or Mohegan) Indians, 66."* They followed the route taken by Captain Schuyler, went down the Sorel or Richelieu to the rapids above Chamblée, and penetrated to Laprairie. A Mohawk deserter left the camp near Chamblée, and informed the French of the approach of the invaders. The latter were thus prepared for the reception of the former, and well defended their fort at Laprairie. After several skirmishes, the expedition returned to Albany toward the close of August, with a loss of nineteen white men and savages. "Thought by all," says Major Schuyler, in his journal, "to have killed about two hundred French and Indians."†

From this time the two brothers were engaged almost continually in public life. The former became first a member, and then President of his Majesty's Council for the Province of New York. For a short time he was acting governor of the colony, and for many years he was chief commissioner for Indian affairs. In 1710 he went to England with four Indian chiefs, who were representatives of four nations that composed the Iroquois confederacy. These, and the nations they represented, were much attached to Schuyler, whom they familiarly called "Brother Queder." They were taken to Britain for a twofold purpose: First, to have these heads of the tribes impressed with the greatness of the English nation, and thereby detach the wavering ones from the French interest; and, Secondly, to arouse the British government to the necessity of assisting the Americans in expelling the French from Canada, whose

* Major Schuyler's "*Journal of the Expedition.*"

† Colden, in his "*History of the Five Nations,*" says the French lost two captains, six lieutenants, and three hundred men.

hostility to the English colonists, and whose influence over the savage tribes were daily increasing. Colonel Schuyler bore an address to Queen Anne from the Colonial Assembly of New York, and he and his confederate "kings," as they were called, were treated with distinuished honor.*

Captain John Schuyler, meanwhile, was serving his country faithfully in both civil and military employments. In September, 1698, Governor Bellomont sent him to Canada with a message to Count Frontenac, respecting the designs of the latter toward the Five Nations and the English. He visited Quebec and Montreal; "felt the pulse" of the Indians on his journey; made careful observations of the strength and condition of the French, and gave the governor of Canada an exalted idea of the great military power which the Earl of Bellomont might command—"One hundred thousand men, rather more than less," he said. This mission was successful, and in May, the following year, he and John Bleecker were appointed commissioners to hold a general council with the Five Nations at Onondaga Castle. He was an Indian commissioner for a great many years, and his name appears frequently in the colonial records of the period between 1701 and 1730 as one of the most active of the servants of the government in keeping the Iroquois in alliance with the English. He was chosen to a seat in the Colonial Assembly in 1705, and held that position until 1713. From that time until the kindling of our old war for independence, the name of Schuyler appears almost continually among those of the representatives of the people in the legislature of the province of New York.

Captain John Schuyler was married to Elizabeth Staats,

* For an interesting account of this embassy, see Drake's *Book of the Indians.*

widow of John Wendell, in April, 1695. The ceremony was performed by Dominie Dellius, minister of the Dutch Church at Albany. In that church they were buried, the wife in 1737, and the husband ten years afterward. Their eldest son, JOHN, was born early in the autumn of 1697, and was baptized on the 31st of October, when Robert Livingston, Jacob Staats, (the child's uncles by marriage,) and his aunt, Maria Schuyler, who held him in her arms, were the sponsors. Being the eldest son, he was heir-expectant to the real estate of his father, which, before his death, became large in amount, he having purchased several valuable tracts from the Indians in the vicinity of Albany, and in the Mohawk country.

This son of the active Captain Schuyler does not appear prominent in history. He married his cousin Cornelia, youngest child of Stephen Van Cortlandt, of New York, by whom he had reasonable expectations of considerable wealth, that aristocratic Dutch family then ranking among the most opulent in the province. He appears to have lived the quiet life of a gentleman of leisure. He died in 1741, six years before his father's death, and was buried in the little family cemetery of Colonel Peter Schuyler, at *The Flats*, (now Watervliet,) as the place of that gentleman's residence was called. He left five small children, his eldest son, PHILIP, the subject of this memoir, being only eight years of age. PHILIP was born at the family mansion in Albany, on the 20th of November, 1733, and, like Dr. Franklin, was baptized on the day of his birth.

## CHAPTER II.

At the period of Philip Schuyler's birth, the political and social aspect of the province of New York was peculiar and interesting. The atmosphere of free thought and action, composed of the congenial ingredients of the spirit of barbaric life in the neighboring forests, a traditional and inherent hatred of oppression and undue restraint, and a sense of equality of condition that had for a hundred years more and more distinguished the inhabitants of the province, nurtured into strength and activity, in his youth and early manhood, those physical and mental qualities which gave him preëminence during a long and eventful life.

Democracy in its broadest and purest sense—the idea of civil government lodged in the hands of the people—found in the province of New York a most congenial soil for its germination, efflorescence and fruitage. The seed was wafted across the Atlantic by gales of persecution, from almost every land in western Europe, where the rights of conscience had been assailed—where the sanctities of private life and the shrine of the spirit had been invaded. These found lodgment and took root upon the shores of the broad and beautiful bay of New York, (then New Amsterdam,) while Dutch power, tempered with that divine toleration which had made Holland an asylum for the persecuted, bore rule in New Netherland.

And when the wicked Kieft, in his perplexity and fear, unintentionally called the elements of representative government into actual activity by asking the heads of twelve families to sit in council with him concerning a war with the Indians, which his unrighteousness had provoked, the inhabitants of that province presented a truly sublime spectacle. The Hollanders and Swedes upon Manhattan and in Nova Cæsarea, the Waldenses upon Staten Island, and the Walloons and English upon Long Island, who had found in these forest regions a sure refuge from persecution, lived in harmony and sweet accord, unmindful of the diversity of creeds that shaped the forms of their worship of Almighty God. From the vineyards of France, from the sunny valleys of Piedmont, from the picturesque banks of the Rhine, from stormy England—stormy in fact and figure—and from the sterile soil and intolerant spirit of the Pilgrim land on the shores of Massachusetts Bay, refugees soon came, and the wise and generous Hollanders who held the sceptre of governmental power gave all a hearty welcome, nor questioned them concerning the secrets between man and his Maker. "The government favored no curious inquiry into the faith of any man," but considered that an expressed desire for citizenship implied a willingness to take a solemn oath of allegiance to the commonwealth, and that oath was the only test. When it was once taken, the allegiance carried with it all the sanctions of a sacrament; and citizenship, as in some other colonial communities, did not rest chiefly nor at all upon particular church membership.

Such was the broad base upon which rested a commercial and cosmopolitan republic in the New World, seated at the open door to a vast inland trade and future civilization; while another republic, greater in numerical strength, physical force, and breadth of domain and influence flourished deep in the interior. That republic was the Iroquois confederacy of five nations of Indians, whose origin must be sought among the primitive people of the earth, and whose league was formed long before Cavalier and Puritan, Hollander and Huguenot, inspired the free air of the western continent. They called themselves *Aquanuschioni*—"united people," and they claimed to have sprung from the soil on which they dwelt, like the trees of the wilderness.*

With these people the early settlers of New Netherland, and for a hundred years the Schuyler family in particular, had much to do as traders in peace, and as allies or as enemies in war. In their political arrangements they exhibited features in common with the Hollanders. Their confederacy was composed of separate independent communities, having distinct municipal laws, like the United Provinces of Holland, and no one nation held a preëminent position in the constitution of the league. They were originally five republics, confederated for mutual defense and conquest, and they were known as the Five Nations until they were joined by the Tuscaroras, a community of Southern Iroquois, who were expelled from the Carolinas early in the last century. Then they became the SIX NATIONS, whose history is closely interwoven with that of New York and Pennsylvania for three quarters of a century. They were called respectively Mohawks, Oneidas, Onondagas, Cayugas, Senecas and Tuscaroras; and each nation was divided into three tribes, distinguished by separate

* *Iroquois* is a purely French word, composed, however, of the Indian expressions *Hiro* and *Koné*. The former, signifying "I have said it," was used at the close of every speech made by the Indians to the discoverers of the St. Lawrence; the latter expresses the sound of a cry of joy or other emotion. So the French called these tribes with whom they became first acquainted *Hiro-Koné*, and the name was written IROQUOIS.—*Charlevoix.*

TOTEMS, or heraldic insignia representing the animals after which the separate families were named.

The SIX NATIONS fancifully called their confederacy the Long House. The eastern door was kept by the Mohawks, the western by the Senecas, and the great council fire was with the Onondagas, at the federal metropolis or chief village, near the present city of Syracuse. Each tribe was governed by its own sachem or civil head, whose position and authority depended wholly upon his ability and faithfulness, in the opinion of his people. They were warlike, and yet agriculture was so extensively practiced, especially among the Senecas, that the confederacy was sometimes called *Konoshioni*—" cabin builders." They had a war-path along the borders of the Alleghany mountains, and by this they made military excursions to the distant domains of the Catawbas and Cherokees, in the beautiful upper country of the South, and caused the fierce Shawnees of the Ohio valley to tremble. They made hostile expeditions against the New England Indians on the east, and the Eries, Andastes, and Miamis on the West; and when the Dutch began the settlement of New Netherland, all the Indians on Long Island and the northern shore of the Sound, and on the banks of the Connecticut, Hudson, Delaware and Susquehanna rivers, were tributaries and in subjection to the Five Nations. At the same time they inhabited villages, cultivated extensive fields and orchards, and traded far and near with the French and English.

The Iroquois possessed an exalted spirit of liberty, and they spurned with disdain every foreign or domestic shackle of control. Almost a hundred years before Jefferson wrote the Declaration of Independence, GARANGULA, a venerable Onondaga sachem, said to the governor-general of Canada, who had menaced the league with distruction, " WE ARE

BORN FREE. We neither depend on *Yonondio* nor *Corlear.* We may go *where* we please, and carry with us *whom* we please, and buy and sell *what* we please."*

Such were the people with whom the Dutch settlers in the interior of New Netherland were brought into immediate contact; and from the hour when the latter established a trading house at Albany, or Beverwyck, to the close of the old war for independence, the Six Nations occupy a large space in the history of the province. And from the reign of William and Mary until far into that of George the Third, the name of Schuyler appears prominent among Indian commissioners, for that family were peerless in their influence over the dusky tribes of New York, except when Sir William Johnson ruled like a nabob in the Mohawk valley.

The innate love of freedom possessed by the Dutch, and its practical illustrations in the daily life of the Mohawks, who held continual intercourse with the settlers at Albany, made the idea of democracy a fixed principle in the minds and hearts of those settlers and their posterity. For twenty years after the change from Dutch to English rule they had felt the unrelenting heel of oppression. Then they were made glad by the presentation of a CHARTER OF LIBERTIES, by the liberal minded Dongan, by which they were allowed to adopt a Declaration of Rights, establish a representative government, and fearlessly assert the great

* Drake's *Book of the Indians.* YONONDIO was the name they gave to the governors of Canada; and they called those of New York CORLEAR, in honor of a humane Dutchman of that name, who lived at Schenectada, and was greatly beloved by the Mohawks. Because of kind services rendered, the governor of Canada invited him to his capital. On his way Corlear was drowned in Lake Champlain. For a long time the Indians, in memory of their friend, called it Corlear's Lake, and in their speeches and treaties designated the governor of New York by the title of "Corlear."

doctrine of the Revolution, that led to independence almost a hundred years later, that TAXATION AND REPRESENTATION ARE INSEPARABLE. They were steadfast in their support of the principles of popular sovereignty represented by Jacob Leisler, when the mongrel aristocracy of New York city pursued him with scorn, malice and falsehood, and murdered him upon the scaffold. And five-and-forty years later there was great joy among the Dutch throughout the province when, two years after Philip Schuyler was born, the liberty of the press was vindicated by the triumphant acquittal of John Peter Zenger, the publisher of a democratic newspaper, who was tried for a libel because he had spoken the truth in his *Journal* concerning the English governor and public affairs.

That trial, which took place in the summer of 1735, was the commencement of a stormy period of forty years in the political history of New York, during which time the opposing elements of democracy and aristocracy contended vigorously for ascendancy in the social and religious life of the province. From the departure of Cornbury until the arrival of Colonel Cosby, in 1732, the royal representatives, six in number, unable or unwilling to resist the will of the people, as expressed by the popular assembly, allowed democratic principles to grow and flourish. When Cosby arrived they had taken deep root in the popular heart, for Rip Van Dam, an honest Dutch merchant, "the man of the people"—who for thirteen months after the death of Montgomerie had been acting governor of the province, by virtue of his senior membership in the council, encouraged and fostered its growth.

Between Van Dam and Cosby there was no affinity, and they soon quarreled. Two violent parties arose—as violent, perhaps, as the Liesler and anti-Leisler parties—

namely, the Democratic, which sided with Van Dam, and the Aristocratic, which supported the governor. Each party had the control of a newspaper, and the war of words raged violently for a long time. The governor, unable to compete successfully with his opponents, ordered Zenger, the publisher of the Democratic paper, to be arrested on a charge of libel. He was cast into prison and confined there for thirty-five weeks, when he was tried by a jury, was nobly defended by the eminent Andrew Hamilton of Philadelphia, and was acquitted.

This verdict was greeted with applause by a great majority of the people, and the magistrates of New York presented the freedom of the city, in a gold box, to Mr. Hamilton, "for his learned and generous defense of the rights of mankind and the liberty of the press." Thus was distinctly drawn the line of demarcation between the Republicans and Loyalists—the Whigs and Tories—in the province of New York, which appeared prominent until the war for independence was closed in 1783. That verdict gave immense strength to republican principles, not only in New York, but throughout the Anglo-American colonies, for sagacious men saw in the liberty of the press the wings of free thought plumed for a wide and glorious flight. "The trial of Zenger in 1735," said Gouverneur Morris to Dr. John W. Francis, "was the germ of American freedom—the morning star of that liberty which subsequently revolutionized America."

It was in the midst of the contentions of these political parties, and the excitement caused by the hostile attitude of the French in Canada and in the east, that the youth and early manhood of Philip Schuyler were passed; and as he belonged to, and was connected by blood and marriage with most of the wealthier and more influential families in the province, he must have been early impressed by the current disputes which agitated society, and stirred by desires to participate in the active scenes of public life.

During the earlier years of Philip Schuyler's life, society at Albany was favorable to the development of every good and noble quality in its members. It was more purely Dutch than at New York, and had not yet become contaminated by the presence of troops and the general introduction of artificial manners and extravagant habits. That ancient town, in the course of a century, had gradually expanded from a trading post and hamlet to quite a stately inland city of three hundred and fifty houses, with its mayor, and recorder, and aldermen, and representatives in the colonial Legislature. It had two houses of worship, one in which the English, and the other the Dutch language was used. It was next in size and wealth to New York, then containing eight times as many buildings, and a mixed commercial population, rapidly increasing in wealth and importance.

The houses in Albany were very neat within and without. They were built chiefly of stone or brick, and covered with white pine shingles, or tiles from Holland. Most of them had terraced gables fronting the street, with gutters extending from the eaves beyond the side-walks to carry off the rain water. "These," says Kalm, the Swedish naturalist, who visited Albany in 1748, "preserve the walls from being damaged by the rain; but it is extremely disagreeable for the people in the streets, there being hardly any means of avoiding the water from the gutters." On that account the streets were almost impassable during a storm of wind and rain.

The streets were broad, and some of them were paved, and lined with shade trees. In proportion to its population, the town occupied a large space of ground. Every house had its garden and pleasant grass plat in the rear, bearing fruit and vegetables in abundance. Before every door a tree was planted, which was often interesting as a memento of the birth of some beloved member of the family. Some of these had now reached a great size, and they were of almost every variety suitable to the climate. These formed agreeable shade for the porches or "stoops," which were elevated a little above the street and furnished with spacious seats. "It was in these," says Mrs. Grant, of Laggan,* "that each domestic group was seated in summer evenings to enjoy the balmy twilight or the serenely clear moonlight. Each family had a cow, fed in a common pasture at the end of the town. In the evening the herd returned altogether, of their own accord, with their tinkling bells hung at their necks, along the wide and grassy street to their wonted sheltering trees, to be milked at their masters' doors. Nothing could be more pleasing to a simple and benevolent mind than to see thus, at one view, all the inhabitants of a town, which contained not one very rich or very poor, very knowing or very ignorant, very rude or very polished individual—to see all these

* Mrs. Grant was the daughter of Duncan McVickar, a Scotch officer in the British army, who came to America when his child was an infant. He remained in the service here until she was thirteen years of age. During the last years of their residence in America, she was much among the Schuylers and Van Rensselaers at Albany and its vicinity. Every thing made a deep impression on her mind, and under the title of "*Memoirs of an American Lady*" she has given charming sketches of society at Albany before the Revolution.

She afterward married Mr. Grant, a young chaplain in the army, and resided many years at Laggan. She is generally known as "Mrs. Grant of Laggan," to distinguish her from her cotemporary, Mrs. Grant of Carron. Mrs. Grant's volume, from which we quote, was published in 1808. She has fallen into many errors respecting the names and relationship of the Schuyler family, and in that particular her book is wholly unreliable. But her sketches of life and character are faithful.

children of nature enjoying in easy indolence or social intercourse,

'The cool, the fragrant, and the dusky hour,'

clothed in the plainest habits, and with minds as undisguised and artless. These primitive beings were dispersed in porches, grouped according to similarity of years and inclinations. At one door were young matrons, at another the elders of the people, at a third the youths and maidens, gayly chatting or singing together, while the children played round the trees, or waited by the cows for the chief ingredient of their frugal supper, which they generally ate sitting on the steps in the open air."*

There the gossip of either sex, who delights in retailing slander or idle talk from house to house was unknown, for intercourse was so free, and open hearted friendship so prevalent, that there was no aliment for the sustenance, nor a sphere of action for such a creature. And the politician proper, whose dogmatism is so offensive, seldom disturbed these social gatherings. These, even so late as the beginning of the present century, took their pipes and chairs every pleasant afternoon, and, seating themselves in the Market House, settled, in their respective opinions, the nature and tendency of the public affairs of the colony and of the realm.

In Albany, at certain times, the gayety of a colonial court would appear. That was when the governor of the province, with his secretary and others, ascended the Hudson and visited the city to hold conferences with the chiefs and sachems of one or more of the Six Nations. On these occasions the Van Rensselaers, the Schuylers, the Wessels, the Tenbroecks, the Lansings, the Staats', the Bleeckers,

* *Memoirs of an American Lady.*

the Ten Eycks, and other leading families, kept open house, and the most generous hospitality prevailed. Balls, parties, and simple amusements of every kind then known, were interspersed with the proceedings of grave conferences with stately savages, while the governer remained.

There, too, at the close of the hunting season, the Indians were seen coming by scores, with the spoils of the forests and the inland waters ; for at that time there was no place in the British colonies, except the Hudson's Bay settlements, where such quantities of furs and skins were bought of the Indians as at Albany. The merchants or their clerks spent the whole summer at Oswego, on Lake Ontario, the chief trading place in the Indian country ; and the dusky hunters and trappers would frequently come from the banks of the St. Lawrence and beyond, laden with beaver skins belonging to themselves or to French traders, notwithstanding a heavy penalty was incurred by carrying furs from Canada to the English settlements. This intercourse between vigorous, sinewy, barbaric rudeness, rugged as the gnarled oak, and a beautiful, simple civilization, untouched by the rheum or the canker of luxurious life, acting and reäcting upon each, gave strength and force to one, and tenderness and polish to the other, and thus worked in salutary harmony.

Notwithstanding there was great equality in Albany society, there was a peculiar custom prevalent until near the time of the kindling of the Revolution, which appeared somewhat exclusive in its character. The young people were arranged in congenial companies, composed of an equal number of both sexes. Children from five to eight years of age were admitted into these companies, and the association continued until maturity. Each company was generally under a sort of control by authority lodged in the hands of a boy and girl, who happened to possess some natural preeminence in size or ability. They met frequently, enjoyed amusements together, grew up to maturity with a perfect knowledge of each other, and the results, in general, were happy and suitable marriages. In the season of early flowers, they all went out together to gather the gaudy blossoms of the May apple ; and in August they went together to the forests on the neighboring hills to gather whortleberries, or later still, to pluck the rich clusters of the wild grape, each being furnished with a light basket made by the expert Indian women.

Each member of a company was permitted to entertain all the rest on his or her birthday, on which occasion the elders of the family were bound to be absent, leaving only a faithful servant to have a general supervision of affairs, and to prepare the entertainment. This gave the young people entire freedom, and they enjoyed it to the fullest extent. They generally met at four o'clock in the afternoon, and separated at nine or ten in the evening. On these occasions there would be ample provisions of tea, chocolate, fresh and preserved fruits, nuts, cakes, cider and syllabub.

These early and exclusive intimacies naturally ripened into pure and lasting friendships and affectionate attachments, and happy marriages resulted. So universal was the practice of forming unions for life among the members of these circles, that it came to be considered a kind of apostacy to marry out of one's "company." Love, thus born in the atmosphere of innocence and candor, and nourished by similarity of education, tastes, and aspirations, seldom lost any of its vitality ; and inconstancy and indifference among married couples were so rare as to be almost unheard of exceptions to a general rule. They usually married early, were blessed with high physical and mental health, and the extreme love which they bore to their offspring made those parents ever dear to each other under the discipline of every possible vicissitude. The children were reared in great simplicity ; and except being taught to love and adore the great Author of their being and their blessings, they were permitted to follow the dictates of their nature, ranging at full liberty in the open air, covered in summer with a light and cheap garment, which protected them from the sun, and in winter with warm clothing, made according to the dictates of convenience, comfort and health.

The summer amusements of the young were simple, healthful and joyous. Their principal pleasure consisted in what we now call *pic-nics*, enjoyed either upon the beautiful islands in the river near Albany, which were then covered with grass and shrubbery, tall trees and clustering vines, or in the forests on the hills. When the warm days of spring and early summer appeared, a company of young men and maidens would set out at sunrise in a canoe for the islands, or in light wagons for "the bush," where they would frequently meet a similar party on the same delightful errand. Each maiden, taught from early childhood to be industrious, would take her work basket with her, and a supply of tea, sugar, coffee, and other materials for a frugal breakfast, while the young men carried some rum and dried fruit to make a light cool punch for a mid-day beverage. But no previous preparations were made for dinner except bread and cold pastry, it being expected that the young men would bring an ample supply of game and fish from the woods and the waters, provisions having been made by the girls of apparatus for cooking, the use of which was familiar to them all. After dinner the company would pair off in couples, according to attachments and affinities, sometimes brothers and sisters together, and sometimes warm friends or ardent lovers, and stroll in all directions, gathering wild strawberries or other fruit in summer, and plucking the abundant flowers, to be arranged into boquets to adorn their little parlors and give pleasure to their parents. Sometimes they would remain abroad until sunset, and take tea in the open air ; or they would call upon some friend on their way home, and partake of a light evening meal. In all this there appeared no conventional restraints upon the innocent inclinations of nature. The day was always remembered as one of pure enjoyment, without the passage of a single cloud of regret.

The winter amusements in Albany were few and simple, but, like those of summer, pure, healthful, and invigorating. On fine winter days the icy bosom of the Hudson would be alive with skaters of both sexes, and vocal with their merry laugh and joyous songs and ringing shouts ; and down the broad and winding road from the verge of Pinkster Hill, whereon the State capitol now reposes, scores of sleighs might be seen every brilliant moonlight evening, coursing with ruddy voyagers—boys and girls, young men and maidens—who swept past the Dutch Church at the foot, and halted only on the banks of the river. It was a most animating scene, and many a fair spectator would sit or stand on the margin of the slope until ten or eleven o'clock, wrapped in furs, to enjoy the spectacle.

Evening parties, the company seldom numbering over a dozen, were quite frequent. These were often the sequels of quilting parties ; and *princktums*, games, simple dances and other amusements were indulged in, but never continued very late. The young men sometimes spent an evening in conviviality at one of the two taverns in the town, and sometimes their boisterous mirth would disturb the quiet city at a late hour. Habitual drunkenness, however, was extremely rare, and these outbreaks were winked at as comparatively harmless.

Among these people the slavery of Africans was so softened by gentleness and mutual attachments, that it appeared truly patriarchal, and a real blessing to the negroes. It was a most beautiful example of the relations of master and servant as they should be—each interested in the comfort and welfare of the other. They stood in the relative position of friends, and the freedom of speech and action that existed between them was that of intimate companions rather than that of a superior and inferior. "I have nowhere," says an eye witness of society there at the time we are considering, "I have nowhere met with instances of friendship more tender and generous than that which here subsisted between the slaves and their masters and mistresses. The slave has been known, in the course of hunting or of Indian trading, at the imminent risk of his life, to carry the disabled master through unfrequented wilds with labor and fidelity scarce credible; and the master has been equally tender, on similar occasions, of the humble friend who stuck closer than a brother; who was baptized with the same baptism, nurtured under the same roof, and often rocked in the same cradle with himself."

The influence of the negro women was often very great in the families of their masters, especially those who were faithful and were truly beloved; and they sometimes exerted quite as much authority over the children as the parents themselves. They were uniformly faithful and true; and in their case slavery, aside from the abstract principle involved, was a happy lot.

The religion of the Albanians was a clear perception

and recognition of the duties and privileges of responsible and dependant creatures, and the overruling providence of a just and loving Father Supreme; and none appeared to doubt the great truths of revelation and the doctrines of Jesus of Nazareth. Their piety, based upon this religion, was more emotional than demonstrative, for they seldom evinced fervor or enthusiasm in their devotions. Their religious observances were performed regularly and quietly, and bigotry and asceticism found no dwelling-place among them. While they were firm in their own belief they were extremely tolerant, even to the extent of practical indifference. Their piety was a prevailing sentiment, manifested in their entire every-day life by an exemplary walk and conversation; and mothers were the principal religious teachers of the children.

Industry and frugality ranked among the cardinal domestic virtues of this exemplary community. The females were peculiarly active in household duties, and spent much time in the open air, in both town and country. Every family had a garden, and after it was broken up by the plough or spade in the spring, this became the exclusive domain of woman, in which no man's hand was seen as a cultivator. In these every kind of vegetable for the table, and flower to please the eye, known in the colony, was cultivated with skill and care by her delicate hands; and it was a common thing to see, before sunrise on a warm spring morning, the mistress of a family, in simple dress, with an umbrageous calèche on her head, carrying in one hand a little Indian basket with seeds, and in the other a rake or hoe, to perform her garden work. Half the day or more these fair gardeners, perhaps beautiful in form, gentle in manner, and refined in thought and conversation, would ply the implements of husbandry, winning healthful vigor for mind and muscle from the needful exercise, the fresh earth, the breath of plants and flowers, and the pure air. Most of the gardens were plain and arranged in beds, part of them devoted to edible plants and part to flowers. The Schuylers, and one or two other families in the city and vicinity, and Van Rensselaer, the Patroon, on the northern border, had very large gardens, laid out in fanciful European style; and among the beautiful flowers and fragrant shrubs the females of these families might be daily seen, not as idle loiterers, but as willing and industrious workers.

In their houses the women were extremely neat. "They rise early," says Kalm, "go to sleep late, and are almost over nice and cleanly in regard to the floor, which is frequently scoured several times in the week." Tea had been but recently introduced among them, but was extensively used; coffee, seldom. They never put sugar and milk in their tea, but took a small piece of the former in their mouths while sipping the beverage. They usually breakfasted at seven, dined at twelve or one, and supped at six; and most of them used sweet milk or buttermilk at every meal. They also used cheese at breakfast and dinner, grated instead of sliced; and the usual drink of the majority of the people was small beer and pure water. The wealthier families, although not indulging in the variety then seen upon tables in New York, used much fish, flesh, and fowl, preserves and pastry, nuts and fruits, and various wines at their meals, especially when entertaining their friends or strangers. Their hospitality toward deserving strangers was free and generous, without formality and rules of etiquette; and they never allowed their visitors to interfere with the necessary duties of the household, the counting-room, or the farm.

Trading, trafficking, and hunting formed the chief business at Albany. The young men generally accompanied their elders on long trading and hunting excursions in the interior until they arrived at a marriageable age, or were resolved on matrimony. Then the *boy*, as all were called until after marriage, began to consider the new responsibilities he was about to assume, and receiving from his father an outfit consisting of forty or fifty dollars, a negro boy, and a canoe, he would start for the wilderness north and west, arrayed almost like the sons of the forest. His stock in trade generally consisted of coarse fabrics, blankets, guns, powder, lead, rum, and trinkets suitable for the taste and wants of the Indians. Their food provided for the excursion was only a little dried beef and maize, for they depended for more ample supplies for daily consumption upon the fowling-piece and the fishing-hook. They slept in the open air in the depths of the forests, where bears, wolves, and panthers were numerous, or in poisonous fens, where the malaria and the serpent threatened them with death, and insects annoyed. Prone to observation, they became expert in knowledge of trees, shrubs, plants and soils, and many a young hunter and trader gained, during those excursions, that practical knowledge of the topography and soil of the virgin country which enabled him to select desirable tracts of land for purchase, and to become a wealthy proprietor of broad domains in after years.

Generally successful, the trader returned with plentiful winnings, which pleased the parents of the maid he loved, and became the foundation of his fortune. His aspect and character would be much modified. "It is utterly inconceivable," says Mrs. Grant, "how even a single season spent in this manner ripened the mind and changed the whole appearance, nay, the very character of the countenances of these demi-savages, for such they seem on returning from among their friends in the forests. Lofty, sedate and collected, they seem masters of themselves and independent of others; though sunburnt and austere, one scarcely knows them till they unbend. By this Indian likeness I do not think them by any means degraded. One must have seen those people (the Indians) to have any idea what a noble animal man is while unsophisticated.

"The joy that the return of these youths occasioned was proportioned to the anxiety their perilous journey had produced. In some instances the union of the lovers immediately took place, before the next career of gainful hardships commenced. But the more cautious went to New York in winter, disposed of their peltry, purchased a larger cargo of Indian goods, and another slave and canoe. The next year they laid out the profits of their former adventures in flour and provisions, the staple of the province; this they disposed of at the Bermuda Islands, where they generally purchased one of those light-sailing cedar schooners, for building of which those islanders are famous, and proceeding to the Leeward Islands, loaded it with a cargo of rum, sugar and molasses. They were now ripened into men, and considered as active and useful members of society.

"The young adventurer had generally finished this process by the time he was one or (at most) two and twenty. He now married, or if married before, which was pretty often the case, brought home his wife to a house of his own. Either he kept his schooner, and, loading her with produce, sailed up and down the river all summer, and all winter disposed of the cargoes he obtained in exchange to more distant settlers, or he sold her, purchased European goods, and kept a store. Otherwise he settled in the country, and became as diligent in his agricultural pursuits as if he had never known any other."*

Such is a brief outline of the character and condition of the society in which Philip Schuyler was nurtured for the active duties of life. Frankness, generosity, patriotism, rectitude, sobriety, and others of the sterner Christian virtues, were lessons imparted by the every-day life of his people ; and from these he learned that divine maxim of truth, manifested in the lineaments of his own character during a long life, that goodness is the soul of greatness.

* *Memoirs of an American Lady*

# CHAPTER III.

The father of Philip Schuyler died in the autumn of 1741, and was interred at The Flats, (now Watervliet,) in the family burying-place of his cousin, Colonel Philip Schuyler, son of the eminent first mayor of Albany. Philip was then only eight years of age, and was the eldest of five children that were left to the care of their mother. Their grandfather, Captain John Schuyler, was seventy-three years old, and enfeebled by the severe labors he had performed and the hardships he had endured in military life on the frontier and as Indian commissioner. The entire duties of guardian and guide for the orphans were therefore laid upon the mother, Cornelia Van Cortlandt Schuyler, a person of superior excellence, and then in the prime of early womanhood.

According to the English laws of primogeniture, Philip inherited all of the large real estate of his father, and upon him the hopes of the family were naturally suspended. His mother, fully equal to the responsibilities imposed upon her, and sensible of the importance of the trust committed to her keeping, trained him with anxious care and solicitude, and was rewarded at every step by earnest filial affection, displays of great goodness of heart, and promises of an honorable career.

Mrs. Schuyler was an indulgent mother, but a firm disciplinarian, and she never allowed her authority to be questioned by her children. Philip frequently mentioned an illustrative example that occurred when he was about ten years of age. On one occasion, not satisfied with some food that was set before him at dinner, he refused to eat it and asked for another dish. His mother, regarding his dislike as whimsical, ordered a servant to carry the dish away, and nothing else was given him. At supper the same dish was set before him, and it was again refused. He went to bed fasting, and the next morning the same dish was given him for breakfast. All this while his mother had not uttered a word of reproof, nor exhibited the least unkindness of manner. Hunger had subdued his rebellious spirit, and conscience made him penitent. He ate the obnoxious food cheerfully, begged his mother to forgive him for his obstinacy, and resolved never again to defy her authority. This kind of maternal discipline had a powerful effect, and was reproduced in the character of the son in an eminent degree.

And now a dark and ominous cloud gathered in the northern horizon of the colony and filled the inhabitants with alarm. The banner of hostility was again raised upon the St. Lawrence, and the savages of the north were preparing to go out upon the old war paths which led to the frontier settlements of New York. For thirty years after the treaty at Utrecht the colonists had enjoyed comparative repose. The English and French governments had been at peace, and their respective colonists in America had lived in as much accord as national antipathies and dissimilarities would allow. The sword had been kept in its scabbard and the hatchet in its grave, and the benign influence of traffic was apparently smoothing the way for a real friendship between the Canadians and the people of New York, when the torch of war was suddenly kindled in Europe, and speedily lighted up the forests of America.

A contest had arisen between Maria Theresa, Empress of Hungary, and Louis the Fifteenth, King of France, concerning the occupancy of the throne of Austria as the seat of the German empire, just become vacant by the death of the Queen's father, Charles the Sixth, who, full twenty years before, had publicly settled his dominions on his daughter. Louis was resolved that Charles Albert, Elector of Bavaria, should be elevated to that throne, while the English people enthusiastically favored the claims of the Hungarian Queen ; and the King of England, as Elector of Hanover, espoused her cause. A contest, called in Europe the war of the Austrian succession, ensued, in which nearly all the continent became involved.

France declared war against England in the spring of of 1744, and for almost four years the contest raged in both hemispheres. In America it was called King George's war, and the loyal colonists, sympathizing with their fellow subjects in England, heartily espoused the cause of their sovereign. The peace that had so long rested upon the hills and valleys of America was suddenly banished, and the excitement of hostile sentiments and preparations prevailed all over the middle, northern, and eastern colonies. For a time it was uncertain where the flame would be first kindled, and anxiety and continual alarm harassed the people. The whole frontier of New York and New England was exposed to invasion by the French and their savage allies ; and from every point between Niagara and Quebec came intelligence of tampering with the Indians in the English interest by French emissaries, and of hostile preparations.

Albany, the chief frontier town, was in the programme of every scheme of invasion, because it was the key to the Hudson river and the provincial capital at its mouth, so much coveted by the Gallic power on the St. Lawrence; and it was continually menaced with the terrible blow dealt upon Schenectada fifty years before. Every family and every individual had an important interest at stake, and from the dawn of morning until the falling of the evening shadows the war was the great topic which occupied the thoughts and speech of all, from the mere child, listening with wonder, to the mature and aged, who planned and prepared to execute. The bud of young Schuyler's life was then just developing into the blossom of youth, and his plastic mind was continually impressed with words and deeds that left ineffaceable records of memory there, to be consulted in future years.

At length the great question was decided, and the chief theatre of war was prepared in the far east, where the fortress of Louisburg, the great stronghold of French power on this continent, reposed. It was upon the island of Cape Breton, which lies westward of the entrance to the Gulf of St. Lawrence, and had been constructed by the French at an expense of five and a half millions of dollars. On account of its great strength it was called the Gibraltar of America; and the sagacious William Shirley, then governor of Massachusetts, under whom young Schuyler served in after years, perceived its immense importance in the coming contest. Plans for its capture were speedily formed by the Legislature of Massachusetts, and other colonies cheerfully lent their coöperation. Rhode Island, New Hampshire, and Connecticut furnished their proper quota of troops, New York sent artillery, and Pennsylvania provisions. Thus common danger was extending the idea of a necessity for a union of the Anglo-American colonies ten years before it assumed a practical form in a colonial convention at Albany.

Preparations for the expedition against Louisburg occupied several months, and then, after vainly waiting for some time in expectation of aid from Commodore Warren, who was in the West Indies, the colonial forces, thirty-two hundred strong, under the general command of William Pepperell, sailed for Louisburg on the 4th of April, 1745. They were joined at Canseau by Warren early in May, and on the 11th of that month, the combined forces, four thousand strong, landed a short distance from the Louisburg fortress. Their appearance was unexpected to the French, and at first great consternation prevailed in the town and garrison. A regular siege was commenced on the last day of May, and on the 28th of June the French surrendered the fortress, the city of Louisburg, and the island of Cape Breton into the hands of the English.

Although this great and important victory was achieved almost entirely by the colonial troops, the British government awarded the whole of the prize money, amounting to at least a million of dollars, to the officers and crews of the royal ships-of-war. The two commanders, Warren and Pepperell, were each rewarded with the title of baronet, but the British ministry, with a mean spirit of jealousy toward the colonies, used every effort to depreciate the services of the provincial troops, and to deprive them of their share of the glory of the conquest also. This injustice was never forgotten, yet the loyalty of the colonists was too ardent and sincere to be seriously diminished by it.

Who can tell how much the recollection of this injustice, quickened by subsequent oppression, served to make Richard Gridley, the engineer, and David Wooster, the brave young Connecticut captain, earnest patriots and uncompromising opponents of the crown in the war for independence which broke out thirty years afterward.

Flushed with this great victory in the east, Shirley contemplated the complete conquest of the French colonial dominions. He urged the ministry to send over a sufficient land and naval force for that purpose, and to defend the prizes already won, for it could not be doubted that the mortified and exasperated French would put forth all their energies in efforts to regain what they had lost. Shirley's general plan was to send a British fleet and army, with New England troops, up the St. Lawrence, to attack Quebec, while colonial forces from New York, and provinces southward of it, should rendezvous at Albany, and proceed against the French fort at Crown Point, on Lake Champlain, and the city of Montreal on the St. Lawrence. The ministry appeared to listen favorably, and promised the desired aid. The Massachusetts Assembly agreed to the measure, and a large body of New England troops were speedily collected at Boston, and waited long for the regulars from England. For reasons not satisfactorily explained, the whole summer of 1746 passed away before any troops from abroad arrived, and the fleet of Warren did not come at all.

Shirley was disappointed but not disheartened, and he proposed to detach a portion of the New England troops to join the other provincials at Albany in an attack upon Crown Point. George Clinton, the governor of New York, warmly seconded the proposition. Through the influence of the Schuyler family and others, he had succeeded, as we shall observe presently, in not only securing the friendship of the Six Nations, but in engaging them to render active assistance in the contest; and the enterprise appeared to promise abundant success. But before the plan could be carried into effect intelligence came from the east that Louisburg was in danger, French troops and Indian war-parties being on their march toward it. The New Englanders were accordingly directed to hasten toward Cape Breton, but when they were on the point of embarking from Boston, tidings came that a large French fleet and army were upon the coast of Nova Scotia. It was an armament consisting of forty vessels, under the Duke D'Anville, conveying more than three thousand disciplined troops and a formidable train of artillery, for the recovery of the fortress and the desolation of the English settlements. The provincials were dismayed. To proceed would have been madness, and for a moment the deepest gloom settled upon the colonists, for it appeared as if they were doomed to destruction. But the strong arm of God's providence, which had so often and so long preserved them in the midst of many perils, was not now withdrawn. Storms wrecked many of the French vessels, and disease soon wasted hundreds of the Gallic troops; and D'Anville, thoroughly dispirited, abandoned the enterprise without striking a blow.

The pious New Englanders regarded this as a special deliverance, and hymns of joy and thanksgiving went up from ten thousand homes, unmixed, however, with any expressions of gratitude or respect for the parent State, whose neglect, but for this deliverance, would have insured their ruin.

Meanwhile the settlers on the extreme northern frontiers had been terribly smitten by bands of French and Indian marauders, and an expedition quite formidable in numbers had swept down the valley of the Hudson as far as Saratoga, within about thirty miles of Albany, leaving there a horrible record, and spreading the wildest alarm among the settlements below. This expedition, consisting of upwards of five hundred Frenchmen and Huron Indians, accompanied by some disaffected warriors of the Six Nations, left Montreal on the afternoon of the 4th of November, 1745, under the command of M. Marin, an active French officer, and proceeding up the Sorel from Chambleé, crossed Lake Champlain to Fort St. Frederic at Crown Point, which was then commanded by M. Vaudreuil. They arrived there on the 20th, and Marin prepared to cross the country to attack some English settlements on the Connecticut river, which was the original object of the expedition, when the Indians expressed a reluctance to go eastward on account of the lateness of the season, and their lack of preparation for the rigors of winter weather. Marin was disappointed, for he was unwilling to return empty of military achievements. On the suggestion of Father Piquet, the French Prefect Apostolique to Canada, who met the expedition at Crown Point, and the representations of the Iroquois who were with Marin, that officer determined to lead his party southward, toward Orange, as Albany was yet called by the French, and cut off the advancing English settlements. They passed up Lake Champlain and Wood Creek, crossed the country to the Hudson river, destroyed Lydius' lumber establishment on the site of Fort Edward, and approached the thriving settlement of Saratoga, seated on the flats at the junction of the Fish Creek and Hudson river.

The scattered village of Saratoga consisted of about thirty families, many of them tenants of Philip Schuyler, who owned mills and a large landed estate there; and near it, upon a hill across the river, was a small fort in a dilapidated condition, and without a garrison. Marin, with his motley horde of white and dusky savages, accompanied by Father Piquet, having laid waste nearly fifty miles of settlement, approached the village stealthily on the night of the 28th of November, when the inhabitants were asleep.

They burnt the fort and most of the houses, plundered everything of value, murdered Mr. Schuyler and a few others, and took captive one hundred and nine men, women and children, including negroes.

Beauvais, one of the officers who accompanied Marin, knew and respected Mr. Schuyler. He went to his house and requested him to surrender, assuring him at the same time that he should suffer no personal injury. Schuyler was a brave and high spirited man, and refused to surrender. He called Beauvais a dog, and fired a fusee at him. Beauvais again begged him to surrender, when Schuyler fired a second time. The incensed Beauvais instantly returned the fire with fatal effect. The house, which was of brick and pierced for muskets to the roof, was entered, pillaged and burnt, together with the body of Mr. Schuyler, and, it was believed, some persons who were concealed in the cellar.

On the following morning the marauders chanted the *Te Deum* in the midst of the desolation they had made, and then turned their steps toward Canada. A part of the prisoners were distributed among the savages, and the remainder were carried to Montreal, where the whole party arrived on the 9th of December.*

* Among the Schuyler papers is a manuscript of twenty-two foolscap pages, in the French language, containing a complete narrative of this expedition, entitled "Journal de la Campagne de Sarastogue, 1745." It is in the peculiar handwriting of the time, and was evidently written immediately after the occurrence by a participant in the expedition. The following is the entry concerning the death of Schuyler, the substance of which is given in the text. It will be seen that Schuyler is spelt Skulle:

"Sortant du moulin, nous allâmes a la maison du nommé Philippe Skulle, brave homme qui nous aurait fort embarassé s'il eut eu vue douzaine d'hommes aussi vaillans que luy. Beauvais qui le connoissait et qui l'aimoit, s'etoit rendu à sa maison le premier et en lui disant son nom l'invita fort à se rendre qu'il n'aurait point de mal. L'autre luy repondit qu'il étoit un chien et qu'il le voulait tuer en effet luy tira un coup de fusil. Beauvais luy reitera sa prière de

The murdered Schuyler was young Philip's uncle, from whom he inherited the fine estate at Saratoga, which he owned when it was desolated by order of Burgoyne more than thirty years afterward. The circumstances of his death caused the fiercest indignation as well as alarm throughout the province, and his brother, Colonel Peter Schuyler, who had been Indian commissioner for many years, importuned Governor Clinton for a detachment of three hundred of the militia of the lower counties to defend the frontier, and also to have the fort at Saratoga rebuilt and garrisoned.* The Commissioners of Indian affairs also urged the governor to take other measures for the security of the frontiers in connection with the friendly Six Nations; and a letter from Doctor Cadwallader Colden, who resided in the vicinity of Newburgh, was received by Clinton at about the same time, giving alarming suggestions concerning an expected attack by the Indians on the western borders of Ulster County. Coincident with these movements, the Massachusetts people sent an earnest request for

se rendre à quoi Phillipe repondit par des coups de fusils, enfin Beauvais las d'être exposé à son feu, lui tira son coup et le tua; nous entrâmes aussitôt, et tous fut pillé dans l'instant—cette maison étoit de briques percée de creneaux jusques à rez de chaussée, les sauvages nous l'avoit annoncée comme un espèce de corps de garde on il y avoit des soldats—ou y fit quelques domestiques prisonniers, on dit qu'il y a eu du monde de brulé qui s'étoit retiré dans la cave.

* Fort Saratoga stood upon a hill on the east side of the Hudson, opposite the present Schuylerville. It was rebuilt in the spring of 1746, in quadrangular form and strongly palisaded, and named Fort Clinton. At each corner of the fort were the houses of the officers, and timber barracks for the soldiers were within the palisades. A French account of it says it was twenty-five *toises* (one hundred and fifty feet) in height, meaning, no doubt, its height above the level of the river. The English, unable to defend this fort against the attacks of the French and Indians, burned it at about the 1st of December, 1747. A French officer (Villiers), who visited it three weeks after its destruction, saw twenty chimneys then standing. He reported that the English had ninety batteaux there which they took away with them.

New York to join with the New England colonies in a confederation for mutual welfare. These things were pressed upon the governor, and by him upon the representatives of the people, at a moment auspicious for their receiving attention. The public service had been neglected in consequence of the almost incessant quarrels between the chief magistrate and the assembly, causing supplies asked for to be refused, and the best interests of the commonwealth, in a time of great danger, to be made shuttlecocks for the amusement or profit of partisan players.

Governor Clinton was a son of the Earl of Lincoln, had spent most of his life in the navy, loved ease and good cheer, and evidently came to America to mend his fortune—impaired by extravagance—by genteel frugality in a society more simple than he found at home. He was a good-humored, kind-hearted man, and the ten years of his administration might have passed happily, had not unwise advisers influenced him at the beginning, and rancorous party spirit cursed the province. The old politicians who survived the administrations of Cosby and Clarke were as violent in their mutual animosities as ever, and the governor, after trying for awhile to propitiate the favor of both with no success, made the wealthy, able, and influential James De Lancey, then chief justice of the province, his confidant and guide. They finally quarreled over their cups and became personal and political foes, and from that hour Clinton found no peace in his public life. De Lancey was implacable. He was a politician of most exquisite mould, and bore almost absolute sway over the colonial assembly and the people. At the table where their friendship was broken he had taken an oath of revenge, and he pursued Clinton with the tenacity of a hound. He aimed to thwart every effort of the governor toward placing the province in a state of proper defense, for the evident purpose of making him, by his seeming inefficiency, unpopular with the people, while the governor, having the advantage of power, dealt severe blows of retaliation in return.

By these personal disputes and public agitations which disturbed the waters of society in New York, a hitherto obscure man was cast up to the surface, and for thirty years he held a conspicuous place in the history of the province, especially in that portion that pertained to the Indian tribes within its borders. That man was William Johnson, a nephew of Admiral Sir Peter Warren, and then in the prime of young manhood. His uncle, by marriage with Miss Watts of New York, became possessed of many broad acres upon the Mohawk river, and Johnson came from Ireland to take charge of the princely domain. For several years his ambition lay dormant, and he was content to reside in obscurity near Fort Hunter, surrounded by the Mohawk savages.

The quarrels between Clinton and De Lancey wrought a change in Johnson's aspirations and fortunes as sudden as it was great. Colonel Schuyler, who had long and faithfully exercised the duties of Indian commissioner, and was greatly beloved by the Six Nations, unfortunately for the public good attached himself to the interests of De Lancey. The governor was offended, and as Johnson, who had become a favorite with the Indians, had given Clinton full proofs of his friendship, upon him the office held by Colonel Schuyler was conferred, strictly on party grounds. That office became to Johnson the door of entrance to honors, fame and fortune ; and thus the man with whom Philip Schuyler the younger had so much to do in after years, in connection with the Iroquois confederacy, was first presented to public view.

The foray against Saratoga, and the imminent danger that every where overhung the province, hushed the voice of party spirit for a while; and when, early in 1746, the governor, by his message, demanded from the Legislature provision for constructing six new block houses on the northern frontier; the punctual payment of their militia garrisons, and the appointment of twenty-five men to be posted in two others at Schenectada; notified them that the Six Nations had refused to act in the war; urged an alliance with the New England colonies to lessen the expense of repurchasing the aid of the Iroquois confederacy; insisted upon more money to strengthen the hands of the Indian commissioners; demanded a further aid of provisions for a garrison at Oswego, and a quota of men to garrison Louisburg till others should arrive from England; and declared that "the enemy could not be more industrious for the ruin of the colony than he could be careful to preserve it in the quiet possession of his Majesty's subjects," scarcely a murmur of opposition was heard. The assembly proceeded to vote for the services recommended, and an increase in the amount of paper money to be issued.

Soon after this a scene occurred at Albany that must have made a deep and lasting impression upon young Schuyler. He was then nearly thirteen years of age, quite precocious, and vigilant and acute in his observations of passing events. Intelligence had come from England that the British ministry had determined to send an expedition against Canada, and desired aid from the colonies in men and supplies. This was the project of Governor Shirley already mentioned. It gave the people joy. The assembly voted a most loyal address to the governor. Bounties were raised for volunteers, and for the purchase of ammunition and provisions; exportation of provisions was forbidden;

the Six Nations were invited to meet the governor at Albany in council, and the other colonies were requested to join in collecting presents to conciliate them; artificers were impressed for the public works, and other measures for vigorous coöperation were planned.

A few days after the assembly adjourned, in July, the governor departed for Albany, with Dr. Colden and Philip Livingston, of his Majesty's council, and Captain Rutherford, who commanded in the north. They arrived at Albany on the 21st of July, and after being cordially received by the corporation, the regular troops in the city, and the militia, the governor took up his abode in the fort, on account of the prevalence of the small pox in the town.

Commissioner Johnson, meanwhile, had made great exertions to arouse the Mohawks to war against the French. He flattered their pride by dressing like them, and gained their further good will by feasting them. He was very successful, and on the 8th of August he appeared on the hills that overlooked old Albany, dressed and painted like the savages, at the head of a large number of them. Preparations having been made for their formal reception, they were led down to the fort, where the chiefs were treated with wine. It was a large and imposing gathering of the noblest sons of the forest, who came with their best appointments to hold friendly communion with "Corlear," as the governors of New York were styled. And there were many other braves there besides those of the Mohawk valley. Chiefs and warriors came from the Delawares, the Susquehannahs, the River Indians, and the Mohegans of the Connecticut valley. All the people of the town flocked to see the spectacle, and many came for the purpose from the neighboring settlements.

The council was satisfactory to all parties. The Indians

generally promised to lift the hatchet against the French, and were dismissed with presents, and Johnson was furnished with arms and directed to send out war parties from Schenectada and his own settlement near the lower Mohawk Castle, to annoy the French and their savage allies, who brooded in the forests northward of the English homes on the borders of the wilderness.

From this time no actual hostilities of importance occurred within the province of New York or on its frontier for several years; but the annals of New Hampshire for two years thereafter present a long and mournful catalogue of plantations laid waste and colonists slain or carried into captivity by the French and Indians. Pillage appeared to be the chief object of the invaders; "and their prowess," says an elegant English writer, "was directed less against States and armies than against dwelling-houses, families, rural industry and domestic life."*

In April, 1748, a treaty of peace was concluded at Aix-la-Chapelle, in western Germany, when it was mutually agreed that all prisoners should be released, and all acquisitions of property or territory made by either party should be restored. Louisburg, therefore, passed back into the hands of the French, and France and England were both immense losers by the conflict. But the American colonists, heavy as were their pecuniary and industrial sacrifices during the war, were great gainers, for their latent strength was developed, and the incalculable advantages of union were discovered and appreciated. They were tutored for great achievements in the future—achievements in which Philip Schuyler bore a conspicuous part.

* Grahame's Colonial History of the United States, i. 183.

## CHAPTER IV.

Philip Schuyler was little more than fourteen years of age when the war was closed by treaty, and its attendant alarms had mostly ceased. He had studied the ordinary branches of a plain education under the instructions of his mother, for the schools of Albany were very indifferent. He also had the advantage of listening to the conversation, and perhaps actually receiving instruction from educated French protestants, who, as well as their fathers, had ever been welcome visitors in the mansion of Colonel Schuyler at The Flats. There was also a holier tie than that of mere friendship that linked the Schuylers in sympathy with those people, a brother of the colonel having married a polished and well-educated daughter of one of the Huguenot refugees, who held the first rank in society in the provincial capital.

Under the colonel's hospitable roof young Philip spent much time during his childhood and youth with the good "Aunt Schuyler," the charming matron whose characteristics of mind and heart have been so beautifully portrayed by Mrs. Grant of Laggan, for he appears to have been a special favorite with her and her husband, whom the Mohawks loved so well. It appears evident, from a sentence contained in a letter of his, in after life, that he received some instructions in the science of mathematics from one of those Huguenots, who may have been employed as a private tutor in some wealthy families at Albany. From his earliest years Philip had exhibited a great fondness for numerals; and long before he left home for a wider range in intellectual culture, he was complete master of all arithmetical rules laid down in the books then in use or expounded by the tutors in schools.

The subject of education, considered so important by the early Dutch settlers, had, after the conquest of New Netherland by the English, received less and less attention until the period in question, when nearly all schools were neglected, and there was no institution in the province where an academic education might be acquired. Chief Justice Smith, a resident and cotemporary historian, when alluding to the action of the Legislature of New York in 1746, in authorizing the raising of twenty-two hundred and fifty pounds, by lottery, for founding a college, says: "To the disgrace of our first planters, who beyond comparison surpassed their eastern neighbors in opulence, Mr. De Lancey, a graduate of the University of Cambridge, (England,) and Mr. Smith, were for many years the only academics in this province, except such as were in holy orders; and so late as the period we are now examining, (1750,) the author did not recollect above thirteen more, the youngest of whom had his bachelor's degree at the age of seventeen, but two months before the passing of the above law, the first toward erecting a college in this colony, though at a distance of above one hundred and twenty years after its discovery and the settlement of the capital by Dutch progenitors from Amsterdam."* "The persons alluded to," says Judge Smith, in a note, "were Peter Van Brugh Livingston, John Livingston, Philip Livingston, William Livingston, William Nicoll, Benjamin Nicoll, Hendrick Hansen, William Peartree Smith, Caleb Smith,

* History of the Province of New York; by William Smith.

Benjamin Woolsey, William Smith, jr., John M'Evers, and John Van Horne. These being then in the morning of life, there was no academic but Mr. De Lancey on the bench or in either of the three branches of the Legislature, and Mr. Smith was the only one at the bar." All of these were afterward the cotemporaries of Philip Schuyler in public life—some with him and some against him in the arena of political strife.

At that time commerce engrossed the attention of the principal families in the province, for it was the surest road to wealth and social distinction; and the sons who were generally destined for its avocations, were usually sent from the writing-school to the counting-room, and, in due time, on a voyage to the West India Islands. This practice was introduced by the French refugees, who had settled in the province near the close of the preceding century, they having brought with them money, arts, manners, education, and all the essential elements of thrift and progress, and had become the chief merchants of New York.

Although young Schuyler was not specially designed for mercantile life—for large landed estates awaited his care when he should arrive at his majority—his education appears to have been directed toward that end. At the age of about fifteen years, he was placed in a school at New Rochelle, in Westchester County, then in charge of the Reverend Mr. Stouppe, a native of Switzerland and pastor of the French Protestant church at that place. The settlement was composed almost entirely of the families of those Huguenots who fled from France to avoid persecution between the years 1680 and 1700, the minions of the Pope having persuaded the profligate Louis the Fourteenth to break the great green seal that held the solemn edict of Henry the Fourth, made ninety years before, which proclaimed toleration to all the Huguenots of his kingdom. In the great Protestant exodus that ensued, the strongest foundations of the French State were sapped. Eight hundred thousand of her best citizens—skillful agriculturists and artisans, and virtuous families—fled from her borders, and carried the secret arts of France into other countries. Fifty thousand cunning workmen took refuge in England, and gave that realm the benefit of their skill, while large numbers crossed the Atlantic, and sought quiet homes in a strange land, where the rights of conscience were held sacred. Those who settled in the province of New York were nearly all from La Rochelle. They soon separated, the artisans remaining in the city, and the tillers of the soil seating themselves in the country, some on the Hudson above the Highlands, and a large number upon a beautiful spot purchased for them by Jacob Leisler on the banks of Long Island Sound. That spot they solemnly dedicated as their future home, and named it New Rochelle, in remembrance of the loved city in their birthland from which they had fled. They soon built a church edifice and established a school, and there (the only place within the English colonies,) the French language was taught.

Young Schuyler entered upon his studies at New Rochelle with a great deal of zeal. Very soon the hand of disease was laid heavily upon him, and for a whole year he was confined to his room with hereditary gout. It was the first appearance of a malady that tormented him all his life, notwithstanding he was always active and temperate in eating and drinking. The fortitude of the youthful martyr was sufficient to sustain him, and during the whole period of his sufferings he hardly relaxed his studies for an hour. Mathematics and the exact sciences were his favorites.

These he pursued with a devotional spirit, and he acquired a thorough knowledge of the French language, then seldom learned except by the sons of merchants engaged in trade with the West Indies.

How long Philip remained at New Rochelle can not be determined, for there is no record to answer. Probably not more than two years, for as early as the summer of 1751, when he was in his eighteenth year, he was deep in the wilderness on the borders of the Upper Mohawk, doubtless on one of those wild trading and hunting excursions in which all young Albanians engaged. He was then a tall youth, with a florid complexion, a benevolent cast of features, a fine, manly deportment, and distinguished for great kindness of manner. The red men of the forest admired and loved him, and whenever he visited them, in company with Colonel Johnson, or with Albany merchants in their summer tours to Oswego, they always gave him some testimonial of their regard. On one of these occasions, when Philip was about twenty years of age, some of the Oneida chiefs met him at the carrying place between Wook creek and the Oneida lake, while he was on his way to Oswego, and sought and obtained his assistance in nullifying a sale of much of their lands westward of Utica, which had been made to scheming white speculators by the dissolute young men of the nation. The latter had been bribed by a little money and a great deal of rum to make the transaction. Schuyler was successful, and the domain was saved to the nation. The chiefs, to testify their gratitude, exchanged names with him, a custom then common among them, by which they considered both parties honored. Several of them assumed his surname, and the last of the General's children, who survived him more than half a century,* remembered that almost sixty years afterward, full-blooded Oneidas, named SCHUYLER, came to Utica to sell their beautifully embroidered moccasins, and partook of the holy communion at the same table with herself in the Episcopal church. From the time of these friendly services to the Indians until his death, no man except Colonel Johnson ever exercised a greater influence over the more easterly tribes of the Iroquois confederacy than Philip Schuyler.

After his eighteenth year Philip usually visited New York each autumn, and spent several weeks with friends and relatives in the metropolis. Society there was quite different in many of its aspects from that in Albany. There was far less of the staid Dutch element in its character, and it displayed in prominent lines the cosmopolitan features of commercial marts. Being the seat of the colonial government, the tone of the best society was marked by courtly gaiety of manner and the appearance of considerable luxury. New York was one of the most social places on the continent. The inhabitants consisted principally of merchants, shopkeepers, and tradesmen; and there was not so great an inequality of wealth and position as in many other places. They were sober, honest, industrious and hospitable, though intent upon gain ; and were generally frugal and temperate, except the richer sort, whose tables were furnished with the greatest variety of meat, vegetables and liquors.

Their amusements were simple and rational. The men were not given to extravagant gaming nor the cruel practice of horse racing. They usually collected in weekly evening clubs for conversation, smoking, and the indul-

* Mrs. Catharine Van Rensselaer Cochrane, his youngest child, who died at Oswego, New York, on the 26th of August, 1857, aged 76 years.

gence of games of chance for amusement ; and the women of all ages were amused in summer by aquatic excursions on the neighboring waters, and in winter by concerts of music and assemblies for dancing, which were held in a large room in the Exchange at the foot of Broad street. On such occasions they assembled and retired early ; and there might always be seen many handsome women, "scarce any of them distorted shapes," and all well dressed.

At about this time theatrical performances were introduced into New York for the first time. As usual, they were exceedingly attractive, especially to young people, and the little theatre fitted up in Nassau street, south side, between the present Fulton and John streets, with room enough for only about three hundred persons, was usually crowded on the nights of performance, which occurred tri-weekly. The theatre was opened at about the middle of September, 1753, under the management of Lewis Hallam, who had been with his company performing at Williamsburg, in Virginia, and at Annapolis and other places in Maryland. Young Schuyler, who was always a welcome visitor in the choicest circles of New York, not only on account of his own excellence of character and easy and refined manners, but because of his relationship by intermarriages with families in the city who held the highest social position next to the governor, appears to have been present at one of the earliest, perhaps the very earliest of these performances. Writing to a friend in Albany on the 21st of September, he says :

"The schooner arrived at Ten Eyck's wharf on Wednesday, at one o'clock, and the same evening I went to the play with Phil. You know I told you before I left home that if the players should be here I should see them, for a player is a new thing under the sun in our good province. Phil.'s sweetheart went with us. She is a handsome brunette from

Barbadoes, has an eye like that of a Mohawk beauty, and appears to possess a good understanding. Phil. and I went to see the grand battery in the afternoon, and to pay my respects to the governor, whose lady spent a week with us last spring, and we bought our play tickets for eight shillings apiece, at Parker and Weyman's printing-office, in Beaver street, on our return. We had tea at five o'clock, and before sundown we were in the theatre, for the players commenced at six.* The room was quite full already. Among the company was your cousin Tom and Kitty Livingston, and also Jack Watts, Sir Peter Warren's brother-in-law. I would like to tell you all about the play, but I can't now, for Billy must take this to the wharf for Captain Wynkoop in half an hour. He sails this afternoon.

"A large green curtain hung before the players until they were ready to begin, when, on the blast of a whistle, it was raised, and some of them appeared and commenced acting. The play was called *The Conscious Lovers*, written, you know, by Sir Richard Steele, Addison's help in writing the *Spectator*. Hallam, and his wife and sister, all performed, and a sprightly young man named Hulett played the violin and danced merrily. But I said I could not tell you about the play, so I will forbear, only adding that I was no better pleased than I should have been at the club, where, last year, I went with cousin Stephen, and heard many wise sayings which I hope profited me something.

"To-morrow I expect to go into Jersey to visit Colonel Schuyler,† who was at our house four or five years ago, when he returned from Oswego. He is a kinsman and good soldier, and as I believe we shall have war again with the French quite as soon as we could wish, I expect he will lead his Jerseymen to the field. I wish you and I, Brom.,

* On the 20th of November, [1753,] the following curious note appeared on the play bills:

"N. B. Gentlemen and ladies that intend to favor us with their company are desired to come by six o'clock, being determined to keep to our hour, as it would be a great inconvenience to them to be kept out late, and a means to prevent disappointment."—Dunlap's *History of the American Theatre*, page 14.

† Grandson of the first Schuyler, of Albany, and second son of Arent Schuyler, who settled in New Jersey. When an incursion into Canada was projected in 1746, he was put in command of a New Jersey regiment, and was at Oswego for two years, when he returned to private life. He went with his regiment to the same fort in 1755. He was made a prisoner on parole in 1756, but was ordered to Canada in 1758, where he was soon exchanged and returned home. He was soon in the north again with his regiment, and in September, 1760, he entered Montreal as a victor. He died in 1762, near Newark, New Jersey.

could go with him. But I must say farewell, with love to Peggy, and sweet Kitty V. R. if you see her."*

This, and another short letter, comprise all of the writings of General Schuyler, in manuscript or published, that I have seen bearing date earlier than that of his commission as captain, in 1755. Indeed very little is known of his career up to that time, for no biographical sketch of him was written during his life, and he left behind no continuous diary or journal containing any notice of his earlier years.

Schools in New York, at this time, were of a low order. "The instructors want instruction," said a cotemporary, "and through a long, shameful neglect of all the arts and sciences, our common speech is extremely corrupt, and the evidences of a bad taste, both as to thought and language, are visible in all our proceedings, public and private."† There was nothing more generally neglected than reading among all classes, imitating, in this respect, society in England at that time, when education was regarded as pedantry, and a student outside of the liberal professions was a great rarity. Philip Schuyler, who had acquired much useful knowledge and a great variety of information from books, as well as observation, was therefore looked upon almost as a prodigy in New York, and men of culture delighted to have him visit them. Among these he best loved the society of Mr. Barclay, rector of Trinity Church, Mr. Johnson, his assistant, and Mr. Smith, the historian. With the latter he became very intimate, and they were constant correspondents for years before the Revolution, and even after Mr. Smith had taken an opposing position

* Autograph Letter of Philip Schuyler to Abraham Ten Broeck. † Smith.

in politics and espoused the cause of the king in the quarrel.

Only two newspapers were published in New York at this period, and they were very indifferent ones. They contained very little reading except advertisements and a meagre record of current events, but were much improved a few years later, when Hugh Gaine's *Mercury* became a vehicle through which some of the ablest essayists of the province were enabled to reach the public ear.

In libraries the people were very deficient. In the City Hall, a strong brick edifice, two stories in height, which stood upon the site of the present custom-house, were a thousand volumes, which had been bequeathed to the *Society for the Propagation of the Gospel in Foreign Parts*, by Dr. Millington, Rector of Newington. That library was sent to New York in 1730, and, as evidence of the scarcity of books in America at that time, it may be mentioned that the secretary of the society, in his letter to Governor Montgomerie, stated that they were sent "for the use of the clergy and gentlemen of New York, and the neighboring governments of Connecticut, New Jersey, and Pennsylvania, upon giving security to return them." The greater part of these were theological works, and at the time we are considering many of them were missing. With the movement for the establishment of a college in New York a desire for a public library appears to have arisen, and in 1754 a considerable sum was subscribed for that purpose, and seven hundred volumes of new and well selected books were purchased. This was the origin of the New York Society Library, one of the most flourishing of the literary institutions of that city at the present time.*

* The largest private library known in the province previous to the Revolution was that of Governor Montgomerie, which contained 1,341 volumes

Religion, morals and metaphysics received due attention, but in different degrees. Theology had always been a favorite topic for meditation, and at about the middle of the last century it became almost as popular as politics as a theme for public discussion in the province, because of recent ecclesiastical movements in England that deeply concerned the American colonists. Every Protestant sect was legally tolerated in the province, while the Episcopalians, dwelling under the shadow of the established church in England, and claiming precedence, looked with very little favor upon the dissenters. The dislike was mutual, and no love was wasted.

Nationality, likewise, had a separating influence, and the old hatred that existed between the English and Dutch had not disappeared, but was greatly modified. The bulk of the inhabitants of New York city consisted of the descendants from the original Dutch planters and traders, and there were two churches in the city wherein the gospel was preached in the language of their fathers, by Ritzema and De Ronde, who were both strict Calvinists. These two churches were associated under one incorporation styled the Reformed Protestant Dutch Church of the city of New York.

There were also two Episcopal church edifices in the city. Trinity Church, first erected in 1697 and rebuilt in 1737, contained seats for two thousand hearers, but strangers and proselytes had so augmented the congregation

of a standard character. The first law library of which we have any account was that of Broughton, the attorney-general in 1704, which contained only thirty-six volumes. The library of Judge Smith, the historian, and that of his father, the eminent jurist, who died in 1769, contained about a thousand volumes of law and miscellaneous books and pamphlets. Of the latter they had a large collection, dating back to the civil wars in Charles the First's time.

that in 1752 St. George's chapel was erected on Beekman street, in what was then considered "a new, crowded, and ill-built part of the town." In the face of much opposition from the Church of England party, a Presbyterian church was founded in 1719, under the pastoral charge of Mr. Anderson, a Scotch minister, but they did not erect a church edifice until 1748. At this time the French church had become torn by dissensions, and its membership reduced to a handfull. There were also in the city two German Lutheran churches, and a Quaker and an Anabaptist meeting-house, a Jewish synagogue, and a Moravian congregation. The latter was a new sect in America, just planted by Count Zinzendorf and others, and the congregation in New York then consisted principally of female converts from other religious societies.

But the Episcopalians took the lead in influence, the aristocracy being chiefly members of that church. They enjoyed the advantages of special privileges granted by their church charter and laws connected with it, the violent, weak, and dissolute Governor Fletcher, who became the tool of the aristocracy and was hated by the people, having procured the passage of an act by the Assembly which virtually made the doctrines and rituals of that church the established religion of the province. With profane and perhaps drunken lips, he piously declared to the Assembly that "neither heresy, sedition, schism or rebellion should be preached among them, nor vice and profanity encouraged." His views were seconded by the successor of the Earl of Bellomont, Edward Hyde, (Lord Cornbury,) the licentious robber of the public treasury, who persecuted all denominations of Christians except those of the Church of England. From his time until the kindling of the old war for independence, in whose blaze the rubbish of despotic systems of every kind in the colonies was consumed, the sum of five hundred dollars of the annual salary of the rector of Trinity Church was unrighteously levied upon all the other clergy and laity in the city.

At about the time in question, a sharp controversy commenced between the episcopal and dissenting writers of the province, and continued for several years, continually increasing in acrimony. The chief cause of the controversy was the alarm felt in the colonies concerning a scheme proposed in 1748 by Dr. Secker, Archbishop of Canterbury, for establishing episcopacy and curtailing the Puritan or dissenting influence in the political and religious affairs of the American colonies. The throne and the hierarchy were in a measure mutually dependent, and Dr. Secker's proposition was warmly approved by the British cabinet.

The colonists, viewing episcopacy in its worst light, as exhibited in the early days of the American settlements, had been taught to fear such power, if it should happen to be wielded by the hand of a crafty politician, more than the arm of civil government, and they regarded the archbishop's scheme as a weapon of contemplated tyranny. The eminent Whitefield had been for years crossing and re-crossing the Atlantic on errands of mercy, and arousing the colonists to a right sense of their duties and privileges. He had taught lessons concerning religious freedom with power to thousands whose minds had never been agitated by reflections and speculations upon such subjects ; and all over the land there was a general awakening to truths of vast importance, secular and spiritual, hitherto undiscovered or unrecognized. These truths imparted strength to the recipients, and with the recent vindication of the liberty of the press in the acquittal of Zenger, they made many bold in their enunciation of maxims concerning the freedom of conscience, and the right of every man to the exercise of private judgment in matters relating solely to himself and his God.

The public mind was prepared to act when the notes of alarm were sounded, and Whitefield was among the first to send them over the land. He had learned the secret of Archbishop Secker's scheme, and the fact that the integrity of Puritanism in New England had been approached with the bribe of a bishop's mitre for several dissenting divines, and he exclaimed to Dr. Langdon, of Harvard college, "I can not leave this town without acquainting you with a secret. My heart bleeds for America. O, poor New England! There is a deep laid plot against both your civil and religious liberties, and they will be lost. Your golden days are at an end. You have nothing but trouble before you. Your liberties will be lost if you are not vigilant and brave!"

From other points alarums were sounded, and the pens of ready writers caught up the strain and put forth valiant words and hard arguments in opposition. Among the most powerful and industrious of these writers in the province of New York was William Livingston, (afterward governor of New Jersey,) a native of Albany, then about thirty years of age, and already eminent as a lawyer in the provincial capital. He commenced his task behind the curtain of anonymity, and dealt heavy blows in favor of Presbyterianism and against episcopacy, in a weekly periodical called the *Independent Reflector*, first published late in 1752.

For some time the *Reflector* was devoted to the exposure and censure of local social and political abuses, and the suggestion of ideas practically beneficial to the people. The talent displayed, the truths put forth, and the interests disturbed by this serial attracted general attention immediately, and provoked the strongest opposition. The editor spared no party, social, political, or religious ; and he was denounced in private circles as an infidel and libertine, and in the pulpit as the Gog and Magog of the Apocalypse. The mayor, who had felt his lash, recommended the grand jury to present the *Reflector* as a libel, and the author was publicly charged with profanity, irreligion, and sedition.

It was not until the spring of 1753 that the Episcopalians and their interests were assailed in the *Reflector*. The occasion was the effort (which proved successful) to place the College about to be established under the control of the Episcopalians. Mr. Livingston was one of the small minority of the trustees who were not of that denomination, and had opposed the measure because the Episcopalians were greatly in the minority in the province, and the money having been raised by a general tax. Accordingly, in March he opened his batteries with great force against the measure. His language was bold and defiant, but dignified and unexceptionable. He caught up the alarm notes of Whitefield, and in several numbers he most ably discussed the subject of Christianity and its mission, and its relations to society and the civil power, drawing illustrations for his arguments from the past history of the Church of England and events around him. Violent opposition immediately appeared, and Barclay, Johnson, Auchmuty, and other churchmen answered the strictures of the *Reflector* in the columns of Gaine's *Mercury*. The subject was considered of sufficient importance to compose almost the entire theme of a letter written at the close of June, 1753, by the Reverend Samuel Johnson to Dr. Secker, the Achbishop of Canterbury. "Among other pernicious books," he said, "the *Independent Whig* grows much in vogue, and a notable set of young gentlemen of figure in New York have of late set up for writers in that way in a weekly paper called the *Independent Reflector.** Several worthy gentlemen of the Church in that province have of late been embarked in the design of erecting a college as a seminary of the Church, though with a free and generous toleration for other denominations, upon which these Reflectors have been indefatigable in their paper, and by all possible means, both public and private, endeavoring to spirit up the people against us, and to wrest it out of the Church's hands and make it a sort of a free-thinking, latitudinarian seminary.† We have several of us been writing in the Church's defense against them, and endeavoring, not without some success, to defeat their pernicious schemes."

Finally, through the influence of the civil authority, the clergy, and the aristocracy, the printers of the *Independent Reflector* (Parker and Weyman,) were induced to refuse to print it any longer, and it was closed with the fifty second number, on the 22d of November, 1753. But the controversy continued for more than ten years, in various

* It was known that Livingston was the sole conductor of this work, and his articles were signed with different initials. But there were some able contributors besides himself, over different signatures, and as John Morin Scott, William Peartree Smith, and William Smith, the historian, coincided with him in sentiment, these have been named as his coadjutors. In the letter here quoted, Mr. Johnson speaks of Mr. Smith (the young man who bore it,) as one who had written against the *Reflectors.*

† In the spring of 1754, the trustees of the college, stimulated by an offer of a tract of land whereon to build an edifice, made by Trinity Church, on condition that the head of the college should always be a member of the Church of England, and the prayers of the church always to be used in it, petitioned Lieutenant Governor De Lancey for a charter containing such provisions. Livingston alone entered a protest against the prayers of the petitioners, believing that this college scheme was a part of the great plan arranged for uniting Church and State in the colonies. But the act of incorporation, with these sectarian provisions, was passed, and the Reverend Samuel Johnson, the writer of this letter, was appointed to the presidency.

ways, and through various vehicles. The synod of Connecticut voted thanks to Livingston for his championship; while in Gaine's paper he was lampooned in a poem of almost two hundred lines. Livingston wrote anonymously, and the poet thus referred to the author:

> "Some think him a *Tindall*, some think him a *Chubb*,
> Some think him a *Ranter*, that spouts from his *tub*;
> Some think him a *Newton*, some think him a *Locke*,
> Some think him a *Stone*, some think him a *Stock*—
> But a *Stock* he at least may thank Nature for giving,
> And if he's a *Stone*, I pronounce it a *Living*."

Young Schuyler was in New York when the forty-sixth number of the *Reflector* appeared, which contained the editor's "creed" in thirty-nine articles. In a letter to a friend, whose name does not appear in the manuscript, he said: "I send you the forty-sixth number of the *Independent Reflector*, which is making a notable stir here. The clergy, and all churchmen, are in arms against it, and our friend, Will. Livingston, who is the principal writer, is thought by some to be one of the most promising men in the province. I esteem the Church and its liturgy, but I believe he is right in opposing the ridiculous pretensions of the clergy, who would make it as infallible as the Popish Church claims to be. I wish liberty of conscience in all things, and I believe our friend is right when he says, '*Our faith, like our stomachs, may be overcharged, especially if we are prohibited to chew what we are commanded to swallow.*'"

The foregoing glance at the social and religious aspect of New York, at the period we are considering, will be found essential as we proceed in our researches concerning the development of events that led to the old war for independence, in which Philip Schuyler bore a conspicuous and noble part, because in these elements we may perceive the philosophy of the history of those times.

A brief delineation of some of the most prominent material characteristics of the city of New York, the metropolis of the province, is equally necessary for the same reasons, because the quarrel was based upon interests involving principles of a moral and material character.

New York city, at that time, contained about thirteen thousand inhabitants, of whom about two thousand were negroes, who were mostly held in easy servitude as bond slaves. There were about twenty-five hundred buildings in the city, many of them of brick, covered with tiles, and most of them presenting an aspect of comfort and thrift. Fine country residences, surrounded by gardens and pastures, embellished the suburbs, and some of the town residences were comparatively palatial. The city was almost a mile in length, and about half a mile in its greatest breadth. Some of the streets were paved with huge pebbles, as in rural cities and villages at the present, but nearly all of them were irregular in their linear relations and course. Its markets were well supplied with fish, flesh, and vegetables of every kind, the latter being chiefly raised by Dutch farmers on Harlem Plains, near the northern end of the island. "No part of America," says a cotemporary writer,* "is better supplied with markets abounding with greater plenty and variety. * * * Our oysters are a considerable article in support of the poor. Their beds are within view of the town; a fleet of two hundred small craft are often seen there, at a time, when the weather is mild in winter; and this single article is computed to be worth, annually, £10,000 or £12,000."

The merchants of New York were justly compared to

* William Smith.

a hive of bees gathering honey for others, for the largest portion of the profits of their trade centered in Great Britain. They were not allowed to traffic except with Great Britain or its colonies; and acts of Parliament forbade various domestic manufactures, so that many necessary articles which the colonists might have made for themselves were imported from England.

They exported to the British West Indies bread, peas, rye, meal, Indian corn, apples, onions, boards, staves, horses, sheep, butter, cheese, pickled oysters, beef and pork. Of flour alone they shipped about eighty thousand barrels a year. Their returns consisted chiefly of rum, sugar, and molasses from the islands, and cash from Curaçoa, and the balance in this trade was always in favor of the New York merchants. They imported cotton from St. Thomas and Surinam, lime-juice and Nicaragua wood from Curaçoa, and logwood from the Bay of Honduras. They exported flax seed to Ireland and logwood and furs to England, but the balance was always largely against the colonists. The importation of dry goods alone from Great Britain was so great that they often found it very difficult to make remittances. They were consequently drained of gold and silver by the British merchants. The annual importation of goods from Great Britain by the colony of New York, at that time (1753 to 1760), was estimated at not less than one hundred thousand pounds sterling.

The city of New York, incorporated more than sixty years before, was divided into seven wards, under the government of a mayor, recorder, aldermen and assistant aldermen, who formed a common council. The mayor, sheriff and coroner, were annually appointed by the governor, and the recorder, holding a patent from the same officer, was dependent upon his pleasure for the term of his official career. The annual revenue of the corporation was nearly two thousand pounds a year, and the standing militia of the island consisted of twenty-three hundred men. The city had also, in reserve, one thousand stand of arms for seamen, the poor, and others, in case of an invasion.

A strong fortification was upon the lower end of the island, on the site of the old Fort Amsterdam, called Fort George, in which was the governor's house, three stories in height and pleasantly fronting the bay ; also brick barracks, originally built for the accommodation of the independent companies. A large battery had just been erected eastward of the fort, built of stone, cedar joists and earth, on which ninety-two cannon were mounted ; and in front was Nutten (now Governor's) Island, which was made a demesne for the governors by an act of the colonial assembly, on which the erection of a strong castle was then under discussion, it being an eligible point for an enemy to plant batteries to bombard the town. A greater portion of the palisades and block-houses erected during the alarm caused by the enemy's inroads on the northern frontier in 1745, extending from the East river to the Hudson, nearly on a line with the present Chambers street, were yet remaining, "a monument to our folly," says Judge Smith, "which cost £8,000."

Such was New York at the opening of the French and Indian war, a little more than a hundred years ago, during which the province became the theatre of the most stirring scenes of that contest.

## CHAPTER V.

In the old family Bible that belonged to General Schuyler may be seen, in his hand-writing, this record: "In the Year 1755, on the 17th of September, was I, Philip John Schuyler, married (in the 21st Year, 9th Month, and 17th Day of his Age,) to Catharine Van Rensselaer, aged 20 Years, 9 Months, and 27 Days. May we live in peace and to the glory of God."

This was the "sweet Kitty V. R." mentioned in Philip's letter in the preceding chapter. She was a daughter of Colonel Johannes Van Rensselaer, of Claverack, in the present Columbia county, New York. They were married by that excellent minister of the Reformed Dutch church in Albany, Dominie Frelinghuysen. She was delicate but perfect in form and feature; of medium height, extremely graceful in her movements, and winning in her deportment; well educated, in comparison with others, of sprightly temperament, possessed of great firmness and tenacity of will, and was very frugal, industrious and methodical.

The benediction implored by the husband in his marriage record appears to have been granted in full measure, for his spouse, who bore him fourteen children, and was his companion for eight-and-forty years, was all that a man could desire as the wife of his bosom, the joy and solace of his life, and the mother of his offspring. They loved each other tenderly, bore the burdens of life together lovingly and patiently, enjoyed God's blessings abundantly and thankfully, and ended their pilgrimage almost at the same time, only the space of twenty months separating them on earth. Of her it might have been truthfully said, at every period of her life, she was

> "A Being breathing thoughtful breath,
> A Traveler between life and death;
> The reason firm, the temperate will,
> Endurance, foresight, strength and skill;
> A perfect Woman, nobly planned
> To warn, to comfort, and command;
> And yet a Spirit still, and bright,
> With something of an angel light."

Mrs. Grant, in her admirable sketches of persons and events during her residence with "Aunt Schuyler" at the Flats, has given a brief outline of the portraiture of Philip as it was impressed upon her memory ten years after his marriage. He was then known as "Philip Schuyler of the Pasture," to distinguish him from a kinsman of the same name, who lived with the Colonel at the Flats as his expectant heir. "He appeared," says Mrs. Grant, "merely a careless, good humored young man. Never was any one so little what he seemed with regard to ability, activity and ambition, art, enterprise and perseverance, all of which he possessed in an eminent degree, though no man had less the appearance of these qualities. Easy, complying, and good humored, the conversations, full of wisdom and sound policy, of which he had been a seemingly inattentive witness at the Flats, only slept in his recollection, to wake in full force when called forth by occasion."

Mrs. Grant's picture of society and of domestic life at the Flats is so charming, and also so useful in forming a truthful estimate of the home life of young Schuyler and his youthful wife, (for their own household was modeled in a manner after that of "Aunt Schuyler's," under whose roof they spent much time,) that no apology is needed for giving it here almost entire. At this time "Aunt Schuyler" was on the evening side of life, and was so corpulent that she moved about with difficulty, yet she entertained her guests with delightful ease, and enjoyed society with a zest that many might envy. "After the middle of life," says Mrs. Grant, "she went little out; her household, long since arranged by general rules, went regularly on, because every domestic knew exactly the duties of his or her place, and dreaded losing it as the greatest possible misfortune. She had always with her some young person, 'who was unto her as a daughter,' who was her friend and companion, and bred up in such a manner as to qualify her for being such, and one of whose duties it was to inspect the state of the household, and 'report progress' with regard to the operations going on in the various departments. For no one better understood, or more justly estimated, the duties of housewifery. Thus those young females who had the happiness of being bred under her auspices very soon became qualified to assist her instead of encroaching much on her time. The example and conversation of the family in which they lived was to them a perpetual school of useful knowledge, and manners easy and dignified, though natural and artless. They were not, indeed, embellished, but then they were not deformed by affectation, pretensions, or defective imitation of fashionable models of manners. They were not, indeed, bred up 'to dance, to dress, to roll the ey , or troll the tongue;' yet they were not lectured with unnatural gravity or frozen reserve. I have seen those of them who were lovely, gay, and animated, though, in the words of an old familiar lyric,

'Without disguise or art, like flowers that grace the wild,
Their sweets they did impart whene'er they spoke or smiled.'

"Aunt," continues Mrs. Grant, "was a great manager of her time, and always contrived to create leisure hours for reading; for that kind of conversation which is properly styled gossiping she had the utmost contempt. Light, superficial reading, such as merely fills a blank in time, and glides over the mind without leaving an impression, was little known there, for few books crossed the Atlantic but such as were worth carrying so far for their intrinsic value. She was too much accustomed to have her mind occupied with objects of real weight and importance to give it up to frivolous pursuits of any kind. She began the morning with reading the Scriptures. They always breakfasted early and dined two hours later than the primitive inhabitants, who always took that meal at twelve. This departure from the ancient customs was necessary in this family, to accommodate the great number of British as well as strangers from New York, who were daily entertained at her liberal table. This arrangement gave her the advantage of a long forenoon to dispose of. After breakfast she gave orders for the family details of the day, which, without a scrupulous attention to those minutiæ which fell more properly under the notice of her young friends, she always regulated in the most judicious manner, so as to prevent all appearance of hurry and confusion. There was such a rivalry among domestics, whose sole ambition was her favor, and who had been trained up from infancy, each to their several duties, that excellence in each department was the result both of habit and emulation; while her young protégés were early taught the value and importance of good housewifery, and were sedulous in their attention to little matters of decoration and elegance which her mind was too much engrossed to attend to; so that her household affairs, ever well regulated, went on in a mechanical kind of progress that seemed to engage little of her attention, though her vigilant and overruling mind set every spring of action in motion.

"Having thus easily and speedily arranged the details of the day, she retired to read in her closet, where she generally remained till about eleven, when, being unequal to distant walks, the Colonel and she, and some of her elder guests, passed some of the hotter hours among those embowering shades of her garden, in which she took great pleasure. Here was their Lyceum; here questions in religion and morality, too weighty for table-talk, were leisurely and coolly discussed, and plans of policy and various utility arranged. From this retreat they adjourned to the portico, and while the Colonel either retired to write, or went to give directions to his servants, she sat in this little tribunal, giving audience to new settlers, followers of the army left in hopeless dependence, and others who wanted assistance or advice, or hoped she would intercede with the Colonel for something more peculiarly in his way, he having great influence with the colonial government.

"At the usual hour her dinner party assembled, which was generally a large one; and here I must digress from the detail of the day to observe that, looking up as I always did to Madame with admiring veneration, and having always heard her mentioned with unqualified applause, I look often back to think what defects or faults she could possibly have to rank with the sons and daughters of imperfection inhabiting this transitory scene of existence, well knowing, from subsequent observation of life, that error is the unavoidable portion of humanity. Yet of this truism, to which every one will readily subscribe, I can recollect no proof in my friend's conduct, unless the luxury of her table might be produced to confirm it. Yet this, after all, was but comparative luxury. There was more choice and selection, and perhaps more abundance at her table than at those of the other primitive inhabitants, yet how simple were her repasts compared with those which the luxury of the higher ranks of this country offer to provoke the sated appetite. Her dinner party generally consisted of some of her intimate friends or near relations ; her adopted children, who were inmates for the time being ; and strangers, sometimes invited merely as friendly travelers, on the score of hospitality, but often welcomed for some time as stationary visitors, on account of worth or talents, that gave value to their society ; and lastly, military guests, selected with some discrimination on account of the young friends, who they wished not only to protect, but cultivate by an improving association. Conversation here was always rational, generally instructive and often cheerful.

"The afternoon frequently brought with it a new set of guests. Tea was always drank early here, and, as I have formerly observed, was attended with so many petty luxuries of pastry, confectionery, etc., that it might well be accounted a meal by those whose early and frugal dinners had so long gone by. In Albany it was customary, after the heat of the day was past, for young people to go in parties of three or four, in open carriages, to drink tea at an hour or two's drive from home. The receiving and entertaining of this sort of company, generally, was the province of the younger part of the family, and of those, many came, in summer evenings, to the Flats, when tea, which was very early, was over. The young people, and those who were older, took their differing walks, while Madame sat in her portico, engaged in what might comparatively be called light reading—essays, biography, poetry, etc., till the younger party set out on their return home, and her domestic friends rejoined her in her portico, where, in warm evenings, a slight repast was sometimes brought; but they more frequently shared the last and most truly social meal within. Winter made little difference in her mode of occupying her time. She then always retired to her closet to read at stated periods.

"The hospitalities of this family were so far beyond their apparent income that all strangers were astonished at them. To account for this it must be observed that, in the first place, there was perhaps scarce an instance of a family possessing such uncommonly well-trained, active, and diligent slaves as that which I describe. The set that were staid servants when they were married had some of them died off by the time I knew the family, but the principal roots, from whence the many branches then flourishing sprung, yet remained. There were two women who had come originally from Africa while very young. They were most excellent servants, and the mothers or grandmothers of the whole set, except one white wooled negro-man, who, in my time, sat by the chimney and made shoes for all the rest.

"The great pride and happiness of these sable matrons was to bring up their children to dexterity, diligence, and obedience, Diana being determined that Maria's children should not excel hers in any quality which was a recommendation to favor; and Maria equally resolved that her brood, in the race of excellence, should outstrip Diana's Never was a more fervent competition. That of Phillis and Brunetta, in the Spectator, was a trifle to it, and it was extremely difficult to decide on their respective merits; for though Maria's son Prince cut down wood with more dexterity and dispatch than any one in the province, the mighty Cæsar, son of Diana, cut down wheat and thrashed it better than he. His sister Betty, who, to her misfortune, was a beauty of her kind, and possessed wit equal to her beauty, was the best seamstress and laundress by far I have ever known ; and the plain, unpretending Rachel, sister to Prince, wife to Titus, alias Tyte, and head cook, dressed dinners that might have pleased Apicius. I record my humble friends by their real names because they allowedly stood at the head of their own class, and distinction of every kind should be respected.

"Of the inferior personages in this drama I have been characterizing it would be tedious to tell ; suffice it that, besides filling up all the lower departments of the household, and cultivating to the highest advantage a most extensive farm, there was a thorough-bred carpenter and shoemaker, and a universal genius who made canoes, nets, and paddles, shod horses, mended implements of husbandry, managed the fishing, in itself no small department, reared hemp and tobacco, made cider and tended wild horses, as they call them, which it was his province to "break." For every branch of domestic economy there was a person allotted—educated for the purpose ; and this society was kept immaculate in the same way that the Quakers preserved the rectitude of theirs—and indeed in the only way that any community can be preserved from corruption—when a member showed symptoms of degeneracy he was immediately expelled, or, in other words more suitable to this case, sold.

"The habit of living together under the same mild though regular government produced a general cordiality and affection among all the members of the family, who were truly ruled by the law of love ; and even those who occasionally differed about trifles had an unconscious attachment to each other, which showed itself on all emergencies. Treated themselves with care and gentleness, they were careful and kind with regard to the only inferiors and dependents they had, the domestic animals. The superior personages in the family had always some good property to mention or good saying to repeat of those whom they cherished into attachment and exalted into intelligence; while they, in their turn, improved the sagacity of their subject animals by caressing and talking to them. Let no one laugh at this, for whenever a man is at ease and unsophisticated, when his native humanity is not extinguished by want or chilled by oppression, it overflows to inferior beings and improves their instincts to a degree incredible to those who have not witnessed it.

"The Princes and Cæsars of the Flats had as much to tell of the sagacity and attachments of the animals as their mistress related of their own. * * * Each negro was indulged with his raccoon, his gray squirrel or muskrat, or perhaps his beaver, which he tamed and attached to himself by daily feeding and caressing him in the farm-yard One was sure about all such houses to find these animals, in which their masters took the highest pleasure. All these small features of human nature must not be despised for their minuteness. To a good mind they afford consolation."*

Such was the pattern of a home after which Philip Schuyler and his wife arranged their own, though on a less extensive scale at first, for his fine mansion, yet standing at the head of Schuyler street, in Albany, where hospitality was dispensed to friends and strangers with almost princely plenitude for forty years, was not erected until about 1765. As the elder son he came into possession of the real estate of his father when he attained his majority

* *Memoirs of an American Lady.*

in the autumn of 1754, and his residence, during the earlier years of his married life, was in the family mansion at Albany, with his mother and sister. The property which he received by entail was large, but his nature was too noble to be governed by the selfishness which the laws of primogeniture allowed and which universal practice sanctioned, and he generously shared his patrimony with his brothers and sister. This act was more remarkable because his life and experience were intimately connected with the aristocracy of the province, who held the largest landed estates in the country. With these the justice of primogeniture laws was never questioned, nor their privileges ever refused by the fortunate elder son ; and a relinquishment of these privileges and advantages for the benefit of others was a thing unknown. But Philip Schuyler was innately just, noble and generous, and his act was nothing but a natural manifestation of these qualities. His sense of right and the fraternal yearnings of his spirit would have been outraged by any other course ; and so, governed by his natural impulses, and with a beautiful loyalty to conscience which no pecuniary advantages could bribe, he divided his houses and lands, and gave to each of his mother's children an equal share with himself.

The nuptials of Philip Schuyler, like those of his great compatriot and friend, George Washington, were celebrated at the close of the most active duties of a campaign in which he had been engaged. The treaty at Aix-la-Chapelle had secured nothing but a hollow truce for the colonists. Peace reigned in Europe, but war was again raging between the English and provincials on one side and the French and Indians on the other, in the forests of America. Blood had already flowed profusely near the banks of the Monongahela and of Lake George ; and the shifting scenes of political events in the New World, and especially in the province of New York were now grand and imposing, for the magnificent drama of the FRENCH AND INDIAN WAR—the memorable Seven Years War, performed upon two continents and the stormy ocean that separated them—was in full progress.

Rightly to understand that drama, we must become familiar with the leading facts in the history of its rehearsals in the colonies, and view, if only in hurried glances, the progress of its preparations until the curtain was lifted and the actors appeared in character before the great audience of nations. To do this let us go behind the scenes for a moment, and in the green room of retrospection hold familiar conversation with individual players. With the acts of the drama that were performed in the Old World we need have little to do except to observe the links of their connection with the plot; for Philip Schuyler, whose life and times we are delineating, and who now, for the first time, appeared as a public actor, had no part in transatlantic scenes. His sphere of action and influence was in the colony in which himself and family for three generations had lived. From the colonial governor he received his first commission as a military officer, and among colonial troops he first drew his sword in defense of his country and the honor of the British realm.

## CHAPTER VI.

THE treaty of Aix-la-Chapelle, as we have observed, was practically only a contract for a truce. The treaty of Utrecht, made in 1713, guaranteed to England all Nova Scotia included in ancient Acadie, and to the Five Nations of Indians, subject to Great Britain, the peaceable enjoyment of all their well-defined rights and privileges. But so indefinite were the terms of the treaty of Aix-la-Chapelle in 1748, notwithstanding the treaty of 1713 was held as its basis, the real difficulties which gave rise to the last war remained unsettled. The agreement that boundaries should remain as before the war was so vague in terms, considering the fact that for almost thirty years those very boundaries had been a subject for contention, that interpretation was difficult. As early as 1721, France had erected Fort St. Frederick on Crown Point, within territory always claimed by Great Britain and the Five Nations; and before the signing of the treaty of Aix-la-Chapelle, in 1748, the French had constructed almost twenty forts and several stockades and trading places on soil claimed by the British crown. France, at that time, was putting forth all her energies in carrying forward schemes of aggrandizement at various points in the Mediterranean, the East and West Indies, and in North America. She doubtless intended the peace to be only a truce, so that whilst England was inactive she might strike deeper the roots of her dominion, especially in the New World, for her Jesuit priests, with the banner of the cross in one hand and the truncheon of secular enterprises in the other, had penetrated the wonderful vallies of the Great West, and revealed their boundless wealth to their nation.

At the time we are considering the French in America were not more than one hundred thousand in number, and scattered in trading settlements for nearly a thousand miles along the St. Lawrence and our immense lakes, and also at points on the Mississippi and its tributaries, and the Gulf of Mexico ; whilst the English numbered more than a million, and occupied the Atlantic seaboard, in the form of agricultural communities, more than a thousand miles in a line eastward of the Alleghany Mountains and far northward toward the St. Lawrence, from the St. Mary's in Florida to the Penobscot in Maine.

The trading posts and missionary stations of the French, deep in the wilderness, at first attracted very little attention, but when, after the capture of Louisburg, in 1745, they built strong vessels at the foot of Lake Ontario, and commenced the erection of a cordon of fortifications more than sixty in number between Montreal and New Orleans, the English perceived the necessity of arousing to immediate and vigorous opposition. Disputes soon arose, and these resulted in hostile action. The territorial question was revived, and both parties appeared to be in a mood to settle it by a passage at arms. A peaceful company of speculators brought the matter to issue in this wise :

In 1749 King George of England conveyed, by grant, six hundred thousand acres of land on the southeast bank of the Ohio river to an association composed of London merchants and Virginia speculators, giving them, at the same time, the exclusive privilege of trafficking with the Indians. The association was called *The Ohio Company*, and, anxious to bring their domain into market, they sent surveyors to explore and settle the boundaries of it. At the same time English traders penetrated the country northward of the Ohio, as far as the Miami villages, to traffic with the willing Indians. The jealousy of the French traders was aroused, and at Piqua, an Indian village, a skirmish ensued between traders of the two nationalities, when the first blood was shed in the cruel war that ensued.

In 1753, the governor of Canada detached twelve hundred French soldiers to occupy the Ohio valley, to the exclusion of the English. They built a fort, first on the south shore of Lake Erie, near the village of that name, then on the Venango (French Creek), near the present village of Waterford, and a third at the junction of the Alleghany river and French Creek, at the village of Franklin. *The Ohio Company* complained of this intrusion, and as their land lay within the chartered limits of Virginia, the lieutenant-governor of that province, Robert Dinwiddie, felt called upon to espouse their cause. He resolved to first try diplomacy, and accordingly, in the autumn of 1753, he sent George Washington, then a young man less than twenty-two years of age, to confer with Le Gardeur de St. Pierre, the commander of the French troops, and to present to him a letter of remonstrance against his occupancy of English soil.

It was late in autumn when Washington, with only two or three attendants, departed upon his perilous journey of full four hundred miles towards Lake Erie, though a dark wilderness and many tribes of savage men. Ice, snow, floods, all lay in his path, yet he accomplished his undertaking to the satisfaction of those who sent him. His mission, however, seemed unfruitful. St. Pierre received him courteously, treated him hospitably four or five days, and then gave him a written answer to Dinwiddie in a sealed envelope. Washington had heard the important fact of the hostile designs of the French from the lips of officers made incautious by a free use of wine, and with this information, and a knowledge of the strength and position of the French posts, he returned to Williamsburg with St. Pierre's letter to Dinwiddie. That letter simply informed the Virginia magistrate that the commander of the French was acting under the orders of the Marquis Du Quesne, the governor-general of Canada, and that he should not withdraw his troops from the Ohio country, as Dinwiddie demanded.

Dinwiddie was a wrong-headed, avaricious Scotchman, and had already made the Virginians restive under royal rule. He was concerned in the *Ohio Company*, and resolved to make war upon the French intruders, but when he evoked the civil aid of the province, in giving sanction to an expedition and providing means for its support, he found powerful opposition in the Legislature and among the people. Their patriotism was appealed to, and at length the Legislature voted fiftv thousand dollars for the support of troops enlisted for an expedition. The other colonies were invited to coöperate, but none responded affirmatively except North Carolina, from whose bosom, on the recommendation of her Legislature, four hundred volunteers were soon on their way toward Winchester. A few volunteers from South Carolina and New York hastened toward the seat of war, while in Virginia a regiment of six hundred men was formed, with Colonel Joshua Fry as commander, and Major Washington as his lieutenant. These rendezvoused at Alexandria, and, with Washington at the head of the advanced corps, marched toward the Ohio at the beginning of April, 1753.

In the meantime the *Ohio Company* had sent thirty

men to construct a fort at the junction of the Alleghany and Monongahela rivers. They were attacked and driven away by some French troops, who completed the fortification and named it Du Quesne, in honor of the governor of Canada. Washington was within forty miles of that point, with the advanced guard, when intelligence of the event reached him, with the information that a strong force of the enemy were on their way to intercept him. He fell back to a place called the Great Meadows, and there erected a stockade, which he named Fort Necessity. While it was in progress he sent out a party to attack the advanced guard of the French. They were successful. At the dead of night the Virginians fell upon the sleeping Frenchmen, and Jumonville, their commander, and nine of his men were slain. Of fifty who formed the detachment only fifteen escaped.

Two days after this event Colonel Fry died, and the command of the expedition fell upon young Washington. With about four hundred men he proceeded toward Fort Du Quesne. He had not advanced far when he was informed that a brother of the slain Jumonville, with at least a thousand Indians and some Frenchmen were marching to avenge the death of his kinsman. Washington immediately fell back to Fort Necesssity, where he was attacked by fifteen hundred foes. After a conflict of ten hours he was compelled to capitulate, on the 4th of July, but on honorable terms, and he and his men returned to Virginia. Thus was inaugurated the French and Indian War, which afterward raged vigorously in northern New York.

While these military operations were in progress, a civil movement of great importance was seen at Albany, the residence of Philip Schuyler. It was the meeting of the representatives of seven of the Anglo-American colonies, to consult upon a plan for a federal union, so as to oppose a strong front to the common enemy seated upon the St. Lawrence and the lakes. This was really the primal object of the members of the convention ; a secondary and important one was to strengthen the bond between the English and the Six Nations.

The necessity for such union, and such friendship with the Indians, had been felt for some time, yet the home government, when it proposed the convention by a circular letter addressed by Lord Holderness to all the colonies, did not contemplate a permanent political union ; only a temporary confederation in time of danger against a menacing enemy. In that letter his lordship declared the chief design of the convention to be the renewal of treaties with the Six Nations.

Only seven of the thirteen colonies responded to the call, namely, Massachusetts, New Hampshire, Connecticut, New York, Rhode Island, Pennsylvania and Maryland. Delegates from these provinces assembled at the old City Hall, in Albany, on the 19th of June, 1754, and the convention was organized by the appointment of James De Lancey, the lieutenant governor of New York, as their president.* Chiefs of the Six Nations had come with tardy steps, and only one hundred and fifty were in attendance. Hendrick, the great Mohawk warrior, who was slain

* The following are the names of the commissioners from the several States: *New York.*—James De Lancey, Joseph Murray, William Johnson, John Chambers, William Smith. *Massachusetts.*—Samuel Welles, John Chandler, Thomas Hutchinson, Oliver Partridge, John Worthington. *New Hampshire.*—Theodore Atkinson, Richard Wibird, Mesheck Weare, Henry Sherburne. *Connecticut.*—William Pitkin, Roger Wolcott, Elisha Williams. *Rhode Island.*—Stephen Hopkins, Martin Howard. *Pennsylvania.*—John Penn, Benjamin Franklin, Richard Peters, Isaac Norris. *Maryland.*—Benjamin Tasker, Benjamin Barnes.

in battle near Lake George the following year, was their principal speaker.

De Lancey opened the business of the convention by a speech to the Indians, interpreted by Colonel Myndert Schuyler, one of the commissioners, and was responded to by Hendrick. That powerful, white-haired warrior, a noble specimen of his race, arose with grave mien, and advancing a few steps, held up the chain belt which had been given him by the lieutenant-governor and the chief magistrates of other colonies, and said: "We return you all our grateful acknowledgments for renewing and brightening the covenant chain. We will take this belt to Onondaga, [the federal capital of the Six Nations,] where our council-fire always burns, and keep it so securely that neither thunder nor lightning shall break it. There we will consult over it, and we hope when you show this belt again, we shall give you reason to rejoice at it. In the meantime we desire that you will strengthen yourselves, and bring as many into this covenant chain as you possibly can." Then, his eyes flashing indignation at the remembrance of the past, when the French swept down the Hudson valley to Saratoga, and there were no forts to impede their progress, he said:

"You desired us to open our minds and hearts to you. You have asked us the reason of our living in this dispersed manner. The reason is, your neglecting us these three years past." Then casting a stick behind him, he continued: "You have thus thrown us behind your back and disregarded us, whereas the French are a subtle and vigilant people, ever using their utmost endeavors to seduce and bring our people over to them. Look at the French! They are *men;* they are fortifying everywhere. But, we are ashamed to say it, you are like *women,* bare and open, without any fortifications. It is but one step from Canada hither, and the French may easily come and turn you out of doors."

Through this neglect during the political strife in the province, that had raged violently for several years, the Six Nations had become extensively disaffected. Full one half of the Onondagas had withdrawn and joined a settlement near the site of Ogdensburgh, at the mouth of the Oswegatchie, under the protection of the guns of the old French fort *Presentation.* Even some of the Mohawks uttered loud complaints, but through the influence of Hendrick, and one or two others, they were retained as fast friends of the English.

While the business of the convention was in progress, that body, responding to an invitation of the Massachusetts delegates, took into consideration the expediency of forming a federative union of the colonies. The subject was referred to a committee consisting of one member of each delegation present.* Several plans were proposed, when Dr. Franklin, whose fertile mind had conceived the necessity of a union and the form of a confederation, arose and submitted a draft of a scheme for the consideration of the convention. The subject was debated "hand in hand." Franklin observed, "with the Indian business, daily, for twelve consecutive days;" and at length a report, as substantially drawn by him, was adopted, the Connecticut delegates alone dissenting.

Franklin's plan of union, having, in many respects, a remarkable similarity to the Federal Constitution formed by himself and others thirty-three years afterward, proposed

* The committee consisted of Hutchinson of *Massachusetts*, Atkinson of *New Hampshire*, Pitkin of *Connecticut*, Hopkins of *Rhode Island*, Smith of *New York*, Franklin of *Pennsylvania*, and Tasker of *Maryland.*

a grand council of forty-eight members—seven from Virginia, seven from Massachusetts, six from Pennsylvania, five from Connecticut, four each from New York, Maryland, and the two Carolinas, three from New Jersey, and two each from New Hampshire and Rhode Island. The number of forty-eight was to remain fixed, no colony to have more than seven nor less than two members; but the apportionment to vary within those limits, with the rates of contribution. This council was to have the general management of civil and military affairs. It was to have control of the armies, the apportionment of men and money, and to enact general laws in conformity with the British Constitution, and not in contravention of statutes passed by the imperial Parliament. It was to have for its head a president general, appointed by the crown, to possess a negative or veto power on all acts of the council, and to have, with the advice of the council, the appointment of all military officers and the entire management of Indian affairs. Civil officers were to be appointed by the council, with the consent of the president.*

The seat of the proposed federal government was to be Philadelphia, then a central city in the colonies, and where, it was alleged, the representatives would be "well and cheaply accommodated." It was also suggested that if the whole journey to the seat of government had to be performed on horseback, (much of it could be accomplished by water,) "the most distant members, namely, the two from New Hampshire and from South Carolina, might probably render themselves at Philadelphia *in fifteen or twenty days!*"†

The plan of union was doomed to a singular fate. Franklin was greeted at New York, when he went down

* Pitkin's *Political and Civil History of the United States*, i. 143.

† *Life and Writings of Franklin*, iii. 42.

the Hudson from the council at Albany, with every demonstration of joy as the mover of American union, but the several colonial assemblies, viewing it with the jealous eye that watched over the individual liberties of the colonies, rejected it as too aristocratic—too much *prerogative* in it—partaking too largely of the centralization of power; while the Lords of Trade, to whom it was submitted, did not approve of it nor recommend it to the King, because it was too democratic. Perhaps some minds among them may have been sagacious enough to perceive the danger it might work to the integrity of the British realm.

The Board of Trade had already proposed a plan of their own:—a grand assembly of colonial governors and certain select members of their several councils, with power to draw on the British treasury, the sums thus drawn to be reimbursed by taxes imposed in the colonies by the British Parliament. This proposition found no favor with the colonists, and Massachusetts gave her agent in England special instructions "to oppose everything that should have the remotest tendency to raise a revenue in America for any public use or services of government."

The capacious mind of Franklin conceived, at this time, an empire more magnificent than the one contemplated in the union of the then existing colonies. The convention ordered the committee charged with the preparation of a plan of union, to report a representation of the affairs of the colonies. This able paper, it is believed, was drawn by Franklin, for it embodies the ideas expressed by him in a communication made to Governor Pownall not many years afterward. It proposed "that the bounds of those colonies which extend to the South Sea, (the Pacific Ocean,) be contracted and limited by the Alleghany or Appalachian mountains, and that measures be taken for settling, from time to time, colonies of his Majesty's Protestant subjects westward of said mountains, in convenient cantons to be assigned for that purpose." But the war just kindling prevented, for the time, putting into execution Franklin's grand idea of a federal and expanding Union.

The convention at Albany had just closed its labors, when a cry for help was raised along the New England frontier. The Indians, incited by the French, commenced murderous depredations there; and those in the Ohio country, inflamed by French emissaries, lifted the hatchet and lighted the brand for a war of extermination against the advancing English settlements. Clouds of danger were thickening on every hand, and yet some of the colonies were tardy in their preparations for the impending storm. Governor Shirley, of Massachusetts, put forth all his energies and accomplished much, while in Virginia disputes about precedence between the regimental officers and the captains of independent companies ran high, and in a degree paralyzed efforts for the public good; and Governor Dinwiddie made matters worse by his ignorance and obstinacy. The assembly of New York, awake to the perils that threatened, voted twenty-five thousand dollars for the military service, and the authorities of Maryland voted thirty thousand dollars for the same. The British government sent over fifty thousand dollars for the use of the colonies, and, to allay discontents, appointed Governor Sharpe, of Maryland, commander-in-chief of all the provincial troops. Yet the year 1754 closed without any efficient preparations for a conflict with the French.

The British government, meanwhile, had perceived that a very severe contest was about to be commenced between their colonists in America and those of the French, and resolved to extend aid to the former, notwithstanding the two nations were at peace. When the British ministry called the attention of the French court to transactions in America, the latter expressed the most pacific intentions and promises for the future, while its actions were in direct opposition to its professions. The British resolved no longer to be diverted by this duplicity, and at the close of 1754, sent General Edward Braddock, a brave but haughty and self-sufficient Irish officer, with two regiments, commanded by Colonels Halkett and Dunbar, to assume the chief command in America and coöperate with the provincials as circumstances might require. He arrived in the Chesapeake in February, 1755, and, at his request, six of the colonial governors met him in convention at Alexandria, in April following, to assist in arranging a vigorous campaign against the French.*

Three separate expeditions were planned—one against Fort Du Quesne, at the forks of the Ohio, to be led by Braddock in person ; a second against fort Niagara, at the mouth of the Niagara river, and Fort Frontenac (now Kingston), at the foot of Lake Ontario, to be commanded by Governor Shirley ; and a third against Fort St. Frederick, at Crown Point, on Lake Champlain, under General William Johnson, of the Mohawk region, where he had acquired great ascendancy over the more eastern nations of the Iroquois confederacy. A fourth expedition had already been arranged by Governor Shirley, and Governor Lawrence, of Nova Scotia, designed to drive the French out of that province and all other portions of Acadie. The im-

* Shirley, of *Massachusetts;* Dinwiddie, of *Virginia;* De Lancey, of *New York;* Sharpe, of *Maryland;* Morris, of *Pennsylvania;* and Dobbs, of *North Carolina.* Admiral Keppel, commander of the British fleet that bore Braddock's thousand men to America, was also present.

perial government sanctioned these extensive preparations, and when the flowers first bloomed upon the New England hills, in the spring of 1755, the colonies began to glow with the warmest enthusiasm.

James De Lancey, a man of great energy and large fortune, was now acting governor of the province of New York. He had been the uncompromising political adversary of Governor Clinton for several years, and, as we have before observed, their quarrels interfered seriously with the public welfare. Clinton had become extremely unpopular. "Easy in his temper, but incapable of business," says a cotemporary, "he was always obliged to rely upon some favorite. In a province given to hospitality he erred by immuring himself in a fort, or retiring to a grotto in the country, where his time was spent with his bottle and a little trifling circle, who played billiards with his lady and lived upon his bounty. He was seldom abroad; many of the citizens never saw him; he did not even attend divine worship above three or four times during his whole administration."* At length, thoroughly wearied with the defensive warfare which he was compelled to continually wage with his opponent, he resigned his commission and returned to England in the autumn of 1753.

Clinton was succeeded by Sir Danvers Osborne, brother-in-law of the Earl of Halifax. He had lately been bereaved of his wife, whom he passionately loved, and with a heavy heart he crossed the Atlantic. On his arrival he was received with acclamations, but he soon learned that the people were, in a measure, arrayed against the government on the subject of taxes, and that his situation as the representative of the crown would be a most uneasy one. On the 10th of October he took the oaths of office, and

* *History of New York*, by William Smith.

with the shouts of welcome for himself he heard execrations of his predecessor. "I expect like treatment before I leave the government," he said, sorrowfully, and retired to his lodgings more gloomy than ever.

Osborne had received from the city council an address, in which they said "We are sufficiently assured that your excellency will be as averse from countenancing as we from brooking any infringements of our inestimable liberties, civil and religious." This implied jealousy distressed him, and when, on the following day, he communicated to his council his instructions from the King, first to inform the assembly that they were required "to recede from all encroachments upon the prerogative," and then to insist upon their affording permanent and indefinite support to the government, while all public money was to be applied by the governor's warrant, with the consent of the council, and the assembly never to be allowed to examine the accounts, he was informed that the latter would never comply. He sighed, turned about, and reclining against the window frame exclaimed in plaintive voice, "Then what have I come here for?" And to De Lancey he said, "I believe I shall soon leave you the government; I find myself unable to bear the government of it." He went home in a mood of deepest melancholy, and towards morning he hanged himself upon his garden fence. Thus were the reigns of government left in the hands of De Lancey.

De Lancey's position was a delicate one. He had been the leader of the opposition in the assembly, and he was now compelled to become a Janus—rebuke the assembly publicly for not obeying instructions in granting required supplies, and to confederate with them privately in measures directly opposed to the will of the crown. The assembly, in turn, lauded the governor for his virtues and abilities, boasted of their attachment to the crown, and declared that nothing should be wanting to promote the King's service and render his administration easy and happy. At the same time they firmly resisted every movement in the way of taxation without their consent, while De Lancey, with well dissembled zeal, joined Shirley and Dinwiddie, Sharpe and Morris, Braddock, Dunbar, and Gage, in urging the British government to put in action a scheme of general taxation in America by act of Parliament. Thus urged, the imperial government resolved to assert its full authority in the American colonies, and to raise funds for American affairs by a stamp duty and a duty on products of the foreign West Indies.

While politicians in and out of the New York Legislature were playing disreputable games, in which the best interests of the commonwealth were more or less involved, the people at large, alarmed by the kindling war, became clamorous for measures that should provide defenses against the foe, both inland and upon the sea. These clamors became so loud and importunate that, on the advice of his council, De Lancey issued a proclamation on the 10th of January, 1755, directing the Assembly to convene on the 4th of February following, almost six weeks earlier than the time to which they had adjourned. In his message he stated that preparations for war against the French in America were absolutely necessary, and that he should expect them to make all proper provisions for putting the province in a suitable state of defense. He informed the assembly of the armament on the way under General Braddock; urged them to strengthen the fortifications at New York, and to take immediate measures for erecting others at the northward. "Our northern frontier," he said, "demands your most serious attention. The city of Albany is in such a condition as draws a reproach upon us from our own Indians at the same time that it greatly discourages them." He urged them to take care to secure that city against the foe, for if it should be once taken, nothing, he thought, could prevent the enemy penetrating into New Jersey and Pennsylvania. He also desired them to provide for the building of a strong fortification higher up on the Hudson ; to adopt more compulsory regulations for bringing the militia into active service; and concluded by saying, "I flatter myself you will not risk losing your all by an ill-timed parsimony."

The Assembly took prompt action, for there was great alarm abroad. Utterly disregarding the royal instructions, which prohibited the further issue of paper money by the colony, unless bills for the purpose were submitted to and approved by the crown, they authorized the emission of £45,000 in bills of credit, to be sunk at short intervals by a tax. They also subjected the militiamen to such duties and penalties as the executive should prescribe ; authorized the levy of eight hundred men and the impressment of artificers ; prohibited the exportation of provisions to the French colonies, and provided funds for arming the troops, and for making presents to the Indians to secure their cooperation.

It was at this juncture that Shirley sent out his envoys to arouse the colonies to a war of extermination against the French, or at least to achieve the conquest of Canada. His envoy to New York was Thomas Pownal, who afterward became governor of Massachusetts. He appeared at about the middle of March, and soon afterward the assembly passed bills for levying eight hundred men for the proposed expedition against Crown Point, under William Johnson. The patriotism of the young men of the colony was appealed to, and then, for the first time, Philip Schuyler, who had lately attained to his majority, appeared in the arena of public life, under the sanction of the following commission:

"To PHILIP SCHUYLER, ESQUIRE:

"Whereas, by an act of the Legislature of this province, passed on the third of May instant, provision is made for raising and subsisting eight complete companies of volunteers, to consist of one captain, two lieutenants, four sergeants, three corporals, one drummer, and eighty-nine private men, to be employed in building one or more forts on his Majesty's lands to the northward of Albany, in conjunction with the forces to be raised by the other governments; the whole to be commanded by William Johnson, Esq., Major-General and Commander-in-Chief of the said forces. And as an inducement to officers and men to engage in this service, the following pay and other advantages are granted by the act: To every captain who shall raise such a complete company, to be paid on the first muster thereof, one hundred pounds. To each able-bodied man a bounty of thirty-two shillings and sixpence, a blanket, a good lapelled coat, a felt hat, one shirt, two pair of Oznaburg trowsers, one pair of shoes, and one pair of stockings. To captains eight shillings per diem, lieutenants six shillings, sergeants one shilling and eightpence, corporals one shilling and sixpence, drummers one shilling and sixpence, and each private man one shilling and threepence per day. And you being represented to me as a person able to raise such a company and fit to be employed in this service, I have therefore thought fit to authorize, and I do hereby authorize and impower you to beat up for volunteers, and to raise such a company within this province, whom you are to enlist according to the directions herewith given you, on the completion and muster whereof you shall receive my commission to command such company, and from thenceforth to be entitled to pay. And all officers, civil and military, are required to give you all due encouragement. And for your so doing this shall be your warrant.

"Given under my hand, in the city of New York, this fifth day of May, 1755. "JAMES DE LANCEY."

Young Schuyler set about the business of recruiting immediately, and very soon the full complement of one hundred men responded to his call. They were chiefly young men, belonging to the most respectable families in

Albany and its vicinity. Some of them became distinguished militia officers in the army of the Revolution twenty years later. Schuyler reported himself to General Johnson's adjutant-general, and soon afterward received the following commission from acting governor De Lancey:

"To PHILIP J. SCHUYLER, ESQUIRE, GREETING:

"Whereas the several governments of the Massachusetts Bay, New Hampshire, Connecticut, Rhode Island, and this province, have respectively raised a body of men to be employed in an expedition for erecting a strong fort or forts on his Majesty's lands near Crown Point, and for removing the encroachments of the *French* in that quarter, the said forces to be commanded by the Honorable William Johnson, Esq., Major General and Commander-in-Chief of the said expedition; and reposing especial trust and confidence in the care, diligence, and circumspection, as well as in the loyalty, courage, and readiness of you to do his Majesty good service, I have nominated, constituted and appointed, and do, by virtue of the powers and authorities to me given by his Majesty, hereby nominate, constitute, and appoint you, the said Philip J. Schuyler, to be *Captain* of the company raised by you for the service aforesaid, in the regiment of the province whereof William Cockcroft, Esq., is colonel. You are therefore to take the said company into your charge and care as captain, and duly to exercise both the officers and soldiers of that company in arms. And as they are hereby commanded to obey you as their captain, so are you likewise to observe and follow such directions, from time to time, as you shall receive from me, or any other your superior officer, according to the rules and discipline of war, in pursuance of the trust reposed in you; and for so doing this shall be your commission.

"Given under my hand and seal-at-arms, in New York, the fourteenth day of June, in the twenty-eighth year of his Majesty's reign, Anno Domini one thousand seven hundred and fifty-five.

"JAMES DE LANCEY.

"GEO. BANYAR, Secretary."

## CHAPTER VII.

THE troops destined for the expedition against Niagara and Frontenac, under Governor Shirley, and against Crown Point, under General Johnson, were ordered to assemble at Albany. The call for volunteers and levies had been cheerfully responded to, and the larger portion of the number summoned were at Albany at the close of June. Those who were to be led by Shirley consisted of certain regiments of regulars furnished by New England, New York, and New Jersey, and a band of Indian auxiliaries. Those who were to follow Johnson consisted chiefly of militia regiments, comprising between five and six thousand men, supplied by New England and New York.

Johnson's lieutenant was Phineas Lyman, of Connecticut, then thirty-nine years of age, who had served his province faithfully in a legislative capacity, and by its authority was commissioned a major-general. He reached Albany with his own regiment at about the middle of June. There he was joined by the eight New York companies, (among which was that of Captain Schuyler,) and three hundred Mohawks, under Hendrick; and with an energy and skill which, in comparison with Johnson, entitled him to the post of chief commander, he arranged the expedition. Johnson, meanwhile, was collecting artillery, boats, and military stores, but so great was the delay that the provincials became tired of inaction and very discontented.

Shirley, meanwhile, had arrived, and taken up his line of march through the Mohawk valley for Oswego.

To prevent the discontented troops from desertion, General Lyman moved up the Hudson, through its rich and beautiful valley, then covered with a forest, where now the smiles of cultivation are seen on every side. It was during the hot days of July, and the troops made short marches. They were five days in making a journey of a little more than fifty miles to a point on the Hudson known as the "great carrying place," in allusion to the isthmus of twenty-five miles between that river and Lake Champlain, which connects the peninsula of New England with the continent, over which the dusky warriors of Canada sometimes carried their canoes when they penetrated the country of the Iroquois. There, on the bank of the river, General Nicholson, who commanded an expedition against Canada in the summer of 1711, built a rude stockade, and upon its site General Lyman, while waiting for General Johnson, employed his troops in the erection of quite a strong timber and earth fortification, of irregular quadrangular form, with bastions at three of the angles, and the fourth resting upon the high bank of the river. The ramparts were sixteen feet in height, and twenty-two feet in thickness, and upon these the general mounted six cannon. One of its sides was protected by a creek, the other by the Hudson river; and in front of the other two sides a deep fosse was excavated. On the whole it was a strong and well-built fortification, and, in honor of the commander, it was called Fort Lyman. But Johnson, who was ever ready to bend the supple knee to the power from which he might receive honors and emoluments, afterward ungenerously named it Fort Edward, in honor of the Duke of York, grandson of the reigning sovereign, and brother of the prince who, a few years later, became King George the Third.

On the 8th of August Johnson left Albany with the artillery and stores ; also the New York troops under Lieutenant Colonel William Cockroft, (Captain Schuyler's chief,) and a few of the Connecticut troops left behind by General Lyman. He reached Fort Edward on the 14th, and there, a week later, he held a council of war, to determine what route should be taken to Crown Point. It was unanimously decided that by the way of the Lake of the Holy Sacrament, as Lake George was then called, appeared to them the most eligible, and that they would proceed immediately in that direction.

While these preparations for the campaign in the north were in progress, Braddock was on his way toward Fort Du Quesne, and the eastern expedition, under General Winslow, had performed its mission. Winslow had sailed from Boston toward the close of May with three thousand men, and at the head of the Bay of Fundy, where he landed, was joined by Colonel Monckton, with three hundred British regulars from a neighboring English garrison. There Monckton, Winslow's superior, took the chief command, and in June had conquered the country and placed the whole region under martial rule. So far good, according to the ethics of war, but the cruel sequel deserves, as it has received, universal reprobation. The English decided upon the total destruction of the French settlements in all Acadie, and under the plea that they would be likely to aid their brethren in Canada, that innocent and happy people were seized in their homes, their churches and their fields, conveyed on board the British fleet, without regard to the sanctities of the family relations or the claims of gentle woman and helpless childhood, and borne away. Families were thus separated for ever; and to compel those who had escaped the hand of ruthless violence, and fled to the woods for safety, to surrender to the invader, their growing crops and garnered food were totally destroyed, and starvation or captivity were the dreadful alternatives offered to them. The Acadians were completely peeled. Those who were carried away became helpless beggars in the English colonies, to die heart-broken in strange lands. In one short month, their paradise, into which no Satan had ever before intruded, was changed to a desert of despair, and a happy, unoffending people, were crushed into the dust.

Braddock, with about two thousand men, left the Potomac at Cumberland toward the middle of June, and made his weary way over the Alleghanies to attack Fort Du Quesne. His force was composed of British regulars and American provincials; and young Washington had consented to become his aid, with the rank of colonel. To him was given the command of the provincials. Anxious to reach his destination before the garrison could receive reinforcements, Braddock made forced marches with twelve hundred men, leaving Colonel Dunbar, his second in command, to follow with the remainder and the wagons.

Braddock was a bigoted disciplinarian of the European school, and he spurned the advice of Colonel Washington, when he ventured to propose methods, dictated by experience, to meet the Indians in their native forests. He would listen to no suggestions, especially from a provincial officer, and on the 9th of July, at about mid-day, while marching in fancied security, just after crossing the Monongahela, he fell into an ambuscade. Dusky warriors arose from the ravines and behind the huge forest trees on every side, and poured terrible storms of bullets and arrows upon his doomed army. Even then, had Braddock been willing to shape his tactics to the exigencies of the moment, his army might have been saved and perhaps victorious, but he obstinately persisted in maneuvering according to European rules, while his troops were falling around him in scores. For three hours a deadly conflict raged in the forest. The slain covered the ground. Every mounted officer but Washington was killed or maimed, and finally the really brave Braddock fell mortally wounded. Washington remained unhurt, took the chief command, rallied the provincials, and gallantly covered the retreat of the regulars, who fled when their general fell. The enemy did not follow, and the remnant of the army was saved. Braddock was carried off the field, and a week afterward he died. Then, by torch-light, Colonel Washington read the impressive funeral service of the Anglican Church over his body, and it was buried beneath a road, where the Indians might not discover and desecrate it. The flying troops were received by Colonel Dunbar, and Washington, with the southern provincials, went back to Virginia. Thus ended in utter defeat an expedition to which all others of the campaign were secondary.

The expedition against Niagara and Frontenac, under the personal guidance of General Shirley, although not so disastrous as that under Braddock, was equally unsuccessful. The main body of Shirley's troops were not assembled at Oswego, the point of general rendezvous for an attack on these forts, until late in August. Shirley was informed of Braddock's defeat while on his march through the upper Mohawk valley, and the intelligence spread consternation throughout the army. Many of the boatmen and sledge men, hired to transport provisions and stores to Oswego, began to desert; and the Indians, also alarmed, showed signs of serious defection. Much time was consumed in efforts to conciliate and reassure them, for, as on all occasions, the savages were unwilling to remain with what appeared to them the weaker party. Many bands of Indians fell off, and when, on the 21st of August, Shirley arrived at Oswego, his forces was so much reduced by desertion, and the fidelity of the Indians was so insecure, that he hesitated about proceeding further. He finally moved forward, but a succession of heavy rains so damaged his munitions of war that he abandoned the expedition, and leaving Colonel Mercer, with a garrison of seven hundred men, at Oswego, instructed to build two additional forts for the defense of that station, he marched the remainder of the army back to Albany.

The alarming intelligence of Braddock's disaster and the failure of Shirley somewhat dispirited the troops under Johnson, and a feeling generally prevailed that the expedition against the French at Crown Point would also prove an utter failure. But the New England people had entered into this scheme for expelling the French from Lake Champlain with a great deal of earnestness, their borders being peculiarly exposed to incursions from the north while Crown Point was in possession of the enemy. For this reason the troops at Fort Edward, who were chiefly from the East, were ready to press forward.

Leaving a sufficient garrison to hold Fort Edward, Johnson set out on the 26th of August, with the main body of the army, for the Lake of the Holy Sacrament, a distance of about seventeen miles, and arrived at its head on the evening of the 28th. With the same loyalty that caused him to change the name of Fort Lyman to that of Fort Edward, Johnson now called the beautiful sheet of water, upon whose margin he stood, Lake George, "not" he said "in simple honor of his majesty, but to assert his undoubted dominion here." "I found," he said, "a mere wilderness; never was house or fort erected here before." He at once commenced a clearing for a camp of five thousand men, but, with strange indolence or lack of sagacity, not a spade or pick was employed in making intrenchments. There his camp lay, with the open lake on one side and the sheltering forest on the other, completely exposed to the attacks of a vigilant and stealthy enemy.

Slowly wagon after wagon brought artillery, boats, and stores to that camp, while the soldiers spent day after day in utter idleness, notwithstanding Indian scouts brought the intelligence that a party of French and savages were erecting a fort at Ticonderoga, twelve miles further into the country of the English than the post against which this expedition was pressing. This intelligence startled Johnson, and he resolved to construct a rude fort at the head of the lake, and then, with part of his troops, proceed in bateaux to its foot, march over through the forest, and take possession of Ticonderoga before the enemy could complete their works, rest there until joined by the remainder of his forces, and then attack Crown Point.

Johnson was leisurely preparing for this movement, when scouts brought intelligence that the enemy in considerable numbers were pushing through the forests from South Bay, an expansion of the narrow part of Lake Champlain near Whitehall. The report was true. A force of almost two thousand men, consisting of French regulars, Canadians, and Indians, under the Baron Dieskau, an able and experienced general, was advancing toward the English settlements. He had arrived at Quebec in the spring, with about two thousand regulars, and intended to go up the St. Lawrence and Lake Ontario, capture Oswego, and hold in awe the whole Iroquois confederacy. Information of Johnson's expedition against Crown Point caused him to change his plan, and with a part of his troops to go up Lake Champlain to assist in the defense of Fort St. Frederick. He waited there for the approach of Johnson until, wearied with inaction, he determined to press forward and meet his enemy. With the vigilance of an accomplished disciplinarian, he made himself acquainted with the condition and movements of his opponents ; and when he arrived at South Bay he resolved to cut a road through the woods in the direction of Fort Edward, attack and capture the garrison there, and then, with quick movement, fall upon Johnson's exposed camp at the head of Lake George. This accomplished, he intended to turn southward, desolate Albany and Schenectada, and cut off all communication with Oswego. Dieskau believed his plan could be accomplished with comparative ease, and under this impression he moved forward.

Sunday, the 7th of September, was a beautiful day. The sun shone in splendor upon the provincial camp that lay upon the rising ground at the head of Lake George ; and when the sermons for the day were over, the soldiers sauntered listlessly in the shade along the margin of the forest, and the Mohawk braves forgot to be vigilant under the influence of the feeling of security that prevailed. The scouts were out upon the mountains and in the ravines, but no alarm disturbed the quiet of the camp, and the sun went down that night as it had gone down many nights before, leaving an unwise general to sleep in fancied safety, without a battery or a trench for defense.

The evening wore away and the camp-fires were burning feebly, when, at midnight or past, scouts came in hot haste to the general's tent to inform him that the woods between South Bay and Fort Edward were swarming with

French and Indian warriors. Johnson immediately sent swift couriers first to Fort Edward, and then to New England and to the authorities of his own province, with information of his peril and a call for help. Massachusetts was the first to respond, by raising, in addition to her troops already in the field, several hundred more. But before they could reach the scene of danger all danger was past.

On the morning of the 8th, General Johnson called a council of war, and as the enemy were seen making their way in the direction of Fort Edward, it was resolved to send a detachment of a thousand men to the relief of the garrison there. Colonel Ephraim Williams, of Massachusetts, was chosen to command the relief corps, and he was joined by Hendrick and two hundred of his Mohawk warriors. At nine o'clock in the morning they started in the direction of Fort Edward.

Meanwhile the cowardice or extreme caution of the Indians with Dieskau foiled that general. Full three hundred of them were discontented warriors of the Six Nations, who had emigrated to Canada, and the other three hundred were Abenakes. The Iroquois, as they approached Fort Edward, heard that there were cannon upon its ramparts. They had learned to dread that destructive engine, and refused to attack the fort. The Abenakes joined in the refusal, but all agreed to attack the unfortified camp at the head of the lake. Dieskau, therefore, turned his face in that direction. His scouts soon brought him intelligence of the advancing troops under Williams, and his whole force was placed in ambuscade, according to Indian custom.

Williams, unsuspicious of danger, had marched about three miles from the camp, when his party fell into the ambush, which was in crescent form. French and Indians rose upon them on every side, and poured deadly vollies upon the bewildered provincials and Mohawks. Hendrick, who was advanced in years and quite corpulent, was the only man on horseback. He had shrewdly remarked in the morning, when told of the number of the detachment, "If they are to fight, they are too few; if they are to be killed, they are too many." And he had objected to the proposition of making three divisions, saying, as he put three sticks together, "Unite them and you can not break them; take them one by one, and you can break them easily." Johnson, guided by the opinion of Hendrick, ordered the whole detachment to march in one body.

Hendrick fell almost at the first fire, and his braves turned back upon the advancing provincials. Williams mounted a rock for the purpose of reconnoitering, when he, too, fell mortally wounded. The slaughter soon became dreadful, and the surviving provincials and Indians, under the general command of Lieutenant Colonel Whiting, of New Haven, retreated in good order toward the camp, frequently delivering galling fires upon the pursuers. As they drew near the camp, their retreat was covered by a party of three hundred men, under Lieutenant Colonel Cole, sent out by General Johnson for the purpose.

When Johnson heard the din of battle in the forest, and its sounds approaching nearer and nearer, he was aroused to a sense of real danger, and at once ordered breastworks of trees to be raised. At the same time some field pieces that had been sent from Fort Edward were placed in battery, and some heavy cannon and a howitzer, intended for use at Crown Point that were lying upon the shore of the lake, were dragged up the bank and placed upon the rude breastwork. These hasty preparations for defense were scarcely finished when the fugitives appeared with the enemy in hot pursuit.

It had been Dieskau's plan to rush forward suddenly, and enter the camp with the flying provincials, but when within a short distance of the breastworks, his Indians, from rising ground, saw the cannon, they halted. The Canadians also faltered. The Baron, with his regulars, after brief hesitation, rushed forward to attack the center of the camp, where he was received with severe vollies of musketry. He had hoped for aid in this assault from the Canadians and Indians, whom he had placed on his flanks, but they were shy, and a bombshell from the howitzer, and a heavy fire of grape shot from the larger cannon, under the direction of Captain Eyre, of the engineer corps of Braddock's army, soon caused the two wings to flee. And yet, for more than four hours did Dieskau and his regulars, with no other weapon than the musket, sustain the severe conflict. Three times the baron was wounded, but he would not retire, and nearly all of his brave men perished. Resolved on death or victory, he ordered his servant to place his military dress near him. Faint with fatigue and loss of blood, he sat upon a stump in the midst of the leaden storm. At length the provincials, leaping over the breastworks, put the shattered enemy to flight. Dieskau remained, unable to flee ; and as a provincial soldier who discovered him approached, he put his hand in his pocket to offer him his watch as a bribe to allow him to escape. Believing the baron to be feeling for his pistol, the provincial shot him severely in the hip, and in that condition he was made prisoner and carried into the American camp, where General Johnson also lay wounded in the fleshy part of his thigh, from a ball sent in the beginning of the action. The battle, during the whole conflict, was conducted by General Lyman, and the credit of the victory properly belonged to that brave and energetic man.

Hendrick's Indians wished to pursue the fugitives and take revenge for the loss of their leader, and Lyman strongly recommended pursuit. Had that course been taken, no doubt the whole body of the enemy might have been slain or made prisoners. But Johnson, with his usual indecision, refused permission to pursue, and the best fruits of the victory were lost.

Just at evening the fugitives were met and attacked by a party of two hundred men, under Captain M'Ginnis, a mere lad, from New Hampshire. The enemy fled in dismay, but the young leader was killed at the moment of his victory. The Americans lost on that day about two hundred and sixteen killed and ninety-six wounded.* The loss of the French and their allies was much greater. The French major-general was killed; also St. Pierre, to whom Washington carried a letter from Dinwiddie. He commanded the Indians in this engagement.

General Lyman, with much vehemence, urged General Johnson to push forward immediately and take possession of Ticonderoga and Crown Point, a matter of easy accomplishment while the French were panic stricken by the disasters at Lake George. But Johnson, having none of the qualities of a good general, did not know how to profit by success. General Shirley and the authorities of New Eng-

* The muster roll of the following companies that were in Johnson's army at that time, are preserved in the archives of the State of New York:

| Captains. | | | Officers. | Rank and File. |
|---|---|---|---|---|
| Philip John Schuyler's | company, | Albany, | 3 | 89 |
| Edmund Matthews' | " | " | 3 | 97 |
| Isaac Corsa's | " | Westchester, | — | 95 |
| Pieter Vanderburgh's | " | Dutchess, | 3 | 78 |
| William M'Ginnis's | " | Schenectada, | 3 | 89 |
| Samuel Dimock's | " | Seabrook, Ct., | 3 | 97 |
| John Slap's | " | Dunham, Ct., | 3 | 97 |
| Street Hall's | " | Wallingford, Ct., | 3 | 97 |

land, and even a council of war of his own army, urged him to advance, but in vain. He pleaded his expectation of being shortly attacked by a more formidable force with artillery; and he spent the whole autumn in his camp, employing the men, under the direction of Captain Eyre, in the useless labor of building a fort there, to which, when completed, he gave the name of William Henry, in honor of two English princes. It was an irregular quadrangle of about three hundred feet on each side. It was commenced in September and completed by the close of November. Johnson then placed six hundred New York troops in the fort as a garrison, disbanded the New England militia, and returned to his home amid the barbarians of the Mohawk valley, to await the rewards which he was certain to receive through the influence of friends at court and the ungenerous maxims of military ethics which then prevailed. He was careful not to divide the honors of the event. With a meanness paralleled only by his own incapacity, he did not even mention, in his report to the Lords of Trade, the name of General Lyman, the real leader in the victory. And it was immediately after the battle that, with evident jealousy of Lyman, he sought to hide his name in oblivion by changing the name of Fort Lyman to that of Fort Edward. The imperial government, elated by this, the only cheering event in the disastrous campaign of the year, created Johnson a baronet and gave him twenty thousand dollars wherewith to support the dignity of the title.* The honor and the emolument were unworthily bestowed. They were given to an avaricious and immoral man and unskillful gen-

* The appointment was thus announced in the *London Gazette*:

"WHITEHALL, November 18, 1755.

"The King has been pleased to grant unto William Johnson, of New York, America, Esquire, and his heirs male the dignity of a baronet of Great Britain.

eral, while another, pure, and noble, and brave, was suffered to go unnoticed, either by his general or by the King whom he served.

We have no record of the special part (if any) which Captain Schuyler and his company performed in the battle at Lake George. Two or three days after the engagement, he set out for Albany charged with special duties which were particularly pleasing to him. One from his general was to make arrangements for the reception of the French prisoners at Albany ; and the other was the more pleasing commission of his affections, to marry one to whom he had been for some time affianced. That marriage, as we have already observed, was solemnized on the 17th of September, nine days after the battle. For a week the young soldier was allowed to remain with his bride in the enjoyment of nuptial festivities, in which, no doubt, the best elements of society in Albany participated. Then he repaired to the camp at Lake George, and remained there until the dismissal of the New England troops, a few weeks later, when he was employed in the important service of making Fort Edward a safe dépôt of military stores.

The wounded Baron Dieskau, and his aide-de-camp, Lieutenant Colonel Bernier, of the Royal Swedish regiment, arrived in Albany during Captain Schuyler's bridal festivities, and at once received his personal attentions. The captain was almost the only officer in Johnson's army who could speak French fluently, and as Dieskau could not speak English, they had become quite intimate at headquarters before Schuyler left for Albany. The number of French prisoners including the Baron was twenty-nine. Twenty-one of them were sent to Fort Edward by General Johnson on the 15th, to be joined by six others there in a batteau voyage down the Hudson under a proper guard.

Dieskau and Bernier followed the next day. The latter was slightly wounded, the former seriously. He was carried on a litter to Fort Edward, and from there to Albany in a batteau.

Dieskau was a brave old Saxon, and always acted according to the motto on his arms "BOLDNESS WINS." He had been a great favorite with the celebrated Marshal Saxe, with whom he had long served, and by whom he was made the executor of that great soldier's last will. He had come to Canada with Vaudreuil, (lately appointed governor general of that province,) in the spring of 1755, as commander-in-chief of all the French forces in America. He had expected, as Burgoyne, twenty years later, boasted he should, to eat his Christmas dinner a conqueror in Albany. He was there long before Christmas, a prisoner, with wounds which caused his death at Surenne, in France, on the 8th of September, 1767.

Like Burgoyne, Dieskau experienced the most generous hospitality in Albany, and at the hands of the same man—Philip Schuyler. Before leaving his mother and his bride for the northern camp, Captain Schuyler made ample provisions for the prisoners, and especially for the Baron and his aide-de-camp; and he enjoined his family to do all in their power, during his absence, to alleviate the sufferings of the brave and unfortunate old general. How well his injunctions were heeded, and how gratefully the kind attentions of his family were accepted by the prisoners, the following letter, written in French, by Dieskau's aide-de-camp to Captain Schuyler, fully attests:

"ALBANY, October 5, 1755.

"I have received, sir, and dear friend, the letter which you have done me the honor to write to me from your camp. It is full of politeness and sentiment. As to the portion intended particularly for me, I am truly sensible; and I should esteem myself infinitely happy to be able to give you some marks of my gratitude, and of the esteem and friendship which are due to you.

"I have read the letter to the Baron Dieskau. It has confirmed him in the good opinion of you which, you know, he has reason to entertain. He is still as when you left him—still suffering, and uncertain how his wounds will end at last. He charges me to pray you, in his behalf, to present his compliments to Mr. Johnson, and to assure him of the extent of his gratitude to him.* His greatest desire is to be able to write to him himself. I pray you add to the Baron's wishes my very humble respects.

"One can add nothing to the politeness of Madame, your mother, and Madame, your wife. Every day there comes from them, to the Baron, fruits and other rare sweets, which are of great service to him. He orders me, on this subject, to express to you all that he owes to the attentions of these ladies. If it was permitted me to go out, I should already have been often to present to them his respects and mine.

"The Baron has been much pleased to learn by your letter that General Johnson esteems you, and gives you marks of his consideration and goodness. If he shall have the happiness to be restored to health, and to see your General again, he will himself be the proclaimer of all the good words which should be said of you, and which in justice he owes you, for the trouble and care that you have had for him.

"I pray you, my dear Captain, to say many things to Engineer Eyre on the part of the Baron and myself. For the good will I bear you, I wish you might secure his particular friendship. He is an officer of distinction, and if you love the trade of war seek his instructions. We knew him long before we saw him, because of his merits and reputation, and the Baron, who is a connoisseur in these things, has a great regard for him. To facilitate your access to him, say to him that the Baron prays him to extend to you the friendship he bears for himself.

"I do not know yet when, if at all, we will go to New York; but if we are ever there, give us news of you, I pray you; and if you shall ever come there, you know beforehand how much pleasure it will give the Baron to see you, and to renew his sentiments of friendship. As for me, I owe too much to yours, not to seek every means to merit your friendship. I have the honor to be, my dear captain, your very humble and very obedient servant, "BERNIER."

"Salute, I pray you, on my part, Colonel Cole, and all those gentlemen by whom I have the honor to be known."†

* General Johnson lent the Baron fifty guineas when he left Lake George for Albany.

† Translation of autograph letter.

## CHAPTER VIII.

Governor Shirley, the successor of Braddock as commander-in-chief of the British forces in America, was a splendid theorist, but knew very little about war practically. He had pursued the profession of the law with indifferent success, until, upon the tide of politics, he was borne into office, and by great self-reliance, industry, and assurance, he gained a commanding position in the colonies. At a convention of colonial governors held at New York in December, 1755, he submitted a plan of a campaign for 1756, which was adopted by the convention and approved by the home government. It was proposed to employ ten thousand men in an attack upon Crown Point, six thousand in an expedition against Fort Niagara, three thousand against Fort Du Quesne, and two thousand to menace Quebec, by crossing the wilderness by way of the Kennebec and Chaudiére rivers, over which Arnold marched nineteen years later. Shirley's plan also contemplated the expulsion of the French from Toronto and Frontenac, on the north shore of Lake Ontario, and to take possession of that great inland sea, and cut off Montreal and Quebec from the interior posts of Niagara, Du Quesne, Detroit, Michillimackinac, and those on the waters of the Mississippi.

The British government had resolved to declare war against France, and to prosecute the campaign with vigor. Extensive preparations were accordingly made. Shirley, who had offended Lieutenant-Governor De Lancey and his friends by not inviting them to the grand council in New York, became a victim to their intrigues. Through their representations the blame of Braddock's defeat, and other disasters of the campaign of 1755, were laid upon the shoulders of Shirley, and a strong party in England, irritated thereby, caused him to be superseded in that office.

The successor of Shirley was the Earl of Loudoun, a man totally unfit for any command whatever. He was indolent and ever unready, and his conduct in the administration of military affairs in America justified the comparison made by a gentlemen in conversation with Dr. Franklin, who said his lordship "reminded him of St. George upon the tavern signs—always on horseback but never gets forward." General Abercrombie was his lieutenant, who, not at all remarkable for skill and forethought, was nevertheless a better officer than his superior.

England did not proclaim open hostility to France until the middle of May, 1756, but her ships of war, with no justification but a pirate's right, founded upon might, not only despoiled French commerce, but in opposition to the righteous declaration of Frederick of Prussia, that "free ships make free goods"—that by the law of nations the property of an enemy can not be taken from on board the ships of a friend—forbade neutral vessels to carry merchandise belonging to her antagonist, and seized it when so carried. Thus, under cover of a legal representation made to the King in 1753, by the eminent Murray, (afterward Lord Mansfield,) the British government commenced that system of warfare upon the commerce of neutrals which became a chief cause of the last war for American independence sixty years afterward.

Spring had passed and summer had begun before Loudoun was ready to sail for America. Abercrombie, with some regulars, departed toward the close of April, and arrived at New York early in June. There he lingered for some time and then ascended the Hudson to Albany, where he met Shirley and received information of the exposed condition of Oswego, and the general alarm of the country on account of the depredations of the Indians. There, also, was General Winslow, with seven thousand men, whom he had been commissioned by Shirley to lead against Crown Point, and who were anxious to press forward, for the whole frontier was menaced by the French and Indians. But instead of acting promptly for the public good, Abercrombie took his ease; instead of stimulating the patriotism of the provincials, he cast fire-brands among the troops and the people by asserting the right of the regular officers to command those of the provincial army of the same rank, and insisting upon the propriety of quartering the soldiers upon the inhabitants. These assumptions caused serious disputes and mutual dislikes. "Go back again," said Sybrant Van Schaick, the mayor of Albany, to the troops, when he became utterly disgusted with them; "go back, for we can defend our frontiers ourselves." But Abercrombie would not allow them to move backward or forward, but with at least ten thousand men, regulars and provincials, he lay in supineness at Albany, waiting for the Earl of Loudoun and casting up useless fortifications.*

Meanwhile an active officer had been performing signal

* Fort Frederick, built in 1746, when Cornelius Schuyler was mayor of Albany, was in excellent condition, though quite an inefficient fortification. Kalm described it, in 1748, as "a great building of stone, surrounded with high and thick walls." A drawing of it before me shows it to have been quadrangular, with bastions, and apparently very strong. Its position was a bad one, as there were several hills westward of it that completely commanded it.

service in the interior with a handful of men. It was Colonel John Bradstreet, who, ten years earlier, was lieutenant-governor of St. John's, Newfoundland. Shirley had perceived the great importance of keeping open a communication with Oswego, where an English garrison was maintained. For this purpose forty companies of boatmen were placed under the command of Bradstreet. With these, and about two hundred provincial troops, he penetrated the country toward Oswego at the close of spring, suffering many hardships on the way. He went up the Mohawk to the site of Fort Stanwix, which he assisted in building two years afterward. Then he crossed a portage to Wood creek, and passed through Oneida Lake to the Oswego river. After leaving the lake he found vigilant enemies, for the French and Indians were hovering around the fort at Oswego with the intention of making it a prey. But Bradstreet, cautious and brave, made his way to the fort, and placed in it provisions and stores for five thousand men for six months.

Captain Schuyler, whose industry, judgment, and faithfulness in the performance of his duties at Fort Edward during the preceding winter, had won for him the warmest esteem of Shirley, accompanied Bradstreet as commissary, on the strong recommendation of the commanding general; and thus commenced that intimate relationship which existed between Bradstreet and Schuyler while they both lived. The latter was only twenty-three years of age when this expedition was undertaken, but his knowledge of the country, obtained in his previous hunting and trading excursions, made him a most valuable aid. He shared with the common soldiers and the batteau-men the perils and privations of the campaign; and when, on the 3d of July, as Bradstreet and his party were just commencing their march from Oswego to Albany, they were attacked by a party of French regulars, Canadians, and Indians, nine miles up the Oswego river, he displayed an intrepidity and humanity creditable alike to a soldier and a true man. He was one of eight men who, with Bradstreet at their head, reached a small island in the river, and drove thirty of the enemy from it. One of them, a French Canadian, was too badly wounded to flee, and as a batteau-man was about to dispatch him with a tomahawk, Captain Schuyler interposed and saved his life. Just then forty of the enemy returned to the attack. Bradstreet and his party had been reinforced by six men, and the French and Indians were received so warmly that they were compelled to flee. A few minutes afterward seventy of the enemy appeared upon the shore, and at the same time six more of Bradstreet's men joined him. For a while the contest was warm and the result doubtful. The enemy poured a cross fire upon Bradstreet, and twelve of his followers were wounded. The French were finally compelled to retire, for the third time, and did not renew the attack.

About four hundred of the enemy were now seen approaching the river on the north side, a mile above, with the apparent intention of crossing and surrounding the provincials. Bradstreet immediately quitted the island, and at the head of two hundred and fifty men marched up to confront them.

Owing to accident, there was only one batteau at the island when Bradstreet resolved to leave it, and it was hardly sufficient to carry his party over. The wounded Canadian begged to be taken in, but was refused. "Then throw me into the river," he cried, "and not leave me here to perish with hunger and thirst." The heart of Captain Schuyler was touched by the poor fellow's appeal, and handing his weapons and coat to a companion-in-arms, he bore the wounded man to the water, swam with him across the deep channel, and placed him in the care of Dr. Kirkland with the approbation of Bradstreet. The man recovered ; and when, in 1775, Schuyler, as commander-in-chief of the northern army, sent a proclamation into Canada inviting the French inhabitants to join the patriots, that soldier was living near Chamblée, and gladly enlisted under the banner of Ethan Allen, that he might see and thank the preserver of his life. His wish was gratified, and he made himself known to Schuyler in his tent at *Isle aux Noix.*

Captain Schuyler joined Bradstreet and his party as soon as his wounded prisoner was in the hands of the surgeon, and he was in the severe engagement which occured in a swamp half an hour afterward. The enemy had crossed the river in considerable numbers. Bradstreet attacked them boldly, and drove them from their skulking places in the swamp to the bank of the river, leaving them the alternative of captivity or the perils of the flood. Many of them rushed into the river and were drowned, and others were slain. In this engagement the provincials lost twenty killed and twenty-four wounded. Of the enemy full a hundred perished by weapon and flood, and others escaped to the forests. "This repulse," said a letter-writer of the time, "will doubtless check the incursions of the French, shake their Indian interest, strengthen our own, and secure our future convoys in their passage to Oswego."

Bradstreet was soon afterward joined by some of Shirley's grenadiers on their way to the fort, and also by two hundred men from the garrison. Thus reinforced he would have gone in quest of the main body of the French, who were eastward upon the shore of Lake Ontario, but excessive rains prevented. He made his way back to Albany with his command, where he arrived on the 13th of July, and communicated to Abercrombie the important intelligence that a French army was on its way to attack Oswego. But, notwithstanding the way was opened, and Colonel Webb, with the forty-ninth regiment, was ordered to hold himself in readiness to march to its defense, nothing was done. Abercrombie kept his ten thousand men at Albany until the arrival of the Earl of Loudoun, at the close of July. His lordship appeared to require rest after a sloop voyage from New York of one hundred and sixty miles, and he, too, loitered in Albany, until want of employment and close quarters in hot weather generated disease in the camp and caused universal dissatisfaction in the army.

While these inefficient commanders were wasting time and energy at Albany, and producing great irritation by giving superior command over the provincials to the regular officers, and treating the former with contempt, the more active French were accomplishing their designs. The Marquis de Montcalm, a field-marshal of France, and an active officer, had succeeded Dieskau in the supreme command. He visited Ticonderoga in July, obtained accurate information of the strength of the forces and the weakness of the commanders at Albany, and immediately hastened to Montreal to collect troops for an expedition against Oswego. He assembled about five thousand Frenchmen, Canadians, and Indians at Frontenac, (now Kingston, in Upper Canada,) and with these, and thirty pieces of cannon, he crossed Lake Ontario, and landed within a few miles of Oswego early in August. On the 11th he appeared before Fort Ontario, on the east side of the river, and demanded the surrender of the garrison. Their commander, Colonel Mercer, refused compliance. Montcalm commenced a regular seige, and at midnight of the 12th he opened his trenches. After a brave resistance, Mercer spiked his cannon and retreated to Fort Oswego, on the opposite side of the river. Montcalm's guns were immediately brought to bear upon that old fortification. Colonel Mercer was killed, and on the 14th the garrison, sixteen hundred in number, surrendered. Among the prisoners was Colonel Peter Schuyler, of New Jersey, mentioned in Philip's letter on page 69. He was released on parole. Forty-five of the garrison had been slain, and the remainder, except some officers, were sent down the St. Lawrence, prisoners of war. The post, with all its cannon, vessels of war, ammunition, and stores, fell into the hands of the French. The forts were demolished, and the whole country of the Six Nations was laid open to the incursions of the enemy. Oswego was left a solitude ; and Colonel Webb, who had advanced as far as the Oneida portage, informed of the fact, fled to Albany, terror giving speed to his movements.

The sluggish blood of Loudoun was somewhat stirred by these events. It was caused only by the excitement of feverish alarm, however. He had troops enough to have conquered Canada in that single campaign, under an efficient leader, but they were leashed to his unreadiness and incapacity. After loitering at Albany a few weeks longer, recalling the troops on their way toward Ticonderoga, and uttering ungenerous and wicked complaints against the provincials, expecting therewith to cover his own imbecility, he dismissed them to their homes, and ordered the regulars into winter quarters. A thousand of them went to New York, where he opened afresh the bitter controversy of the colonists with the home government by demanding quarters for his troops. When Mayor Cruger, in the name of the people, demurred at the demand made for free quarters for the officers, Loudoun uttered a coarse oath, and said, "If you do not billet my officers upon free quarters this day, I 'll order here all the troops in North America under my command, and billet them myself upon the city." Loudoun spoke by authority, for an order in council, after more than half a century of recommendation from the Board of Trade, was passed in July, 1756, establishing a rule, without limitation, that troops might be kept in the colonies and quartered on them at pleasure, without the consent of the colonial Legislatures. This order, virtually establishing a standing army in the colonies, to be maintained, in a great measure, by the people, was the magnetic touch that gave vitality to that sentiment of resistance which soon sounded the tocsin of revolution. The authorities of New York yielded temporarily to Loudoun's demand, under a silent but most solemn protest.

Military operations, under Loudoun's administration, were quite as inefficient elsewhere as in the province of New York. Washington was at the head of fifteen hundred volunteers and drafted militia, but was made powerless by official interference; and the only important achievement on the part of the English during the year, excepting the operations of Bradstreet, was the severe chastisement of the Delawares in Western Pennsylvania, by some provincial troops, under Colonel John Armstrong, of that province. The chief rendezvous of the Indians, near the Kittanning mountains, thirty-five miles from Fort Du Quesne, was assailed by Armstrong and his party, with whom was Captain (afterward general) Hugh Mercer of Virginia, on the night of the 8th of September. The leading chief of the savages was killed, the town was destroyed, and the offending Delawares were completely humbled. Thus ended the campaign of 1756. The French still held in possession almost all of the territory in dispute and the most important of their military posts.

Captain Schuyler was so thoroughly disgusted with the military operations of the year that he left the service at the end of the campaign, and remained in private life during the stirring events in northern New York in 1757. Yet he was not an indifferent nor an idle spectator. Between himself and Colonel Bradstreet there was a strong attachment, and Captain Schuyler was frequently employed as counselor, and sometimes as efficient actor in providing supplies for the army. He had also become a favorite with Sir William Johnson, and it is believed that the baronet offered him the position of a deputy superintendent of Indian affairs, when, in the spring of 1757, Sir William expected to take the field with Mohawk warriors.

Loudon called a military council at Boston in January, 1757. It assembled on the 19th, when his Lordship proposed to confine the operations of that year to an expedition against Louisburg, and to a defense of the northern frontiers. The northern colonies, and especially those of New England, were disappointed. Their favorite scheme was the expulsion of the French from Lake Champlain, and, if possible, from the territory south of the St. Lawrence. The New England representatives in the council urged the importance of such a result, but in vain. Loudon was imperious, and had very little respect for the opinions of any provincial. Wiser and better men than he acquiesced in his plans, but deplored the poverty of his judgment and his lack of executive force. But the general ardor of the colonists was not abated, and the call for troops was so promptly responded to, that at the opening of summer more than six thousand provincials were in arms. Much might have been done toward wiping out the disgrace of the previous year, had efficient men been at the head of civil affairs in England, and a good general controlled military operations in America. The silly Duke of Newcastle, who was ignorant of the fact that Cape Breton, on which the fortress of Louisburg was situated, was an island, was the prime minister of England. He read Loudoun's dispatches "with great attention and satisfaction," and praised his "great diligence and ability," while Loudoun himself was doing all in his power to disgust the colonists by laying an embargo upon all ships in North American ports, preventing the exportation of wheat, and, as was alleged, sharing in the enormous profits of the contractors who supplied the army and navy with flour.

Loudoun resolved to go to Louisburg in person. He ordered Colonel Boquet to watch the frontiers of the Carolinas ; gave General Stanwix control of the western theater of war, with about two thousand troops ; and making General Webb his second in command, sent him, with six thousand men, to defend the frontiers of New York and keep the French from Forts William Henry and Edward.

After impressing four hundred men at New York, Loudoun sailed for Halifax on the 20th of June. He arrived at his destination ten days afterward, and found himself at the head of a well-appointed army of ten thousand men, with a fleet of sixteen ships of the line and several frigates. With his usual procrastination he laid out a parade at Halifax, planted a vegetable garden for the use of his armament, exercised his troops in mock battles, and thus consumed the precious summer months. His officers, among whom was Charles Lee, afterward a major-general in the continental army under Washington, became mortified and exasperated ; and Major General Lord Charles Hay expressed his contempt so loudly as to be arrested.

He said that the commander-in-chief was "keeping the courage of his Majesty's soldiers at bay, and expending the nation's wealth in planting cabbages, when they ought to have been fighting the enemies of their king and country in reality."

August came, and Loudoun was about to sail for Louisburg, when he was informed that the French had one more ship than he, and a reinforcement in the garrison. This alarmed his lordship, and he changed the plan of the campaign and sailed for New York, to be met on the way by intelligence of disasters on Lake George and the failure of all his weak plans.

The vigilant and active Montcalm had again carried away trophies of victory from the English. The French partisans in the field were vigilant, active, and brave. Marin, who in 1745 desolated Saratoga, was upon the war-path with Canadians and Indians. Early in the summer, with two hundred men, he penetrated almost to Fort Edward, and his savage allies carried back to Ticonderoga the scalps of forty provincials. Meanwhile Montcalm was preparing a powerful armament at Ticonderoga. Toward the close of July he was at the foot of Lake George with more than eight thousand men, (of whom almost two thousand were Indians,) and a train of artillery, and proceeded to besiege Fort William Henry, at the head of the lake, then garrisoned by five hundred men, under Colonel Munro, a brave English officer, who was supported by an intrenched camp inclosing nearly two thousand provincial soldiers.

Montcalm appeared before Fort William Henry on the 2d of August, and planted a battery of nine cannon and two mortars, and then demanded a surrender. Colonel Munro. confident of efficient aid from Colonel Webb, then at Fort Edward with four thousand men, and to whom he had sent an express on the approach of Montcalm, promptly refused. But that confidence in his commanding general was sadly misplaced. For six days Montcalm continued the siege, and every hour Munro expected aid from Fort Edward, for expresses, at great peril to the riders, were sent to General Webb daily. But no reinforcements were sent. Even Sir William Johnson, who had obtained Webb's reluctant consent to hasten toward Lake George, and had proceeded several miles with a corps of provincials and Putnam's Rangers, was ordered back. Nothing was sent to Munro but a letter filled with exaggerations and advice to surrender. This fell into Montcalm's hands just as he was about to raise the siege and retire. He then made a peremptory demand for a surrender, at the same time sending Webb's letter in to Munro. That brave officer still hesitated, notwithstanding half his cannon were useless and his ammunition was exhausted. But he was compelled to yield. Montcalm made honorable terms, for he respected a brave soldier. The English were to depart under an escort, on a pledge not to serve against the French during the next eighteen months. To insure the fulfillment of the capitulation on the part of the victors, Montcalm called the Indian leaders into council and obtained their acquiescence. The garrison marched out on the 9th of August and retired to their intrenched camp, where the ruins of Fort George may now be seen, and the French took possession. That night was one of anxiety for the captives. From English suttlers the Indians procured liquor. Intoxication followed. Their passions were inflamed, and in the morning, when the prisoners on parole departed for Fort Edward, the savages fell upon them to plunder and destroy. The French could not restrain them, and in great confusion and terror the survivors fled to Fort Edward. The fort and all its appendages were laid in ruins, and for nearly a hundred years nothing marked its site but the remains of its intrenchments. Now an immense hotel occupies the ground, and thousands spend the summer months there in gayety, unconscious of the sanguinary associations that cluster around the locality.

Webb was undoubtedly a coward. When Fort William Henry fell he sent his own baggage to a place of safety far down the Hudson, and would have retreated to the Highlands had not young Lord Howe, who arrived at Fort Edward on the 7th, persuaded him that he and his command were in no immediate danger. And Loudoun, utterly confused, proposed to encamp on Long Island, two hundred miles from Lake George, "for the defense of the continent."

The position of affairs in America now alarmed the English people. The government of the aristocracy had paralyzed the energies of the whole empire, and both America and England were humbled by the events of the summer of 1757. "We are undone," said Chesterfield, "at home by our increasing expenses; abroad by ill-luck and incapacity." In America there was much irritation. Thoroughly imbued with democratic ideas, and knowing their competency, unaided by royal troops, to assert and maintain their rights, they regarded the interference of the home government, in their quarrel with the French, as an impediment to their success. Some of the royal governors were rapacious, others were incompetent, and all were distinguished by a haughty demeanor toward the colonists, highly offensive to their just dignity as freemen. They demanded money as a master would command the service of his slave; and the arrogant assumption of superiority by the English officers disgusted the provincial officers and troops, and often cooled the ardor of whole regiments of brave Americans.

The people of England yearned for a change in the administration of public affairs, and the popular will at length prevailed. William Pitt, by far the ablest statesman England had yet produced, was called to the position of prime minister in June, 1757, after a struggle of eleven weeks, during which time the realm had no ministry. "Give me your confidence," said Pitt to the King, "and I will deserve it." "Deserve my confidence," the King replied, "and you shall have it."

Pitt knew that it was the voice of the people that had called him to the head of affairs, and for the welfare of that people and the realm, he wrought. Patriotism, energy, and good judgment marked every movement of his administration, especially in measures for prosecuting the war in America. He could not hear from Loudoun, or know what he was about, so he recalled him, and gave the chief command in America to Abercrombie. Relying upon the spontaneous patriotism of the colonists, he obtained the King's order that every provincial officer, of no higher rank than colonel, should have equal command with the British, according to dates of commission. Instead of demanding aid from the colonies, he issued a letter to the several governments, asking them to raise and clothe twenty thousand men. He promised, in the name of the Parliament, to furnish arms, tents, and provisions for them ; and also to reimburse the several colonies all the money they should expend in raising and clothing the levies. He arranged such an admirable militia system for home defense, that a large number of the troops of the domestic standing army could be spared for foreign service. A large naval armament, for American waters, was prepared and placed under the command of Admiral Boscawen; and twelve thousand additional English troops were allotted for service in America.

The liberal offers of the minister and the generous preparations of strength had a magical effect in the colonies. New England alone raised fifteen thousand men; New York furnished about three thousand; New Jersey one thousand; Pennsylvania about three thousand, and Virginia over two thousand. Royal American troops, as they were called, organized in the Carolinas, were ordered to the North, and when, in May, 1758, Abercrombie took formal command of the army, he found fifty thousand men, regulars and provincials, at his disposal—a number greater than the whole male population in the French dominions in America at that time.

The scheme for the campaign of 1758 was extensive. Shirley's plan of 1756 was revived, and its general outlines were adopted. Three points of assault—Louisburg, Ticonderoga, and Fort Du Quesne—were designated, and ample preparations were made for powerful operations against them. Upon Louisburg the first blow was to be struck, and General Jeffrey Amherst, a man of good judgment and discretion, was appointed to the command of a land force of more than twelve thousand men, destined for that enterprise. These were to be borne by the fleet of Admiral Boscawen. Abercrombie, assisted by Lord Howe, whom Pitt had chosen as "the soul of the enterprise," was to lead an army by way of Albany to attack the French on Lake Champlain, while General Joseph Forbes was commissioned to lead another army over the Alleghany mountains to capture Fort Du Quesne.

The first of these expeditions was very successful, and

gave encouragement to the actors in the others. Boscawen arrived at Halifax with his fleet of forty armed vessels, and the land forces under Amherst, early in May. General Wolfe, a young man but thirty-one years of age, but who had already won imperishable laurels in the army, was Amherst's lieutenant. He, too, like Howe with Abercrombie, was chosen to be the active spirit of the enterprise, and well did he acquit himself on this occasion and afterward.

The expedition left Halifax on the 28th of May, and on the 8th of June the troops landed, without encountering much opposition, on the shore of Gabarus bay, near the city of Louisburg. Their appearance was unexpected to the French, who, in alarm, fled from their outposts and retired within the fortress. The attack upon that fortress and the French shipping soon commenced, and the contest, in various forms, continued for fifty days. The French made a vigorous resistance, but were finally compelled to yield, when nearly all the shipping in the harbor was destroyed. The fort, town, and the island of Cape Breton, on which they stood, with the adjoining island of St. John, (now Prince Edward,) and their dependencies, were surrendered to the English by capitulation on the 26th of July. Five thousand prisoners were the immediate results of the triumph, and the spoils consisted of a large quantity of munitions of war. The English, by this victory, became masters of the eastern coast from their own possessions almost to the mouth of the St. Lawrence; and when Louisburg fell the French dominion in America began to wane. From that moment its decline was continuous and rapid.

Quebec had been included in the scheme of conquest. Its reduction was to follow that of Louisburg; but when the victory at the latter was accomplished, the season was too far advanced to attempt Quebec. Indeed, disasters on Lake Champlain, which we shall presently consider, caused the reception of a message by Amherst which called him in that direction rather than to the more northern field of operations.

## CHAPTER IX.

Captain Schuyler again appeared in public life in the spring of 1758, in connection with his friend, Colonel Bradstreet, who had been active at Albany during the previous year as deputy quartermaster general. Lord Howe, whose regiment was quartered on Long Island, had spent much of the winter at Albany, (where Abercrombie remained,) making preparations, first for a winter attack upon Ticonderoga, and finally for the next summer's campaign. His was a lovely character, and he had endeared himself to the soldiers and the people. At the Flats he was "Aunt Schuyler's" frequent and most welcome visitor. Her husband had died of pleurisy in Februrary, 1757, but the hospitalities of his house were continued by his widow.

After the death of Colonel Schuyler, Philip and his wife, with their infant children, spent much time at the Flats. The younger of the infants at the beginning of 1758 was Elizabeth, who became the wife of the eminent Alexander Hamilton, and lived to the age of more than ninety-six years. It was there that Captain Schuyler and Lord Howe formed an intimate relationship as friends. Their mutual attachment, growing out of wise appreciation, was very strong ; and when the former was assured that his noble friend was appointed Abercrombie's lieutenant, and would be the active spirit of the expedition against the French on Lake Champlain, he resolved to join the provincial army, and share the fortunes of the campaign. At the urgent solicitation of Colonel Bradstreet, he accepted the office of deputy commissary with the rank of major.

As early as March, when Bradstreet, warmly supported by the zealous Howe, proposed an expedition against Frontenac, Major Schuyler entered upon his duties, and from that time until the close of the campaign he was continually in the public service. It had been determined that a strong force should march upon Frontenac as soon as the army should be established upon Lake Champlain, and to promote this enterprise the New York officers and soldiers bent their best energies. But these were continually paralyzed by the indolence and absurd interferences of the commander-in-chief, and it was late in June before the army destined for the capture of Ticonderoga had collected at Fort Edward, the designated place of rendezvous.

Lord Howe was a Lycurgus of the camp. He introduced stern reforms, which commended themselves to the common sense of his associates, but which caused the incredulous shaking of the big-wigs of the elders, who made innovation and sacrilege convertible terms. He labored to conform the methods of the service to its wants in this new country. Laying aside pride and prejudice, he applied for advice to those whose experience and observation entitled them to respect. He forbade in his own regiment all displays of gold and scarlet in the rugged marches of the army, and led the proposed new fashion himself, by wearing a plain short-skirted ammunition coat. He ordered the muskets to be shortened, that they might be used with more freedom in the forests; and to prevent the discovery of his corps by the glitter of the barrels, he directed that portion of their weapons to be painted black. To preserve the legs of his men from briers and the bite of insects he caused them to wear buckskin or strong woolen cloth leggins, such as were used by the Indians. The innovation most deprecated by the young men of his corps, who took great pride in their long, abundant powdered hair, was his order for them all to have their locks cut short, that they might not become wet and produce maladies when the owners slept upon the damp ground or marched in storms. But Lord Howe, whose hair was fine and abundant, set the example in this as in other movements, and had his own locks cropped short. He also abolished the use of chairs, tables, and other things used in the tents, because it would be almost impossible to carry them through the wilderness which the army was about to penetrate ; and he set his officers an example one day, when he had invited them to dine with him. They found him in his tent to welcome them. The ground was covered with bear skins, and there was a log for each of the guests to sit upon, after the manner of his lordship. Presently his servants set a large dish of pork and beans in their midst, when his lordship took a sheath from his pocket, containing a knife and fork, and with them he proceeded to distribute the food. The guests sat in awkward surprise, for they had neither knife nor fork. They were soon relieved by the host presenting each with a similar sheath and contents. To each man of his regiment he also furnished a quantity of powdered ginger, with orders to mix it with their water when on weary marches, and not to stoop down, as was customary, and drink from the streams. This precaution saved many lives, and kept off agues when these troops were in swampy places.

Through the activity of Bradstreet, assisted by Major Schuyler, the batteaus for carrying the troops over Lake

George were ready by the time the necessary stores arrived from England, and before the end of June Lord Howe led the first division of four thousand men to the head of the lake. Abercrombie arrived there with the remainder at the beginning of July. His entire force at the head of the lake then consisted of seven thousand regulars, nine thousand provincials, and a heavy train of artillery. Montcalm then occupied Ticonderoga with less than four thousand men.

The provincial troops were chiefly from New England, New York, and New Jersey ; and among the former were Stark, of New Hampshire, and Putnam, of Connecticut, the former now promoted to captain, and the latter to major. These were men who were afterward to fill a conspicuous place in the history of their country. There was Gage, likewise, who, in later years, was the executor of his royal master's will in oppressing the Bostonians. Five hundred rangers were under his command. And there was the bold Rogers, too, the ever brave partisan, at the head of four hundred others, gallant like himself, who all the spring had been scouting among the mountains, and performing deeds of daring which the world knows little of. With a part of these he had passed over Lake George in five whale-boats, and in company with Captain Jacob (Nawnawapateonks,) and a party of Mohegan Indians had fully reconnoitered the French works at Ticonderoga.

Before sunrise on the morning of the 5th of July, the whole armament under Abercrombie proceeded to embark on Lake George, in nine hundred batteaus and one hundred and thirty-five whale-boats. The artillery was placed upon rafts, and before ten o'clock the immense flotilla moved majestically down the lake, led by Lord Howe in a large boat, accompanied by a guard of rangers. Bradstreet was in the boat with Lord Howe; Schuyler remained at the head of the lake, to superintend the forwarding of supplies for the use of the army.

Seldom has a scene more imposing than this been looked upon in America. The day was bright and warm, the waters of the lake still and clear as crystal, and around them lay the lofty, everlasting hills, covered with the green forest from their summits to the water's edge, and echoing the sounds of martial music, which, toward evening, fell faintly and mysteriously upon the ears of the French scouts in the direction of Ticonderoga. In that stately procession the regular troops occupied the centre of the flotilla, and the provincials formed the wings. Over all waved the bright banners of the regiments; and floating proudly from a staff in the barge of the commander-in-chief, was the royal flag of England with its union crosses.

As the flotilla approached the narrows of the lake an order for silence went from boat to boat. The trumpet, fife, and drum were dismissed; the oars were all muffled, every voice was subdued to a whisper, and as the sun went down in glory, and the bright stars came out in a serene sky, the movement of the armament was so silent that not a scout upon the hills appears to have observed them.

The flotilla reached Sabbath-day Point, a low promontory on the western shore, just as the twilight was fading into night, and there the army landed and rested five hours. Lord Howe pitched his tent there, and during the evening he sent for Captain Stark. Reclining upon his bear skin bed, he talked with the Captain long and seriously respecting Ticonderoga, the French works there, the best mode of attack, and the probabilities of success. They supped together; and before Stark left, Lord Howe gave orders for the rangers to carry the bridge at the falls between

Lake George and the plains of Ticonderoga on the following day.

Soon after midnight the army moved silently on ; Lord Howe, doubtless meditating upon the chances of war and the glory to be won, had not slept, and at early dawn, accompanied by Colonel Bradstreet and Major Rogers, he pushed forward to within a quarter of a mile of the landing place at the foot of the lake. There he discovered a French picket. The whole army soon afterward appeared, and the first intimation that the French outposts received of the proximity of an enemy, was the full blaze of their scarlet uniforms in the morning sun. At twelve o'clock the landing was effected in a cove on the western side of the lake.

The outlet of Lake George forms a winding, rapid river, less than four miles in length, and falling, in that distance, about one hundred and sixty feet. It connects Lake George with Lake Champlain, having a mountain over eight hundred feet in height on the western side of its mouth, and a rocky promontory, rising more than a hundred feet, on the eastern side. This promontory was called Ticonderoga, and upon its highest point the French had built a fort, which they named *Carillon.** It was substantially built of limestone, with which the promontory abounds, and was constructed with so much skill that a small garrison might make a respectable defense against quite a large army. On the extreme point of the promontory was a grenadier's battery. Northward of the fort were marshes and wet meadows, over which it was difficult to pass, and the only solid

* Ticonderoga, or Tionderoga, is a corruption of Cheonderoga, an Iroquois word signifying *sounding water*, in allusion to the roar of the falls in the outlet of Lake George. The French named their fort Carillon for the same reason, that word, in their language, signifying chime, jingling, noise, brawling, scolding, racket, clatter, riot.

way, from the northwest, was over quite a narrow isthmus. Across this the French had placed extensive outworks. They had also built mills at the falls, and posted some troops there; and they had stationed a picket guard at the foot of Lake George.

Such was the position of the belligerents on the morning of the 6th of July, when the troops under Abercrombie landed and took up their line of march toward Ticonderoga in four columns, leaving behind their artillery, provisions, and baggage. The French advanced guard fled when the British landed, setting fire to the bridges and carrying alarm to the fort. This movement, and intelligence that Montcalm was in hourly expectation of a strong reinforcement under De Levi, caused Abercrombie thus to disencumber his army and press forward to an immediate attack. But the country was covered with such a dense forest, in which lay occasional morasses, that the progress of the British was very slow. Their guides were incompetent, and the moving columns, following these bewildered leaders, frequently encountered each other and became broken and confused. In this manner they had proceeded about two miles, and were crossing a brook within sound of the rushing waters of Cheonderoga, when the right center, commanded by Lord Howe in person, came suddenly upon a French party of about three hundred men, who had lost their way and had been wandering in the forest for twelve hours. A skirmish immediately ensued. Both parties fought bravely, but the wearied Frenchmen were overcome. Some of them were killed, some were drowned in the stream, and more than one half of them were made prisoners. At the first fire Lord Howe was struck by a musket ball and expired immediately. His fall produced dismay in his soldiers, and the British columns, broken, confused, and fatigued, marched back to the landing to bivouac for the night.

Early on the morning of the 7th, Colonel Bradstreet, with Rogers' rangers, advanced, rebuilt the bridges, and before noon took possession of the saw mills. Abercrombie then advanced to that point with the whole army, and sent out Clerk, his chief engineer, to reconnoiter the French works. He was accompanied by Captain Stark with a part of Rogers' rangers. All returned the same evening. Clerk reported the French works to be deceptive. They appeared strong, but were in reality very weak and unsubstantial. The practiced eye of Stark had a different perception, and he averred that the works were well finished, and that preparations for defense were ample. With his usual contempt for the provincials, Abercrombie paid no attention to Stark's opinion, and resolved to press forward to the attack the next morning, without waiting for his cannon. This was his fatal mistake.

At daybreak of the 8th, Sir William Johnson joined Abercrombie with four hundred and forty Indians, and before sunrise the British forces were moving toward the French works, New Jersey and Connecticut troops forming a rear guard.

Through his scouts Montcalm had watched these movements. On the day that the British landed he called in all of his troops at outposts, and prepared for a desperate defense. His force in Fort Carillon and upon the out-works did not exceed three thousand men, but on the evening of the 7th, De Levi returned from an intended expedition against the Mohawks, with four hundred followers. With this reinforcement Montcalm felt confident, notwithstanding he had not yet completed an important battery. On the morning of the 8th, when the drums beat to arms, he placed himself just within the trenches. With quick eye he discerned every movement, and with ready skill directed every maneuver.

The British approached the French lines in three columns. Abercrombie kept at a safe distance in the rear. As the army approached the out-works, the French, completely hidden in their trenches, and well defended by a deep *abatis*, (composed of felled trees, their tops lying outward from the embankments,) opened a sudden and incessant fire from swivels and small arms. The British were entangled in the projecting limbs, logs, and rubbish, yet they pressed forward with the greatest intrepidity, while officers and men were swept down as with a mower's scythe. For four hours, in the face of a most destructive storm of iron and lead did they strive to cut their way, and the carnage was dreadful. Some did, indeed, mount the parapet, and scores fell within a few feet of the trenches. Never was British valor more strikingly displayed than on that occasion, and had Abercrombie brought up his artillery, or possessed a tithe of the activity and courage of Montcalm, he would have secured a victory. But as the moments sped on, and he heard that his brave regulars were rapidly diminishing (for he had remained, like a coward, at the mills), he ordered a retreat to be sounded. The British had then lost two thousand men, and in the conflict had become much disordered. The retreat became a flight, and when Abercrombie was sought for to rally them he could nowhere be found. He had hurried back to the landing place on Lake George, in "extremest fright," and the army, in consternation, followed. They would have rushed pell mell into the boats but for the alertness and influence of Colonel Bradstreet, who had the command of the flotilla.

Meanwhile a courier had been dispatched in a whale-boat, with the following hurried letter from Abercrombie's aide-de-camp to Colonel Cumming, who had been left in charge of a detachment at the head of the lake :*

"FRENCH ADVANCED GUARD, July 8, 1758.

"COLONEL CUMMING :

"You are hereby directed not to send any more provincial troops down the lake, but stop them all there, as likewise all the stores that have been ordered down, except as many men as is necessary to bring all the empty batteaus down immediately, which you are to forward without any loss of time. All the wounded are to be forwarded to Fort Edward. You will observe the above orders. Our army, who have behaved with the utmost intrepidity, were obliged to give way to batteries and the strongest intrenchments. Forward the wounded to New York as soon as possible.† Send this note to Captain Read. Forward the heavy artillery to New York as soon as possible. Collect the provincial troops at Fort William Henry, as we hope to advance again soon. Finish all your stockaded forts immediately, and particularly the hospital. Keep a good watch, and defend your post to the last. You will soon have a large body of troops down at your post. Give all the assistance to the sick and wounded you can.

"I am, dear Cumming, your most humble servant,

"JAMES CUNNINGHAM, Aide-de-camp."

* Autograph letter.

† Among the wounded was Captain Charles Lee, afterward the second major-general in the army of the Revolution. He was then distinguished for his recklessness, bad manners, and worse morals. On the march of the troops from Albany, he commanded a small detachment that encamped at the Flats, the residence of "Aunt Schuyler." He had neglected to procure the customary warrants for impressing horses and oxen, and obtaining necessary supplies for the army. Without authority he seized what he wanted, and did not spare even Mrs. Schuyler, the friend and benefactor of the army; and when remonstrated with he answered by coarse oaths. Her domestics were enraged, but she remained calm, and quieted their excitement. When the wounded at Ticonderoga were brought down, she caused her great barn to be converted into a hospital, and a room was furnished in her house for the use of a surgeon. Among the surgeon's patients was the rapacious and ill-mannered Lee. Mrs. Schuyler treated him with the utmost kindness, and never made the least hint concerning his past misconduct. Lee was charmed, and "he swore," says Mrs. Grant, "that he was sure there would be a place reserved for Madame in heaven though no other woman should be there, and that he should wish for nothing better than to share her final destiny."

Two days before this courier was sent, another boat had passed over the lake, but upon a different errand. It conveyed the body of the young Lord Howe, who fell, as we have seen, in the first encounter with the French in the forests at Ticonderoga. Its arrival upon the sandy beach at the head of the lake was the first intimation to Colonel Cumming and his command of the great loss the army had sustained. None grieved more sincerely than Major Schuyler, and he asked and received permission to convey the dead body of his friend to Albany for interment. It was carried on a rude bier to Fort Edward, and thence to Albany in a batteau. Major Schuyler caused it to be entombed in his family vault, and there it lay many years, when the remains were placed in a leaden coffin and deposited under the chancel of St. Peter's church, in that city. They rest there still. We have observed that Lord Howe, as an example for his soldiers, had cut his fine and abundant hair very short. When his remains were taken from the Schuyler vault for reëntombment, his hair had grown to long, flowing locks, and was very beautiful.

Lord Howe was not quite thirty-four years of age when he died. "With him," observes Mante, "the soul of the army seemed to expire."* In England intelligence of his death caused a profound sensation, and there was sincere

* "A few days after Lord Howe's departure, in the afternoon, a man was seen coming on horseback from the north, galloping violently, without his hat. Pidrom, as he was familiarly called, the Colonel's [Schuyler] only surviving brother, was with Aunt Schuyler, and ran instantly to inquire, well knowing he rode express. The man galloped on, crying out that Lord Howe was killed. The mind of our good aunt had been so engrossed by her anxiety for the event impending, and so impressed by the merit of her favorite hero, that her wonted firmness sunk under the stroke, and she broke out into bitter lamentations. This had such an effect on her friends and domestics that shrieks and sobs of anguish echoed through every part of the house."—*Mrs. Grant's Memoirs of an American Lady.*

mourning throughout the colonies. The general court of Massachusetts Bay, as a testimonial of their respect for his character, appropriated two hundred and fifty pounds sterling for the erection of a monument to his memory in Westminster Abbey.*

On the morning of the 9th, Abercrombie's broken army retreated across Lake George as rapidly as possible, as the frightened chief could not feel safe until that little sea, thirty-eight miles in length, was between himself and the dreaded Montcalm. At the head of the lake a council of war was held. Colonel Bradstreet, burning with indignation because of the defeat at Ticonderoga, and hoping nothing from a general who, while he calumniated his army as broken-spirited, exhibited none of the characteristics of a good general, urged the importance of attempting his long cherished scheme of capturing Fort Frontenac, at the foot of Lake Ontario. He offered to conduct the expedition himself, and by his strong appeals he wrung from the council a reluctant consent. Abercrombie, after some hesitation, commissioned him to lead three thousand men against that fortress, and "he rather flew than marched with them," says a cotemporary, "through that long route from Lake George to Albany, and thence again up the stream of the Mohawk river."

At Albany Bradstreet was joined by Major Schuyler and his kinsman by marriage, Dr. John Cochran, who became surgeon-general of the northern department in the war for independence. At the Oneida carrying-place he

* "Lord Howe was a grandson of George the First, his mother being the natural daughter of that monarch and his mistress, Lady Darlington."—*Grahame.* His father was Sir E. Scrope, second Viscount Howe, in Ireland. His brothers, Richard and William, were British commanders in America during the earlier years of the war for independence. The former succeeded to his brother's title.

found General Stanwix, who was about to commence the erection of a fort where the village of Rome now stands. That officer placed under Bradstreet's command an additional force of twenty-seven hundred men, eleven hundred of them New Yorkers. He was also joined there by forty warriors under Red Head, a renowned war-chief of the Onondagas. With this strong force, eight pieces of cannon, and three mortars, Bradstreet pushed forward to Oswego, by way of Wood Creek, Oneida Lake, and the Onondago or Oswego river.

Major Schuyler, accompanied by Dr. Cochran, a corps of provincial soldiers, and a large number of carpenters and other artificers, had made much quicker marches than the main body of Bradstreet's army, and arrived at Oswego several days in advance of them. That place presented a picture of utter desolation. There was scarcely a vestige of the forts to be seen, and no memorial of the French occupancy remained but a huge rude, cross. Schuyler immediately commenced the construction of a rude but strong schooner, to bear the cannon and howitzers, the powder and balls of the expedition over Lake Ontario, light whaleboats only having been transported from Albany by the army for their use. This schooner, incredible as it may seem, was completed within three weeks after the keel was laid. It was named *The Mohawk*, and did good service in carrying the heavy ordnance to Frontenac.

Bradstreet and his army embarked in open boats upon Lake Ontario, and creeping along the southeastern shores, landed within a mile of Fort Frontenac on the evening of the 25th of August. M. de Noyan, the commander of the fort, was taken completely by surprise. The fortification was a quadrangle, strongly built, and mounted with sixty pieces of cannon. But the garrison was small, and a feeling of absolute security caused them to be ill prepared for defense. Couriers were immediately sent by Noyan to M. de Vaudreuil, at Montreal, for aid. That officer caused the *generale* to be beaten, and without regard to the harvest then ready for the reapers, he levied fifteen hundred men—soldiers, farmers, and Indians—and sent them toward Frontenac under Fabert, the major of the town. But succor was not timely. At the close of the second day Bradstreet opened batteries at so short a distance from the fort that almost every shot took effect. The Indian auxiliaries of the French soon fled in dismay, and on the evening of the 27th Noyan was compelled to surrender the fort and all its dependencies. Bradstreet allowed the chaplain of the garrison to carry away all the sacred vessels belonging to the chapel; and Noyan, who was permitted to go to Montreal, agreed to effect an exchange of himself for Colonel Peter Schuyler, of New Jersey, who had been made a prisoner at Oswego the year before, released on parole, but afterward reclaimed.

There were only about one hundred men in the fort, who became prisoners of war; but the captors found there forty six pieces of cannon, sixteen small mortars, together with a prodigious collection of military stores, provisions, and merchandise, intended chiefly for Fort Du Quesne and the interior dependencies. Nine armed vessels, carrying from eight to eighteen guns each, also fell into their hands. After destroying the fort and seven of the vessels, and such stores as he could not carry away, Bradstreet loaded the two remaining vessels with spoils, and with his whole army returned to Oswego. Major Schuyler had remained there, and joined the victorious colonel in his march back to the Oneida carrying place. There Bradstreet found General Stanwix engaged in building a fort, which he had commenced on the 23d of August, for the security of the Indian country. He lent his aid to that officer for a time, and then returned with his main army to Lake George, after losing five hundred men in the wilderness by sickness.

The capture of Frontenac was a most important event in the history of the war, and should have secured for Bradstreet greater honors than he ever received. It facilitated the fall of Du Quesne in the west, discouraged the French, and gave great joy and confidence to the English. The resources of Canada were almost exhausted, and there was a cry for peace, "no matter with what boundaries." "I am not discouraged," wrote Montcalm, in evident disappointment, "nor are my troops. We are resolved to find our graves under the ruins of the colony."

The sagacious mind of Pitt comprehended the value of this conquest. He "appeared accurately informed of the inland geography of America," says Smith, the historian, whose letter to Governor Morris, in England, bore the first intelligence of the event to the British cabinet. Pitt perceived that Bradstreet had secured the dominion of Lake Ontario, and an easy way to the possession of Niagara and the country beyond, and he looked with confidence to the operations then in progress toward Fort Du Quesne.

Nor was that confidence disappointed. The command of the expedition was entrusted to General Joseph Forbes, and in July he had about nine thousand men at his disposal, including the Virginia troops, under Colonel Washington, at Fort Cumberland. Forbes was taken ill at Philadelphia, and this circumstance, and his perversity of will and judgment, caused most disastrous delays in the progress of the expedition. Contrary to the advice of Washington and other provincial officers, Forbes insisted upon the construction of a new road over the mountains, instead of following the one made by Braddock three years before. So slow were his movements that in September, when it was known that not more than eight hundred men were in garrison at Fort Du Quesne, and its conquest might be easily accomplished, Forbes, with six thousand troops, was yet eastward of the Alleghanies. Major Grant, of the British army, a brave but injudicious officer, had been detached with eight hundred of Colonel Bouquet's advanced corps, part regulars and part provincials, to reconnoiter the condition of Du Quesne and the surrounding country. With foolish recklessness he displayed his force near the fort, and invited an attack. It was accepted, and before he was aware of his danger he was surrounded by a large force of French and Indians, and furiously assailed. Three hundred of Grant's men were slain or wounded, and himself and nineteen officers were made prisoners and carried to Canada.

This was on the 21st of September. Forbes still moved on slowly and methodically, and when the main army joined Bouquet's advance, on the 8th of November, they were yet fifty miles from Fort Du Quesne. Winter was approaching, the troops were discontented, and at a council of war it was resolved to abandon the enterprise and return. At that moment three prisoners were brought to head-quarters, who assured the general that the French garrison at Du Quesne was extremely weak and illy supplied, for they had relied upon the provisions and stores which Bradstreet had captured at Frontenac. Washington was immediately sent forward with his Virginians, and the whole army made preparations to follow. When the advance were within a day's march of the fort, Indian scouts discovered them, and their fears, magnifying the numbers of the Virginians, caused them to tell a most alarming tale to the commander at Du Quesne. The garrison was then reduced to five hundred men, and was short of provisions. They were seized with panic, and on the 24th of November they set fire to the fort and fled down the Ohio in open boats, leaving everything behind them. Washington and his Virginians took possession of all that was left, on the following day, and raised the flag of England over the smoking ruins. A detachment of four hundred and fifty men were left to repair and garrison the fort, and the remainder of the army hastened back to winter quarters. The name of the post was changed to Fort Pitt, in honor of the great statesman at the head of public affairs ; and around its site is now spread out the manufacturing city of Pittsburg, with full sixty thousand inhabitants.

With the close of this expedition ended the campaign of 1758. On the whole it had resulted favorably to Great Britain ; sufficiently so to encourage Pitt in making vast preparations for the campaign of another year. French pride had been effectually humbled by the loss of three of their most important posts—Louisburg, Frontenac, and Du Quesne—and the weakening of the attachment of their Indian allies. Many of the savage warriors had openly deserted the French ; and at a great council held at Easton, on the Delaware, in Pennsylvania, in the summer of 1758, six tribes had, with the SIX NATIONS, made treaties of friendship or neutrality with the English.

# CHAPTER X.

THE final struggle for the mastery in the New World, between the English and the French, was now at hand. Four years had elapsed since the commencement of the contest, but only during the last campaign had success encouraged the English. Now the future for the colonists appeared bright, and the pride and ambition of England were powerfully excited. Pitt, with wonderful sagacity, surveyed the whole scene of possible conflict, and calculated the chances of future success. He conceived the magnificent scheme of conquering all Canada, and destroying, at one blow, the French dominion in America. That dominion was now confined to the region of the St. Lawrence, for the more distant settlements of the west and south were in the condition of weak colonists cut off from the parent country.

Pitt had the rare fortune to possess the confidence of Parliament and of the colonists, and nothing that he desired was withheld. The former was dazzled by his greatness, the latter were deeply impressed with his justice. He had promptly reimbursed all the expenses incurred by the provincial assemblies during the campaign recently closed, amounting to at least a million of dollars ; and they as promptly seconded his scheme of conquest, which had been communicated to them under an oath of secresy. With great unanimity Parliament voted for the year sixty millions of dollars, and such forces, by land and sea, as had never before been known in England. "This is Pitt's doing," exclaimed Lord Chesterfield, "and it is marvelous in our eyes."

The inefficient Abercrombie, who had wasted the whole autumn at Lake George in criminal supineness, was deprived of his command, and General Jeffrey Amherst, who, with Wolfe, had earned laurels on the eastern shores, was made commander-in-chief of all the British forces in America, and sinecure governor of Virginia. The general operations were to be conducted at separate points. A strong land and naval force, under General Wolfe, was to ascend the St. Lawrence and attack Quebec. Another force, under Amherst, was to drive the French from Lake Champlain, seize Montreal, and join Wolfe at Quebec; while a third expedition, commanded by General Prideaux, was to attempt the capture of Fort Niagara, and then hasten down Lake Ontario and the St. Lawrence to Montreal. A considerable fleet, under Admiral Saunders, was deputed to carry Wolfe up the St. Lawrence, and to coöperate with him in the attack on Quebec.

The French in America, who were to oppose these formidable preparations for the conquest of their remaining territory, were comparatively few in number and weak in supplies. Montcalm was the military commander, but in all Canada he could not muster seven thousand men into the service, and only a comparatively few Indians. Scarcity of food prevailed throughout all the French domain in America, for the able-bodied men had been called from their fields to the camp; and on account of arrearages of pay and a profusion of paper money, the French soldiers were becoming very discontented. "Without unexpected good fortune or great fault in the enemy," Montcalm wrote to the minister, "Canada must be taken this campaign, or certainly the next."

Amherst, on hearing of the disasters at Ticonderoga in the summer of 1758, had hastened to Boston from Louisburg, and then across the country, with four regiments and battalion, to reinforce the defeated general. He arrived at Lake George early in October, too late for further action in the field that season. He returned to New York, and in November received his commission as commander-in-chief. He immediately set about arrangements for the next campaign. When these were completed, he transferred his headquarters to Albany, appointed Colonel Bradstreet quartermaster general of the army under his immediate command, and then collected his forces. They were assembled at the close of May, twelve thousand strong, chiefly provincials, furnished by New York and New England.

The assembly of New York entered into the scheme of conquest with zeal. They voted two thousand six hundred men for the service, and authorized the emission of half a million of dollars in bills of credit. Again, early in July, the assembly, at the request of General Amherst, agreed to loan the crown a large sum, to be reimbursed in the course of the year.

Notwithstanding Amherst used the greatest exertions to enter the field early, it was July before his army moved northward, and it was not until the 22d of that month that it appeared at Ticonderoga. Meanwhile the object of the expedition against Niagara, under Prideaux, had been almost accomplished. Prideaux was accompanied by Sir William Johnson and a few Mohawk Indians. His forces, who were chiefly provincials, were collected at Oswego. From that point he sailed for Niagara, and landed a short distance from the fort, without opposition, on the

17th. Prideaux immediately commenced the siege, and was killed on the same day by the bursting of one of his own guns. The command then devolved upon General Johnson, and he sent a flag demanding the surrender of the fort. The garrison, in hourly expectation of reinforcements, refused, and held out bravely for several days. On the 24th, about fifteen hundred French regulars, and as many Creek and Cherokee Indians, appeared, and were greeted by the garrison with a shout of welcome. Their joy lasted but for a moment. Johnson's troops and the French reinforcement had a severe engagement. The latter were effectually routed, and on the following day, the 25th of July, Fort Niagara and its dependencies, and the garrison of seven hundred men, were surrendered to Johnson. A fortnight afterward Lieutenant Governor De Lancey wrote to the Lords of Trade, saying, "His Majesty is now in possession of the most important pass in all the Indian countries." It was even so. Fort Niagara was the connecting link of French military posts between Canada and Louisiana. It was effectually broken, never to be reunited.

Johnson garrisoned Fort Niagara and returned to Albany, for his prisoners encumbered him, and he could not procure sufficient vessels to carry himself and troops to Montreal to coöperate with Wolfe and Amherst, according to the plan of the campaign.

Amherst took the route by Lake George, over which Abercrombie passed the year before. He was accompanied by Colonel Bradstreet, Colonel Schuyler, of New Jersey, who had been exchanged, and Brigadier General Gage. Among other officers were some who became distinguished as the friends or foes of freedom in the war for American independence in after years. Of these, the most noted were

Balfour, who commanded British troops at Charleston; Loring, father of the British commissioner of prisoners in New York and Philadelphia; Moncrieffe, who was a major in the royal army; Prescott, the petty tyrant, who held Ethan Allen a prisoner in 1775, and ruled with a rod of iron while commanding in Rhode Island two years later; Putnam, a major general in the Continental army; Skene, who was made a prisoner with Burgoyne; Stark, the hero of Bennington; Waterbury, who performed brave exploits on Lake Champlain, and Wooster, the patriot-martyr, who was killed near Danbury.

Major Schuyler remained at Albany, actively engaged in the duties of forwarding supplies for the army. So great was his ability in carrying on his plans, public and private, that he was now invested with the functions of commissary general. He was still an easy, good-natured young man, and no one would have suspected that under that exterior lay qualities hitherto unsuspected, even by himself, that were to exalt him to the position of one of the most honored patriots of the world. They existed, nevertheless, and when occasion called for their exercise they promptly appeared. In business he was always firm and discreet. No one ever saw him hurried, embarrassed, or agitated; and he conducted the affairs of his department at this time with the greatest prudence, judgment, and dispatch.

General Amherst appeared before Ticonderoga on the 22d of July. The French, unable to cope with their enemies, had resolved to confine their operations to the service of delaying the invading armies. In consequence of the withdrawal of troops to assist in the defense of menaced Quebec, the garrison at Ticonderoga at this time was very feeble.

On the morning of the 23d, the French army, under

Bourlamarque, withdrew from their lines into the fort, and three days afterward abandoned and partially demolished it, and fled to Crown Point. General Amherst immediately took possession of Fort Carillon, ordered the works to be repaired, and placed a strong garrison there. While engaged in these repairs, he received information that the French had also, in dismay, abandoned Crown Point, and fled down the lake in their boats. This evacuation occurred on the first of August. Amherst immediately detached a body of troops to occupy the abandoned post, and on the 4th proceeded to its occupation with his whole army.

The French fled to Isle aux Noix, at the foot of the lake. Amherst was about to follow with a detachment of his army, when he was informed that the French were over three thousand strong, and that the lake was guarded by four vessels, mounted with cannon and manned by numerous pickets, under the command of M. le Bras, a skilful officer of the French navy. Amherst immediately gave orders for the construction of several vessels of war, which he placed in charge of Captain Loring. When these were equipped, he embarked with his whole army, chiefly in batteaux, near the middle of October, resolved to drive the enemy beyond the St. Lawrence. Heavy tempests arose upon the lake, and he was compelled to turn back. He abandoned the enterprise, landed at Crown Point, put his army into winter quarters there, and proceeded to erect that strong and costly fort whose picturesque ruins may yet be seen by voyagers upon Lake Champlain. Captain Loring, however, braved the storm with his little fleet, went down the lake, destroyed the French flotilla, and thus gained the complete command of Champlain.

A more successful expedition was in progress in the meantime. As soon as the ice of the St. Lawrence came floating into the Gulf in the spring of 1759, Admiral Saunders prepared to sail from Louisburg to Quebec with the British army under Wolfe. The entire armament consisted of eight thousand men in transports, under a convoy of twenty line-of-battle ships, and as many frigates and smaller armed vessels. Admiral Holmes was Saunders' lieutenant; and in the army and navy engaged in this expedition were several officers who were conspicuous in the war for American independence, in the royal service.

The whole force was under the command of Wolfe. It arrived off the Isle of Orleans, just below Quebec, on the 26th of June, and on the following day landed there. Quebec then, as now, consisted of an upper and lower town, the former within fortified walls on the top and declivities of a high rocky promontory; the latter lay upon a narrow beach at the water's edge, and was slowly creeping up the St. Charles river. Upon the heights of the promontory, three hundred feet above the water, was a level plateau called the Plains of Abraham. The town was strongly garrisoned, and at the mouth of the St. Charles, where it enters the St. Lawrence, at the base of the promontory, the French had moored several armed vessels and floating batteries. Along the north bank of the St. Lawrence, from the St. Charles to the Montmorenci river, a distance of seven miles, lay the French army under Montcalm, in a fortified camp. This army was composed chiefly of French Canadians and Indians. The former had been pressed into the service, and all agricultural operations devolved upon old men, women, and children. Montcalm trusted more to the natural strength of the position in which his camp and the city lay, than in his troops for the successful defense of the province.

Wolfe, with amazing skill and vigor, prepared for a

siege. On his left lay his fleet at anchor, and over the beautiful island stretched the tents of his army. All went on quietly until the following night, which was dark and tempestuous, when a fleet of fire-ships, hurried forward by a furious storm of wind and the ebbing tide, came blazing in wrath upon the English ships. The sailors of the fleet, with great adroitness, grappled each incendiary vessel as it came, and towed it free from the shipping. No harm was done by the fire.

On the 30th the English, after some skirmishing, took possession of Point Levi, opposite Quebec, and proceeded to plant batteries there. These were within a mile of the city. From them red hot shot and blazing bombshells were sent upon the lower town. These set on fire full fifty houses in one night, and almost destroyed that part of the city. The citadel, higher up and strong, was beyond the injurious effects of this severe cannonade and bombardment.

Wolfe was eager to gain the prize he so much coveted, and he resolved to attack Montcalm in his fortified camp. On the 10th of July he had landed a large force, under Generals Townshend and Murray, below the Montmorenci, and formed a camp there. On the last day of the month, General Monckton, with grenadiers and other troops, crossed from Point Levi, and landed upon the beach above Montmorenci, at the foot of the great cataract, where the water, after passing for a mile over a rocky bed in a series of roaring rapids, leaps into a dark chasm two hundred feet below.

Murray and Townshend were ordered to force a passage across the Montmorenci above the falls, and coöperate with Monckton. The latter was too eager for attack to await their coming. He rushed up the steep bank, but was soon repulsed, and was compelled to take shelter behind a block-house on the beach just as a heavy thunder storm, which had been gathering for several hours, burst upon the combatants. Darkness fell before the storm ceased, when its voices were rivalled by the roar of the rising tide, which warned Monckton and his men to take to their boats. More than four hundred of the English had perished before this hasty embarkation. In general orders the next day, Wolfe, while he uttered severe censure for rashness, praised Monckton's regiment as one able to cope with the whole Canadian army.

Several weeks had now passed since the English landed upon the Isle of Orleans, and yet nothing of importance had been accomplished. Wolfe was becoming very impatient. Day after day he expected Amherst with reinforcements. They came not. He could not even hear from Amherst. He was informed of the fall of Niagara, the flight of the French from Ticonderoga and Crown Point, but still no aid came for him. Every hour difficulties more and more appalling were gathering around Wolfe. At length, early in September, exposure, fatigue, and anxiety had wasted his strength and produced a violent fever. Prostrate in his tent he called a council of war, and while his brow and hand were hot with disease, he laid before his officers three desperate plans of attack upon the vigilant enemy. They dissented from all, and at the suggestion of Townshend it was resolved to scale the heights of Abraham and draw the French out into open battle. Wolfe acquiesced, though with faint hopes of success. A plan was speedily matured, and, feeble as he was, the commander-in-chief resolved to lead the assault in person. He considered the enterprise a most hazardous one, and he wrote to Pitt, saying, "In this situation there is such a choice of difficulties that I am at a loss myself how to determine. The affairs of Great Britain require most vigorous measures, but then the courage of a handful of brave men should be exerted only where there is some hope." These words gave England unpleasant emotions.

On the 8th of September the camp at the Montmorenci was broken up, and the attention of Montcalm was diverted from the real designs of the English by seeming preparations to attack his lines. Already, having secured the posts on Orleans, Wolfe had marched the portion of the army at Point Levi, up the river, and embarked them on transports which had passed the town in the night for that purpose. Bougainville, who had been sent by Montcalm to watch the movements of the English and prevent a landing, was completely deceived; and when, in several vessels of the fleet, the whole army appeared to be retreating up the river, there was great joy in Quebec and in the French camp. De Levi was sent with three thousand men to defend Montreal, and the Canadians felt confident that the lateness of the season would compel the British fleet to leave the river soon.

It was the pleasant evening of the 12th of September when the whole army destined for the assault moved several miles up the river, above the intended landing place. Leaving their ships at midnight, they embarked in flatboats, and with muffled but unused oars, moved silently down at the speed of the current, followed by the ships soon afterward. Black clouds were then gathering in the sky, and before the flotilla reached its destination the night was intensely dark.

Wolfe was in good spirits, and yet there was evidently in his mind a presentiment of his speedy death. At his evening mess, before leaving the vessel, he composed and sang impromptu that little campaigning song, which has been chanted in many a British tent since, commencing—

> "Why, soldiers, why
> Should we be melancholy, boys?
> Why, soldiers, why,
> Whose business 't is to die!"

And as he sat among his officers, and floated softly down the river in the gloom, a shadow seemed to rest upon his heart, and he repeated in low, musing tones, that touching stanza of Gray's Elegy in a Country Churchyard—

> "The boast of heraldry, the pomp of power,
> And all that beauty, all that wealth e'er gave,
> Await alike the inevitable hour—
> The path of glory leads but to the grave."

At the close he whispered "Now, gentlemen, I would prefer being the author of that poem to the glory of beating the French to-morrow."

At dawn, on the 13th of September, almost five thousand British troops were drawn up in battle array on the Plains of Abraham, three hundred feet above the St. Lawrence. They had landed cautiously in a cove, which still bears the name of Wolfe, and were led up a ravine and steep acclivity by the commander-in-chief, who was at the head of the main division, followed by Colonel Howe with light infantry and a corps of gallant Highlanders. This was a strange apparition to the French. The sergeant's guard at the brow of the acclivity were instantly dispersed, and in hot haste communicated the startling intelligence, first to the garrison in Quebec, and then to Montcalm, at Beauport. That commander was incredulous. "It can be but a small party come to burn a few houses and return," he said; yet, ever vigilant, he did not wait for confirmation. He was speedily undeceived. He soon saw the imminent danger to which the town and garrison were exposed, and he immediately abandoned his intrenchments and led the greater part of his army across the St. Charles to confront the invaders. Messengers were dispatched to to call back De Bougainville and De Levi, and at ten o'clock Montcalm had his army in battle order on the higher part of the plains of Abraham, near the town.

Both parties were deficient in heavy guns. The French had three field pieces, the English only one, and that was a light six-pounder which some sailors had dragged up the ravine. The two commanders, in the order of battle, faced each other. Wolfe was on the right, at the head of the grenadiers who were repulsed at the Montmorenci. They burned with a desire to wipe out the stain of that event. Montcalm was on the left, at the head of three of his best regiments. Wolfe ordered his men to put two bullets into each of their muskets, and reserve their fire until the enemy should be within forty yards of them. They obeyed. Their double-shotted guns did terrible execution. The French were thrown into utter confusion, and were then attacked by the terrible English bayonet.

Wolfe was urging on his battalions in this bayonet charge when he was slightly wounded. He staunched the blood with a handkerchief, and whilst cheering on his men received a more severe bullet wound in the groin. A few minutes afterward a third bullet struck him in the breast, and he fell mortally wounded. It was at this moment that victory for the English was secured by the confused rout of the French. As Wolfe was being carried to the rear, an officer on whose shoulder he was leaning exclaimed, "They run! they run!" The dim eyes of the expiring hero lighted up, and he asked "Who runs?" "The enemy, sir; they give way everywhere," said the officer. Wolfe gave an important command for a movement to cut off the fugitives, and then feebly exclaimed, "Now, God be praised, I die happy!" These were his last words. He soon afterward expired.

Montcalm was also mortally wounded. "Death is certain," said his surgeon. "I am glad of it," replied Montcalm. "How long have I to live?" he inquired. "Ten or twelve hours—perhaps less," was the reply. "So much the better; I shall not live to see the surrender of Quebec!" the dying general said. That night he "spent with God," and expired in the morning. His remains were buried in the grounds of the Ursuline convent at Quebec. Wolfe's were conveyed to England and laid in his family vault, and his government erected a monument to his memory in Westminster Abbey. Massachusetts, grateful for his services, decreed a marble statue of him. Almost seventy years afterward, an English governor of Canada caused a noble obelisk of granite to be erected in the city of Quebec "To the memory of Wolfe and Montcalm."

General Townshend succeeded Wolfe in the command of the army. The French had left five hundred of their comrades dead on the field when they fled. Townshend took possession of their position, and commenced the erection of batteries to storm the city. Some of the French officers desired to renew the conflict and hold out to the last; but the inhabitants within the walls would not submit to such total destruction of life and property as would result from a siege. A capitulation was agreed upon, and five days afterward the city of Quebec was surrendered to the English, and the remains of Montcalm's army, under De Levi, fled to Montreal. General Murray was left to defend the half demolished city, and the British fleet, fearing frost and ice, left the St. Lawrence, carrying away about a thousand prisoners.

Thus brilliantly, for the English, ended the campaign of 1759. Intelligence of the repulse of the grenadiers at the Montmorenci reached England on the 16th of October, and added to the gloom occasioned by Wolfe's desponding letter to Pitt. On the evening of the same day a vessel arrived with news of the victory on the Plains of Abraham, and the King set apart a day for public thanksgiving. "The incidents of dramatic fiction could not be conducted with more address," wrote Horace Walpole, "to lead an audience from despondency to sudden exultation, than accident prepared to excite the passions of a whole people. They despaired, they triumphed, and they wept, for Wolfe had fallen in the hour of victory." But the conquest of Canada was not yet completed.

When the ice left the St. Lawrence in the spring of 1760, De Levi, at the command of Vaudreuil, the governor general of Canada, proceeded with ten thousand men, composed of French regulars, Canadians, and Indians, to attempt the recovery of Quebec. Admiral Saunders had left abundant provisions and much heavy artillery there, and Murray, when the fleet departed, had seven thousand men under his command for the defense of the city. These were reduced one half by disease during the winter. De Levi approached on the 27th of April, and on the 28th the brave but weak Murray went out with his whole force, less than three thousand, to attack him. The English were defeated, lost all their artillery, and came near being cut off in their retreat to the town. In this engagement they lost a thousand men.

De Levi followed up his success vigorously. He commenced a siege, encamped a large force on the heights of

Point Levi, and brought six French frigates up to assist in beleaguring the city by land and water. Meanwhile Pitt had sent a fleet, under Lord Colville, to coöperate in defense of the city. Colville approached with two ships of the line, destroyed the French vessels in the presence of De Levi, and spread great alarm in the French army. Believing these vessels to be only the van of a large squadron, he raised the siege at the middle of May and retreated precipitately to Montreal, leaving behind him most of his artillery and stores. Murray started in pursuit of the fugitives, but their flight was so rapid that he could not overtake them.

Montreal was the last remaining stronghold of the French, and Amherst might easily have had possession of all Canada before De Levi besieged Quebec. But he preferred to follow the systematic and tardy plan which he had formed for the reduction of the province, to a quick and energetic expedition. So he spent the whole summer in making great preparations for the invasion. Vaudreuil, meanwhile, gathered all the moral and material power, at his command at Montreal, for the final struggle.

Amherst's movements, though slow, were effectual. At the head of almost ten thousand men, and a thousand Indian warriors, under Sir William Johnson, he proceeded to Oswego, thence over Lake Ontario and down the St. Lawrence. At the mouth of the Oswegatchie river (now Ogdensburgh) he took possession of a French fort with a feeble garrison, and moving on, appeared before Montreal on the sixth of September. On the same day Murray arrived from Quebec with four thousand troops ; and on the next Colonel Haviland, who had marched from Crown Point, appeared with three thousand more. Haviland had taken possession of Isle aux Noix on the way. Vaudreuil perceived the folly of attempting resistance against such a crushing force, and on the 8th he signed a capitulation surrendering into the hands of the English, Montreal and all Canada, which was then defined as a region covering not only the present provinces of that name, but part of the country south and west of the more westerly of the great lakes. General Gage was appointed governor of Montreal, and General Murray went down the St. Lawrence with four or five thousand men to garrison Quebec.

The French still held the post of Detroit, on the connecting waters between Lakes Erie and St. Clair ; and Amherst, feeling that the conquest of Canada was not absolutely complete while the lilies of France waved over any garrison in the province, however insignificant, sent Major Rogers, five days after the capitulation, with two hundred of his rangers, to plant the English flag in the far interior. At ruined Frontenac the party were well treated by the Indians. Creeping along the north shore of Lake Ontario, they made their way slowly to Niagara, and there furnished themselves with proper costume for the wilderness. In the chilly month of October they went over Lake Erie in open boats to its southern shore, and with cattle furnished by Colonel Boquet, proceeded by land to Detroit in the midst of savage tribes. At the mouth of a river, according to Rogers' journal, whose locality can not now well be defined, they were met by a deputation of Indian chiefs residing upon the great peninsula of Michigan. They informed Rogers that he was within the domain of Pontiac, the famous Ottawa emperor, and advised him to wait for his coming. That haughty prince, when he came, demanded to know how he dared to enter his country without his leave. Rogers explained that he came not as the enemy of the Indians, but to remove the French; and after some hesitation the Partisan and his rangers were suffered to pass on to take possession of Detroit. This was accomplished at the close of November, 1760.*

* "I landed half a mile from the fort," says Rogers in his journal "and drew up my party in front of it in a field of grass. Here Captain Campbell joined us with a French officer bearing Captain Beleter's compliments, and informing me that the garrison was at my command. Lieutenants McCormick and Leslie, with thirty-six Royal Americans, immediately took possession of the fort. The troops of the garrison piled their arms, the French colors were taken down, and the English flag hoisted in their place. Upon this, about seven hundred Indians, who were looking on at a distance, gave a shout, exulting in their prediction being verified, that the crow represented the English instead of the French."

# CHAPTER XI.

COLONEL BRADSTREET, still holding the office of quartermaster general under Amherst, followed his commander to Oswego early in July. He had suffered much from the sickness that so severely smote his camp the year before, and feeling still feeble when the present campaign was opened, he thought it prudent to commit his private affairs to the hands of some friend in whom he could confide. For this important trust he chose Philip Schuyler, and he addressed to him the following letter:

"ALBANY, July 6, 1760.

"DEAR SIR: As all my private affairs are in my leather portmanteau trunk, I hereby commit it to your care and protection, to the end that it may be delivered safe to my wife and children, now at Boston, in case of my decease this campaign, and by your own hand, in which you will ever oblige your faithful friend,

"JOHN BRADSTREET."

Colonel Bradstreet appears, on further reflection, to have considered Mr. Schuyler the most trustworthy of all his friends with whom, in the event of his death, he might leave the settlement of his public accounts, and on the succeeding day he addressed the following letter to him:

"Your zeal, punctuality, and strict honesty in his Majesty's service, under my direction, for several years past, are sufficient proofs that I can't leave my public accounts and papers in a more faithful hand than in yours to be settled, should any accident happen me this campaign; wherefore, that I may provide against it, and that a faithful account may be rendered to the public of all the public money which I have received since the war, I now deliver you all my public accounts and vouchers, and do hereby empower you to settle them with whomsoever may be appointed for that purpose, either in America or England. And for your care and trouble therein, as well as for your faithful and useful services to the public, I am persuaded, on your producing this paper, you will be properly rewarded, if settled in America, by the commander-in-chief, if in England, by the administration. The accounts are clear, and vouchers distinct and complete up to this time, except trifles. I am, sir, your faithful, humble servant,

"JOHN BRADSTREET."

Too feeble in health to accompany Amherst's expedition down the St. Lawrence, Bradstreet remained at Oswego in the exercise of his official duties, and at the end of the campaign was joined at Albany by his family, who came from Boston. The intercolonial war had now ceased, though the French and British continued hostilities upon the ocean, and the Indian tribes on the western and southern frontiers of the English colonies, having tasted blood, made frequent havoc of life and property among the settlers. The provincial forces, except those that appeared necessary to repel these savage inroads, were disbanded, and all industrial pursuits were resumed.

As quartermaster general, Colonel Bradstreet had many accounts to settle with the home government at the close of 1760. He preferred to go to the source of authority for the purpose rather than transact his business with agents in America. His feeble health and the cares of a family made it difficult for him to cross the Atlantic, and again he turned to his young friend, Philip Schuyler, as his most trustworthy agent.

At Bradstreet's solicitation, Mr. Schuyler went to England early in 1761. In return for the confidence which that officer had reposed in him, Mr. Schuyler, by a power of attorney, constituted his "good friend, Colonel John

Bradstreet," his agent for the management and disposition of his property during his absence or in the event of his death. They had purchased broad acres of land together in the Mohawk valley, near the present city of Utica, and the business of each was well known to the other. The power of attorney was executed on the 16th day of February, 1761, in the city of New York, whither Mr. Schuyler had gone for the purpose of embarkation for England.

The precise date of his departure is not on record, and the name of the vessel can only be conjectured from a vague letter of the captain of a French privateer, to which reference will be made presently. That name was *The General Wall*, and was a packet. As soon as Schuyler went on board he became interested in the management of the vessel, especially in the mathematical features of the navigator's art, and he applied himself diligently to its study. That application was timely and fortunate, for the captain soon died, and the passengers and crew, with common consent, made Mr. Schuyler the commander.

On the voyage they met a dismantled slaver in great distress. She had been driven about upon the ocean for several days in a severe storm. Her water and provisions were exhausted. Schuyler transferred the crew to his own vessel, and ordered the hatches of the slaver to be opened, to give the two hundred negroes a chance for their lives. A few days afterward he met a vessel laden with horses, bound for the West Indies, and he requested the captain to seek the slaver and feed the miserable starvelings on horse-flesh.

Not long after this, Schuyler's vessel was captured by the French privateer *La Biscayen*, of Bayonne, commanded by M. Lafargue, who placed his lieutenant on board the prize. The latter officer appears to have made immediate arrangements for the ransom of his prisoners, demanding from Schuyler fifty pounds sterling as his share of the ransom money. But the Frenchmen's prize was soon lost, for the captors and the captives were seized by an English frigate, and conveyed to London.

On the 13th of April Lafargue addressed a polite letter to Schuyler. After first disclaiming all collusion with his brother officer in making the extortionate demand for his ransom, he reminded Schuyler of the good treatment he had received at the hands of the writer while he was a prisoner; and then, coming to the main object of his letter, he implored him to use his influence in procuring the release of his two brothers, who were officers of another privateer of Bayonne, commanded by Lafargue's brother-in-law, that had been captured by an English frigate.*

Intelligence of Schuyler's escape reached his friends at the middle of May, and gave them great joy, for the ocean was swarming with privateers. William Smith, the historian, his warm personal friend, wrote to him from New York on the 15th of May, saying:

"The packet arrived last night, and another sails suddenly in the morning, so that I have only time for a word. I congratulate you most heartily on your escape and arrival, and extreme good fortune in saving your papers. Colonel De Lancey† forwarded your letters to Mrs. Schuyler and Colonel Bradstreet by express before I got mine from the post office. I shall write to her by the first post.

"We are surprised by the late changes among the principal officers. What is Lord Stirling about? I am sorry to find him unnoticed in the American preferments. Pray let us know every thing on your side that concerns us. What sort of folks have the plantation affairs in their hands."

Much uneasiness was then felt in the colonies in respect

* Autograph letter.

† Oliver De Lancey, brother of James De Lancey, and commander of a corps of loyalists in the war for independence.

to the future. George the Second had died in the autumn of 1760, and his grandson had ascended the throne, at the age of less than twenty years, as George the Third. His mother appears to have been quite enamored of the Earl of Bute, a gay but poor and unprincipled Scotch adventurer, who had been the prince's tutor, and had great influence over the young king. The eminent Pitt was actually treated with indifference, and the changes to which the writer of the foregoing letter alluded was the retirement of that great statesman from the head of the imperial cabinet, and his place substantially supplied by the shallow Bute. From that hour the rapid alienation of the colonies from the crown began.

William Alexander (Lord Stirling) was yet in England, whither he went with Governor Shirley in 1756, and by the advice of friends had taken measures to obtain from government a recognition of his title of Earl of Stirling, derived from his father, who had been attainted because of his participation in the rebellion of 1716, when the son of James the Second made an attempt to obtain the sovereignty of England. Alexander failed in securing the legal recognition of his title, but his right to it was so generally conceded that he was ever afterward addressed as Lord Stirling. He and Schuyler had become warm personal friends when the former was at Albany in 1756, as Shirley's military secretary, and now they again met as friends in England. They returned to America in the same vessel, and in the struggle for freedom which soon afterward commenced in the colonies they were compatriots and fellow soldiers.

Mr. Schuyler laid the accounts with which he had been entrusted, and which he had arranged in perfect order for Colonel Bradstreet, before the proper committee of Parliament, and he was highly complimented for their accuracy and neatness. "There was then but one man in England who could compute faster than himself."* Having completed his business, visited some of the principal places in England, and made the acquaintance of several leading men there, Mr. Schuyler returned home toward the close of summer, to find public feeling deeply stirred by causes which speedily brought about an open rupture between the colonies and the parent country.

For a hundred years the colonists had been subjected to oppressive commercial restrictions, the first oppressive navigation act bearing the date of 1660, the year when Charles the Second ascended the throne. In the weakness of their infancy the colonists had been compelled to submit to those restrictions, though often with a bad grace. But as they increased in numbers, and circumstances taught them to perceive their rapidly augmenting strength, they felt their manhood stirring too strongly within them to submit any longer without uttering a protest. Their industry and commerce were becoming too productive and expansive to be confined within the narrow limits of those restrictions which the Board of Trade had from time to time imposed, and they determined henceforth to regard them as mere ropes of sand. They resolved no longer to submit to laws which declared that all manufactories of iron and steel in the colonies should be considered "a common nuisance," to be abated within thirty days after notice being given, or the owner should be subjected to a fine of one thousand dollars; that prohibited the "erection or contrivance of any mill or other engine for slitting or rolling iron, or any plating forge to work with a tilt-hammer, or any fur-

* Statement of Mrs. Catharine Van Rensselaer Cochran, General Schuyler's youngest and last surviving child.

nace for making steel in the colonies;" that forbade the exportation of hats from one colony to another, and allowed no hatter to have more than two apprentices at one time; that burdened imported sugar, rum, and molasses with exorbitant duties; and that forbade the Carolinians cutting down the juicy trees of their vast pine forests, and converting their wood into staves and their sap into turpentine and tar, for commercial purposes.

During many long and gloomy years the colonists had struggled up, unaided and alone, from feebleness to strength. They had erected forts, raised armies, and fought battles cheerfully for England's glory and their own preservation, without England's aid and often without her sympathy. During the Seven Years' War, whose turmoil was now ended in America, did they cheerfully tax themselves and contribute men, money, and provisions. They lost, during that war, twenty-five thousand robust young men, besides many seamen. That war cost the colonies, in the aggregate, full twenty millions of dollars, besides the flower of their youth; and in return Parliament granted them, during the contest, at different periods, only about five and a half millions of dollars. And yet the British ministry, in 1760, while the colonists were so generously supporting the power and dignity of the realm, regarded their services as the mere exercise of the duties of subjects to their sovereign, and declared that, notwithstanding grants of money had been made to them, they expected to get it all back, by imposing a tax upon them after the war, in order to raise a revenue. Even the generous Pitt used language of this kind in a letter to the governor of Virginia. It was the language of a minister who saw the treasury of his country empty—exhausted by a long and expensive war, not yet ended, and with enormous demands upon it, which called for taxation in every conceivable form—and who always maintained that his government had the *right* to tax the colonies.

The resignation of Pitt (who was disgusted with some of his shallow and corrupt colleagues) at that crisis was a most unfortunate occurrence for England, for while the Earl of Egremont, a weak and passionate man, was his nominal successor, the Earl of Bute was the controling power in the cabinet, because of his connection with the King and his mother. And around Bute moved satellites obsequious alike to himself and the monarch. The most fawning of these was Doddington, who had been raised to the peerage as Lord Melcombe. "He was to Bute," says Bancroft, "what Bute was to George the Third." He wished Bute joy, on the resignation of Pitt, "of being delivered of a most impracticable colleague, his Majesty of a most imperious servant, and the country of a most dangerous minister." He said, "men of the city are not to demand reasons of measures; they must, and they easily may be taught better manners." Lord Barrington said of the weak King, "He is the best and most amiable master that ever lived since the days of Titus. * * * God has ordained him with the prerogative, and left to his servants the glory of obedience." Such were the men who surrounded the young monarch and gave direction to the government of England—the great public interests of a people who, by their moral and material strength, had just taken the foremost rank in the family of nations.

The importance of the American colonies was now acknowledged, and the parent government viewed them with mingled feelings of pride and jealousy. Secret agents were dispatched to ascertain and report to the ministry the real condition of the colonists. Some of these gave such fabulous accounts of their wealth and great resources that the government resolved to draw much revenue from them ; and the democratic tendency of the people, who seemed to inhale a love of liberty with the free air of their fresh world, was so magnified that the government was alarmed. Long and anxious were the councils of the advisers of the young King, and the Board of Trade, in whose charge the general affairs of the colonies rested, proposed to annul all the colonial charters, reduce each colony to a royal government, and vigorously enforce all existing revenue laws. At the same time the dignitaries of the established church, acting in concert with the government, proposed plans for making the doctrines and rituals of the Church of England the state religion in America.

The first act which revealed the intentions of the Parliament to enforce the oppressive revenue laws was the authorization of writs of assistance. These were general search warrants, which not only allowed the King's civil and naval officers, who held them, to break open any citizen's store or dwelling to search for suspected contraband goods, but compelled sheriffs and other local officers to assist in the work. The sanctities of private life might thus be invaded, as a cotemporary asserted, "by the meanest deputy of a deputy's deputy." The political maxim of the English constitution, that every man's house is his castle, was thus violated, and the people subjected to the most obnoxious form of petty tyranny. They resolved not to submit to it.

In Massachusetts, where American commerce had first budded more than a century and a quarter before, and had now become vastly important, the first firm voice of opposition to the writs of assistance was heard. A question arose whether the persons employed in enforcing the revenue laws should have power to invoke generally the assistance of all the executive officers of the colony. Chief Justice Hutchinson appointed a day when arguments upon the question would be heard in the old Town Hall in Boston. The court for the purpose was held in February, 1761. It was argued on one side that the revenue officers in America had like powers with those of England, and to refuse a writ of assistance to them would be in effect to deny that the Parliament of Great Britain was the sovereign legislature of the British empire.

It was argued on the other hand that such an act was in violation of the British constitution, and therefore void. "No act of Parliament," said the fiery James Otis, of Barnstable, then advocate general of the colony, "can establish such a writ." With burning words and vehemence of manner that were but faint expressions of his feelings, that wonderful man, then properly named the "great incendiary of New England," portrayed the nature and effects of these writs, which compelled the whole government and the oppressed people to render aid in enforcing the unrighteous revenue laws for the colonies. "I am determined," he said "to sacrifice estate, ease, health, applause, and even life, to the sacred calls of my country in opposition to a kind of power which cost one king of England his head and another his throne. These writs," he exclaimed, "are the worst instrument of arbitrary power, the most destructive of English liberty and the fundamental principles of law."

The majority of the judges believed Otis to be right; and when, according to John Adams, who was present, the orator exclaimed "to my dying day I will oppose, with all the power and faculties that God has given me, all such instruments of slavery on one hand and villainy on the other," the whole audience seemed ready to take up arms against the writs of assistance and kindred measures. "Then and there," said Adams, "American independence was born; the seeds of patriots were then and there sown."

Hutchinson, ambitious of royal favor, and grasping for the emoluments of office which that favor might secure to him, took sides with the crown, and thereby planted in his own side that thorn of popular distrust which finally led to his ignominious flight to England. Great discontents followed, and the fires of the Revolution began to kindle all over the land.

The province of New York, at this time, was powerfully agitated, not so much by religious controversies, which before the war had occupied a large space in the public mind, nor by the writs of assistance which had inflamed Massachusetts, but because a blow had been struck at the independence of the judiciary. Lieutenant Governor De Lancey had died suddenly, at the close of July, 1760, after spending several hours at a dinner party on Staten Island, and the government devolved temporarily on Dr. Cadwallader Colden, the president of the council. Colden was then seventy-three years of age. On hearing of the death of De Lancey, he came from his rural retreat in Orange county and took up his residence at the province house in the fort at New York. General Monckton, who had lately been appointed governor of the province, was too much engaged in military affairs to pay any attention to civil duties, and he joined in a recommendation for the appointment of Colden as lieutenant governor.

The chief justice of the province had lately died. As the other judges had some doubts as to the validity of their commissions, since the demise of the late King, they and the people urged Dr. Colden to fill the vacant seat of the chief justice immediately, that processes might not cease.

Colden's reply was ambiguous. He was contemplating his own aggrandizement, and had resolved to compliment the Earl of Halifax, the secretary of state for the colonies, by desiring him to nominate a chief justice. This was done, and more. Through the influence of Governor Pownall, Pratt, a Boston lawyer, was not nominated but actually appointed chief justice of New York, to hold his office, not, as before the late sovereign's death, "during good behavior," but "at the pleasure of the King."

The assembly and the people were startled by this blow at the independence of the judiciary. They held this new tenure of judicial power to be inconsistent with liberty in America. To make the King's will, they said, the tenure of office, is to make the bench of judges the instrument of the royal prerogative. The administration of justice throughout all America will thus be subjected to an absolutely irresponsible power. The assembly rebelled against this encroachment on the rights of the people, and resolved that while the judges should hold office by such tenure they would grant them no salary. They in effect declared that the people were the true source of all authority. "For some years past," wrote Colden, complainingly, to the Board of Trade, "three popular lawyers,* educated in Connecticut, who have strongly imbibed the independent principles of that country, calumniate the administration in every exercise of the prerogative, and get the applause of the mob by propagating the doctrine that all authority is derived from the people."

The old question of church and state was now revived in New York. It was strongly suspected, what subsequently proved to be the fact, that the Episcopal clergy

* These were William Livingston, John Morrin Scott, and William Smith, the historian.

were in secret communication with Dr. Secker, Archbishop of Canterbury, on the subject of the establishment of episcopacy in America, and the extension of the ecclesiastical dominion of the Church of England over the colonies. Dr. Johnson, the president of King's College in New York, had this project deeply at heart, and in his zeal he revealed sufficient to alarm the fears of the more timid or watchful opponents of the scheme. The colonists opposed it on political grounds only. They knew that if Parliament could create dioceses and appoint bishops, it would introduce tithes and crush so-called heresy. They remembered the character of the hierarchy from the oppression of which the ancestors of the Puritans had fled, and, conscious of the natural alliance between a banded church and state in all measures affecting each other, it was fair to conclude that if the British government was assuming the character of a tyranical master, the church would necessarily be its abettor. They also knew, from the teachings of all history, that the most implacable tyrant was an ecclesiastical one.

For these reasons, those who espoused the cause of the people in their opposition to the oppressive measures of government (and among them was found Philip Schuyler) were vigilant in watching and active in thwarting every movement that tended to episcopacy in America. In the popular discussions of the rights of the people in the province of New York, the ecclesiastical topic formed an elemental and substantial part for many years. The controversy was sometimes upon the ecclesiastical topic alone, and ran high. The newspapers and pamphlets were the principal vehicles by which the sentiments and the arguments of the controversialists were conveyed to the people at large. Art was sometimes evoked to aid the pen. One example will suffice to illustrate the character of this auxilliary and the spirit of the opposition. The *Political Register* for 1769, when the religious controversy we are considering was at its height, contained a picture entitled "An attempt to land a Bishop in America." A portion of a vessel called *The Hillsborough* (in allusion to the Earl of Hillsborough, then the colonial secretary) is seen. She is lying at a wharf, on which is a crowd of earnest people, some with poles pushing her from her moorings. One holds up a book inscribed "Sidney on Government;" another has a volume of Locke's Essays; a third, in the garb of a Quaker, holds an open volume inscribed *Barclay's Apology*, and from the mouth of a fourth is a scroll bearing the words "No lords, spiritual or temporal, in New England." Half way up the shrouds of the vessel is seen a bishop in his robes, his mitre falling, and a volume of Calvin's works, hurled by one on shore, is about to strike his head. From his mouth issues a scroll, inscribed, "Lord, now lettest thou thy servant depart in peace!" In the foreground is a paper, on which is written, "Shall they be obliged to maintain bishops that can not maintain themselves?" Near it is seen a monkey in the act of throwing a stone at the bishop.

As we have already observed, the war had ceased in America, but was continued by the French and English on the ocean and among the West Indies with almost uninterrupted success for the latter. Guadaloupe fell into the hands of the British; and at the close of 1762 General Monckton, with fresh laurels on his brow, produced his commission as governor to the council of New York, and then sailed from the capital of that province with two line-of-battle ships, a hundred transports, and twelve thousand regular and colonial troops, the latter led by General Lyman, the former lieutenant of General Sir William Johnson. Gates, afterward a major-general in the Revolutionary army, accompanied Monckton as his aid, and was honored as the bearer of his general's dispatches to the British government announcing his capture of Martinique. With him went also Richard Montgomery, who, the leader of an invading army, was killed at Quebec at the close of 1775. He was then a captain in the service. Both he and Gates were afterward the friends and companions-in-arms of Philip Schuyler.

Monckton was successful every where in the West Indies. Grenada, St. Vincent's, St. Lucie, and every island of the Caribbean group possessed by the French were speedily passed into the hands of the British. Meanwhile Spain had, by secret treaty with France, known as the Family Compact, (the sovereigns of each empire being Bourbons,) become a party in the contest. Spain commenced hostilities against Great Britain before the latter power, contrary to the advice of Pitt, who had information of the compact, had declared war. At once the British cruisers commenced forays upon Spanish colonial commerce. It was utterly cut off in a very short time, and in August, 1762, the Havana, the key to the Gulf of Mexico, was taken by a British armament.

The finances of France were now almost ruined. Loss after loss was weakening the prestige of her arms and sapping her moral and material strength, and she was compelled to abandon the contest, and with it all claim to territorial possession on the North American continent. Finally, on the 3d of November, 1762, a preliminary treaty was negotiated at Fontainebleau, and definitely concluded at Paris, on the 10th of February, 1763, by which all the vast region east of the Mississippi river (except the island of New Orleans, which, with Louisiana, had been ceded by

France to Spain,) was given up to the British. Spain, then in possession of Florida, gave it for the Havana, and the sovereignty of the whole eastern half of North America, from the orange groves of the Gulf of Mexico to the polar ice, was vested in the British crown.

But the Indians on the southern and western frontiers, incited by French emissaries, were yet restless and unsubdued. Those on the borders of the Carolinas were making frequent bloody forays upon the settlements. Mutual wrongs, inflicted by the Virginians and Carolinians, and the warlike Cherokees — the bold mountaineers of the southern country—kindled a fierce war in the spring of 1760. In the course of a few weeks, the whole frontier of the Carolinas was desolated by the savages. General Amherst heeded the calls of the southrons for aid, and in April, Colonel Montgomery, with some British regulars and provincial troops, marched from Charleston and laid waste a portion of the Cherokee country. Yet these bold highlanders were not subdued. The following year Colonel Grant led a still stronger force against them, burned their towns, desolated their fields, and killed many of their warriors. Then they humbly sued for peace. It was granted at a treaty in June, 1761, and comparative repose was vouchsafed to the frontier settlers for several years.

Meanwhile French emissaries were stirring up the northwestern tribes to hostilities against the English. The cloud of danger soon became most portentous. Pontiac, the sagacious chief of the Ottawas, who met Rogers on his way to Detroit, and who had been an early ally of the French, secretly confederated several of the Algonquin tribes, in 1763, for expelling the English from the country west of the Alleghanies. That wily chief had professed attachment to the English. There appeared safety on the borders of his dominions, and emigration began to pour a living flood into the wilderness. Pontiac became alarmed at this subtle invasion. He saw in the dim future his whole land in possession of the pale faces, and his race driven away or extinguished. With patriotic impulse he resolved to strike a deadly blow for kindred and country. Secretly he confederated the savage tribes ; adroitly he eluded the vigilance of the white man ; and within a fortnight, in the summer of 1763, all the frontier posts west of Oswego, possessed by the English, fell into his hands, except Niagara, Fort Pitt, and Detroit. Boquet saved Fort Pitt ; Niagara was not attacked ; and Detroit, after sustaining a siege almost twelve months, was relieved by a provincial force, under Colonel Bradstreet, in May, 1764. Soon after this, the power of the Indians was completely broken, and the last act in the drama of the French and Indian war was closed.

## CHAPTER XII.

After the peace of 1763, Mr. Schuyler was called into the service of the colony in various civil employments. At the same time he was assiduously engaged in the management of his own private affairs, the operations of which were constantly increasing. With Colonel Bradstreet, Philip Livingston, and later, with Sir Henry Moore, the governor of the colony, he was a frequent purchaser from the Indians and others of lands in the Hudson and Mohawk vallies. He had an interest in lands about Fort Edward, and in the Van Rensselaer estate in Columbia county. He also had large tracts of land in Duchess county and in the manor of Cortland. His ample Saratoga estate was the most valuable of all, for it was improved, and had mills of considerable importance at the falls of the Fish Creek. He had a schooner named *Mohawk*, in trade on the Hudson; also two or three sloops; and he was active in efforts to promote emigration from Europe to the wild lands of the west.

When in London, in 1761, Mr. Schuyler became acquainted with the eminent surgeon, Professor Thomas Brand, with whom he kept up a correspondence for some time. At the close of 1763 he wrote a letter to that gentleman, in which he laid before him a plan for a settlement at Detroit, which had been proposed by Colonel Bradstreet, in which Mr. Schuyler appears to have taken great interest.

The object of that portion of Schuyler's letter was to engage the coöperation of the ministry in promoting emigration to America, and especially to the western wilderness lately wrested from the French. In his reply to that letter, in March following, Professor Brand informed him that schemes for settlement did not in the least occupy the attention of the ministry or the people. The chief objection, he said, was the fact that the war had cost so many lives that none could then be spared from England for the purpose of settlement in the New World. "But Germany," he added, "might and would supply us upon a proper proposal, and even a colony of Jews would be of service and of public benefit."*

Professor Brand seems not to have been aware that at that very time the ministry were casting obstacles in the way of emigration to America, and especially of Germans, who were generally liberty loving men. Some had already gone into New England, and more into Pennsylvania. The emigration of French Roman Catholics to Maryland, which had commenced, was discouraged; and the easy terms upon which wild lands might be procured were so materially changed that, toward the dawning of the Revolution, the vast solitudes west of the Alleghanies were seldom penetrated by any but the hunter from the seaboard provinces. This conduct of the government proceeded from the narrow and unwise policy toward the colonies, based chiefly upon a jealousy of their increasing strength and importance, which marked the first ten years or more of the reign of George the Third, and formed one of the counts of the indictment of that monarch, when he was arraigned, by the Declaration of Independence, in 1776, before the bar of the nations. "He has endeavored," says that Declaration, "to prevent

* Autograph letter.

the population of these States, for that purpose obstructing the laws for the naturalization of foreigners; refusing to pass others to encourage their migration hither, and raising the conditions of new appropriations of lands."

In another part of his letter, Professor Brand informed Mr. Schuyler that the latter had been elected a member of the Society of Arts, in London, and that a gold medal had been voted by the Society "to Mr. Elliot, of New England, for discovering iron ore in the American black sand, and that in a very great proportion." Then, after inquiring how he shall send him papers and transactions, whether there is a library at Albany, or charts of the country about that city, he begs him to continue to write to him, for Schuyler had evidently given him a great deal of information concerning the resources of his country.

In 1764, Mr. Schuyler was appointed by the General Assembly of New York, one of the commissioners to manage the controversy on the part of his province respecting the partition line between that colony and Massachusetts Bay, and he was actively engaged in that discussion in 1767, with associates and opponents of the first rank and character.* He also became involved in the fierce controversy between New York and the New Hampshire Grants, as the present State of Vermont was called, which continued until the kindling of the war for independence.

These disputes grew out of the confusion produced by royal charters. The western boundary of the colonies of Massachusetts Bay and Connecticut were, by their charters, upon the "South Sea," or Pacific Ocean; while Charles the Second had granted to his brother, the Duke of York, the province of New Netherland, which lay along the Hudson river, directly west of those colonies. Here was direct and

* Chancellor Kent.

palpable conflict, which nothing but mutual concessions and compromises could settle. It was an open question when the Duke obtained possession of his domain by conquest in 1664. Commissioners then settled it by agreeing that the partition line between New York and the New England provinces should be at twenty miles eastward of the Hudson river, and running parallel with that stream. This line was first established between New York and Connecticut, and more than a hundred years afterward, by precedent, between New York and Massachusetts Bay. This controversy being concluded, New Hampshire appeared, and, pleading those precedents, asked to have its own partition line formed by the extension of those of its sister colonies directly northward. New York had reluctantly yielded a similar claim to Massachusetts, and now that province emphatically protested against the new claim, declaring that its eastern boundary, north of the Massachusetts line, was the Connecticut river.

Meanwhile, Governor Benning Wentworth, of New Hampshire, who had been authorized to issue patents for unimproved lands within the limits of his province, yielded to the numerous applications of settlers who were penetrating the country westward of the Connecticut river, and made grants of lands to them. Some of these settlers had even crossed the Green mountains, and built their pioneer fires on the wooded shores of Lake Champlain.

Wentworth's first grant for a township was in 1749. It was named Bennington, in honor of the governor, and occupied an area six miles square, having for its western boundary a line parallel with that between New York and Massachusetts. This grant brought the territorial question between New York and New Hampshire to an issue. The authorities of New York protested against the grant.

Wentworth paid no attention to it, and at the commencement of the French and Indian war, he had issued patents for fourteen townships west of the Connecticut river. That war absorbed all minor considerations for the time ; but when, in 1760, Canada passed into the hands of the English, the dispute between New York and New Hampshire was revived. Immigration began to pour its living flood into the beautiful Green mountain region, and in the course of four or five years Wentworth issued patents for no less than one hundred and thirty-eight townships of the size of Bennington. These occupied a greater portion of the present State of Vermont, and the territory was called the *New Hampshire Grants* from that time until the kindling of the war for independence. And the hardy yeomanry who first appeared in arms for the defense of their territorial rights, and afterwards as patriots in the common cause when the Revolution broke out, were called *Green Mountain Boys.*

Lieutenant Governor Colden, acting chief magistrate of New York in the absence of General Monckton, perceiving the necessity of asserting the claims of that province to the country westward of the Connecticut river, wrote an energetic letter to Governor Wentworth, protesting against his grants. He also sent a proclamation among the people, declaring the Connecticut river to be the boundary between New York and New Hampshire. But protests and proclamations were alike unheeded by the governor and the people until the year 1764, when the matter was laid before the King and council for adjudication. The decision was in favor of New York. Wentworth immediately bowed to supreme authority, and ceased issuing patents for lands westward of the Connecticut. The settlers, considering all questions in dispute to be thus finally disposed of, were contented, and went on hopefully in the improvement of their lands. Among these settlers in the Bennington township were members of the Allen family, in Connecticut, two of whom, Ethan and Ira, were conspicuous in public affairs for many years, as we shall hereafter have occasion to observe.

The authorities of New York, not content with the award of territorial jurisdiction over the domain, proceeded, on the decision of able legal authority, to assert the right of property in the soil of that territory, and declared Wentworth's patents all void. They went further. Orders were issued for for the survey and sale of farms in the possession of actual settlers, who had bought and paid for them, and, in many instances, had made great progress in improvements. In this, New York acted not only unjustly, but very unwisely. This oppression, for oppression it was, was a fatal mistake. It was like sowing dragons' teeth to see them produce a crop of full-armed men. The settlers were disposed to be quiet, loyal subjects of New York. They cared not who was their political master, so long as their private rights were respected. But this act of injustice converted them into rebellious foes, determined and defiant. A new and powerful opposition to the claims of New York was created. It was now no longer the shadowy, unsubstantial *government* of New Hampshire, panoplied in proclamations, that opposed the pretensions of New York; it was an opposition composed of the sinews and muskets and determined wills of the *people* of the Grants, backed by all New Hampshire —aye, by all New England. New York had given them the degrading alternative of leaving their possessions to others or of repurchasing them. As freemen, full of the spirit of true English liberty coming down to them through their Puritan ancestors, they could not submit to this alternative, and they preferred to defend their rights even at the expense of their blood. Foremost among those who took this decisive stand was Ethan Allen, who became the leader in the border forays and irritating movements that ensued.

The governor and council of New York at length summoned all the claimants under the New Hampshire Grants to appear before them at Albany, with their deeds and other evidences of possession, within three months, failing in which, it was declared that the claims of all delinquents should be rejected. The people of the Grants paid no attention to the requisition. Meanwhile speculators had been purchasing from New York large tracts of these estates in the disputed territory, and were making preparations to take possession. The people of the Grants sent one of their number to England, and laid their cause before the King and council. He came back in August, 1767, armed with an order for the Governor of New York to abstain from issuing any more patents for lands eastward of Lake Champlain. But as the order was not *ex post facto* in its operations, the New York patentees proceeded to take possession of their purchased lands. This speedily brought on a crisis, and for seven years the New Hampshire Grants formed a theater where all the elements of civil war, except actual carnage, were in active exercise.

In these violent disputes between the authorities of New York and the people of the Grants, Mr. Schuyler was frequently an active participant, first, indirectly, as one of the commissioners for settling the partition line between New York and Massachusetts, then as colonel of the militia of Albany, and for several years as member of the New York General Assembly. Of course, those who upheld the claims of New York incurred the bitter resentment of the New England people; and as Mr. Schuyler was among the most prominent of them, he was most thoroughly disliked by those who regarded New York as an oppressor. This resentment was yet felt when the war for independence commenced, and it frequently appeared in the relations between General Schuyler and the New England officers and troops, when he was commander-in-chief of the northern department of the continental army.

Another dispute, far more important, because more general and momentous, occupied the minds of the leading men not only of New York but of all America during the period we have just been considering. It was a quarrel between Great Britain and her American colonies, because the former claimed and asserted the right to tax the latter, by imposts or otherwise, without their consent. The first overt acts of resistance, as we have seen, were in opposition to the writs of assistance, in 1761. The next movement of the British Parliament that called for opposition on the part of the colonies was the reënactment of the sugar act, and the adoption of kindred measures, which seriously interfered with the trade of the colonies with the West Indies.

Then came the famous Stamp Act. George Grenville had boasted in the House of Commons that he could procure a revenue from America. He was raised to the head of the treasury, and forthwith proceeded to redeem that promise. In a small room in Downing street, late in September, 1763, he and Lord North, and another member of the treasury board, directed the first secretary of the treasury to "write to the commissioners of the stamp duties to prepare the draft of a bill to be presented to Parliament for extending the stamp duties to the colonies." It was done, and early in 1764 the American assemblies were informed of the fact by their respective agents. This intelligence created mingled sentiments of alarm, aversion, and indignation throughout the colonies. "Taxation without representation," they said, "is tyranny." Even Grenville doubted the propriety of taxing the colonies without allowing them a representation in Parliament ; yet, bolder than all ministers before him, he resolved on trying the experiment. But he made that trial with caution. It was more than a year after notice of the minister's intentions was given that a stamp act became law.

Unalarmed by the gathering storm in America, the King, in his speech on the opening of Parliament early in 1765, recommended the carrying out of Grenville's scheme and the enforcement of obedience in the colonies. On the 22d of March following, the King cheerfully gave his signature to an act that declared that no legal instrument of writing should thereafter be valid in the colonies unless it bore a government stamp, for which specified sums should be paid, from sixpence to two pounds sterling. The protests of colonial agents, the remonstrances of London merchants trading with America, and the wise suggestions of men acquainted with the temper and resources of the Americans, were set at naught. The infatuated ministry openly avowed their intention "to establish the power of Great Britain to tax her colonies ;" and even the chimney-sweepers of London, Pitt said, spoke of "*our* subjects in America."

Intelligence of the passage of the Stamp Act produced intense excitement throughout the colonies. Nowhere did the flame of resentment burn more fiercely than in New York, and nowhere were its manifestations more emphatic. Colden, the acting governor, then seventy-seven years of age, was a liberal minded man, but, true to his sovereign, as his representative he felt it his duty to discountenance all opposition to the acts of the imperial legislature. But his opposition was like a breath opposed to the strong wind. Associations calling themselves Sons of Liberty were organized at various places in the province, and though not numerous at first, were very active and potent as centers of opposition. The press spoke out without reserve through its correspondents. Although the assembly, when charged with contemplating independence, "rejected the thought," the germ was swelling in the people's hearts. "If," said a newspaper writer at New York, "the interests of the mother country and her colonies can not be made to coincide; if the same operations of the constitution may not take place in both; if the welfare of the mother country necessarily requires the sacrifice of the most valuable rights of the colonies—the right of making their own laws, and disposing of their own property by representatives of their own choosing—if such really is the case between Great Britain and her colonies, then the connection between them ought to cease, and sooner or later it inevitably must cease."

The pulpit, especially in New England, denounced the scheme as unholy; and to the exhortation of the churchman to loyalty toward "the Lord's anointed," the dissenter responded, "the people are the 'Lord's anointed.'" In the city of New York a committee of correspondence, to communicate with other Sons of Liberty, was chosen, with Isaac Sears, their great leader, at the head, and measures were adopted to compel the appointed stamp distributor to resign his commission. In several other places popular excitement created mobs, and violence ensued; stamp distributors were insulted and abused, and before the first of November, 1765, the day on which the act was to go into effect, there were no officers courageous enough to attempt to execute its commands.

Meanwhile, pursuant to an invitation sent out to the several colonial assemblies by that of Massachusetts, a convention of delegates met in the city of New York on the first Tuesday in October, to deliberate upon the subject of the act. In that congress nine colonies were represented.* Robert R. Livingston, John Cruger, Philip Livingston, William Bayard, and Leonard Lispenard were there in behalf of New York. Timothy Ruggles, of Massachusetts, who afterward proved disloyal to the principles of popular liberty, was chosen president of the congress, and John Cotton was appointed clerk. The congress continued in session fourteen days, and adopted a *Declaration of Rights*, written by John Cruger; a *Petition to the King*, penned by Robert R. Livingston, and a *Memorial to both Houses of Parliament*, prepared by James Otis. These are still regarded as model state papers. Only the president of the congress, and Mr. Ogden, of New Jersey, afterward a famous loyalist, withheld their signatures in approval of the proceedings.

General Gage was now commander-in-chief of the British army in America, and had his headquarters at Fort George, in New York, where a strong garrison was stationed. In view of impending troubles, Colden caused the fort to be strengthened; he also replenished the magazine. These measures became known, and increased the indignation of the people. Their boldness also increased. In defiance of the armed ships riding in the harbor, and of

* Massachusetts, New York, New Jersey, Rhode Island, Pennsylvania, Delaware, Connecticut, Maryland, and South Carolina. The assemblies of New Hampshire, Virginia, North Carolina, and Georgia, wrote that they would agree to whatever might be done by the congress.

the troops in the garrison, they appeared before the fort and demanded the delivery of the stamps deposited there, to their appointed leader. A refusal was answered by shouts of defiance, and half an hour afterward the lieutenant governor was hung in effigy near where the fountain in the City Hall Park now is. After that effigy was paraded through the streets, it was taken back to the fort and there consumed in a bonfire made of the wooden fence that surrounded the Bowling Green. Colden's coach, which the mob had dragged from his carriage house, was cast upon the pile, and all were consumed together. Every effort of the Sons of Liberty to restrain the mob from injuring private property was ineffectual, and excesses were committed disgraceful alike to the city and the civilization of the day. During this excitement the military were prudently kept within the fort. Colden, alarmed, ordered the stamps to be delivered to the mayor and common council of the city, the corporation agreeing to pay for all stamps that might be destroyed or lost.

In other places the first of November was observed as a day of fasting and mourning. Funeral processions paraded city streets, and bells tolled funeral knells. The flags of vessels were placed at half-mast, and the newspapers exhibited the broad black-line tokens of grief. The courts were all closed, because no business could be legally transacted without the stamps; legal marriages ceased; ships remained in port, and all business was suspended. There was a lull in the storm that for months had been raging in the colonies.

The tempest was not subdued. It was gathering renewed strength for a more furious blast. It soon went forth. The Sons of Liberty were more active than ever. Mobs began to assail depositories of stamps and insult the custodians. The more moderate classes took milder but effectual methods for demonstrating their disapprobation. Merchants formed non-importation associations, and agreed to refrain from all purchases of goods in England until the obnoxious act should be repealed. Domestic manufactures were commenced in almost every family; in nearly every household was heard the hum of wheels and the clatter of shuttles. Rich men and women, who commonly walked in broadcloths and brocades, now appeared, on all occasions, in homespun garments. That wool might not become scarce, the use of sheep-flesh for food was discouraged, and in various ways the colonists practically asserted their independence of the mother country.

These demonstrations alarmed the ministry and the British people. They were powerful protests against the coercive measures of the government; and the sentiments of the colonists, embodied in the papers put forth by the congress, were respectful but firm words, spoken manfully in the ears of the British ministry, demanding a retrogressive policy. These were seconded by the London merchants, whose trade was ruined; and early in January a bill to repeal the Stamp Act was introduced into Parliament. On the 18th of March, 1766, the obnoxious act was repealed, and the joyful intelligence thereof reached New York in May following.

On the repeal of the act, London warehouses were illuminated and shipping in the Thames were decorated. In America the measure was celebrated by bonfires, illuminations, and other demonstrations of joy. The city of New York was filled with delight. Bells rang out merry peals, cannon roared, and placards every where appeared, calling a meeting of the citizens to celebrate the event. Hundreds assembled, and marching through "the fields" to where the

City Hall now stands, they fired a royal salute of twenty-one guns. At Howard's, where the Sons of Liberty feasted, an immense table was spread. Twenty-eight "loyal and constitutional toasts" were drunk with delight; the city was illuminated in the evening, and several bonfires were lighted.

Again, on the King's birth-day (the 4th of June), another celebration was held under the auspices of Sir Henry Moore, the governor. The chief magistrate, the council, military officers, and the clergy, dined at the "King's Arms," near the Bowling Green, where General Gage resided. The people had a grand feast in "the fields." They roasted an ox whole. Twenty-five barrels of beer and a hogshead of rum were opened for the populace at the expense of the city. Twenty-five pieces of cannon, answering to the number of the King's years, ranged in a row on the site of the present City Hall, thundered a royal salute; and in the evening twenty-five tar barrels, hoisted upon poles, were burned, and gorgeous fire-works were exhibited at the Bowling Green. The Sons of Liberty feasted that day at Montagnie's, and with the sanction of the governor they erected a mast, and placed upon it the inscription, "*To his Most Gracious Majesty, George the Third, Mr. Pitt, and Liberty.*"

On account of his advocacy of the Repeal Bill, the Americans idolized Pitt. At a meeting in New York, on the 23d of June, the citizens present signed a petition praying the assembly to erect a statue in his honor. That body complied, and at the same time voted an equestrian statue to the King. Both were set up in 1770. That of Pitt was made of marble, and erected at the intersection of Wall and William streets; that of the King was made of lead, and placed in the center of the Bowling Green, the head of the horse and the face of the sovereign being toward the west. Six years afterward the King's statue was pulled down in contempt by the people of New York, and a little later that of Pitt was mutilated by the British soldiery.

The allelujahs of popular joy were soon succeeded by murmurings of popular discontent. With the repeal of the Stamp Act was connected a measure, originated by Pitt, called the Declaratory Act, which solemnly affirmed that the British Parliament had the right to "bind the colonies in all cases whatsoever." Sagacious minds at once perceived in this declaration the egg of tyranny concealed, and while the people were mad with joy because of the repeal, they were solemnly warned that out of that egg would proceed a brood of oppressive measures. The liberal press of England declared the same, and when Pitt pleaded as an excuse that it was an expedient measure to accomplish the repeal of the Stamp Act, he was answered with scorn; and he who yesterday rode on the top wave of popularity, to-day was engulphed in popular distrust.

The imperial government was incensed and alarmed by the extravagant rejoicings on account of the repeal of the Stamp Act, and instead of conciliating the colonists by just measures, it was resolved to obtain their submission by coercion. A large portion of the House of Lords, the whole bench of Bishops, and many of the Commons, were favorable to strong measures, and the ministry were prevailed upon to mature other schemes for taxing the colonies. To preserve quiet and maintain the laws, troops were ordered to America, and a Mutiny Act, as it was called, which provided for the quartering of these troops at the partial expense of the colonists, whom they were sent to overawe, was passed. Pitt, who was soon afterward called to the head of the ministry, and was created Earl of Chatham, opposed the measure as unjust and unwise, and thus he partially regained the friendship of the Americans.

Early in June Governor Moore informed the assembly that he hourly expected troops from England as a reinforcement for the garrison, and that he desired that body to make immediate provisions for them, according to the requirements of the Mutiny Act. The assembly murmured, and the Sons of Liberty, aroused by this new phase of oppression, resolved in solemn conclave to resist the measure to the utmost. The troops came. Mutual hostility at once appeared; and a little more than a month after the mast was erected by the Sons of Liberty with so much good feeling it was cut down by the insolent soldiery. It was reërected the next evening, dedicated as "The Liberty Pole," and a flag was displayed from its summit. Again it was prostrated, and between the people and the soldiery there was the bitterest animosity.

The New York assembly steadily refused compliance with the demands of the Mutiny Act. Twice they were prorogued by the governor. At a session late in the autumn of 1766, he said, "I am ordered to signify to you that it is the indispensable duty of the King's subjects in America to obey the acts of the Legislature of Great Britain. The King both expects and requires a due and cheerful obedience to the same. I flatter myself that, on a due consideration, no difficulties can possibly arise, or the least objection be made to the provisions for the troops, as required by the act of Parliament."

The assembly, unmoved by his appeal, replied that they understood the act to refer to soldiers "on the march;" and after referring to the specific requisitions of the governor, they remarked, "we can not consent, with our duty to our constituents, to put it in the power of any person (whatever confidence we may have in his prudence and integrity) to lay such burdens on them."

This determined action of the assembly was followed by an immediate prorogation. But the press, untrammeled by such official interferences, spoke out boldly. "Courage, Americans," said William Livingston, in a New York paper, "liberty, religion, and science are on the wing to these shores. The finger of God points out a mighty empire to your sons. The savages of the wilderness were never expelled to make room for idolators and slaves. The land we possess is the gift of Heaven to our fathers, and Divine Providence seems to have decreed it to our latest posterity. The day dawns in which the foundation of this mighty empire is to be laid, by the establishment of a regular American constitution. All that has hitherto been done seems to be little beside the collection of materials for this glorious fabric. 'T is time to put them together. The transfer of the European family is so vast, and our growth so swift, that before seven years roll over our heads the first stone must be laid." How wonderfully prophetic! Seven years from that time the first Continental Congress assembled in Philadelphia.

The ministry were amazed at the rebellious conduct of the Americans, and especially of the New York assembly, and resolved to bring that refractory legislature into humble obedience. They determined not to recede a single line from their claim to the right of taxing the colonies, and in the spring of 1767 Charles Townshend, Pitt's Chancellor of the Exchequer, coalesced with Grenville, while Pitt was absent on account of the gout, and presented new taxation schemes for the consideration of Parliament. In June a bill passed that body for levying duties upon tea, glass, paper, painters' colors, et cetera, imported into the colonies, with the avowed object of drawing a revenue from the Americans. Another was soon afterward passed for establishing a Board of Trade or Commissioners of Customs in the colonies, to be independent of colonial legislation, and having general powers of search and seizure similar to those in England, the salaries of the commissioners to be paid out of their own collections. This was soon followed by another, which suspended the functions of the New York assembly—forbidding them to perform any legislative act whatsoever until they should comply with the requisitions of the Mutiny Act concerning the billeting of troops. These acts were framed and passed with the erroneous impression that the colonists objected rather to the *mode* than to the *right* of taxation.

These acts caused a closer union of sentiment throughout the colonies, and the leading men every where took the ground occupied by Otis in 1761, that taxes on trade, if designed to raise a revenue, were just as much a violation of their rights as any other tax. The twenty-five or thirty colonial newspapers began to teem with essays on colonial rights; and on the 3d of December, 1767, appeared the first of the able series of "Letters from a Farmer in Pennsylvania to the Inhabitants of the British Colonies," written by John Dickinson, of Philadelphia, which was designed to show the danger of allowing any precedent of Parliamentary taxation to be established upon any ground or to any extent. These letters brought Dr. Franklin, then colonial agent in London, to the same way of thinking, (for he had been disposed to make a distinction between internal and external taxation,) and he caused an edition of them to be published in England.

## CHAPTER XIII.

During the period of intense excitement in the colonies which we have been considering, Mr. Schuyler was an active but conservative politician. He espoused the cause of his countrymen at the beginning of the dispute, with a clear understanding of the merits of the controversy, but his judgment, his love of order, and his social position, made him cautious and conciliating until the time arrived for radical and decisive action.

Business called him frequently to the city of New York, and there he mingled freely with men of every degree. His social qualities, his strict integrity, his enlightened and liberal views upon all subjects which challenged his attention, made him a welcome guest in every family. He was intimate with Sir Henry Moore, the governor, and their families visited each other. Dr. Johnson, of Kings' College, loved him for his sterling virtues, and politicians of every kind considered his friendship a favor and honor.

As the attorney of Colonel Bradstreet, we find Mr. Schuyler in New York in March, 1766, conferring with General Gage, at Fort George, and receiving for his principal between seven and eight thousand dollars, due him for monies advanced to persons who had supplied the Indians with various articles during that officer's expedition to Detroit, in 1764. We also find him, as revealed by his correspondence, an adviser and mediator in family feuds among his friends; a guardian and protector of the weak and wayward of his kindred; and as a valued counselor of those who were involved in serious or delicate troubles. At the time when he was in New York, in communication with General Gage, and a guest of the governor, we find him the confidential adviser of the afterward eminent Peter Van Shaack, who, while a student in college, privately married a daughter of the opulent Henry Cruger. Her angry father refused to sanction the marriage, and kept them apart. In the midst of his sorrow, a letter from Schuyler, then in New York, appears to have affected him most salutarily. "The approbation of good men," said the sufferer, "is a powerful incentive to virtue. You have exactly expressed the sentiments of *my* heart. However happy her presence would make me, without her affections I would not wish to have her person, or to assert my legal right to it on conditions that will ever be but secondary to me." The father soon became reconciled.

Mr. Schuyler appears not to have been an enrolled member of the association of the Sons of Liberty at Albany, yet he affiliated with Jeremiah Van Rensselaer, Abraham Tenbroeck, Jelles Fonda, Myndert Rosenboom, Robert Henry, Volkert P. Douw, Thomas Young, and other active members in his native city and the Mohawk valley, in their opposition to the Stamp Act. He was in New York in the beginning of May, 1766, when the joyful news was brought by Major James (who came passenger in the *Hynde*, from Plymouth,) of the repeal of the Stamp Act, and he feasted with the Sons of Liberty at Howard's, where "twenty-eight loyal and constitutional toasts were drank." Twenty-four of these were personal and the remainder were exceedingly loyal, such as "The King"—

"The Prince of Wales and the royal family"—" Sir Henry Moore and the land we live in"—and " Perpetual union between Great Britain and her colonies." Before the dinner he went with a large number of the Sons of Liberty, who, on the invitation of the rector, repaired to Trinity Church to hear a congratulatory discourse on the occasion. On the following day a convention of the Episcopal clergy was held at the same place, and Dr. Auchmuty, after sermon, greeted them with a congratulatory speech suitable to the occasion.

Sir Henry Moore was a gay, affable, good-natured, well-bred gentleman, and courteous in the highest degree. He was very popular and fond of company, and he and his family spent much time with the leading inhabitants of New York and its vicinity, and higher up the Hudson, in social enjoyments. The governor made frequent visits to Albany, and was always the guest of Mr. and Mrs. Schuyler. Their spacious and beautiful mansion had been recently erected within the southern suburbs of Albany (yet standing at the head of Schuyler street), and there they had just commenced the dispensing of that generous hospitality which continued for almost forty years. They then had five living children ; and Colonel Bradstreet, who was separated from his wife, (the widow of his cousin, Sir Simon Bradstreet, of Dublin,) was an inmate of the family.

Sir Henry and his family visited Albany in the summer of 1766, and at that time Mr. Schuyler and the governor rode up the Mohawk valley, on horseback, to the baronial residence of Sir William Johnson (now Johnstown) and consummated a joint purchase of lands from the Indians in that wild region. The governor and his family were there again in October, and in December Mr. Schuyler and his family were the guests of the governor at the province house, in the fort at New York, where they left their daughter for a visit of several weeks. At that time arrangements were made for securing some Mohawk lands for Sir Henry's friend, Lord Holland, (father of Charles James Fox,) and for the purchase of other lands in the neighborhood of Fort Stanwix. These land transactions and social re-unions continued during the whole administration of Sir Henry, which was ended by his death in September, 1769, when only fifty-six years of age.

In 1767 Mr. Schuyler appears to have been connected with the commissary department. In March the governor consults him, by letter, concerning the regiment of Colonel Mann, stationed at the head of Lake George, and also as to the appointment of commanders of other militia regiments, whose officers were about to resign on account of age, in which he says, "Believe me when I assure you that the persons proposed to succeed them could not have a better recommendation than Colonel Bradstreet's and yours." Among those recommended was Philip Skene, afterward made famous by his connection with affairs at Skenesborough, or Whitehall, at the beginning of the Revolution.

A little later, we find Colonel Mann, who was assistant commissary, complaining to Mr. Schuyler of a lack of provisions for the garrison at the head of Lake George, and requesting him to send some up immediately.

In May, William Smith, who had espoused the cause of the colonists, but who, when the final struggle began, drew back and became an active tory, wrote to Schuyler respecting Townshend's tax measures, and said, "When will these confusions end! What a disjointed empire is this! I am afraid it is too complex for so vast an extent. At all events America must rise. The prosperity and adversity of Britain both conduce to our growth. Would to God we had a little more government here!"

At about this time, Mr. Schuyler, pursuant to the directions of the governor, was active in the formation of a militia regiment, of which he was to be the commander. In August following he received his commission, dated the 20th, in which his district is defined as being bounded "on the south by the north line of the manor of Rensselaerwyck; on the north by Batten Kill or Creek, and the north bounds of Saratoga; on the east by the county of Cumberland and the townships laid out on the same north and south range or line, and on the west by the east bounds of Schenectada." This comprised large portions of the present counties of Saratoga, Rensselaer, and Washington. From that time until the kindling of the Revolution he was known as Colonel Schuyler, and held the office to which he was appointed by Sir Henry Moore.

In the autumn of 1767, the commissioners of New York and Massachusetts Bay, appointed to fix the boundary line between the two provinces, pursuant to acts in 1764, met in conference at New Haven, in Connecticut. William Nicoll, Robert R. Livingston, and William Smith were now the commissioners for New York, and Governor Hutchinson, William Brattle, and Edward Sheafe were the commissioners for Massachusetts. Colonel Schuyler, as an early commissioner, had taken great interest in the controversy, as we have seen, and had been very useful to the new board from his own province. He had laid before them all the mathematical plans and calculations which he had made for his private use, and the field-notes he had taken when personally engaged in the matter. Mr. Smith, in particular, was under great obligation to him, and on his return from the conference, toward the middle of October, he wrote a long letter to Colonel Schuyler, detailing the proceedings in a concise and perspicuous manner. "I brought a sore throat home with me," he said, "and that prevents me from seeing Sir Henry. I wish to know your sentiments soon, as a guide to me in what may be proper to recommend to him."

Colonel Schuyler had now erected a pleasant country mansion on the bank of the Fish Creek, at Saratoga, a short distance from the site of the one burned by the French and Indians in 1745, when his kinsman was murdered; and he had also enlarged and improved his mills there. For some time he had paid much attention to the cultivation of flax and hemp. In a letter to Professor Brand, of London, as early as 1763, he had urged the propriety of encouraging the culture of the latter in the colonies as a matter of national concern. That gentleman, in reply, said, "your observations about hemp are very just, and apply also to iron, which, if the colonies had been encouraged to have supplied us with, and which they could have done, we need not have regarded Russia, upon whom we depended for our naval stores of hemp and iron during the war." Professor Brand adds, "In my next I hope to send you an account of a machine for pulling up trees by the roots, and expeditiously, which has been tried and succeeds. It comes from Switzerland."

Among other improvements at Saratoga, Colonel Schuyler erected a flax mill in the year 1767, the first of the kind in the American colonies. At a meeting of the *Society for Promoting Arts*, of which he was a prominent member, held in New York near the close of that year, he laid before them a statement concerning his mill, and a calculation of the difference of the work done by it and by the hand. The society, considering his enterprise of great public importance, decreed that a medal should be given to him, and voted him their "thanks for executing so useful a design in the province." At the same meeting a proposition for "setting up the business of silk throwing was read, but judged improper, at least at present, for the colony."

The time was now at hand when the assembly would expire by its septennial limitation. Writs for a new election were issued, and in the newspapers, in caucuses of politicians, in hand-bills, and in public assemblies much was said in opposition to the system of open voting that then prevailed, and the preponderance of lawyers in the Legislature. Much complaint was also made of the practice of self-nomination—"stump candidates," as they are now called in the western States—and their solicitation of votes. Squibs like the following appeared in the newspapers, and indicated a strong feature in public sentiment:

"A CARD.—Jack Bowline and Tom Hatchway send their Services (damn Compliments,) to the Freeholders and Freemen of the city of New York, and beg they would, in order to try how the Land lies, take an Observation, and they will find: *First*, That the good People of this city are supported by *Trade* and the *Merchants*. *Second*, That the *Lawyers* are supported by the *People*.

"SHIP DEFIANCE, February 20, 1768."

*Reply.*—"A CARD: Mr. Axe and Mr. Hammer, being selected by a number of their brother Freeholders and Freemen of the city of New York to return their hearty thanks to their good friends Mr. Hatchway and Mr. Bowline, have consented, and think proper to do it in this Public Manner, and to assure them that the "*Leather Aprons*" (a very respectable body) are clearly of the Opinion that it is *Trade*, and not *Law*, that supports our Families. And honest Jack Jolt, the Cartman, says he never got Sixpence for riding Law-Books, though he gets many Pounds from the Merchants. So, with many thanks for your sensible, good Card, we say as you say, 'No Lawyers to the Assembly.'

"TRADESMEN'S HALL, February 29, 1768."

At the close of 1767, Colonel Schuyler was requested to represent his native city and county in the colonial assembly. A seat in that body, says Chancellor Kent, "was very important, and an evidence of character as well as of influence, inasmuch as the members were few and chosen exclusively by freeholders, and held their seats for seven years."

Colonel Schuyler at first hesitated, chiefly because his private affairs demanded his whole attention. But his warmest friends urged him to accept the nomination. They knew the weight that his unexceptionable character, his extensive connections, and his deserved popularity would have in the councils of the state at that critical moment, when the tempest clouds of revolution were hovering in the political sky. "Let me persuade you," wrote William Smith, then a member of the assembly, at the middle of January, 1768, "not to refuse your services to your country—one session, if no more. After seven years we shall both abandon to ease. I will promise to leave you in full possession of your wolves, foxes, snow, (a small sailing vessel), mills, fish, and lands at Saraghtogue, and give no disturbance while the remaining sands run out." Alas! at the end of seven years Colonel Schuyler was in the midst of a most stormy career of political life, and about to enter upon military duties of the most arduous and responsible kind; while his friend, an apologist for the crown and a practical enemy to republicanism in America, was his fierce political antagonist, preparing himself, by acts of opposition to the popular will, for exile in Canada.

Colonel Schuyler accepted the nomination, much to the satisfaction of the people. "Having been yesterday informed of your being unanimously requested to serve as member of the assembly for the city and county, by the principal people of Albany, and of your acquiescence thereto," wrote Sir William Johnson, from "Johnson

Hall," on the 29th of February, "I have only to congratulate you thereupon, and to assure you of my approbation of their choice, and that I am, sir, your well wisher, etc." Little did Sir William think that, a few years later, this budding statesman would be the virtual controller of the lives and fortunes of the baronet's family.

On the 3d of March, 1768, Colonel Schuyler and Jacob H. Teneyck were elected representatives of the city and county of Albany. The certificate of this election, signed by Harmanus Schuyler, high sheriff of the county, and six others, is dated the same day.

Colonel Schuyler, expecting soon to be called to New York to attend to his duties as a legislator, made preparations for the accommodation of himself and family there. A kinswoman, to whom he wrote on the subject of a boarding place for his children, replied that a widow in Hanover Square was "willing to take two of them, at fifty pounds a year, two pounds of tea and one loaf of sugar each, their stockings and clothes mended; but new work must be paid for making." But he was soon relieved from suspense, by a letter from Sir Henry Moore, at the middle of March, who wrote: "I have already mentioned to the gentlemen of the council that I do not think the assembly should meet on the return of the writs, as I have no particular business to lay before them, and their meeting will be put off by proclamation, so that I hope you will not have your plans broken in upon, and your own private business interrupted."

Toward the close of the previous year, Colonel Schuyler had entertained some strange guests at his mansion. These were the famous Attakullakulla, or the "Little Carpenter," principal chief of the Cherokee nation of Indians, and eight subordinate chiefs and warriors, who arrived in

New York in December, with Captain Schemerhorn and an interpreter. They were on their way to visit Sir William Johnson, to seek his mediation for the conclusion of a peace between the Cherokees and the Six Nations. General Gage took an interest in the embassy, and on the 15th of December sent them in a sloop to Albany, where, at his request, they were received by Colonel Schuyler and forwarded to Sir William. They attempted to ascend the Mohawk in batteaus, but the frost closed it, and they made their way on horseback, suffering much from the inclemency of the weather, so seldom felt in their southern homes. Colonel Schuyler and two or three others accompanied them as far as Fort Johnson, and then dispatched a guide to lead them the remainder of the journey. The embassy was successful, and the embassadors returned to New York at the close of March.

The new assembly, of which Colonel Schuyler was a member, did not meet until the 27th of October, 1768. Philip Livingston, of New York city, was Speaker, and the Legislature was composed of some of the most noted men of the province.* Colonel Schuyler was then thirty-five years of age. Although he was among the youngest members of that body, and had never had an hour's experience

* The following are the names of the members of the New York assembly when Colonel Schuyler first entered it:

*New York City*—Philip Livingston, James De Lancey, Jacob Walton, James Jauncey, Isaac Low, John Cruger, John Alsop. *Albany City and County*—Jacob H. Teneyck, Philip Schuyler. *Kings County*—Simon Boerum, John Rapelye. *Queens County*—Zebulon Seaman, Daniel Kissam. *Suffolk County*—William Nicoll, Eleazer Miller. *Richmond County*—Henry Holland, Benjamin Seaman. *Westchester County*—John Thomas, Frederick Philipse. *Borough of West Chester*—John De Lancey. *Duchess County*—Leonard Van Kleeck, Dirck Brinckerhoff. *Ulster County*—Charles Dewitt, George Clinton. *Orange County*—Henry Wisner, Selah Strong. *Manor of Rensselaerwyck*—Abraham Tenbroeck. *Manor of Livingston*—Peter R. Livingston. *Manor of Cortlandt*—Pierre Van Courtlandt.

in a deliberative assembly, he at once took an honorable, conspicuous, and influential position as a legislator, and particularly as a member of special committees. Prompt in action, extremely methodical, tireless in labor, determined in purpose, candid, fearless, and perfectly reliable, he challenged and received the respect and confidence of the whole House, and the approval of his constituents and of the people at large.

Colonel Schuyler entered upon life as a legislator at a most remarkable and important period in the history of his country. The people in all the provinces were intensely excited by current political events. They stood firm upon the rock of truth—the great principles of justice between man and man—and with a full consciousness of integrity, and firm reliance upon the Divine Protector, they had uttered the voice of remonstrance so vehemently, and raised the arm of resistance so defiantly, that the ire of the home government had become hot and implacable. Massachusetts had sent forth, in the name of the Speaker of the assembly, a Circular Letter to all its sister provinces, embodying in it the sentiments expressed in a petition previously addressed to the King, in which the state of the colony was considered in bold words, and the co-operation of all other colonies was solicited. It was a cry for union against an oppressor, and nobly was that cry responded to.

The court and the ministry were alarmed and incensed at the rebellious acts of Massachusetts, and at once determined to send fleets and armies to bring them into submission if necessary. They considered the Circular Letter an incentive to rebellion, and acted promptly on this opinion. Lord Hillsborough immediately sent a copy of it, with a letter, to all of the colonial governors, directing them to exert their utmost influence upon their respective assemblies "to take no notice of it, which," he said, "will be treating it with the contempt it deserves. If they give any countenance to this seditious paper," he continued, "it will be your duty to prevent any proceedings upon it by an immediate prorogation or dissolution." To Governor Bernard, of Massachusetts, he said, "You will, therefore, require of the House of Representatives, in his Majesty's name, to rescind the resolution which gave birth to the Circular Letter from the Speaker, and to declare their disapprobation of that rash and hasty proceeding."

The Massachusetts assembly, consisting of one hundred and nine members—the largest legislature in America—were not easily frightened by ministerial frowns. They had counted the cost of opposition to unrighteous demands, and were prepared to assert their rights. Instead of complying with the governor's requisition, they made that very demand a fresh cause of complaint. Samuel Adams, that staunch old Puritan, whom no gold could bribe nor place propitiate, made, on that occasion, as the creatures of the crown said, "the most violent, insolent, abusive, and treasonable declarations that perhaps ever were delivered." The fiery Otis, full of the spirit that animated him more than six years before, also denounced the measure with bitterest scorn. "When Lord Hillsborough knows," he said, "that we will not rescind *our* acts, he should apply to Parliament to rescind theirs. Let Britons rescind these measures or they are lost forever." In this strain he harangued the house for an hour, until even the most zealous Sons of Liberty trembled with the fear that he would tread upon the domains of treason.

The assembly refused to rescind by an overwhelming majority—ninety-two to seventeen. They sent a letter to the governor, informing him of their action, in which they said, "If the votes of this House are to be controlled by the directions of a minister, we have left us but a vain semblance of liberty." The governor, greatly irritated, proceeded to dissolve them, but before that act was consummated they had prepared a list of accusations against him, and a petition to the King for his recall.

Thus Great Britain, through her representative, struck the first blow against free discussion in America. The Secretary of State, speaking for the King, offered to Massachusetts the alternative of submitting to his mandate or forfeiting its representative government. In that ordeal she acted bravely, and she was sustained by the warm sympathy of her sister colonies, for whom like treatment, on slight provocation, was doubtless in reserve.

New York stood up manfully in defense of the right of free discussion, and when, on the 14th of November, 1768, Governor Moore transmitted Lord Hillsborough's in-instructions against holding seditious correspondence with other colonies, and called upon the Legislature to yield obedience, they boldly remonstrated against ministerial interference with their inalienable privileges. The House refused obedience. The governor threatened to dissolve them. The foremost leaders of the people sustained their representatives, and in newspapers and in hand-bills they expressed their sentiments freely. "Let these truths," they said, "be indelibly impressed upon our minds, that we can not be *free* without being *secure in our property;* that we can not be secure in our *property*, if, without our consent, others may, as *by right*, take it away; that taxes imposed by Parliament do thus *take it away;* that *duties*, laid for the sole purpose of raising money, are *taxes;* that attempts to lay such should be instantly and firmly opposed."*

In the movements in the assembly concerning the Massachusetts Circular Colonel Schuyler was conspicuous. The New York city members, at their own request, were instructed by their constituents to have the Circular read in the asssembly. Possessed with these instructions, says a writer of the day, the city members used them for selfish purposes. They felt sure that the assembly would be dissolved if the Circular should be read, and from time to time, before the business of the session was concluded, they would threaten to make a motion to read.

"The design of this finesse," says the writer alluded to, "was to feel the pulse of the House, in order if a majority appeared against the measure, they would then make the motion, and monopolize the credit of it to themselves with their constituents and the continent; at the same time their seats would be secure, as there would be no dissolution. This being done repeatedly, many of the members saw through the artifice, which greatly incensed them, upon which Colonel Schuyler, a gentleman of great independency of spirit, and a true Son of Liberty, being unable any longer to bear the duplicity of those political hypocrites, got up and observed to the House that he was as determined to read the Circular Letter, and make resolutions asserting the rights of the people of the colony, as any gentleman in the House, but that he conceived it most eligible to go through the business of the session, that the colony might not suffer for the want of the necessary and annual laws, before they came into the resolutions, which would as well serve the cause of liberty as if they were made at the expense of the loss of those laws. But if it was the opinion of the House that the resolutions with which they had been so often threatened by those gentlemen should be made before the business of the session was gone through, as in that case they would immediately be dissolved, he thought, in justice to themselves and their constituents, to save the time of the former and the money of the latter, they should come into them immediately," and therefore made a motion for that purpose.

"Our corrupt politicians found themselves counteracted, and the arguments of the Colonel would work against them with the judicious if

* Leake's *Life and Times of General John Lamb*, p. 43.

they should persist in their former threats, and the other members of the House being fully in opinion with him for deferring the resolutions until the business was finished, prevailed on him to withdraw his motion, which he accordingly did; so the matter was put off for that time. To prevent any member getting the credit of it, the House some time afterward made an order to take it up and go into it."*

Troops, at this time, had been gathered in Boston, to overawe the people and enforce obedience. General Gage had been requested by Governor Bernard to act upon his secret instructions from Lord Hillsborough, and order some soldiers from Halifax. He did so. Meanwhile the governor had refused to order the election of a new assembly, and the people of Massachusetts took the matter into their own hands and called a provincial convention. In that convention every town and district in the province but one was represented. Cushing, late Speaker of the assembly, was chosen chairman. The governor denounced the movement as treasonable. The convention disclaimed all pretensions to political authority, but professed to have met "in this dark and distressing time to consult and advise as to the best manner of preserving peace and good order." The governor warned them to desist, and admonished them to separate without delay. They were firm but respectful. They adopted a petition to the King, and a defense of the province, in the form of a letter to the agent of the colony in England. This was the first of those popular assemblies, which soon assumed all political power, as derived from the people. The movement was approved in the other colonies. New York spoke warm words of encouragement; and from Virginia, where some of the boldest and most patriotic measures of the day had been adopted during the three years preceding, and also from South Carolina, came the injunction, Stand fast!

* *The Watchman, No. V.*, April, 1770.

On the day after the closing of the provincial convention a British fleet arrived at Boston, bearing two regiments from Halifax, and took a hostile attitude while the troops were landing. It was on Sunday morning. Seven hundred troops, with bayonets fixed, colors flying, and drums beating, marched into the doomed town with all the insolence of victors into a conquered city. A part of them encamped on the Common and a part in Faneuil Hall. Every strong feeling of the New Englanders was outraged by this desecration, and a thrill of indignation ran throughout the colonies. The engine of non-importation agreements, which had operated so powerfully against the Stamp Act, was now speedily put in motion again, and organized associations, under the sanction of the assemblies, worked with increased energy. An agreement of the kind, presented by Washington in the Virginia House of Burgesses, was signed by every member present; and the patriotism of the people was every where displayed by acts of self denial.

## CHAPTER XIV.

Colonel Schuyler's position in the assembly was a delicate one. His intimate personal friend, the governor, was now, from the necessities of his position as the representative of the crown, arrayed in hostility to the assembly and the people. Yet in this instance, as in all similar contingencies in his public life, Colonel Schuyler did not allow private friendships to interfere with his duty to his country. He had espoused the cause of the colonists from a sincere conviction of its justice, and from the hour when he entered the assembly he was never known to swerve a line from the path of duty into which these convictions led him.

From the moment when he entered upon his legislative career, he was faithful to the interests of the people. He saw with pain the waste of time exhibited each hour by the indolent and loose manner in which the business of the House was conducted, and he was particularly displeased with the confusion produced by spectators, and those who, by courtesy, were admitted to the floor of the assembly chamber. In order to lessen these evils, he introduced a resolution, on the 3d of November, containing the following rules and regulations for the maintenance of order on the floor:

"No person whatever shall be admitted into the House but such as shall be introduced by a member thereof.

"No member to introduce more than one person at a time.

"If any member shall desire the House to be cleared, the House to be cleared immediately.

"In order that the House may not be disturbed, all persons admitted are to behave orderly and quietly, and that none presume to speak or whisper. And that if any man shall speak, whisper, or stir out of his place, to the disturbance of the House, at any message or business of importance, Mr. Speaker is to present his name for the House to proceed against him."

This resolution was debated and lost by a vote of thirteen to twelve.

On the 14th of November there was a serious riot in New York, growing out of political excitement, in which some of the Sons of Liberty were involved. On the 21st Governor Moore sent a message into the assembly, asking the House to support him in offering a reward for the conviction of the ringleaders. On the following day the House agreed to make provisions for paying a reward, which was immediately offered in a proclamation by the governor. Colonel Schuyler had been appointed, the previous day, chairman of a committee to prepare an address to the governor on that occasion. Always averse to disorders of every kind, in that address he uttered words of reprobation of the acts of his own political friends, loyal ones toward his King, and timely ones in behalf of the people. It was as follows:

"We, his Majesty's most dutiful and loyal subjects, the General Assembly of the Colony of New York, having taken your Excellency's message of yesterday into our most serious consideration, beg leave to assure your Excellency that though we feel, in common with the rest of the colonies, the distresses occasioned by the new duties imposed by the Parliament of Great Britain, and the ill-policied state of the American commerce, yet we are far from conceiving that violent and tumultuous proceedings will have any tendency to promote suitable redress.

"Conscious of the most sincere and affectionate loyalty to the King our sovereign, trusting to his paternal protection, and depending on the justice and equity of the British Parliament, we are preparing decent and proper representations of the state of this colony, to be laid before his Majesty and the two Houses of Parliament, with hopes of redress.

"As an outrage committed against the laws, and a disturbance of the peace and good order of government, may expose this colony to disrepute, and the inhabitants to a disappointment of their just expectations, we thank your Excellency for the opportunity you have given us to express our abhorrence of the late tumultuous proceedings in the city of New York, and for your intention to maintain the public tranquility.

"It is with pleasure that we can assure your Excellency that these disorderly proceedings are, as appears to us, disapproved by the inhabitants in general, and are imputable only to the indiscretion of a very few persons of the lowest class.

"A riot committed in defiance of the magistrates, (whose vigilance on this, as on every occasion, to suppress turmoils has been very conspicuous,) and contrary to the known sense of the inhabitants, at this so critical juncture, has justly demanded the animadversion of government, and we beg leave to assure your Excellency of our ready concurrence in every measure conducive to good order; and that with this disposition we have resolved on a proper provision to enable your Excellency to fulfill the engagement you have entered into by your proclamation; and that we will, on all occasions, endeavor to support the dignity and authority of government."

As this address referred to the obnoxious acts of Parliament in a tone of deprecation, some of the more loyal and obsequious members of the assembly voted to reject it, but the motion was lost by a vote of seventeen to five. This being considered a test vote on the feelings of the House, it was hailed as a triumph by the republican party.

Colonel Schuyler was then appointed, with Mr. Rapelye, a committee to wait on the governor and ascertain when and where he would receive the address. He appointed the next afternoon as the time, and Fort George as the place, and at twelve o'clock on that day the address was presented to the governor by the hands of Colonel Schuyler. Its tone, though loyal and indicative of a desire to support order, had, nevertheless, such a republican ring about it, that the governor was not *officially* very well pleased.

On the 24th of the same month, Colonel Schuyler presented a most important bill. It provided for raising three hundred pounds, currency, within the city and county of Albany, for the purpose of procuring the translation into English of several of the Dutch records remaining in the clerk's office in that county, and to bind up and index the same. Also to bind up and index all other records remaining in the office. The bill was passed ten days afterward, and being carried to the council by Colonel Schuyler and Abraham Tenbroeck, it was concurred in by that body, and received Sir Henry Moore's signature.

At the close of December the New York Assembly, in which was a large majority of Republicans, fully and warmly sympathizing with the popular movements in all the colonies concerning the constitutional rights of the Americans, adopted a series of bold and important resolutions, asserting "the rights and privileges of his Majesty's subjects within the colony of New York." There is reasonable circumstantial evidence to show that Colonel Schuyler was the author of those resolves. They asserted the right of petition as belonging equally to their body and the House of Commons; that the colony lawfully and constitutionally possessed and enjoyed "an internal legislature of its own, in which the crown and people of the colony were constitutionally represented; and that the power and authority of legislation could not lawfully or constitutionally be suspended, abridged, abrogated, or annulled by any power, or authority or prerogative whatever."

They boldly asserted their right to correspond and consult with other subjects out of the colony or in other parts of the realm, either individually or collectively, on any matter wherein their rights or interests, or those of their constituents were or might be affected; and acting upon this conviction, they appointed a committee of correspondence, to report its transactions to subsequent meetings of the House.

To the third resolution, which declared that the assembly had the right to such free correspondence, Captain De Lancey moved as an addition that "the action of Parliament, suspending the Legislature of this colony, is a high infringement of the freedom of the inhabitants of this colony, and tends to deprive them of their natural and constitutional rights and privileges." This addition was not adopted, for the avowed reason, that these views were sufficiently expressed in the original resolution.

Petitions to the King, and to the Houses of Lords and Commons, were also prepared, in which they pronounced the late acts, imposing duties "with the sole view and express purpose of raising a revenue, utterly subversive of their constitutional rights, because as they neither are," they said, "nor, from their peculiar circumstances, can be represented in Parliament, their property is granted away without their consent."

These resolutions and petitions gave great official umbrage to Governor Moore, and at three o'clock in the afternoon of the 3d of January, 1769, he summoned the assembly to attend him in the council chamber in the City Hall at once. They obeyed, when the governor told them that from the address concerning the riots, which they had presented to him on the 23d of November, he thought they were opposed to all immoderate measures, but the extraordinary resolves which they had lately adopted, and the representations of the state of the colony which they had proposed to send his Majesty, showed such intemperate heat, that his duty forbade his countenancing their conduct. His speech was mild and conciliatory, but firm, and was received with the most respectful attention. He concluded by declaring the assembly dissolved.

On the day of the dissolution the governor issued writs for a new election, returnable on the 4th of February. The canvass was conducted with a great deal of warmth, especially in the city of New York. John Morin Scott, one of the most active of the Sons of Liberty, had, in the form of a petition, made grave charges against Mr. Jauncey, one of the city members of the assembly. He afterward made an affidavit concerning matters contained in his petition, and attempted to get it before the House. On the 7th of November a vote was taken in the House to have the affidavit read, when only Colonel Schuyler, his friend Tenbroeck, and Peter R. Livingston voted for it. There was an overwhelming majority against it; and then an unsuccessful attempt was made to declare Scott's charges of corruption, et cetera, "frivolous and vexatious." The bitterness engendered by these movements produced the fiercest partisanship at the election, and before; and on the very day when the assembly was dissolved we find, by the record, that the House was "informed that Whitehead Hicks, mayor of the city of New York, and Elias Desbrosses, one of the aldermen, had bound over to the peace Jacob Walton and Philip Schuyler, Esquires." The assembly had just ordered that those officials should attend the House the next day, and show cause for their action against two members of that body, when the summons of Sir Henry and the dissolution of the assembly put an end to the matter.

The elections were held late in January. On the 16th, Peter R. Livingston, the representative for the manor of

Livingston in the last House, wrote as follows to Colonel Schuyler:

"Since my last I have only to acquaint you that we are all hard at work. I think the prospect has a good aspect, and at all events Jauncey must go to the wall this time. I make no doubt, if we can keep the eople to the promise they have made, that Philip [Livingston] and Scott will be two, and if the opposite party push old John Cruger, I am of opinion that they will push one of the other two out. Our canvass stands well, but there will be a vast deal of cross-voting. The two they all pitch on, of our four, are Philip and Scott, which will put them in. But there is a great deal in good management of the votes. Our people are in high spirits, and if there is not fair play shown there will be bloodshed, as we have by far the best part of the Bruisers on our side, who are determined to use force if they use any foul play. I have engaged from the first day, and am determined to see it out. Lewis Morris certainly comes for the Borough [Westchester]. Henry Holland is obliged to resign for Richmond, as young Browne and young Farmer set up in opposition to each other."*

Livingston adds, in a postcript: "Miss Moore ran away with Captain Dickinson last Friday night. She has been married to him ever since last July." It was Henrietta Moore, daughter of the governor. Captain Dickinson had been stationed at Fort George for some time, and being ordered to another post, his young wife went with him.

Livingston's predictions were not all verified. In New York, "old John Cruger" was substituted for Philip Livingston, who was chosen to represent the manor of Livingston in place of the writer of the above letter. Nathaniel Woodhull, afterward president of the revolutionary convention of the province, was substituted for Miller, of Suffolk; Christopher Billop for Holland; and Lewis Morris for James De Lancey, as representative of the borough of Westchester. There were but few other changes.

Colonel Schuyler was reëlected by a very large majority. On account of his bold stand on the side of the colonists

* Autograph letter.

in the pending dispute, a few opposed him. His freedom of speech in commenting upon the acts of public officers offended a few officials, and these, of course, were among his opponents. Sir William Johnson took offense at remarks reported to have been made by Colonel Schuyler respecting some matters connected with a late treaty with the Indians at Fort Stanwix; and also at his alleged participation in an attempt to pass a law to prevent members of the governor's council voting or otherwise intermeddling in party affairs, supposed by Sir William to be specially intended for himself. The baronet wrote a very courteous letter to Colonel Schuyler on the subject at the middle of January, frankly telling him that if what he had heard should not be disavowed before the election, he should not support him.

The friendship between Colonel Schuyler and Governor Moore was not disturbed by their political differences. Their correspondence during the winter and spring of 1769 exhibits the same cordial feelings, personally, as before the dispute. They were both too generous and high minded to allow political opinions to excite private enmity, and until the governor's death, the following autumn, he had not a warmer personal friend in the province than Colonel Schuyler.

Letters containing generous greetings and congratulations on account of his reëlection were received by Colonel Schuyler, and such confidence had leading men in the province in his qualities of statesmanship, that they turned to him as one of the best fitted of their public men for a contemplated special embassy to England. "Things are drawing to a crisis," wrote William Smith, in February. "I suspect we shall next be obliged to send home special agents as our last shift, and if the Judge (Robert R. Livingston) gets in for Dutchess, and I had a voice, you and him should be urged to see England in this momentous embassy."* But "the Judge" did not succeed in Dutchess, "owing to all the tenants of Beekman and R. G. Livingston voting against him;"† the embassy was never undertaken, and Colonel Schuyler remained to serve his country in a far more useful field.

The new assembly met on the 4th of April. Colonel Schuyler took a leading position in the House at the commencement of the session, and ever afterward maintained it. He was appointed chairman of the usual committee to draw up a response to the governor's opening message. He prepared it, and it was adopted on the 8th. After referring to the governor's speech, in which his excellency said that he should not burden them with much business, the address went on to say that the members of the assembly were the servants of the public, and were ready to attend to all business which the welfare of the colony required. Then referring to the governor's recommendation, pursuant to the command of ministers, that the agent to solicit the affairs of the colony in England should be appointed as in Virginia, the Carolinas, Georgia, and the West Indies, by the governor, council, and assembly, and not by the assembly alone, the address boldly said:

"We could wish that the mode which your Excellency recommends to this House, in the appointment of our agent for this colony, to reside at the court of Great Britain, was evidently calculated for the public benefit. To us it appears replete with difficulties and dangers, that, were they proper to be enumerated in our address, we humbly conceive your Excellency would coincide in sentiment with us that the mode your Excellency points out is by no means consistent with the duty of our station to enter into. You 'll pardon us, therefore, sir, if on this oc-

* Autograph letter, February 11, 1769.

† Autograph letter of Peter R. Livingston to Colonel Schuyler, February, 1769.

casion we declare, with that freedom which is the birthright of Englishmen, that it would be sacrificing the rights and diminishing the liberties of our constituents to adopt any other mode of appointment than that which has been practiced in this colony for many years past. We acknowledge that the mode which your Excellency recommends has taken place in this colony; but the inconveniency has doubtless been as apparent to former assemblies as it is to this. For after having had an agent at the court of Great Britain for a few years, appointed by act of the governor, council, and general assembly, the house of representatives have constantly declined to continue that mode of appointment, and have for many years uninteruptedly exercised the privilege of nominating him, which has been acquiesced in by the crown immediately, and by his several representatives, as governors of this colony, implicatively, amongst whom we have the satisfaction to include your Excellency. We should, therefore, be extremely sorry that any difficulties should, in future, arise in transacting the affairs of this colony by an agent constituted as ours is."

In reference to the governor's requisition for additional provisions for the support of British troops in the colony, the address plainly said:

"The sums that have been already granted for the support of his Majesty's troops in barracks are very considerable. The repeated application of monies to that purpose would effectually ruin a colony, whose trade, by unnatural restrictions and the want of a paper currency to supply the almost total deficiency of specie, is so much declined, and still declining, that its distresses, in a very short time, will become so great that it will be almost equally difficult to conceive as to describe them. In this unhappy situation, your Excellency's requisition for fresh aid demands our most serious consideration.

"We thank your Excellency for the readiness you express to concur with us in any measure for promoting his Majesty's service and the advantage of the colony. We assure you, sir, that nothing will ever be more agreeable to this House than that a perfect harmony should continue to subsist between the several branches of the Legislature."

On presenting this response to the governor's address, Colonel Schuyler said:

"As the repeated resolves and applications of the colonies, relative to Parliamentary taxation, and the embarrased state of our commerce, and several other grievances, have not been attended with the success so ardently wished for, and so mutually conducive to the tranquillity of the British empire; and as the growing distresses of our constituents loudly call for our most earnest attention to measures best calculated to preserve the union between Great Britain and her plantations, and restoring a lasting harmony, founded in mutual affection and interest, I therefore move that a day be appointed for taking the state of this colony into our most serious consideration, and for the appointment of special agents, of approved abilities and integrity, to be sent home, instructed to exert their most strenuous efforts, in conjunction with such agents as the other colonies have sent, or may think proper to send, in soliciting the important affairs of this country at the court of Great Britain, and before the two Houses of Parliament during the course of the next session."*

The subject of religious freedom had engaged much of the attention of Colonel Schuyler during the long years that the topic of episcopacy in America had been discussed, and which was then a prominent subject for disputation. He had been taught to regard hierarchies with disgust, and to yearn for a more liberal spirit among professing Christians. With that full measure of common sense which always distinguished him, he perceived that all primary movements for the general benefit of society must be local and circumscribed, and if founded upon truth would as surely expand as the circles of waves go outward from the point where a pebble is dropped into the still water. With this view, and mingling with his ideas of spiritual needs the practical one of physical and social advancement, he finally brought forward in the assembly a proposition expressive of a scheme which he had long been revolving in his mind. On the 26th of April he arose in his place, and said:

"I move that as the cultivation of the extensive territory in the county of Albany will be highly beneficial to the crown and the colony; and as one of the best means to invite settlers will be to encourage the

* Journal of the Assembly.

worship of God upon generous principles of equal indulgence to loyal Protestants of every persuasion; and as proprietors of large tracts are willing to give small parcels of land for the support of ministers and schoolmasters to aid the new settlers, provided the same can be secured to the pious purposes of the donors; that leave be given me to bring in a bill to enable every church and congregation of reformed Protestants in the county of Albany, without discrimination, to take and hold real estate to the value of a given amount per annum, for the support of the gospel among them."

Leave was given, he brought in a bill, and it soon afterward became a law.

At the beginning of this session, a long memorial from "merchants, traders, and others concerned in or affected by the Indian trade," addressed to Jacob Teneyck and Philip Schuyler, representatives for the city and county of Albany, Jacobus Myndert, representative of the township of Schenectada, and Abraham Tenbroeck and Robert R. Livingston, representatives respectively of the manors of Rensselaer and Livingston, was presented, in which the memorialists, after expressing their satisfaction because the governor had recommended the passage of an act for regulating the Indian trade, set forth their views, based upon stated facts and conclusions. This memorial was referred to a committee of the assembly, of which Colonel Schuyler was chairman, and on the 10th of May he presented a report on the subject, carefully drawn by his own hand. That report, from its completeness and valuable suggestions, excited a great deal of attention, and Colonel Schuyler and Mr. De Lancey were instructed to prepare and bring in a bill for the regulation of the Indian trade. That bill soon became a law, and the regulations adopted under it were in operation until the commencement of the Revolution, and the change in the relative position of all parties concerned was effected by the war.

The power of executive influence over the legislation of the colony had long been deplored, yet no one had nerve enough to take the evil by the horns and accomplish something toward its arrest, until, on the 17th of May, Colonel Schuyler, after some preliminary remarks, said, "I move that it may be resolved by this House, that no member of this House, or that may hereafter be elected to sit herein, holding any place of honor, profit, or trust whatever under the crown, shall have a seat in this House, unless such member shall resign the same within six months next after such resolve (if any) shall be made." By a majority of only one the question on the motion was postponed.

Resolutions were next passed asserting the sole right of imposing taxes to belong to the assembly; also claiming for the people the right of petition and of trial by jury; all of which had been practically questioned by the parent government. It was also resolved, in consideration of ministerial action against the province of Massachusetts, that sending persons for trial to places beyond the high seas was "highly derogatory to the rights of British subjects." These movements, so bold, so indocile, if not rebellious, mortified Governor Moore, (for he found himself absolutely weak in power, the assembly being supported by the people,) and on the 20th of May he prorogued the Legislature to the 7th of July. On the same day the assembly had, with very great reluctance, voted fifteen hundred pounds for the support of the troops in the colony.

At about this time the Massachusetts assembly convened, and resolved that it was inconsistent with their dignity and freedom to deliberate in the midst of an armed force, and that the presence of a military and naval armament was a breach of privilege. They refused to entertain any subject except a redress of their grievances, and the usual business of granting supplies was passed by unnoticed. They solicited the governor to remove the troops from Boston to Castle William, in the harbor, and on his refusal they voted a petition to the King for his recall.

Virginia, over whose councils Lord Botetourt, a kind-hearted, conciliatory, but vain and ambitious gentleman, now presided, gave generous support to Massachusetts in her hour of trial, and sent her words of greeting. These and other measures offended royal authority, and the governor, as in duty bound, dissolved the Virginia assembly.

In other provinces like proceedings occurred, and in the summer of 1769, the antagonisms between the governors of the provinces and their respective Legislatures and people produced much confusion and excitement. To this, in New York, was added great irritation, when it was known that a resolution of Lord North (who had succeeded Townshend as chancellor of the exchequer), that a respectful petition from the assembly of that province should not be received, had been passed by the Parliament. Had intelligence of this insult reached New York before the passage of the resolution to appropriate money for the troops had been acted upon, that measure would not have been proposed even.

The British ministry, baffled in their attempts to draw a revenue from America by coercive measures, now contemplated a resort to milder ones. The non-importation agreements had been generally adhered to faithfully, and their effects upon English commerce made them the instruments again in bringing ministers to their senses. The English merchants were really more injured by the acts of Parliament than the Americans. The exports from England to America, which, in 1768, had amounted to $11,890,000, of which amount $660,000 were the value of *tea* alone, fell, in 1769, to a little more than $8,000,000, the value of tea being only $220,000. The English merchants, therefore, joined their American brethren in petitions and remonstrances ; and under the direction of Lord North, the Earl of Hillsborough sent a circular letter to the colonies, intimating that the duties upon all articles enumerated in the late act would be taken off, as a measure of *expediency* (not of right), except on *tea*. This was unsatisfactory, for it was not the amount of the tax, but the *principle* involved, that caused the contention. The principle was the same, whether the duty was laid upon one commodity or on a dozen ; and so long as the Parliament assumed the *right* to tax the colonies without their consent, so long the Americas would dispute it. The year 1769 closed without any apparent hope for a reconciliation between Great Britain and her colonies, for warnings came with Hillsborough's circular letter exhorting the Americans to not put their "trust in princes," nor their creatures.

## CHAPTER XV.

THE assembly, prorogued until the 7th of July, did not meet until the 21st of November. There was a second prorogation until September, but at that time Governor Moore was seriously ill. His daughter, as we have seen, had left her home with her husband, Capt. Dickinson, and in June his wife sailed for England to meet that daughter in London and to visit her own friends. Sir Henry's illness was brief and fatal. He died on the 11th of September, and the reins of government passed into the hands of Lieutenant Governor Colden for the third time. Sir Henry was beloved by many, and thoroughly respected by all parties; and when Gaine's *New York Mercury* eulogized him for his liberal views, a correspondent, jealous of the deceased governor's character as a churchman, felt it necessary to deny that he ever attended any other than the Episcopal Church.

During the recess Colonel Schuyler was frequently in New York. These visits, and his attentive correspondent and legal adviser, William Smith, kept him fully acquainted with current political measures, which the gazettes did not always reveal. Smith was especially vigilant in watching the movement for establishing episcopacy in the colonies. "The ministerial rebuff to the bishop scheme," he wrote in August, "animates the non-episcopal patriots, and has brought the tories to reason. The two archbishops are commanded to cease their solicitations, for that it was his Majesty's aim rather to heal than foment the distractions of the empire. Will you believe it ! all the sons of ambition begin openly to disavow the project for an episcopate."*

On the 1st of November the leading Sons of Liberty in New York, the most active of whom were Isaac Sears, Alexander McDougal, John Lamb, John Morin Scott, Caspar Wistar, and Samuel Broome, celebrated the anniversary of the day on which the Stamp Act was to go into effect, but which witnessed its utter failure. Colonel Schuyler, who had gone to New York earlier than the opening of the assembly, to transact private business, was present at the dinner, and participated in the proceedings. The toasts drank on the occasion, as given in the published records of the celebration in the newspapers of the day, evince the spirit of those assembled. They drank to the King—his honest counselors—the great and general court of Massachusetts Bay, as first to promote the congress of 1765—the majority in that congress—the patriotic House of Burgesses of Virginia, and all the Houses of Assembly on the continent who had nobly opposed arbitrary power. They also proposed, as a sentiment, that the last resolutions of Massachusetts Bay, and the Commons House of Assembly of South Carolina, in not granting supplies to his Majesty's troops, should be examples to be universally followed in the colonies. With a studied disrespect they made no allusion to Governor Colden, who, politically, was very obnoxious to the great majority of the people.

The assembly convened on the 21st of November. In his speech, Lieutenant Governor Colden intimated that the obnoxious acts of Parliament concerning duties would be

* Autograph letter.

repealed; asked for temperate action on the part of the Legislature, and informed them that in future the regulations of the Indian trade were to be left with the colonists. He then told them that the sum they had voted for the support of the troops was exhausted, and asked for further supplies. To the latter request the House, in an address a few days afterward, replied: "In the present impoverished state of the colony, every requisition for a fresh supply will demand our most serious consideration."

At this juncture an extraordinary coalition between Colden and the powerful De Lancey family appeared, and excited much suspicion among the patriots. Opposite political elements seemed suddenly to strangely assimilate, and the leaven of aristocracy, working with the loyalty excited by the lieutenant governor's assurances of the probable repeal of obnoxious acts, began to work in the assembly. It was evident to sagacious minds that a scheme involving the liberties of the province, perhaps of America, was maturing, and there was general alarm among the people. Suddenly a resolution for the emission of bills of credit—a measure which the true friends of the colony had earnestly desired—found favor with the coalition, notwithstanding it was in contradiction with acts of Parliament. It was supported with the plea that there was a great lack of specie, caused by the interdiction of traffic with the West Indies and the total absence of a paper currency, reducing values, preventing remittances to England, and obstructing provisions for the public service.

An act was finally presented which provided for the issuing of bills of credit, on the security of the province, to the amount of one hundred and twenty thousand pounds sterling, to be loaned to the people, the interest to be applied to the defraying of the expenses of the colonial government. It was simply a project for a monster bank, without checks, and was doubtless intended by the lieutenant governor, and the Tories acting with him, to cheat the people into a compliance with the Mutiny Act, by the indirect method of applying the profits to that purpose, the support of the troops being a part of the "expenses of the colonial government." To still further cover this obscure intention, there was connected with the emission act a provision for granting one thousand pounds from the colonial treasury, and one thousand more to be issued under the act, to be applied to the support of the troops. The resolutions connected with the incipient steps in this measure passed the House, in committee of the whole, by only one majority.

The leaders of the popular party raised a cry of alarm while this measure was pending. On Sunday, the 16th of December, a hand-bill was found distributed over the town, headed, "*To the betrayed inhabitants of the City and Colony of New York;*" and signed "A SON OF LIBERTY." It denounced the proposal to issue bills of credit as a deceptive covering to some wicked design not likely to be acceptable to the King. It declared that the proposition to grant supplies to the troops unqualifiedly was an acknowledgment of the right to exact such subsidies, and a virtual approval of all the revenue acts; and that the scheme was intended to divide and distract the colonies. It pointed the assembly to the firm stand taken by other colonies, and exhorted them to imitate their examples. It hinted at a corrupt combination, the effect of the acting governor's cupidity and the ambitious designs of a powerful family; called upon the assembly to repudiate the act concocted by the coalition; and closed with a summons for the people to assemble in "the fields" (City Hall Park), to express their opinions and insist upon their representatives in the assembly joining the minority, and in the event of their refusal, to send tidings thereof to every assembly on the continent, and publish them to the world.

This hand-bill appeared, as we have observed, on Sunday, and on Monday not less than fourteen hundred people gathered around the Liberty Pole, where they were harangued by John Lamb, a native of the city, an active Son of Liberty, and then thirty-four years of age. By a vote they unanimously condemned the action of the assembly. A committee of seven, appointed for that purpose, bore their sentiments to that body, who, after receiving them respectfully, set about ferreting out the author or authors of the hand-bill. The Speaker laid the offensive document before the assembly, and Mr. De Lancey moved that the sense of the House should be taken "whether the said paper was not an infamous and scandalous libel." When the vote was taken, twenty of the pliant assembly voted that it was so, and only one member voted No. That member was PHILIP SCHUYLER. He boldly faced the gathering storm, and by his vote rebuked, in a most emphatic manner, the cringing cowardice of those of his compeers who had stood shoulder to shoulder with him in former trials; and proclaimed to the world his belief in the truth of the allegations which the assembly pronounced "a false, seditious, and infamous libel." The assembly then resolved that the lieutenant governor should offer a reward of £100 for the discovery of the author or authors of the handbill.

This action of the assembly was denounced in another handbill, signed "*Legion*," in which the "base, inglorious conduct of the assembly," in abandoning the interests of the people, was spoken of in very strong terms. This, also, was voted to be libellous, and the lieutenant governor was authorized to offer £50 for the discovery of the author. After this, further provision for the support of the troops, to the amount of £2,000 per annum, was voted.

On the same day Colonel Schuyler nominated Edmund Burke as agent in England for the colony of New York, but the appointment was not made until December, 1770. Colonel Schuyler also asked leave to bring in a bill to provide for the election of representatives by secret ballot instead of open vote. It was granted, but the ultra royalists defeated the measure. From that time Colonel Schuyler was the acknowledged leader of the opposition in the assembly, and the special favorite of the more conservative patriots, while the common people, regarding him at a distance, contemplated him with reverence.

Mr. Lamb, who harangued the people, at the Liberty Pole, was suspected of being the author of the offensive handbill, and was cited to appear before the assembly. He was soon discharged, for the guilt was fixed by the frightened printer upon Captain Alexander M'Dougall, an energetic Scotchmen, from "the lone Hebrides," a sailor, and who afterward became an active general in the Revolution. He was arrested on a charge of contempt, and refusing to make any acknowledgment, or to give bail, was cast into prison, where he remained about fourteen weeks, when he was arraigned for trial. With the true martyr spirit, he said, "I rejoice that I am the first to suffer for liberty since the commencement of our glorious struggles."

"The imprisoned sailor," says Hamilton, "was deemed the true type of an imprisoned commerce. To soften the rigors of his confinement, to evince a detestation of its authors, and in his person to plead the public wrongs, became a duty of patriotism. On the anniversary of the repeal of the Stamp Act, his health was drank with honors, and the meeting, in procession, visited him in prison. Ladies of distinction daily thronged there. Popular songs were written and sung under prison bars, and emblematic swords were worn. His name was upon every lip. The character of each individual conspicuous in the great controversy became a subject of comment, and the applause which followed the name of Schuyler gave a new value to the popularity his firmness had acquired."*

After M'Dougall had suffered an imprisonment of more than three months, a grand jury was packed by the government. De Lancey, the leader of the loyalists, was present at their sitting, and they found a bill of indictment.

"They have indicted M'Dougall," William Smith wrote to Schuyler, on the 29th of April, 1770, "and mean to ruin him if they dare disoblige the people. He made a grand show yesterday when he was brought down to plead—an immense multitude. He spoke with vast propriety, and awed and astonished many who wish him ill, and added, I believe, to the number of his friends. The attorney will not try him till October, though he pressed hard for a determination in July. I doubt whether it will ever happen, unless the spirits of the people flag, of which at present there is no sign."†

M'Dougall gave bail at this time, and on the 13th of December following he was again arraigned before the House. To the question whether he was the author of the handbill signed "A Son of Liberty," he replied, "That as the grand jury and the assembly had declared the paper a libel he could not answer; that as he was under prosecution in the supreme court, he conceived it would be an infraction of justice to punish twice for one offense; but

* *History of the Republic of the United States, as traced in the Writings of Alexander Hamilton*, i. 35. By John C. Hamilton.

† Autograph letter

that he would not deny the authority of the House to punish for a breach of privilege when no cognizance was taken of it in another court." His enemies were highly offended by this answer, and it was declared a contempt. He was ably defended by George Clinton, an active member of the House, but he was again cast into prison, where he remained until near the close of the session, in February, 1771, when he was released, and was never afterward molested. The indictment for libel was never tried.

The loyalist party gradually gained the ascendancy in the Legislature in 1770 and 1771; and the soldiery, regarding the voting of supplies for their support as a triumph of the crown, became exceedingly insolent. They resolved to cut down the Liberty Pole, and on the night of the 16th of January, 1770, at about midnight, a band of them issued from the barracks, prostrated the mast, sawed it into pieces, and piled it in front of Montagnie's door, where the Sons of Liberty usually assembled. The perpetrators were discovered before their work was finished. The bell of St. George's chapel, in Beekman street, was rung, and at dawn full three thousand indignant people stood around the stump of the Liberty Pole. There, in the grey of early morning, the Sons of Liberty, by resolution, declared their rights, and their determination to maintain them.

For three days the most intense excitement prevailed in the city. In frequent affrays with the citizens the soldiers were generally the losers; and in a sharp conflict on Golden Hill (Cliff street between Fulton street and Maiden Lane,) several of the troops were disarmed and severely beaten. Few persons were wounded, none were killed. Quiet was restored. The people erected another Liberty Pole upon private ground purchased for the purpose. This was well defended by iron bands and rivets full one half its length, and successfully resisted another attempt of the soldiers to cut it down, in March. Early in May the troops went off to Boston, and the greatest cause for public irritation was thus removed. The Liberty Pole remained undisturbed until the British army took possession of the city in the autumn of 1776, when it was cut down by order of Cunningham, the infamous provost marshal, who, it was said, had once been severely whipped at its foot.

In Boston the troops and the people were at variance continually; and finally, on the evening of the 5th of March, there was an open collision. A sentinel was assaulted with ice and other missiles, and the commander of the military guard went with a file of soldiers to defend him. The mob dared the soldiers to fire, while they hurled missiles at them. One soldier, who received a severe blow, fired, and six of his companions followed his example. Three persons were killed, and five were dangerously wounded. The bells rang out an alarm, and in less than one hour several thousands of people were in the streets. A terrible scene of blood would have ensued had not Governor Hutchinson assured the people that right and justice should be vindicated in the morning. The troops were removed to Castle William, and the "Boston massacre," as it was called, became a theme of thrilling interest to the patriots throughout the land.

On the day of the "massacre," Lord North, then the prime minister, proposed to Parliament a repeal of all duties imposed by the act of 1767, except that upon tea. In April an act to that effect was passed, and as tea was a luxury, the ministry supposed that the Americans would not object to the small duty laid upon that article. That duty was retained merely as an assertion of the right to tax the colonies. That, as we have said, was the bone of contention. The principle involved was the topic of dispute.

The non-importation agreements were now brought to bear upon this one excepted article alone, and the people were as strenuous in the defense of their principles, with only this item for complaint, as when they had a dozen.

The merchants of New York, up to this time, had been faithful to the non-importation league, and would have continued so but for a blow received from a quarter least suspected. The Sons of Liberty had formed a general committee of one hundred, and a vigilance committee of fifty, who were to have a special care of the public movements of the patriots, and particularly to see that the requirements of the non-importation league were observed. The former committee, like the assembly, became leavened with Toryism, and when, on the 3d of May, 1770, at a meeting of the citizens of New York, a manifesto against alleged violations of the league in Newport, Rhode Island, was adopted, the Committee of One Hundred disavowed it. This was the first open evidence of defection. Some of the more eminent of the Sons of Liberty immediately withdrew from the committee. The Vigilance Committee denounced their faltering compeers, and the patriots of New England uttered indignant protests. All was in vain. The disaffection of the committee had spread among the merchants at large, and on the 9th of July, 1770, the Committee of One Hundred resolved upon the resumption of importations of every thing but tea, and issued a circular letter, justifying their course. It was received with scorn, and publicly torn and scattered to the winds, in the New England capital; and the sturdier patriots of Philadelphia said, "The old Liberty Pole of New York ought to be transferred to this city, as it is no longer a rallying point for the votaries of freedom at home."

Toward the close of August the leaden statue of the King arrived, and was set up in the Bowling Green with a great parade of loyalty. The marble statue of Pitt was also erected, but with far less enthusiasm than it was voted; and every day there were new manifestations of a lukewarmness in the republican feelings of the colony, as seen upon the surface.

Toward the close of October, John Murray, Lord Dunmore, arrived as the successor of Sir Henry Moore, and was received with great cordiality. He brought the assent of the King to the bill authorizing the emission of a colonial paper currency ; also intelligence of a kindling war between Great Britain and Spain. In his inaugural message he alluded to the latter, and expressed his confidence that the assembly would "please his Majesty by their loyalty during the anticipated contest." His lordship closed his speech with the oft-repeated admonition of the royal governors, that supplies for the troops would be wanting. The assembly was exceedingly complaisant, and Dunmore had the gratification of seeing evidence of a pliant and loyal Legislature, by which he would be saved the perplexities that had afflicted his predecessors for almost half a century.

Dunmore remained at New York only about nine months, when he was succeeded by Sir William Tryon, an Irish baronet, who for a few years had exercised the most annoying petty tyranny as the governor of North Carolina. The assembly was now thoroughly purged of the radical features of republicanism. They complimented the retiring governor, who had been transferred to Virginia; and in a most cringing address, written by Captain Oliver De Lancey, in reply to Tryon's message at the opening of the assembly, on the 7th of January, 1772, welcomed the new chief magistrate. This address appears the more abject when we reflect that the base character of Tryon, whose outrageous conduct had stirred up the people of North Carolina to actual rebellion, was well known, and every true friend of the province despised him and deplored his advent.

"Our most gracious sovereign," said the address, "having been pleased to confer the command of his dominion of Virginia on our late worthy governor, the Earl of Dunmore, who so justly merited our affection and applause, we are all filled with the warmest sentiments of gratitude for his Majesty's paternal goodness, in appointing to represent his royal person a gentleman universally esteemed for his amiable character, distinguished for his attachment to the principles of our happy constitution, and from his long residence in America, acquainted with the true interests of the colonies.

"The respectable light in which your excellency was held among the people who lately experienced the solid advantages of your protection affords us a pleasing presage of being equally happy under your administration. Preferring the calls of duty and the public good to your own ease, health, and every other consideration, you generously exposed your person to fatigue and the most imminent dangers, and by your gallant behavior and prudent conduct rescued a distracted country from anarchy and confusion, and restored to it the blessings of peace and tranquility, by suppressing an insurrection, which, by its pernicious example, might have caused the like disorders in other parts of his Majesty's American dominions, to the destruction of all law and government. This important service, while it gives luster to your character, recommends you to the favor of our most gracious sovereign, and entitles you to public gratitude and approbation, has unavoidably prevented your excellency from paying an earlier obedience to the King's commands and the dictates of your own wishes in repairing to this colony."

During the years 1770 and 1771, Colonel Schuyler was almost continually afflicted with the gout, and he seldom appeared in the assembly. Yet it did not prevent the exercise of his hospitality in his houses at Albany and Saratoga—the former his place of residence in the winter, the latter his better loved dwelling place nearly nine of the other months of the year. Numerous letters of that period show how freely his friends gave notes of introduction to him, commending sometimes utter strangers to his courtesy and hospitality.

During these two years the dispute between the authorities of New York and the inhabitants of the New Hampshire Grants waxed hotter than at any other period. A crisis approached. Officers of the law in behalf of New York and the determined people of the Grants met face to face. A resident of the Grants was taken to Albany for trial in a suit of ejectment. The decision in his case was to effect all others, and Ethan Allen was employed, as the agent of the people, to attend the court and defend their claims. The whole affair seemed to have been prejudged, and presented a solemn farce, for some of the New York judges and many of the lawyers were connected with the speculators. The verdict was, of course, in favor of the New York complainants.

Allen was exceedingly indignant. The sun went down upon his wrath, and in the morning it was not abated. The attorney general at first tried to flatter the sturdy pioneer. He then advised him to go home and persuade his friends to make the best terms possible with their New York landlords; and concluded his exhortation by suggesting that New York had *might* on her side. That suggestion thoroughly aroused the sleeping lion of Allen's nature, and in his accustomed enigmatical way he thundered out, "The gods of the valleys are not the gods of the hills!" "What do you mean?" exclaimed the startled attorney general. "Come to Bennington," said Allen, with a frown, and in a deep undertone, "and you shall understand it."

From that time reconciliation without ample justice was out of the question. The people of the Grants resolved to defend their rights "by *force*," they said, "as *law* and *justice* were denied them." They assembled in convention and made Allen colonel commandant of the district. He became the leader of an organized armed resistance, and was a marked man. The authorities of New York regarded him as a traitor, and offered a reward for his apprehension. The people of the Grants regarded him as a patriot, and kept him safely in the arms of their protection. The New York authorities declared him an outlaw, while his own people leaned upon him as their noblest champion. So matters went on, the dangers of civil war becoming more and more imminent. The quarrel had reached the point of bloody encounters, when the kindling flame of the great Revolution called the attention of the contestants to a broader and more significant field of conflict, in which the people of New York and of the Grants stood shoulder to shoulder as brethren.

In the progress of these disputes Colonel Schuyler still took a great interest. His sense of justice made him discriminate between right and wrong, notwithstanding his indignation against the people of the Grants, who had taken law into their own hands; and, as in the case of the refractory tenants of Van Rensselaer, in after years, he recommended moderation, at the same time he counseled firmness.

The boundary line between New York and Massachusetts was still an unsettled question, and in the autumn of 1771, Colonel Schuyler, accompanied by his wife, went to Boston in a semi-official capacity to confer with the authorities there upon the subject. He found matters in such a disturbed state that it was difficult to ascertain where real authority might be found. However, as Hutchinson was governor, with him he had a long and friendly interview, and came back with a proposition to Governor Tryon which seemed to promise a salutary result. Soon afterward William Smith, who was the leading member of Tryon's council, wrote to Colonel Schuyler, saying: "Mr. Tryon has taken strong hold on the Boston controversy on your motion. I have drawn up a letter for him to Hutchinson, and proposed to divide the stakes between the two ultimate proposals at New Haven."

In the same letter Mr. Smith introduces the Reverend Mr. Drummond as Schuyler's "spiritual guide at Sarahtogue," who, he said, bore ample testimonials of worth. "I think it a good circumstance," says Smith, "that he was ordained in Scotland, for you know that national establishment is closely connected with that of the Netherlands." With an eye to temporal benefits, Smith continues, "Mr. Drummond is said to be a good scholar, and may be useful to your boys. I think he will be so to the public, as he can promote emigration from divers parts of North Britain." He concludes by saying, "If you think him good enough for the illuminated tenants of Sarahtogue, you'll find him liberal in his sentiments and yet orthodox in his life, which is the best sort of orthodoxy."*

Colonel Schuyler was present at the opening of the session, on the 7th of January, 1772, and on the 16th he moved for leave to bring in a bill to vacate the seat of any member unless he had resided six months previous to the election within the district which he represented. This subject had been introduced in the spring of 1769, when, by resolution, Philip Livingston was "dismissed from further attendance upon the House" as representative of Livingston's Manor, because he resided in the city of New York. A petition of the freeholders of the Manor set

* Autograph letter.

forth that non-residents represented boroughs in England; that twenty-one cases like the present might be found recorded in the colonial journals; and that the manor of Livingston had been thus represented for fifty-three years. It also appeared that three dismissals of the kind had occurred, under the management of party tactics, namely, of William Nicoll and Dirck Wessels, in 1701, and of Edward Holland, in 1745. The resolution was passed by a large majority, and Livingston was deprived of his seat. Schuyler voted against it. He approved of the principle of the resolution, but disliked partial legislation. Now he introduced a general bill for accomplishing the same effect.

The assembly, at the session of 1772, were as pliant as ever, and supplies for the troops were freely voted. In February the governor, in a brief message, refused to receive a salary from the colonial treasury. This was pursuant to instructions received from ministers, Parliament, by a special act, having made the governors and judges in the colonies independent of the people in this respect. The Massachusetts assembly at once denounced the act as a bribe to the governors to oppose the people whenever ordered to do so by the crown. In other colonial assemblies, also, the act was denounced, but there being a majority of loyalists in that of New York, no action was taken in the matter. On the contrary, a special mark of affection was shown to Tryon. A division of Albany county being made at that time, the new territory, taken from its western frontier, was called Tryon county, in honor of the governor. The first representatives in the assembly from the new county were Guy Johnson (son of Sir William), and Colonel Hendrick Frey.

On the 24th of March the assembly was prorogued by the governor until the 4th of May following. By proclamations it was prorogued from time to time, and did not meet again until the 5th of January, 1773. The governor's speech on that occasion related chiefly to the territorial boundaries; and the response drawn up by De Lancey was only an echo to it, except an assurance that in the colony there was an increasing attachment to the governor's person and family.

Among Colonel Schuyler's most intimate friends in early life was Henry Van Schaack, who had served with him in the campaign of 1755 as his lieutenant. When the war of the Revolution broke out, Mr. Van Schaack was a Loyalist. For several years he and Colonel Schuyler had differed in their political opinions. Their personal friendship appears to have been undisturbed, however, until in 1772, when a misunderstanding came very nearly causing a duel between the two friends. It seems that Colonel Schuyler had reported to Colonel Guy Johnson (upon erroneous information,) that Major Van Schaack had attempted to influence the action of officers who had been appointed to summon a jury in an important land trial before the supreme court, in which controversy the two gentlemen were probably interested. Van Schaack and Schuyler were of about the same age, and much alike in disposition. They were men of high spirit and marked energy of character, entertaining exalted perceptions of personal honor, and each jealous of his reputation. The former was somewhat impetuous in temper, and the latter was described as "hot, violent, and indiscreet," when his reputation was assailed or his honor impugned.

On being informed of Schuyler's report to Johnson, Van Schaack, conscious of his integrity, indignantly demanded of his accuser his authority for the aspersions, and a personal explanation. Schuyler, with his usual frankness, generosity, and sense of justice, sent him a letter from Saratoga, in which he explained the matter and asked Van Schaack's pardon. He concluded by saying, "Be assured, sir, that I shall never decline a personal explanation (in whatever sense you may use the word) that you may think proper to call on me for. You know where to find me, and I shall be at Albany about the 25th of next month."

Although the friendship of these gentlemen was interrupted for several years by conflicting interests in regard to land patents, and the difference in their political sentiments during the Revolution, it was renewed immediately after the war, and continued through life.*

So gentlemanly and dignified were the manners of Schuyler in public and private, that, notwithstanding his firm hostility to the anti-republican measures with which he was called from time to time to combat, he was on terms of the most intimate personal friendship with his political adversaries. In May, 1772, we find Governor Tryon, writing to him from Fort George, in New York, saying:

> "Mrs. Tryon desires me to present her compliments to you, and to inform you that she accepts the invitation of becoming your guest while at Albany. As you are well acquainted with the passage of vessels to Albany, and know in which I can be best accommodated, I must give you the trouble to employ one for me, and to be here time enough to land me at Albany toward the end of June."†

The chief object of Governor Tryon's visit northward was to hold a council with some of the Mohawk Indians, who had made complaints of the conduct of white people, who, it was alleged, had defrauded them of their lands. The conference was held at Johnson Hall, on the 28th of

* MS. "*Memoirs of the Life of Henry Van Schaak, an officer in the war which subjected the Canadas to the British crown; a Loyalist in the American Revolution, and a Gentleman of the Old School,*" by H. C. Van Schaack.

† Autograph letter.

July, and the savages in attendance were mostly Canajoharies. Tryon was accompanied by his secretary, Colonel Edmund Fanning, (who had made himself very obnoxious in North Carolina,) and Oliver De Lancey.

Whatever professions the governor may have made to the Indians, he seemed perfectly willing to sanction all purchases of land, by fair or foul means, we may imagine, and did not appear less "The Great Wolf" to them, if they understood him, than he did to their red brethren of Western Carolina, who gave him that name because he appeared so voracious. In a familiar letter to William Duer, in September following, Colonel Schuyler said:

> "Vast Indian purchases have been made. Governor Tryon's fees, alone, will exceed £22,000; a good summer's work that. A large premium is offered by the land jobbers at New York to any ingenious artist who shall contrive a machine to waft them to the moon, should Ferguson, Martin, or any eminent astronomer assert that they had discovered large vales of fine land in that luminary. I would apply to be a commissioner for granting the land, if I knew to whom to apply for it."*

Governor Tryon was absent in the Indian country about a month, and during that time his wife, who was a relative of the Earl of Hillsborough, was the guest of Colonel Schuyler and his family at Albany and Saratoga. In a letter to the Earl after his return, Tryon spoke of the contentedness of the settlers at Johnstown, Burnet's Field, and the German Flats, who were "not less seemingly pleased with the presence of their governor than he was with them," and said, "I heartily wish the eastern parts of the province [referring to the New Hampshire Grants,] were as peaceably settled."†

Colonel Schuyler was in good health during the session of 1773, and was very active in his official duties. In

* Autograph letter, September 21, 1773. † Autograph letter.

January we find him one of the committee to examine into the condition of the colonial treasury accounts. Early in February he presented a bill in relation to the commission for settling the boundary line between New York and New Jersey, then in dispute. On the day of its passage (February 5,) he offered a bill, as a substitute for another drawn by a committee "to remedy the evils to which the colony was exposed from the quantities of counterfeit money introduced into it." He proposed to have plates for the paper currency of the colony engraved in a manner that should be difficult to counterfeit. He suggested as a device "an eye in a cloud—a cart and coffins—three felons on a gallows—a weeping father and mother, with several small children—a burning pit—human figures poured into it by fiends, and a label with these words: '*Let the name of the counterfeiter rot*,'" etc., and such other additions as they might think proper: 44,000 to be struck off on thin paper, "to be pasted, glued, or affixed to each of the bills emitted by the act" for the purpose. He proposed that the engraver and printer should make oaths that the plates had not been out of their hands; the plates, when the printing should be done, to be sealed up and given to the treasurer of the colony; the treasurer to give the commissioners a receipt for the paper copies struck off; no bill to be considered genuine without such paper upon its back; commissioners to take oath of fidelity; and a reward to be given for the detection of counterfeiters. This bill became a law, and was effectual in restraining rogues from committing a crime whose penalty was death.

Later in February the subject of the dispute between New York and the New Hampshire Grants was brought before the House, in considering a petition from a resident of the latter territory. A committee was appointed, with

Colonel Schuyler as chairman, to prepare a full statement of "the just rights of New York in the matter." Schuyler's associates were Mr. De Noyelles and Crean Bush, both warm loyalists. The task of preparing the statement was laid upon Colonel Schuyler, and three weeks afterward they made a report which excited a great deal of attention because of its fullness and remarkable perspicuity. It first examined the whole matter historically, citing authorities, etc. The claims of Connecticut and Massachusetts were next examined, and having, as the report averred, "established the right of New York to the disputed territory west of the Connecticut river," they examined "the extraordinary claim of New Hampshire." This statement occupies no less than twenty-six printed pages of the published journal of the House. It was sent to Edmund Burke, the agent of the colony in England, and a few months later Governor Tryon was cited to appear before the King and his council, to give information respecting the boundary troubles.

This statement was the production, chiefly, of James Duane, but Colonel Schuyler being the chairman of the committee, it was attributed to him. It was this, more than anything else, that excited bitter feelings toward him among the New England people, which, as we have already observed, was made so manifest in the war for independence.

# CHAPTER XVI.

In the summer of 1773 the county of Charlotte was formed. It embraced all of northern New York above Albany county as then divided, eastward of the new county of Tryon; and it was the design of Colonel Schuyler's friends to make him the first judge of that district, with two associates. Political intrigue seems to have thwarted this design. In July Councillor Smith wrote to him:

"We have organized the county of Charlotte. It was left to Oliver [De Lancey] to speak to Colonel Reid and others, and form a list of justices, for it was long ago settled in council that the judges should be yourself, Skene, and Duer, in the order I mention them. I learnt from Reid that he, Oliver, and Duer waited upon the governor with a list not only of *justices* but of *judges*, and that Skene was put at the head of it. Oliver dictated this order to Duer, who held the pen. But all is set right I believe. The governor was displeased with this liberty, and declared that you would not serve out of the place first designated and known abroad. All this is *entre nous*, but you will get it from Duer. I told Fanning that in my opinion Skene should be last, if named at all. You see the man, after all his professions of friendship."*

De Lancey's will prevailed. Schuyler, as the governor predicted, would not take a subordinate station upon the bench, and he was left in the field of politics, untrameled by official restraints, to serve his country more profitably than if wearing the mantle of judicial dignity.

It was at this period that fuel was added to the kindling fires of the Revolution by the folly of the British gov-

* Autograph letter, July 5, 1773.

ernment. Early in 1773 a new thought upon taxation entered the brain of Lord North. The East India Company, a powerful monopoly of more than a hundred and fifty years duration, felt most seriously the operation of the non-importation associations in America, by which tea, the trade in which belonged exclusively to the company, was deprived of a market in the American colonies. They found themselves burdened with more than seventeen millions of pounds of tea in their warehouses in England. Unable to pay their annual bonus to the crown, or their private debts, the company sought relief in a permission to ship their teas, free of duty, wherever they could find a market, promising the government an export duty more than equal in amount. The stupid ministry could not perceive, or would not embrace, the opportunity now offered to quiet America and add to the exchequer; but, fearing such concession might be considered submission to "rebellious subjects," gave the company permission to ship their teas free of *export* duty. As this would make tea cheaper in America than in England, it was thought the colonists would not object to paying a small import duty of three pence a pound. But the proposition increased the indignation of the colonists. They saw the parent government making concessions of a pecuniary nature to a vast commercial monopoly, while spurning the appeals of a nation in behalf of a great principle.

The East India Company were as blind as the ministers, and soon after the passage of a bill in accordance with North's proposition, in May, 1773, several of their heaviest tea-ships, fully laden with the herb, were on their way to America. Information of the fact reached the colonies some time before any of the tea-ships arrived; and at no time since the passage of the Stamp Act was popular indignation hotter, and the spirit of defiance more rampant. It was resolved by the people in the principal seaport towns that the tea should not be landed, and appointed consignees were warned not to disregard the popular will by receiving it. The Sons of Liberty became exceedingly active, and late in the autumn a formal reorganization of the societies took place. Their correspondence was renewed, and plans were concerted to destroy the tea should the consignees persist in having the cargoes landed.

Two of the tea-ships first arrived at Boston at the close of November, and in obedience to the wishes of the people the vessels were moored at a wharf, with a guard of twenty-five men stationed near, to see that none of the obnoxious article was landed. Finally, the people, at a public meeting, ordered the commanders of the vessels to leave the port and proceed to sea with their cargoes. The governor interfered, and took measures to prevent their sailing. This aroused public indignation to the highest pitch, and on a cold moonlight evening, the 16th of December, a crowd rushed from an excited meeting in Faneuil Hall at the signal of a savage war-whoop, some disguised as Mohawk Indians, and boarding the ships, broke open the tea chests and cast the whole of the cargoes into the waters of the harbor.

In New York the excitement was equally great. At a public meeting, held on the 20th of October, it was declared that tea consignees and stamp distributors were equally obnoxious; and they denounced the importation of tea so emphatically that some of the commission merchants in London refused to have anything to do with the shipment of the article. A New Yorker, named Kelley, canvassing for a seat in Parliament as representative of one of the English boroughs, ridiculed the reported indignation of the Americans, and gave assurances that no danger need be apprehended from their ire. His offense was noted at home, and on the 5th of November he was burned in effigy in front of the Coffee House, in Wall street.

Concert of action in different cities was evinced by the fact that on the 25th of November, the "Mohawks" of New York city were notified to be in readiness for duty on the arrival of expected tea-ships; and we find the name of "Mohawks" connected with similar movements elsewhere. On the 29th, the Sons of Liberty were formally reorganized, and passed strong resolutions of warning to all who should in any way be concerned in the reception of tea, or even of harboring it should any be landed.

Governor Tryon declared that the tea should be delivered to the consignees, even if it was to be "sprinkled with blood." This declaration was repeated by an officer of the crown in the presence of several Sons of Liberty, when John Lamb, one of the foremost of the patriots, said, "Tell Tryon, for me, that the tea shall not be landed; and if force is attempted to effect it, his blood will be the first shed in the contest. The people of the city are firmly resolved on that head."* The governor undoubtedly received the message, and, taking counsel of his fears or his prudence, wisely refrained from interfering in the matter.

On the 17th of December, the day after the tea was destroyed in Boston harbor, and before intelligence of the event could have reached New York, a large concourse of people assembled in "the fields," pursuant to a public call, and were addressed by Mr. Lamb. Strong resolutions in favor of resistance were passed, and a committee of fifteen were appointed to correspond with their friends in other places. While the business of the meeting was in progress,

* Leake's Life of Lamb, p. 78.

the mayor and recorder of the city appeared, bringing assurances from Governor Tryon that when the tea should arrive it should be publicly taken into the fort, kept there until the proper orders for its distribution by the King, the council, or the owners, should be given, and then it should be sent out as publicly as it was taken in. Lamb saw through the artifice. The act of Parliament demanded payment of the duties when the article should be landed; and Lamb warned the people that suffering the tea to be brought on shore at all would be an infraction of their solemn resolves and the pledges of the non-importation league. He then put the question, Shall the tea be landed? when there was a most emphatic response, thrice repeated, No! The meeting then adjourned "till the arrival of the tea-ships."

During the period of excitement concerning the tea-ships Colonel Schuyler was confined to his house most of the time with the gout, and was not in New York during the session which commenced on the 6th of January, 1774, and ended on the 19th of March following.

"We have finished a long and disagreeable session," wrote Councillor Smith, "in which I wish you had taken a part, not because I wish you trouble, but that you might have shared in the credit which Clinton* has acquired in the course of it. There is a surprising change both within doors and without, the spirit of party being in disgrace, to the confusion of those who led it, and found it necessary to the continuation of their power that the people should not recover their senses. Their impatience under a governor who scorned to be purchased excited them to another effort to humble him, but they found themselves baffled in

* George Clinton, one of the most efficient men during the Revolution, as brigadier general, and as governor of the State, had taken a decided republican stand, with Schuyler, during the two preceding sessions. He had studied law with Mr. Smith, and was now only twenty-five years of age. The troubled sea of politics was consonant with his nature, and he entered upon it with zeal.

our House, as they were before by your good management in the assembly."*

At that time political affairs were in the greatest confusion. There were so many side issues continually presenting themselves, that loyalists upon one question to-day were found to be republicans upon another question tomorrow ; and even Schuyler, staunch Whig as he was, was sometimes suspected of leaning toward the crown and the aristocracy by those who could not comprehend the propriety of personal friendship with political opponents, and because of his conservatism.

Among the people loyalty and timidity developed bitter fruits which distracted the Revolutionary committees, and by adroit management moderate men and royalists gained the ascendancy. Afraid openly to oppose the popular will, they insidiously cast obstacles in the way of efficient coöperation with other colonies. Two distinct parties were formed among professed republicans, marked by a line of social distinction—the *Patricians* and the *Tribunes*, as they were called—the merchants and the gentry, and the mechanics. We shall refer to this matter again presently.

The assembly and the governor were upon amicable terms during the session of 1774. At midnight, at the the close of 1773, the government house in the fort took fire. The flames spread so rapidly that the governor's family escaped with difficulty, and a servant girl, sixteen years of age, perished in the flames. The governor lost all of his personal effects. In his opening speech to the assembly he laid the matter before them, and in addition to making provisions for rebuilding the province house, they voted him a present of twenty thousand dollars in consideration of his misfortune.

* Autograph letter, March 22, 1774.

Late in January the assembly appointed another standing committee of correspondence,* to hold communion with the assemblies of other provinces on the great political questions of the day. In the New York Legislature, and among the Sons of Liberty, committees had been in operation for several years, but Legislative Committees, for intercolonial communication upon the rights of the people, had been suggested by Massachusetts, on motion of Samuel Adams, and acted upon by Virginia only during the preceding year.

Appropriate resolutions were adopted by the New York assembly when the committee was appointed, and the Speaker was instructed to prepare drafts of letters to the Speakers of all the colonial assemblies on the continent, inclosing these resolutions, and requesting them to lay them before their respective Legislatures. They also, by resolution, thanked the Virginia Burgesses "for their early attention to the liberties of America."

In his opening message Governor Tryon had informed the assembly that he was about to leave for England on account of the controversy with the New Hampshire Grants, and on the 19th of March they presented to him a most loyal and affectionate address at the house of Lord Stirling, in Broad street. He sailed for England on the 7th of April, leaving the government in the hands of Colden, his venerable lieutenant, then eighty-six years of age. Eleven days afterward the first of the tea-ships arrived at Sandy Hook, near New York. It was the *Nancy*, Captain Lockyer, which had been terribly storm-tossed and beaten on her

* The committee consisted of John Cruger, James Jauncey, Benjamin Seaman, Frederick Philipse, Zebulon Seaman, Simon Boerum, James De Lancey, Jacob Walton, Isaac Wilkins, Daniel Kissam, John Rapelye, John De Noyelles, and George Clinton.

voyage. "Ever since her departure from Europe," said Holt's *Journal*, when noticing her arrival, "she has met with a continued succession of misfortunes, having on board something worse than a Jonah, which, after being long tossed in the tempestuous ocean, it is hoped, like him, will be thrown back upon the place from whence it came. May it teach a lesson there as useful as the preaching of Jonah was to the Ninevites."

The Sons of Liberty were on the alert when intelligence of the arrival of the *Nancy* reached them. The pilots would not take her into port without consent of the patriots. A committee went down to Sandy Hook and took charge of her ; and on the solicitation of her captain, who wished to refit his vessel, she was allowed to go up to the city. The captain was met at the wharf by a large concourse of citizens. The consignee, awed by the people, advised the captain to return with his cargo as speedily as possible. He was not allowed to go near the custom-house ; and, finally, escorted by a great number of citizens, called out by the ringing of the bells, and with a band playing "God save the King," he was placed on a pilot boat and taken on board his ship, while the colors of the vessels in the harbor were gaily displayed, and a flag was unfurled from the Liberty Pole with a royal salute of artillery. Lockyer, glad to escape, immediately put to sea.

Meanwhile another vessel had arrived, having some tea concealed among its cargo. It was discovered by the Sons of Liberty, and the whole was thrown into the waters of the harbor. The commander, who at first denied having the obnoxious article, took refuge from the fury of the populace on board the *Nancy*, and went with her when she sailed away. In other seaports of the colonies similar proceedings were had when tea-ships arrived ; and all the tea that came to America was either sent back, destroyed, or locked up, so that not a farthing of revenue was ever derived from the plausible scheme of Lord North.

The destruction of tea at Boston produced a powerful sensation throughout the British realm. The exasperated ministry at once proposed retaliatory measures, and the King and Parliament resolved to inflict severe punishment upon Boston for its treasonable and rebellious conduct, notwithstanding full compensation was offered to the East India Company for the tea that had been destroyed. On the 7th of March, 1774, Parliament, by enactment, ordered the port of Boston to be closed against all commercial transactions whatever, and the removal of the custom-house, courts of justice, and other public offices to Salem.

On the 28th of March Paliament leveled a destructive blow against the charter of Massachusetts, by so modifying it as to deprive the people of many of the dearest privileges guaranteed by that instrument. On the 21st of April, a third retaliatory act was passed, providing for the trial in England of all persons charged in the colonies with murders committed in support of government, giving, as Colonel Barré pointedly said, "encouragement to military insolence, already so insupportable." A fourth bill was passed, providing for the quartering of troops in America; and a fifth, called the Quebec Act, making great concessions to the Roman Catholics of Canada, was enacted. The latter excited the animosity of all Protestants.

These measures created unusual indignation. The Americans saw that justice from Great Britain could not be expected, and that they would soon be called upon to support and defend their rights and freedom with their own strong arms. They wisely proceeded to prepare for the inevitable conflict. They commenced arming themselves. They practiced daily in military exercises. The manufacture of arms and gunpowder was encouraged; and in New England, the inhabitants capable of bearing arms were enrolled in companies, and prepared to go to the field at a minute's warning. These formed the vast host of *Minute Men* of the Revolution—an army, as we have else where observed, "strong, determined, generous, and panting for action, yet invisible to the superficial observer. It was not seen in the camp, the field, nor the garrison. No drum was heard calling it to action, no trumpet was sounded for battle. It was like electricity, harmless when latent but terrible when aroused. It was all over the land. It was at the plough, the workshop, and in the counting-room. Almost every household was its headquarters, and every roof its tent. It bivouacked in every church, and mothers, wives, sisters, and sweethearts, made cartridges for its muskets, and supplied its commissariat. It was the old story of Cadmus repeated in modern history. British oppression had sown dragons' teeth all over the land, and a crop of armed men was ready to spring up, but not to destroy each other."*

The Boston Port Bill was to go into operation on the 1st of June. To enforce it, General Gage had been made Governor of Massachusetts. He arrived at Boston on the 12th of May. On the following day a meeting of the inhabitants was called. Samuel Adams presided, and it was resolved to renew non-importation measures in all their stringency, and to discontinue trade to the West Indian colonies, if their sister provinces should concur with them in the expediency of the measure. The object sought to be gained by including all of the West India islands was not only to raise a clamor in the British possessions there, but to arouse those of the French, Dutch, and Danes, whose

* Lossing's *Life of Washington*, i. 140.

respective courts would be immediately called upon to remonstrate.

Paul Revere, one of the most active Sons of Liberty in Boston, bore a letter to those of New York, giving them intelligence of what had been done in Faneuil Hall. But before his arrival, the New York Vigilance Committee, consisting chiefly of Hampden Hall patriots—the most radical of the Sons of Liberty—had written to their friends in Boston, urging them to pursue vigorous opposition measures, and assuring them of the sympathy and support of New York. This letter was dated the 14th.

We have observed that the professed republicans of New York were, at this time, separated by political distractions and social differences. Loyalists and conservatives sought to suppress if not destroy the influence of the radical democrats, and merchants were arrayed against mechanics. The merchants, always timid during commotions, were alarmed by the letter of the Vigilance Committee to the patriots of Boston, and a meeting of their class was summoned at the house of Samuel Fraunces, corner of Broad and Pearl streets, called "The Exchange," on the evening of the 16th of May, "to consult on the measures to be pursued in consequence of the late extraordinary advices received from England"—the retaliatory measures of Parliament. That meeting nominated a Committee of Fifty as representatives of public sentiment in New York. Several well-known loyalists were placed upon it, while more radical Sons of Liberty, like John Lamb, were excluded.

A meeting of the citizens was called on the 19th to ratify the nomination, when Francis Lewis was added, and the committee consisted of fifty-one.

The spirit that ruled in the appointment of that committee may be inferred by the following extract from an ironical letter written by Gouverneur Morris to Richard Penn, on the day after the ratification meeting was held:

"The heads of the mobility," he said, "grow dangerous to the gentry, and how to keep them down is the question. While they correspond with the other colonies, call and dismiss popular assemblies, make resolves to bind the consciences of the rest of mankind, bully poor printers, and exert with full force all their tribunitial powers, it is impossible to curb them. But art sometimes goes further than force, and, therefore, to trick them handsomely, a Committee of Patricians was to be nominated, and into their hands was to be committed the majority of the people, and the highest trust was to be reposed in them by a mandate that they should take care *quod republica non capiat injuriam.* The Tribunes, through the want of good legerdemain in the senatorial order, perceived the finesse, and yesterday I was present at a grand division of the city, and there I beheld my fellow citizens very accurately counting their chickens not only before they were hatched, but before one half of the eggs were laid. In short, they fairly contended about the future form of our government—whether it should be founded on aristocratic or democratic principles."

The first act of the Committee of Fifty-one was to repudiate the strong letter of the 14th to the Boston committee, and to caution the public that it was not official. On the 23d, at a meeting of the Grand Committee, Paul Revere was received, and laid before them the official proceedings of the Boston town meeting of the 13th. They did not concur with the resolutions of that meeting concerning non-intercourse with Great Britain and the West Indies, but favored the assembling of a congress of deputies. They accordingly appointed Alexander M'Dougall, Isaac Low, James Duane, and John Jay a committee to prepare a response to the Boston letter. It was written, it is supposed, by John Jay, and was reported to the Grand Committee the same evening.

"Your letter, enclosing the vote of the town of Boston, and the letter of your Committee of Correspondence," said the response, "were immediately taken into consideration. While we think you justly entitled to the thanks of your sister colonies for asking their advice on a case of such extensive consequences, we lament our inability to relieve your anxiety by a decisive opinion. The cause is general, and concerns a whole continent, who are equally interested with you and us; and we foresee that no remedy can be of avail unless it proceeds from the joint acts and approbation of all. From a virtuous and spirited union much may be expected, while the feeble efforts of a few will only be attended with mischief and disappointment to themselves, and triumph to the adversaries of liberty.

"Upon these reasons we conclude that A CONGRESS OF DEPUTIES FROM THE COLONIES IN GENERAL is of the utmost importance; that it ought to be assembled without delay, and some unanimous resolutions formed in this fatal emergency, not only respecting your deplorable circumstances, but for the security of our common rights. Such being our sentiments, it must be premature to pronounce any judgment on the expedient which you have suggested. We beg, however, that you will do us the justice to believe that we shall continue to act with a firm and becoming regard to American freedom, and to coöperate with our sister colonies in every measure that shall be thought salutary and conducive to the public good. We have nothing to add but that we sincerely condole with you in your unexampled distress, and to request your speedy opinion of the proposed Congress, that if it should meet with your approbation we may exert our utmost endeavors to carry it into execution."*

The Virginia House of Burgesses had, three days before this letter was prepared, made a similar recommendation, but intelligence of the fact had not, of course, reached New York. Indeed the feeling was spontaneous, and was confined to no section of the country. The people everywhere began to long for a closer union against a common oppressor, and Massachusetts and other colonies promptly responded in the affirmative to the suggestion of New York for a general congress.

On the 7th of June, the New York committee sent a second letter to the Boston committee, requesting them to appoint the time and place for the assembling of the proposed congress. Ten days afterward the Massachusetts

* American Archives, i. 297.

assembly adopted and signed a "Solemn League and Covenant," in which all former non-importation agreements and cognate undertakings were concentrated; and a committee was appointed to send the covenant as a circular to every colony in America. They also passed a resolution in favor of a general congress of deputies, and suggested the first day of the ensuing September as the time, and the city of Philadelphia as the place for the assembling of such congress. The people in other colonies acceded to the Boston proposition for non-intercourse, and New York stood almost alone in refusing to adopt those stringent and hitherto successful measures. The Loyalists rejoiced, and Rivington, the Royal Printer, published in his *Gazetteer* the following verse:

"And so, my good masters, I find it no joke,
For YORK has stepped forward and thrown of the yoke
Of congress, committees, and even King Sears,*
Who shows you good nature by showing his ears."

The Committee of Vigilance of the Sons of Liberty were not awed by the more imposing one of the Fifty-one, but were active, vigilant, and untiring. They called a meeting of the inhabitants in "the fields," on the 19th of June, when the refusal of the Fifty-one to accede to the general union in favor of non-importation, proposed by Massachusetts, was denounced, and resolutions were passed expressive of the sympathy and intended coöperation of the people of New York with the suffering Bostonians; also that delegates should be appointed to the proposed general congress, instructed to agree to a vigorous non-intercourse, in accordance with the Boston resolutions.

* Isaac Sears, commonly called King Sears, was one of the earliest and most ardent Sons of Liberty. He was a merchant, and, though radical, was placed on the Committee of Fifty-one. The next year he avenged himself by leading a party that dest oyed Rivington's printing establishment.

The Committee of Fifty-one held a meeting on the evening of the 4th of July, when, on motion of Alexander M'Dougall, Philip Livingston, John Alsop, Isaac Low, James Duane, and John Jay were nominated for delegates to the continental congress. M'Dougall also proposed to ubmit the nominations to the Tribunes or "committee of mechanics for their concurrence." The nomination was approved, but the reference to the mechanics was rejected. This refusal brought forth a handbill the next day (July 5), which called upon the inhabitants of the city to assemble in "the fields" on the 6th, at six o'clock in the evening, to hear matters "of the utmost importance to their reputations and security as freemen."

A great crowd was assembled at the appointed time. M'Dougall was called to the chair, and a series of resolutions, drawn by him, were adopted. These denounced the Boston Port Bill; declared that any attack upon the rights of a sister colony was immediately an attack upon the colony of New York; that the assumption of power to close ports and interrupt commerce was "highly unconstitutional;" pledged the colony to join with the others in a stringent non-importation league, and to be governed by the action of the contemplated general congress, etc. They ordered the resolutions to be printed in the public newspapers, and transmitted to the different counties in the colony, and to the committees of correspondence for the neighboring colonies.

This gathering, so great in numbers and in the importance of its action, was always referred to as THE GREAT MEETING IN THE FIELDS, and it was on that occasion that a student in King's College, known as the "Young West Indian,"—a delicate boy, girl-like in personal grace and stature, only seventeen years of age—astonished the multitude by his logic and eloquence. He had been often seen walking alone under the shadow of large trees on Dey street, sometimes musing, and sometimes talking in low tones to himself. The residents near had occasionally engaged him in conversation, and were deeply impressed by his wisdom. Some of them seeing him in the crowd, urged him to address the meeting. He at first recoiled, but after listening attentively to the successive speakers, and finding several points untouched, he presented himself to the multitude.

"The novelty of the attempt, his youthful countenance, his slender, boyish form, awakened curiosity and excited attention. Overawed by the scene before him, he hesitated and faltered, but as he proceeded almost unconsciously to utter his accustomed reflections, his mind warmed with the theme—his energies were recovered. After a discussion clear, cogent, and novel, of the great principles involved in the controversy, he depicted in the glowing colors of ardent youth the long continued and long endured oppression of the mother country. Insisting upon the duty of resistance, he pointed to the means and certainty of success, and described the waves of rebellion sparkling with fire, and washing back on the shores of England the wrecks of her power, of her wealth, and her glory. The breathless silence ceased when he closed, and a whispered murmur 'It is a collegian! it is a collegian!' was lost in loud expressions of wonder and applause at the extraordinary eloquence of the young stranger."*

That orator was the destined son-in-law of Philip Schuyler, ALEXANDER HAMILTON. This was his entrance upon the theatre of public life, whereon he played a most useful and extraordinary part for thirty years.

* *A History of the Republic of the United States, etc.*, by John C. Hamilton, i. 55.

The Committee of Fifty-one met on the evening of the 7th. They were evidently alarmed at the course of events. They reconsidered their action on the motion of M'Dougall to submit the nomination of deputies to the congress to the committee of mechanics, but proceeded to disavow and condemn the resolutions of the great meeting in "the fields" as seditious and incendiary. These denunciations offended several of the staunch republicans of the committee, and eleven of them instantly withdrew.*

"The political sky at this place," wrote Councillor Smith to Colonel Schuyler two days afterward, "is cloudy. The Committee of Fifty-one, composed of jarring members, ten or a dozen of whom have made a secession from the main body upon the majority's disapproving some late resolves in the Fields, which you have seen in the papers. These were intended to urge the committee to join the common voice of the continent. They have since published other resolves, and to-day the town meets to approve or disapprove them. Those who know the populace say nothing will be done but a motion be made to amend them. Strange that a colony who had the first intelligence of the Parliamentary measures is behind all the rest."†

A committee appointed by the Tribunes, or mechanics, addressed a note to each of the nominees for a seat in the assembly of deputies, requesting to know whether they would support the Massachusetts resolves in that approaching congress. They answered that such a course would be in accordance with their individual opinions, but declared that they gave the assurance not with a view to secure their election, but to express their sentiments upon a question of so great importance.‡ This response was quite satisfactory, and on the 27th of July the gentlemen

* These were Francis Lewis, Joseph Hallet, Alexander M'Dougall, Peter V. B. Livingston, Isaac Sears, Thomas Randall, Abraham P. Lott, Leonard Lispenard, John Broome, Abraham Brasher, and Jacob Van Zandt.

† Autograph letter, July 9, 1774.

‡ Leake's Life of Lamb, page 94.

who were nominated were elected delegates by the unanimous vote of the city. Suffolk county elected William Floyd ; Orange county, Henry Wisner and John Herring ; and Kings county, Simon Boerum. Dutchess and Westchester adopted the New York city delegates as their representatives.

Albany county endeavored to send a deputy from that district in the person of Colonel Schuyler, who had been all the year, thus far in its progress, a great sufferer from the pains of rheumatism and his hereditary malady. We have observed that he could not attend the session of the assembly, and while the stirring scenes which we have just considered were transpiring in New York, he was a prisoner to disease at Saratoga. His friends were anxious that one so useful should be in active public life, and as the time drew near when the great Senate of the people was to assemble, his constituents, and his friends in other districts, earnestly desired his recovery, for no man appeared so eligible for the position as he. Toward the close of July, Councillor Smith wrote to him, saying :

> "The colonies are preparing for the grand *Witenage Mote* [Great Assembly] with great spirit. At Philadelphia a plan is digesting for an American constitution. I know not the outlines of it. I hope it is for a Parliament, and to meet annually. Our people will be the last of all in the appointment of delegates. I wish your county would assist in the choice. Expresses will be sent through the whole colony to call upon the counties for the purpose. * * * The people of England begin to call out for an American Parliament."*

Colonel Schuyler's health improved early in August, so that he rode down to Albany ; and when intelligence that an appointment of delegates to the congress had been made in New York city, his constituents felt more anxious than ever for his recovery. Late in August he received the fol-

* Autograph letter, July 23, 1774.

lowing letter from Jacob Lansing, jr., chairman of the Albany Committee of Correspondence:

"Yours of the 22d instant I have received. These rheumatic pains, attended with a disagreeable fever, are undoubtedly very hard, but we must console ourselves in the days of affliction by hoping we shall get the better of it. I am now requested by the Committee to inform you that, by the majority of votes of that board, you are appointed our delegate for the city and county of Albany, to join the general congress at Philadelphia, which I hope you will accept, and not decline serving, as it is for the welfare of the public. * * * It is proposed to meet on Tuesday next to consider the resolves—whether we are to stand by the resolves made at New York [at the great meeting in the Fields,] or make new ones."*

Colonel Schuyler's health would not permit him to accept the nomination, and Mr. Lansing communicated to the congress the fact that the committee of the city and county of Albany had adopted the New York city delegates as the representatives of their district.† Within sixty-three days after the proposition for a general congress went forth, twelve of the thirteen Anglo-American colonies had responded in the affirmative; and at the beginning of September delegates from all them were on their way toward Philadelphia.

* Autograph letter, August 23, 1774.

† Journals of the Continental Congress, September 5, 1774.

# CHAPTER XVII.

The First Continental Congress assembled in Carpenter's Hall, Philadelphia, on Monday, the 5th of September, 1774. Twelve colonies were represented. Peyton Randolph, of Virginia, was chosen president, and Charles Thomson, of Pennsylvania, was appointed secretary. The regular business of the congress commenced on the morning of the 7th of September, after the Reverend Jacob Duché, of the Church of England, in an impressive prayer, had implored the aid of Divine Wisdom in the work to be performed.

The session of that congress, so strange and bold in its inception—so unmindful of all precedents—so imposing in its array of truly great, because good and courageous men—so important to the cause of free thought and action in both hemispheres—was brief but wonderfully fruitful of results. The deputies remained in session until the 26th of October. They were far from harmonious in their action. There were antagonisms, growing out of geographical and social differences, that at times threatened to defeat the great purposes of the congress. But the deputies debated with courtesy and candor, respected each other's opinions, sought diligently for the way of truth, and finally matured public measures for future action which received the general approbation of the American people.

The congress prepared and signed a plan for a general

commercial non-intercourse with Great Britain and her West India possessions, according to the recommendation of the assembly of Massachusetts. It was called *The American Association*, and was recommended for adoption throughout the country. It consisted of fourteen articles; and in addition to its non-intercourse provisions, it recommended the abandonment of the slave trade, the improvement of the breed of sheep, abstinence from all extravagance in living, cessation of indulgence in horse-racing, etc., and the appointment of a committee in every town, to promote conformity to the requirements of the *Association.* Fifty-two members present signed it, and it was sent forth to the people as a powerful weapon wherewith to combat the wicked enactments of the British Parliament.

The congress also put forth a Declaration of Rights, and an address to the people of Great Britain; another to the several Anglo-American colonies; another to the inhabitants of Quebec, or Canada; and a petition to the King. These were remarkable state papers, and elicited the warmest encomiums from the first statesmen in the old world. But their most significant action was on the 8th of October, when they resolved:

"*That this congress approve the opposition of the inhabitants of Massachusetts Bay to the execution of the late acts of Parliament, and if the same shall be attempted to be carried into execution by force, in such case all America ought to support them in their opposition.*"

Thus it was that the voice of the *nation* spoke out in harmonious and defiant tones. The quarrel of Massachusetts with the home government was then adopted as their own by the other colonies. It was the deliberate expression of the sentiments of the people of the continent, and made a most profound impression upon the civilized world. And when full intelligence of the acts of the congress, after their adjournment, reached England, the great William Pitt manifested his admiration of their wisdom, and said: "I have not words to express my satisfaction that the congress has conducted this most arduous and delicate business with such manly wisdom and resolution as do the highest honor to their deliberation."

The congress "dissolved itself" after a session of fifty-one days; and having declared their opinion that "another congress should be held on the 10th day of May next, unless the redress of grievances which we have desired be obtained before that time," they recommended such deputies to assemble at Philadelphia, and that "all the colonies in North America choose delegates as soon as possible to attend such congress."

At the beginning of 1775, the colonies were in a blaze of excitement. Measures were every where consummated or in progress to enforce the *American Association*, by the appointment of committees of inspection; and provincial congresses, assuming the functions of regular civil government, soon began to germinate, in defiance of known preparations on the part of the British ministry to crush the rising rebellion.

In November, 1774, the Committee of Fifty-one in New York was dissolved, and at a meeting of "freeholders and freemen," held at the City Hall on the 22d of that month, a committee of sixty persons were chosen, "for carrying into execution the Association entered into by the Continental Congress."

On that day, Councillor Smith, who was already beginning to waver in his attachment to the cause of the people, in the shape it was assuming, wrote to Colonel Schuyler, saying:

"You know what spirit prevailed in the Committee of Fifty-one before the congress had published their resolves, letters, etc. Their delegates have become converts to the prevailing sentiments of the congress. The true motives I can not positively as yet pronounce, nor would I be censorious. I am still not without suspicions, and have a little clue. Suppose some of them, who were once opposed to the Liberty Boys, should have reasoned thus at Philadelphia: 'The government favor we have already lost, and the question only is whether we shall court the continent or the merchants of New York. From the last we have less to fear. There is an approaching election, and with part of the trade, part of the Church, all the non-episcopals, and all the Liberty Boys, we may secure places in the assembly and laugh at the discontented.' * * * You 'll not wonder, therefore, to learn that by the interest of the delegates the Committee of Fifty-one is to be dissolved, and a new committee appointed to execute the decrees of the congress, which is to consist of the delegates and such a set as the most active of the Liberty Boys approve, and had (through the mechanics, who were consulted,) chosen in conjunction with the Committee of Fifty-one, from which a set, who formerly dictated all their movements, have retired outwitted and disgusted, and, as they think, betrayed. With this hint you 'll be able to predict what the conduct of some old politicians will be at the next session, and will perceive that the current will set all one way for liberty in both Houses, unless some persons will throw obstacles in the way."*

As soon as the congress adjourned, the Loyalists and the high church party in New York undertook to weaken the *American Association*, by inducing violations of its requirements. Accomplished scholars and able divines, who had been engaged in the controversy about an American episcopate, now resumed their pens. Among the most eminent of these writers were Reverends Dr. Cooper, president of King's College, Dr. Ingles, Dr. Seabury, and Dr. Chandler. Their chief opponents were William Livingston, John Jay, and young Alexander Hamilton. The latter entered the list of political writers at this time, and very soon he was acknowledged to be the chief of all, not excepting the veteran combatant, Livingston, who had

* Autograph letter, November 22, 1774.

battled the church and government party so manfully for many long years. Hamilton's reply to Dr. Seabury, who assumed the character of a "Westchester Farmer," was a masterpiece of reflections and wise conclusions upon the subject of political economy; and at that early day, before cotton, the great staple of our southern States, had been dreamed of as an article of commerce, he foresaw its immense future value. "With respect to *cotton*," he said "you do not pretend to deny that a sufficient quantity of that might be produced. Several of the southern colonies are so favorable to it, that, with due cultivation, in a couple of years they would afford enough to clothe the whole continent."

Colonel Schuyler visited New York in September, for the first time in many months. He was called there by a summons to the bedside of his dying friend, General Bradstreet. He remained in the city, with the exception of one week, until the meeting of the assembly on the 1st of January following.

We have already observed that Bradstreet, from causes which do not appear, was, for several years, alienated from his family. At the time of his death, his wife and four children were living. His son was a major in the British army, and his daughters (Mrs. Agatha Buttar, and Martha and Eliza Bradstreet,) were with their mother in London, under the protecting care of Sir Charles Gould, of the Horse Guards. In an angry moment, Bradstreet had made a will cutting off his family from inheritance of his estate. Colonel Schuyler frequently remonstrated with him on the injustice and cruelty of his act, and finally obtained the General's consent to destroy the will. On the 23d of September, 1774, Bradstreet executed another, in which provision was made for his family.* It was drawn by William Smith. Colonel Schuyler was made sole executor, and immediately after the general's death, he addressed the following letter to the widow:

"DEAR MADAM: Such are the vicissitudes of human life, that a misfortune seldom occurs but what is accompanied by some comfort. Such are the reflections which arise on the death of General Bradstreet, for whilst I mourn the departed friend, I rejoice the returned husband and parent. No characters, Madam, are perfectly free from blemish. The greatest, and almost the only one in his was an unbecoming resentment against his family, for supposed faults of which I have often told him I feared he was too much the occasion. This, however, ought to be for ever eradicated from your memory, as he died in perfect peace with all. Having set his heart at ease on this point, he seemed more cheerful than he had been for a long time before, and met his fate with all the fortitude becoming his character as a soldier, and with all the resignation inspired by a consciousness that the Supreme Being disposes all for the best."†

General Bradstreet was buried in Trinity church-yard, in the city of New York, with military honors. His remains were taken to the church, accompanied by civil and military officers, and the 47th regiment.

The first session of the New York assembly after the Continental Congress had closed its labors commenced on the 10th of January, 1775. There was a clear majority of loyalists or Tories, as the friends of the government were now called, in both Houses, and Colonel Schuyler, as the acknowledged leader of the opposition, nobly seconded by Clinton, Woodhull, Tenbroeck, Boerum, Van Cortlandt, Livingston, De Witt, and Thomas, resolved to have the political issues between the government and the people distinctly drawn and specifically considered.

The venerable Lieutenant Governor Colden, in his mes-

* Substance of an autograph letter (rough draft) of Colonel Schuyler to Sir Charles Gould, October 2, 1774.

† Autograph letter, October 2, 1774.

sage, called the attention of the Legislature to the disturbed state of the colonies; spoke of the "alarming crisis;" and told the assembly that the country looked to them for wise counsel. "If constituents are discontented and apprehensive," he said, "examine their complaints with calmness and deliberation, and determine upon them with an honest impartiality." He directed them to supplicate the throne, and they would be heard; exhorted them to discountenance measures calculated to increase the public distress, and promised them his aid.

The assembly, in its response to the governor's message, took conservative ground. It was drawn by Mr. De Lancey. Colonel Schuyler was one of the committee, and before it was reported he moved to strike out the words "and with calmness and deliberation pursue the most probable means to obtain a redress of our grievances," and to substitute the following: "And consider and examine, with the utmost calmness, deliberation, and impartiality, the complaints of our constituents; and endeavor to obtain a cordial and permanent reconciliation with our parent state, by pursuing the most probable means to obtain a redress of our grievances." This was thought too strong language, and it was negatived. Schuyler voted for the address, which had been slightly amended, for there was nothing in it particularly offensive to a patriot.

On the 26th of January, a question came up which tested the political character of the assembly. On that day Colonel Tenbroeck moved that the House should "take into consideration the proceedings of the Continental Congress, held in the city of Philadelphia in the months of September and October last." The motion was negatived by a majority of only one, the previous question having been called by Colonel Phillipse. Notwithstanding the meagreness of the majority, the result gave great joy to the Tories.

"I have the most perfect satisfaction," wrote a New York Loyalist, to his friend in Annapolis, "in acquainting you that this day was made, in our assembly, a motion for appointing a day for examining the proceedings of the Continental Congress, and that it was thrown out of the House by a majority of one voice. Of this event I heartily wish you joy, and that this example may be adopted by the senators in your province; but my fears almost preclude the hope of such good."

Another wrote, on the 30th, to a gentleman in Boston, saying:

"The enclosed will unriddle the joy that fills the breasts of all the friends to government, decency, and good order. Since the glorious eleven, with Colonel Phillipse at their head, have carried the day, two more members have come, both of which are on the right side, so that there is now no chance of the assembly's aiding or abetting the congress. The friends of the government plume themselves on this victory, and are now open-mouthed against the proceedings of congress, and no one dares among gentlemen to support them. Worthy old Silver Locks (Lieutenant Governor Colden), when he heard that the assembly had acted right, cried out, 'Lord, now lettest thou thy servant depart in peace.'"

On the 31st of January it was agreed to take into consideration the state of the colony, and to enter upon the journals such resolutions as they should pass. It was determined to prepare a petition to the King, a memorial to the House of Lords, and a statement and a remonstrance to the Commons. For the latter service Colonel Schuyler was associated with some of the leading members of the House, and they reported on the 3d of March.

Meanwhile other action, coöperative with the patriots in the sister colonies, was attempted in the House. On the 16th of February, Colonel Schuyler moved that certain letters which had passed between the committees of correspondence of New York and Connecticut, in June, 1774, on the subject of another congress, and also a copy of a letter to Edmund Burke, the agent of New York at the court of Great Britain, written by the assembly committee of correspondence in September, 1774, "be forthwith entered in the journals of the House, and that the clerk be ordered to supply copies for publication in the newspapers. This motion was negatived by a vote of sixteen to nine.

On the following day Colonel Woodhull moved that the thanks of the House should be given to the delegates from New York in the late Continental Congress "for their faithful discharge of the trust reposed in them." This was negatived by fifteen to nine. A motion to tender the thanks of the House to the merchants and inhabitants for their patriotic adherence to the non-importation league, was negatived by the same vote. On the 23d a motion to appoint delegates to the proposed second Continental Congress was negatived by a vote of seventeen to nine. Each of these motions were debated with zeal, and foremost among the speakers who voted in the affirmative were Schuyler and Clinton.

On the 3d of March the committee appointed to prepare a statement of the grievances of the colony presented a timid report, far too delicate in its condemnation of certain acts of Parliament to suit the views of Schuyler and his friends. He spoke out boldly but courteously concerning the hesitation of the committee, and then moved that a certain act of Parliament, "so far as it imposes duties for the purpose of raising a revenue in America—extends the admiralty courts beyond their ancient limits—deprives his Majesty's American subjects of trial by jury—authorizes the judges' certificates to indemnify the prosecutor from damages which he might otherwise be liable to—and holds up an injurious discrimination between the subjects in

Great Britain and in America, is a grievance." He supported his motion with great zeal and was warmly seconded by Clinton. It was adopted in committee of the whole by a vote of seven to two.

Mr. De Lancey, who voted in the negative, now moved that the opinion of the committee of the whole should be taken "whether his Majesty and the Parliament of Great Britain have a right to regulate the trade of the colonies, and to lay duties on articles that are imported directly into the colonies, from any foreign country, which might interfere with the products of Great Britain." It was decided, by the same relative vote, that they had the right, Schuyler and Clinton voting in the negative. Schuyler then moved the following addition to De Lancey's resolution: "excluding every idea of taxation, internal or external, for the purpose of raising a revenue on the subjects in America without their consent." This amendment was defeated.

The committee appointed under the resolution of the 31st of January, to prepare a series of resolves to be placed on the journal of the House, reported on the 8th. These resolutions were five in number, and as there was nothing in them particularly offensive to the republicans, they were adopted without much discussion by a handsome majority, after some amendments had been rejected. But when, on the 24th, the petition to the King was reported, it was so obsequious, so disappointing to the friends of popular liberty, that Schuyler took fire, and offered amendments to almost every paragraph, in language more becoming the dignity of freemen. He moved to strike out of the fifth paragraph the sentence which spoke of the King as "an indulgent father"—that said there were "some measures pursued by the colonies that might be construed to their disadvantage," and which they condemned, and besought him to view them leniently, as "the honest though disorderly struggles for liberty, not the licentious efforts of independence." For these fawning words Schuyler proposed to substitute "And as we have too much reason to suspect that pains have been taken to induce your Majesty to think us impatient of constitutional government, we entreat you, Royal Sir, to believe that our commotions are honest struggles for maintaining our constitutional liberty, and not dictated by a desire for independence. Could your princely virtues, as easily as your powers, have been delegated to your servants, we had not, at this time, been reduced to the disagreeable necessity of disturbing your repose on an occasion which we sincerely lament." This was such a severe commentary on the conduct of the royal governors that the loyal assembly rejected it by a vote of fifteen to eight.

Colonel Schuyler then moved to strike out of the sixth paragraph the passage which spoke of the colonies having, as infants, "submitted hitherto, without repining, to the authority of the parent state," but now thought "themselves entitled to their birthright," which was "an equal participation of freedom with their fellow subjects in Great Britain," and to substitute these words: "Although your Majesty's American subjects have, in some instances, submitted to the power exercised by the parent state, they nevertheless conceive themselves entitled to an equal participation of freedom with their fellow subjects in Great Britain." This more manly and dignified mode of expression did not suit the Tory members, and this amendment was also rejected by a vote of fourteen to seven.

Unflinching in his determination, Colonel Schuyler immediately moved to strike out the parargraph in which they assured the King that they cheerfully acknowledged subordination to the Parliament, and wished "only to enjoy the rights of Englishmen, and to have that share of liberty, and those liberties secured to them, which they were entitled to," and to substitute the words, "Conscious of the incompetency of the colonial Legislatures to regulate the trade of the empire, we cheerfully acknowledge such a power in that august body [the Parliament] as is founded in expediency, and confined to the regulation of our external commerce, with a view to the general weal of all your Majesty's subjects, and in such manner as will leave to us, unimpaired, those rights which we hold by the immutable laws of nature, and the principles of the English constitution; but the exercise of powers incompatible with those rights, not justified by expediency, and destructive of English liberty, induces us," etc. This, also, was negatived by a vote of fifteen to eight.

Colonel Woodhull, Mr. Clinton, and Mr. De Witt, offered substitutes for paragraphs with the same desire to have the petition manly in tone, but they were all voted down.

At the afternoon session of the same day, the memorial to the House of Lords was considered, and Colonel Schuyler offered several amendments, so as to more distinctly enunciate the Whig view of the powers of Parliament, but they were negatived by a strict party vote. Amendments to the representation and remonstrance to the Commons, offered by Clinton, shared the same fate. Thus, in the course of a month, the political ideas considered by the Continental Congress were reviewed by the New York assembly.

These papers, expressive of the feelings of the majority of the representatives, but not of the people of the province, were ordered to be transmitted to Edmund Burke, the agent of the colony; and on the 3d of April the colonial assembly adjourned, never to meet again.

What now was to be done? The republicans of the province of New York, composing by far the greater portion of the inhabitants, labored under severe disabilities. Acting Governor Colden was a Loyalist, and his council held office by the King's will. The assembly, though chosen by the people, continued in existence only by the King's prerogative. They might be dissolved by the representative of the crown (the acting governor) at any moment. There was no legally constituted body to form a rallying point for the patriots as in Massachusetts, where there was an elective council and an annually elected assembly. In all the other colonies there was some nucleus of power around which the people might assemble, and claim to be heard with respect. But in New York they were thrown back upon their own resources, and nobly did they preserve their integrity and maintain their cause, in spite of every obstacle.

The whole continent was now moving in the direction of rebellion. The newspapers were filled with every species of writing which the occasion called forth—epigrams, parables, sonnets, dialogues, as well as grave essays; and the great subject was presented to the public mind in every conceivable form of literary expression, remarkable for point and terseness. The following is a fair specimen of the logic in rhyme which often appeared:

"Rudely forced to drink tea, Massachusetts in anger
Spills the tea on John Bull—John falls on to bang her;
Massachusetts, enraged, calls her neighbors to aid,
And give Master John a severe bastinade.
Now, good men of the law, pray who is in fault,
The one who begun, or resents the assault?"

The warlike demonstrations of the people had alarmed General Gage at Boston, and he commenced fortifying the Neck leading to the main at Roxbury. He also seized and conveyed to that city, quantities of gunpowder found in the neighboring villages, and employed stringent measures to prevent intercourse between the patriots in town and country. Fierce exasperation followed these impolitic measures. Hundreds of armed men assembled at Cambridge. At Charlestown the people took possession of the arsenal, after Gage had carried off the powder. At Portsmouth, New Hampshire, they captured the fort, and carried off the ammunition. At Newport, Rhode Island, the people seized the powder, and took possession of forty pieces of cannon at the entrance to the harbor. In Philadelphia, Annapolis, Williamsburg, Charleston, and Savannah, similar defensive measures were taken.

The excitement in New York was equally intense. Toward the close of the preceding December, the Liberty Boys were called to action by the seizure of arms and ammunition, which some of them had imported, and had consigned to Walter Franklin, a well known merchant. These were seized by order of the collector, because, as he alleged, of the want of cockets, or custom-house warrants, they having been in store several days without them. While they were on their way to the custom-house, some of the Sons of Liberty rallied and seized them, but before they could be concealed they were retaken by government officials and sent on board a man-of-war in the harbor.

Some days afterward a warning letter, directed to Collector Elliot, was thrown into the post-office, informing him that the arms would be called for when wanted. It concluded with these words :

"Do not slight this admonition, or treat it as a vain menace, for we have most solemnly sworn to effect it sooner or later, and you know our nation is implacable. We would not have you imagine that it is in the power of any set, either civil or military, to protect or shield you from our just revenge, which will be soon done, and in such a manner as not to be known until it is fatally experienced by you.

"FROM THE MOHAWK RIVER INDIANS."

This letter, with Elliot's answer, was posted at the Coffee House, and was generally disapproved, as the collector was a just and humane man. But that night a printed hand-bill, supposed (as well as the letter) to have been written by Lamb, was thrown into almost every house in the city. It was an exciting appeal to the people, urging them to resistance.

"In the name of heaven," said the appeal "throw off your suspicions; assemble together immediately, and go in a body to the collector; insist upon the arms being re-landed, and that he must see them forthcoming or abide the consequences. Delays are dangerous; there is no time to be lost. It is not a season to be mealy-mouthed or to mince matters; the times are precarious and perilous, and we do not know but the arms may be wanted to-morrow."

It was in this spirit that the republicans acted every where, and yet the British Parliament, blind to the best interests of the nation, persisted in their hostile attitude to the colonies. When that body assembled, in January, 1775, they presented a scene of great excitement. Dr. Franklin, and others in England, had given a wide circulation to the state papers put forth by the Continental Congress, and the English mind was already favorably influenced in behalf of the Americans. Pitt went on crutches into the House of Lords, from his retirement in the country, to cast the weight of his mighty influence into the scale of justice by action in that House. There he proposed conciliatory measures. They were rejected. Burke, Conway, and Hartley, all in turn, proposed similar measures. They were not only rejected, but the majority in Parliament struck another severe blow at the industry of New England, by prohibiting fishing on the Banks of Newfoundland, a business in which four hundred ships, two thousand shallops, and twenty thousand seamen were engaged. The ministry also attempted to sow dissensions among the Americans, by crippling the trade of the southern and middle colonies, but exempting New York, Delaware, and North Carolina from the oppression, these provinces having, of late, evinced the most loyalty. But the people of these colonies indignantly spurned the bait to win their allegiance, and the scheme for disunion signally failed. The continent was united more strongly than ever by the presence of common dangers and a perception of common interests ; and when the spring of 1775 opened, all hope of reconciliation between England and her American colonies had vanished. Relying upon the justness of their cause, and the favors of the Lord God Omnipotent, the republicans resolved to defy the fleets and armies of Great Britain with which they were menaced.

The flame of war was first lighted in the east. General Gage beheld with alarm the work of the people of Massachusetts, in collecting arms and ammunition. He was informed that some artillery was deposited at Salem, and in February he dispatched Lieutenant Colonel Leslie by water to Marblehead, to seize and carry them to Boston. The whole movement was made in secret. The troops landed at Marblehead on Sunday morning. An express carried the news of danger to the people of Salem. They were worshiping God in their churches. The congregations were immediately dismissed, and rallied around Colonel Timothy Pickering. Led by him, they opposed the British, who had then reached the draw-bridge, near the town. A compromise was effected, by which the troops were allowed to cross the bridge and immediately return, and they marched back without having produced bloodshed or secured their plunder. This ridiculous performance allowed Trumbull, the poet, to write a few weeks afterward:

"Through Salem straight, without delay,
The bold battalion took its way;
Marched over a bridge, in open sight
Of several Yankees armed for fight;
Then, without loss of time or men,
Veered round to Boston back again,
And found so well their projects thrive,
That every soul got back alive!"

But a more serious affair occured soon afterward, when an attempt of a similar character was made. On the 1st of April Gage had three thousand armed men under his command in Boston. He felt confident in his strength, and in the pride of that confidence he felt assured that he could easily repress insurrections and keep the people quiet. He did not like the accumulation of warlike stores in the hands of the people, which he was informed was going on in every direction. He knew full well what effect the boldness of the people's representatives would have upon their constituents—representatives who, in spite of his frowns, had met, ninety in number, and formed a provincial congress, with John Hancock at their head. They had repudiated royal authority; made provision for an army of twelve thousand men; solicited other colonies to follow their example, and augment the army to twenty thousand; and commisioned officers of experience in the French and Indian war to be the generals of the host.

When Gage reflected upon these movements he felt uneasy, notwithstanding his confidence in his balls and bayonets ; and towards midnight, on the 18th of April, he dispatched eight hundred men, under Lieutenant Colonel Smith and Major Pitcairn, to destroy military stores which the republicans had gathered at Concord, less than twenty miles from Boston. The expedition was conducted with the most perfect secrecy, yet vigilant eyes were upon the actors. Dr. Joseph Warren, one of the early martyrs of the Revolution, had been watching Gage's movements with sleepless vigilance. Early in the evening he became aware of the expedition, and as soon as the troops moved from the city, Paul Revere, by Warren's direction, crossed to Charlestown, and made his way toward Concord with all possible dispatch, to arouse the inhabitants and summon the minute-men to the field. The effort was effectual. The clangor of church bells, the roar of cannon, and the sharp crack of musketry, soon heard in all directions, aroused the country ; and when at dawn, on the morning of the 19th, Pitcairn, who led the advance, reached Lexington, a few miles from Concord, he found seventy determined men drawn up on the village green to oppose him. With bitter scorn, as he rode forward, he called them "Rebels !" He shouted "Disperse ! disperse ! Lay down your arms and disperse, ye rebels !" They stood firm, and he ordered his men to fire. Then the first blood of the Revolution flowed. Seven citizens were killed, and several were wounded. The survivors returned a feeble fire, and then, by order of their leader, they dispersed. "Oh what a glorious morning is this !" cried Samuel Adams, who, with John Hancock, had been attainted by royal decree as arch-rebels, and had slept that night in Lexington.

It was indeed a glorious morning. The Source of Day arose in splendor an hour after the delicate grass on the green at Lexington had been sprinkled with the blood of martyrs, and typified the ascension of the Sun of Liberty, which on that day arose and shed its vivifying rays over the continent. While the British troops, spurred on by a sense of gathering danger, were shedding more blood at Concord, in a vain endeavor to execute their master's orders, or were making an inglorious retreat towards Boston, terribly smitten by the exasperated people on every hand, intelligence of the massacre was speeding over the land as fast as fleet horses could bear the messengers; and with one impulse the colonists grasped their weapons and prepared for the inevitable struggle. Deliberation's voice was hushed, and the strong right arm was regarded as the asserter of the people's rights henceforward. The sword was now drawn, and the scabbard was cast away. From the Penobscot to the St. Mary—from the capes of the Atlantic coast to the most shaded valley beyond the Alleghanies where the smoke of the pioneer's camp fires were seen, the sentiment "LIBERTY OR DEATH!" which had just been uttered by the lips of Patrick Henry, vibrated upon the strings of every heart in tune with the song of the angels, over the plains of Bethlehem, when the Prince of Peace was born.

## CHAPTER XVIII.

We have seen how the republicans failed in their efforts, in the New York Assembly, to procure the appointment of delegates to the second Continental Congress, to be convened at Philadelphia in May. Nothing was left for them to do but to appeal to the people. The General Committee of sixty members, many of them of the loyal majority in the assembly, yielding to the pressure of popular sentiment, called a meeting of the freeholders and freemen of the city at the Exchange, to take into consideration the election of delegates to a convention of representatives from such of the counties of the province as should adopt the measure, the sole object of such convention being the choice of proper persons to represent the colony in the Continental Congress.

This movement was opposed by the loyalists as disrespectful to the assembly, who had refused to appoint delegates; but the people were now driven to a point where respect for authorities whose views were not in consonance with the spirit of liberty and free discussion, was almost unknown. They accordingly assembled in great numbers around the Liberty Pole on the 6th, bearing a banner, inscribed, "Constitutional Liberty," and marched in procession to the Exchange. The loyalists soon afterward appeared there in considerable numbers, headed by members of the council and the assembly, with officers of the army and navy, expecting, no doubt, to overawe the republicans. At first there was confusion. This soon subsided, and the meeting proceeded with calmness and dignity to nominate eleven persons to represent the city in a provincial convention to be held in New York on the 20th, who were to be instructed to choose delegates to the Continental Congress.

On the following day the chairman of the Committee of Sixty gave notice of the proposed convention on the 20th to the chairmen of the committees of correspondence in the different counties, advising them to choose delegates to the same. There was a prompt response. In some of the counties the deputies were chosen by the committees of correspondence; in others by a convention of committees chosen in different parts of the county; in others the several towns chose each a delegate; in Orange county the freeholders made the choice, as in the election of assemblymen; and in the city of New York they were chosen by ward meetings. All of these produced at the convention a certificate of their election from proper authorities.

The convention assembled at the Exchange, in New York, on the 20th, and consisted of forty-two members.* Colonel Schuyler was at the head of the delegation from Albany, and took a leading part in the convention. Philip

* These were for the *City and County of New York*—Philip Livingston, John Alsop, James Duane, John Jay, Leonard Lispenard, Francis Lewis, Abraham Walton, Isaac Roosevelt, Alexander M'Dougall, and Abraham Brasher. For the *City and County of Albany*—Philip Schuyler, Abraham Tenbroeck, and Abraham Yates, jr. For *Ulster County*—Charles Dewitt, George Clinton, and Levi Paulding. For *Orange County*—A. Hawkes Hay, Henry Wisner, John Herring, Peter Clowes, Israel Seeley. For *Westchester County*—Lewis Morris, John Thomas, Robert Graham, Philip Van Courtlandt, Samuel Drake, Stephen Ward. For *Duchess County*—Morris Graham, Robert R. Livingston, jr., Egbert Benson. For *Kings County*—Simon Boerum, Richard Stillwell, Theodorus Polhemus, Denice Denice, John Vanderbilt. For *Suffolk County*—William Floyd, Nathaniel Woodhull, Phineas Farring, Thomas Treadwell, John Sloss Hobart. For *Newtown and Flushing*—Jacob Blackwell, John Talman.

Livingston was chosen president of the convention, and John M'Kesson secretary. This was the first provincial convention in New York—the first positive expression of the doctrine of popular sovereignty in that province. They remained in session three days, and chose for delegates to the Continental Congress Philip Livingston, James Duane, John Alsop, John Jay, Simon Boerum, William Floyd, Henry Wisner, Philip Schuyler, George Clinton, Lewis Morris, Francis Lewis, and Robert R. Livingston, to whom were given full power, "or any five of them, to meet the delegates from other colonies, and to concert and determine upon such measures as shall be judged most effectual for the preservation and reëstablishment of American rights and privileges, and for the restoration of harmony between Great Britain and her colonies."

While this convention was in session intelligence of the bloodshed at Lexington was on its way, but did not reach New York until the day after the adjournment. It was then only a vague rumor, but, notwithstanding it was the Sabbath, the Sons of Liberty got together, and speedily unloaded two vessels that were about to sail for Boston with flour for the British troops. Towards evening they secured a large quantity of the public arms, took possession of the City Hall, and placed a guard of one hundred men at its door, and another hundred at the powder magazine, to keep these munitions of war for the use of the people.

On Monday, the 24th, Colonel Schuyler left for Albany in a sloop. Authentic intelligence from Boston had not yet reached New York. It came the following day, at two o'clock in the afternoon. Expresses were immediately sent up the Hudson by a sloop about to sail with a fair wind. Calms succeeded, and it was Friday, the 28th, before the confirmed intelligence reached the committee of correspondence at Albany, and was spread by swift couriers over the Hudson and Mohawk vallies.

Colonel Schuyler was at his seat at Saratoga, when, late on Saturday, the news reached him. That evening he wrote as follows to his friend John Cruger, chairman of the assembly's committee of correspondence, who was preparing for a voyage to England on account of ill-health:

"Of course long ere this you have received the news from Boston. My heart bleeds as I view the horrors of civil war, but we have only left us the choice between such evils and slavery. For myself, I can say with Semprenius:

'Heavens! can a Roman Senate long debate
Which of the two to choose, slavery or death!
No; let us arise at once,' etc.

for we should be unworthy of our ancestors if we should tamely submit to an insolent and wicked ministry, and supinely wait for a gracious answer to a petition to the King, of which, as a member of the assembly who sent it, I am ashamed. I know there are difficulties in the way. The loyal and the timid in this province are many, yet I believe that when the question is fairly put, as it is really so put by this massacre in Massachusetts Bay, whether we shall be ruled by a military despotism, or fight for right and freedom? the great majority of the people will choose the latter. For my own part, much as I love peace—much as I love my domestic happiness and repose, and desire to see my countrymen enjoying the blessings flowing from undisturbed industry, I would rather see all these scattered to the winds for a time, and the sword of desolation go over the land, than to recede one line from the just and righteous position we have taken as freeborn subjects of Great Britain.

"I beg you, my dear sir, if your health shall permit when you arrive in England, to use all your influence there to convince the people and the rulers that we were never more determined to contend for our rights than at this moment—that we consider ourselves not *aggressors*, but *defenders*—and that he who believes that our late assembly truly represented the feelings and wishes of our people is greatly deceived. I have watched the course of the political currents for many months with great anxiety, and have been, for more than a year, fully convinced that unless Great Britain should be more just and wise than in times past, war was inevitable. It is now actually begun; and in the spirit of Joshua I say, I care not what others may do, 'as for me and my house, we will serve our country."

On the following day Colonel Schuyler, as usual, attended public worship. The news from the east had already spread over the neighborhood.

"I well remember," records an eye-witness, "notwithstanding my youth, the impressive manner with which, in my hearing, my father told my uncle that blood had been shed at Lexington! The startling intelligence spread like wild-fire among the congregation. The preacher's voice was listened to with very little attention. After the morning discourse was finished and the people were dismissed, we gathered about General Philip Schuyler for further information. He was the oracle of our neighborhood. We looked up to him with a feeling of respect and affection. His popularity was unbounded; his views upon all subjects were considered sound, and his anticipations almost prophetic. On this occasion he confirmed the intelligence already received, and expressed his belief that an important crisis had arrived which must for ever separate us from the parent state."*

The intelligence from the east came at a moment when the republicans of New York were powerfully stirred by local events. Sears, the great leader of the Liberty Boys, had been arrested for seditious words, because he had advised the people at a public meeting to arm themselves and prepare for conflict. He refused to give bail, and was on his way to prison, when his political friends took him from the officers and bore him in triumph through the town, preceded by a band of music and a banner. The royal government was powerless. The acting governor of the province and the mayor of the city had lost all control, coercive or persuasive. The Liberty Boys, with the emboldened Sears at their head, had closed the custom-house and laid an embargo upon vessels in the harbor.

All power was now in the hands of the people. A new committee of one hundred citizens were chosen in place of the Committee of Sixty, and it was resolved that a provincial congress ought speedily to be assembled, who should

* *The Sexagenary, or Reminiscences of the American Revolution*, page 20.

take the government into their own hands, provide for all contingencies that might arise, and prepare the province for defense against hostile invasion.

A circular letter was sent to the several county committees, proposing the election of deputies to a provincial congress to be held in the city of New York, its sessions to commence on the 21st of May. An address was drawn up to the Lord Mayor and common council of London, explanatory of the views of the republicans in America, setting forth their rights, and expressing their determination to maintain them. A military association was formed, under Samuel Broome ; and a paper, in the form of a league, to be signed by the people at large, was prepared, in which, after declaring their conviction of the necessity of union, they resolved "in the most solemn manner never to become slaves, and to associate, under all the ties of religion, honor, and love to their country, to adopt and endeavor to carry into execution whatever measures may be recommended by the Continental Congress, or resolved upon by the provincial convention, for the purpose of preserving their constitution and opposing the execution of the several arbitrary and oppressive acts of the British Parliament, until a reconciliation between Great Britain and America, on constitutional principles, which is most ardently desired, can be obtained."

Elections were speedily held throughout the province, in a manner nearly the same as in the preceding canvass and on Tuesday, the 23d day of May, about seventy of eighty-one delegates elected assembled at the Exchange, in New York, and organized a provincial congress by choosing Peter Van Brugh Livingston for president, Volkert P. Douw vice-president, and John M'Kesson and Robert Benson secretaries.

While the people of New York were thus moving in

the opening scene of the drama of the Revolution, events of the greatest moment had taken place elsewhere, having the same tendency. Even before the tragedies at Lexington and Concord, Patrick Henry had electrified the Virginia Assembly at Richmond with that great speech whose peroration was "*Give me liberty, or give me death!*" And before his prophecy, that "the next gale that sweeps from the north will bring to our ears the clash of resounding arms!" was fulfilled, he had marched upon Williamsburg, the residence of the royal governor, and compelled him to make full restitution for powder belonging to the province, which had been secretly conveyed on board a British man-of-war lying in the York river. Already the patriots of Charleston and Savannah had seized the arms and ammunition of their respective provinces, and made their governors tremble for their personal safety; and as the intelligence of bloodshed went from colony to colony, steps were taken for the assembling of provincial congresses and abolishing royal rule. Before the middle of June, when the first real *battle* of the Revolution was fought on Breed's Hill, the inhabitants of all the colonies had virtually if not actually repudiated royal authority, and were controlled by that only just government which is based upon a righteous popular will.

Some aggressive enterprises were also undertaken by the republicans, the most important of which occurred in the province of New York, but not by its citizens.

"It has been proposed to us," wrote Joseph Warren, in behalf of the Massachusetts Committee of Safety, to the committee of New York, on the 30th of April, "to take possession of the fortress at Ticonderoga. We have a just sense of the importance of that fortification, and the usefulness of those fine cannon, mortars, and field-pieces which are there; but we would not, even upon this emergency, infringe upon the rights of our sister colony, New York. But we have desired the gentleman who carries this letter to represent the matter to you, that you may give such orders as are agreeable to you."

The proposition alluded to by Warren was made by Benedict Arnold, a druggist and bookseller, of New Haven, Connecticut, and captain of one of the train-bands of that town. On hearing of the skirmish at Lexington, he had hastened to Cambridge with his company of volunteers. Before he left, a plan had been crudely formed by members of the Connecticut assembly, to attempt the surprise of the garrison and the capture of the fort at Ticonderoga, if on inquiry it should be deemed expedient. Of this Arnold had doubtless heard.

While the committee at Cambridge were waiting for an answer from New York, the Connecticut people had moved. One thousand dollars were advanced from the colonial treasury to defray the expenses of the expedition; not, however, by the open sanction of the assembly, but by its tacit consent. A committee of two persons was appointed to proceed to the frontier towns, to make inquiries and act as circumstances should dictate. They were joined by a few more in Connecticut. On their consulting Colonels Easton and Brown, at Pittsfield, in Western Massachusetts, these officers both agreed to join in the enterprise, and the latter immediately enlisted about forty of his regiment as volunteers. The whole party then went on to Bennington, the home of Ethan Allen, whose influence in the New Hampshire Grants was almost boundless. The Green Mountain Boys, as the train-bands were named, were ready to obey his call at a moment's warning. The enterprise suited Allen's nature and aspirations, and he joined the expedition with a strong corps. At twilight, on the 7th of May, the whole party halted at Castleton and held a council of war. Colonel Allen was appointed commander-in-chief, Colonel Easton his lieutenant, and Colonel Seth Warner, of the Green Mountain Boys, the third in command.

Arnold, meanwhile, under the sanction of the Massachusetts committee and the consent of the Massachusetts Provincial Congress, had also been forming an expedition for the same purpose, and had procured for himself the chief command of it. He was commisioned a colonel by the Provincial Congress, furnished with means, and authorized to raise, in western Massachusetts, not more than four hundred men for the expedition. On reaching Stockbridge he was disappointed by finding another expedition already in the field. Engaging a few followers he hastened onward and joined the others at Castleton. Because of his commission, he claimed the right to chief command. His pretensions were disallowed. The Green Mountain Boys declared that they would shoulder their muskets and march home before they would follow any other man than Colonel Allen.

Arnold yielded, but with a bad grace. He joined the expedition as a volunteer, retaining his commission but having no command. With hasty steps they pressed forward, for they feared information of their movement might reach the fort. On the evening of the 9th of May they were on the shores of Lake Champlain, opposite the fortress ; and at dawn the next morning the officers and eighty-three men were upon the beach at Ticonderoga, sheltered by the bluff on which stood the old grenadier's battery built by the French. They dared not wait for the arrival of the remainder of their comrades, for daylight might be fatal to the enterprise.

In the dim light of the early morning, Colonel Allen, with Arnold at his side, followed the lead of a lad who well knew the intricacies of the fort, and went stealthily up the slope to the sally-port. The sentinel then snapped his fusee, and fled along the covered way to alarm the garrison. The invaders followed him closely, and were led by the frightened fugitive directly to the parade within. Arraying themselves in proper order, the New Englanders wakened the sleeping garrison with a tremendous shout, while the gallant leader of the Green Mountain Boys ascended a staircase to the chamber of Captain De Laplace, the commander, and beating the door with the handle of his heavy sword, he cried out, with stentorian voice, "I demand a surrender!"

De Laplace started from his bed, followed by his trembling wife, and opening the door saw and recognized Allen. "Your errand?" he boldly asked the intruder. Pointing to his men, Allen answered, "I order you to surrender immediately!" "By what authority do *you* demand it?" asked the indignant De Laplace. "The Great Jehovah and the Continental Congress," said Allen, with terrible emphasis, at the same time flourishing his broadsword over the head of the now terrified commander, and ordering him to be silent. Although the Continental Congress did not commence its session until several hours after this peremptory demand, and De Laplace doubted Allen's divine authority, while he knew that George was King "by the grace of God," he took counsel of necessity and surrendered to the republicans the fortress and its dependencies, and a large quantity of articles precisely such as the gathering armies of patriots needed. No less than one hundred and twenty iron cannon, fifty swivels, two mortars, a howitzer, a cohorn, a large quantity of ammunition and other stores, and a warehouse full of naval munitions, and abundant provisions, were the spoils of victory. Forty-eight men, women, and children, were sent prisoners of war to Hartford, in Connecticut.

Soon after the surrender was effected, Colonel Warner arrived with the remainder of the expedition, and on the 12th he took possession of Crown Point. Thus a handful of determined men, inexperienced in the art of war, accomplished in the space of three days what expedition after expedition had failed to do in the wars with the French; and at the outset of the Revolution the Republicans had the advantage of the possession of Lake Champlain and the key to Canada.

Arnold now again claimed a right to chief command, but his pretensions were resisted as before. The semi-official committee from Connecticut, having the expedition in charge, formally installed Colonel Allen commander-in-chief of Ticonderoga and its dependencies, and authorized him to remain as such until he should receive further orders from the Connecticut Assembly or the Continental Congress. Arnold reluctantly yielded, sent a protest to the Provincial Congress of Massachusetts, from whom he had received his commission, and then went down the lake in command of a sort of amphibious expedition. We shall meet him frequently hereafter.

The second Continental Congress assembled in Carpenter's Hall on Wednesday, the 10th of May, 1775, when Peyton Randolph was unanimously chosen president, and Charles Thomson secretary. It was agreed that its sessions should be secret. On the 13th there was a representation present from all of the thirteen provinces.

Grave questions arose when the congress had assembled and were prepared for business. Whom did they represent? and what might they do? According to the terms of their appointment, this body was no more a legislative one than the congress of 1774. It was composed of simple committees, met to consult on measures for the public good. No executive or even legislative powers had been delegated to any of these committees, and yet, by the common consent of the continent they were regarded as a governmental power. The nation, not yet crystallyzed into a confederacy, was menaced with imminent danger. The sovereign of the realm to which they belonged had declared them rebels. Clashing interests, geographical divisions, and sectional habits, made them an apparently heterogeneous people, difficult to be brought into social and political affinity.

Shall we confederate? Shall we legislate as well as deliberate? Shall we attempt the exercise of executive power? These were serious questions that arose in the minds of the deputies. They were soon answered by the faith of the people. The great body of the inhabitants of the colonies regarded the General Congress as the arbiter and director of public affairs for the whole continent in sympathy. The Provincial Congress of Massachusetts expressed this, when, seven days before the Continental Congress met, they prepared a communication to that body, saying: "The sudden exigency of our public affairs precluded the possibility of *waiting for your directions* in these important measures;" [raising and providing an army] and by asking for the direction and assistance of congress, and suggesting that an American army should be forthwith raised.

Colonel Schuyler left Albany for Philadelphia on the 9th of May, bearing to the committee at New York a letter from that of his own county, asking advice concerning the supplying with provisions troops from Connecticut in their expected attack upon Ticonderoga. He reached Philadelphia on the 15th, and on the same day took his seat in congress with his colleagues. Franklin, convinced that reconciliation with Great Britain was next to impossible, had lately returned home, and was now in the congress with Samuel and John Adams, of Massachusetts, Jay and Livingston, of New York, Washington, Henry, and Lee, of Virginia, Rutledge, of South Carolina, and almost fifty other patriots of less note—the best men to be found in the colonies.

The congress, somewhat doubtful of their powers, moved cautiously. At the very beginning of this session a question of vital importance was propounded by the New York committee for their solution. Intelligence had arrived that British troops were about to be landed in that city to quiet the rebellion, in imitation of the armed occupancy of Boston the year before. An address had been presented to Lieutenant Governor Colden, which, after commenting upon passing events, requested him to use his influence with General Gage, to prohibit the landing of such troops as had been ordered to that station. Colden assured them that no troops were expected, and suggested that the rumor was put in circulation to justify the calling in of rebel troops from Connecticut, who had collected under Wooster, and were hovering upon the eastern borders of New York. This assurance was false, for troops soon arrived at Sandy Hook but were ordered to Boston.

Meanwhile the New York committee asked the advice of the congress as to their course in the event of the troops attempting to land. With "scrupulous timidity," as Edmund Burke said, the congress recommended the colony of New York to act on the defensive for the present, "so long as may be consistent with their safety and security; that the troops be permitted to remain in the barracks so long as they behave peaceably and quietly, but that they be not suffered to erect fortifications, or take any steps for cutting off the communication between the town and country; and that if they commit hostilities or invade private property the inhabitants should defend themselves and their property, and repel force by force; that the warlike stores be removed from the town; that places of retreat, in case of necessity, be provided for the women and children of New York; and that a sufficient number of men be embodied and kept in constant readiness for protecting the inhabitants from insult and injury."*

This course was doubtless thought to be expedient, but the advice embarrassed the action of the Provincial Congress of New York, who assembled a week later. It recognized the existing royal government in the province, with all its machinery of civil, military, and naval power. It also embarrassed the Continental Congress, for, three days afterward, intelligence reached them of the capture of Ticonderoga and Crown Point. What should be done? They had already resolved to send a humble petition to the King, and make overtures for a reconciliation. They had advised New York to submit conditionally to royal authority, but here was an overt act of rebellion—an actual beginning of offensive war. Must they disclaim it and lose the advantage gained?

An invasion of Canada had been thought of, and now the way for success seemed open. But, for a moment, the congress shrunk from the responsibility, and advised the committees of New York and Albany to remove the spoils taken at Ticonderoga to the head of Lake George, to prevent them from being recaptured by a force from Canada; and that "an exact inventory be taken of all

* Journals of Congress, May 5, 1775.

such cannon and stores, in order that they may be safely returned when the restoration of the former harmony between Great Britain and the colonies, so ardently wished for by the latter, shall render it prudent and consistent with the overruling law of self-preservation."*

On the 15th, the congress appointed Colonel Washington, Samuel Adams, and Thomas Lynch, a committee to consider what posts were necessary to occupy in the colony of New York, and agreed that on the following day the congress should "resolve itself into a committee of the whole to take into consideration the state of America." The latter topic occupied the attention of that august body for many days. While a few among them desired political independence, the greater proportion only wished for reconciliation, for their attachment to *home*, as England was still called, was almost as strong as their love of liberty and sense of oppression. But every day brought them fresh reasons for believing a reconciliation to be doubtful, and every day they felt the necessity more and more of preparing for a conflict of arms. Taking counsel of prudence, they recommended vigorous preparations for war, while holding out to the mother country, with the hand of true affection, the olive branch of peace.

The Provincial Congress of New York met on the 22d of May. The political complexion of that body disappointed the people. The old leaven of Toryism that prevailed in the late colonial assembly was evidently a power in the new conclave. It appeared early in several minor acts, but most decidedly when John Morin Scott moved that as the colony of New York had not given such public testimonials of its cordial accession to the confederacy of the colonies as others had done, by approving of the acts

* Journals of Congress, May 18, 1775.

of the Continental Congress of 1774, "this congress do fully approve of the proceedings of said congress."* This motion met with decided opposition, and elicted a warm debate. It was this debate, on a subject where there could not be a diversity of sentiment among true patriots, that alarmed the republicans.

Doubtless during the few years preceding the kindling of the Revolution, and the earlier period of the contest, there were more active and influential friends of the crown in New York than in any other province. This was owing in part to its geographical and commercial position, but especially to the fact that there were several landed proprietors and wealthy families who naturally felt averse to a change in government, being sensible of greater security for their property under the existing state of things. These were loyal—not all, but a greater portion of them. The exposed situation of the province below the Highlands to attacks from the naval forces of Great Britain was another inducement to be cautious not to offend the government, if not to be actually friendly to the crown. Again, Sir William Johnson and his family, who had unbounded influence over the Indians in the Mohawk region and the interests of many settlers, were naturally loyalists, and for a long time after hostilities had commenced, Toryism strongly prevailed among the inhabitants west of Albany. It was less, probably, than it would have been had Sir William lived to bear rule there when the dispute resulted in blows. He died suddenly at Johnson Hall, in July, 1774, and the mantle of office, as Indian agent, fell upon his son-in-law and nephew, Guy Johnson, whose loyalty was equal to that of Sir William.

Such are some of the reasons why New York, in her

* Journals of the Provincial Congress, May 25, 1774.

representative assembly, moved so tardily to the music of rebellion when the war broke out. She has been taunted for that tardiness, but unjustly. The masses of her people were republican in sentiment from the beginning; and when, finally, Toryism was fairly crushed out of her provincial congress by the popular pressure, no state was more practically patriotic. With a population of only a little more than one hundred and sixty thousand, of whom thirty-two thousand five hundred were liable to do militia duty, New York furnished almost eighteen thousand sturdy soldiers for the Continental Army—over three thousand more than its quota called for by the Continental Congress.

The members of the Provincial Congress of New York subscribed to and recommended the *American Association*, organized by the first congress, and adopted measures to enforce its provisions. They also took into consideration the means for defense, and were earliest, on the motion of Gouverneur Morris, in recommending an emission of paper money by the General Congress for the whole continent, thus recognizing the confederation as complete and the congress as the supreme legislature. They also addressed a circular letter to the inhabitants of Canada, (translated into French by Paul Du Simitiere,) calling upon them to join those of their sister colonies in defense of their liberties and the rights of man.

The Continental Congress also issued an address to the inhabitants of Canada, for the same purpose, at the close of May. They had already, by a series of resolves, based upon a report of the committee of which Washington was chairman, recommended the colony of New York to proceed immediately to erect fortifications at the upper end of York Island and in the Hudson Highlands; to arm and train the militia of the province, that they might be ready to act at a moment's warning; recommended that troops be enlisted to serve during the remainder of the year; and in every way to persevere the more vigorously in preparing for their defense, as it was very uncertain whether the earnest endeavors of the congress to accommodate the unhappy differences between Great Britain and the colonies, by conciliatory measures, would be successful.*

The Provincial Congress of New York acted promptly on these recommendations; at the same time they evinced a most earnest desire for reconciliation. They appointed committees to view the various points near New York and on the Hudson thought to be eligible for fortifications, and they directed another committee to draft a plan for honorable reconciliation with Great Britain, in a spirit of mutual concession. They agreed that Colonel Philip Schuyler was the most suitable person in the colony to be recommended to the Continental Congress as a major general, and Richard Montgomery, Esq., as brigadier general; and they wrote to their representatives in that Congress, saying: "We pray you to use every effort for the compromising of this unnatural quarrel between the parent and child, and, if such terms as you may think best shall not be complied with, earnestly to labor, that at least some terms may be held up, whereby a treaty shall be set on foot to restore peace and harmony to our country, and spare the further effusion of human blood."

"For many reasons," wrote Councillor Smith to Colonel Schuyler, "I think the present the moment in which the greatest blessings may be secured to our country. The last hope of the ministry is to divide us. This is become impossible. We are then at the eve of a change of men, or a change of measures by the same men. The first is ruin to the ministers. They have no way of preventing it but by a change of measures. Could you wish for a better opportunity to negotiate? You

* Journals of Congress, May 25, 1775.

have the ball at your feet. For heaven's sake don't slip so fair a prospect of gaining what you run the greatest risk of losing upon a change ot men. I heard of Dr. Franklin's arrival with extreme anguish. He has connected himself with Lord Chatham. I dread this event and his influence upon your councils, if he aims only, as the great orator, I fear, does, at the destruction of the favorites and the support of our cause only as the instrument to effect it. If that lord was first minister, have you reason to believe that he means more than to exempt you from internal taxation?"

After suggesting what he deemed a feasible plan for reconciliation, embracing the idea of an American Parliament restricted in its operations to making revenue provisions, the writer continued:

"If something of this kind is not the result of your present councils, we shall purchase our redemption with blood and misery, for every nerve of administration will be strained to stand another year at least. And though I think we shall be free at last, yet why not now? Why not immediately? Why raise a military spirit that may furnish unmanageable adventurers on this side of the water unfriendly to a province in which you and I have something to lose. * * * For God's sake be slow. Guard against those who are interested in pushing matters to extremities for their personal safety or private interests. There may be among you those who look for salvation from the number of the obnoxious, as well as for elevation from a change of ministry. Your country wants nothing but a change of measures. I trust myself to your prudence and friendship in this distressing, critical hour. I commend you to the Fountain of Light."*

* Autograph letter, May 16, 1775.

## CHAPTER XIX.

WHILE the general Congress, notwithstanding their desire for reconciliation, was prudently moving on with vigor in preparations for war, the popular assemblies in all the provinces and the great mass of the people were engaged in like preparations. A deceptive token of peace had been held out by the British ministry. To the astonishment of all parties in Parliament, Lord North, in March, offered what he called a Conciliatory Bill for their consideration. It provided that when the proper authorities in any colony should offer, besides maintaining its own civil government, to raise a certain revenue and place it at the disposition of Parliament, it would be proper to forbear imposing any tax on that colony except for the regulation of commerce. The minister found himself immediately exposed to a cross-fire. The ministerial party opposed his proposition because it was conciliatory, and the opposition were dissatisfied with it because it proposed to abate but a single grievance, and was not specific.

When a copy of North's bill was laid before the Congress, on the 26th of May, the significant commentary upon it was a resolution that the colonies should be "immediately put in a state of defense." The proposition to petition the King was vehemently opposed as an imbecile and temporizing measure, calculated to embarrass the proceedings of Congress and to give the ministry time to send fleets and armies while the Americans were vainly waiting to hear words of royal clemency.

There was a decided war spirit in the general Congress. Still they were cautious. Notwithstanding the way for the conquest of Canada was fairly opened, and Ethan Allen and Benedict Arnold were calling for aid to make a successful invasion of that province, the Congress, hoping to gain a greater victory by making the Canadians their allies, sent a loving address to them, and resolved, on the 1st of June, "that no expedition or incursion ought to be undertaken or made by any colony or body of colonists against or into Canada."

But it was difficult to restrain the people. The war spirit was abroad. The patience of supplication was exhausted. Already an army was in the field. When intelligence of the bloodshed at Lexington and Concord went from lip to lip throughout New England, the inhabitants rushed toward Boston from almost every town within fifty miles of that city. Within two days at least twenty thousand men, armed and unarmed, were gathered in that neighborhood. They came also from Connecticut, Rhode Island, and New Hampshire. The veteran Putnam left his plow in the furrow and hastened to Cambridge. His companion-in-arms in the old French war, Captain Stark, soon joined him there; and Gridley and others, who had shared with him the privations and honors of earlier wars, were ready for action. Artemas Ward was appointed by the Massachusetts Committee of Safety commander-in-chief of the motley army so suddenly assembled, and Richard Gridley was made chief engineer. With a determined spirit they commenced piling up fortifications to imprison the British army upon the Boston peninsula. Day by day the position of that army became more and more perilous, notwithstanding a large reinforcement arrived at the close of May, under three experienced generals—Howe (brother of the loved commander whose remains Captain Schuyler bore from Lake George to Albany for burial), Clinton, and Burgoyne. Twelve thousand armed men were on that peninsula at the beginning of June; and in the harbor and surrounding waters were several full-armed ships under Admiral Graves.

Gage felt strong as he looked upon his well-appointed battalions, and he determined to march out and scatter the earthworks of the rebels and their undisciplined host to the winds. On the 10th of June he proclaimed all Americans in arms to be rebels and traitors, and offered a free pardon to all who should return to their allegiance, except those arch offenders, John Hancock and Samuel Adams, whom he intended to send to England to be hanged. The former was then the president of the Continental Congress, and the latter was the most active and determined spirit in that body.

Apprised of the intentions of Gage to send out an invading force, the patriots prepared to meet him. During the brief darkness of a short June night they cast up intrenchments upon Breed's Hill, overlooking Charlestown and menacing Boston. The British generals could hardly credit the testimony of their senses in the morning when this apparition appeared. Delay would now be dangerous, and on the morning of the 17th of June many boats filled with British soldiers crossed the narrow waters between Boston and the Charlestown peninsula. It was a hot, sultry day, and the slopes of Breed's Hill seemed to glow with flame when the scarlet uniforms of the British soldiers were displayed upon them, and heavy platoons were moving slowly up to attack the redoubt, within which lay fifteen hundred provincials. In full view of the anxious, streaming eyes of friends who covered roofs and balconies in Boston, the first real battle of the Revolution was then fought, desperately and courageously by both parties. Breed's Hill was strewn with the slain invaders, while the Americans yet held the redoubt. But their scanty ammunition soon failed, and they were compelled to retreat. In the battle they had lost but few men, but at the moment of retreat one of the noblest of them fell. It was Dr. Joseph Warren, just appointed a major-general, but fighting gallantly as a volunteer under Colonel Prescott, the commander of the redoubt. Near the spot where he fell, and within the lines of the little fortress so nobly defended, the countrymen of Warren have raised a tall granite shaft commemorative of the gallant deeds of himself and his compatriots.

Two days before this conflict — a conflict in which neither party could claim a victory—a conflict known as the Battle of Bunker's Hill,* the Continental Congress, acting upon the sentiment in their petition to the King—"We have counted the cost of this contest, and find nothing so dreadful as voluntary slavery"—had not only voted to raise an army of twenty thousand men, but had adopted the incongruous one before Boston as a Continental Army, and appointed GEORGE WASHINGTON commander-in-chief of "all the forces raised or to be raised for the defense of the colonies." Artemas Ward, then in command of the army, with his headquarters at Cambridge; Charles Lee, a restless adventurer and experienced soldier; Philip Schuyler, who had, a few days before, been placed on a committee with Washington to prepare rules and regulations for the government of the army; and Israel Putnam, a vet-

* General Ward ordered Colonel Prescott to fortify Bunker's Hill, lying a short distance back of Breed's Hill. The expedition for the purpose proceeded in the darkness, and by mistake fortified Breed's Hill, nearer Boston.

eran of the French and Indian wars, were appointed major-generals, and composed the principals of Washington's staff. Seth Pomeroy, David Wooster, and Joseph Spencer, of Connecticut; Richard Montgomery, of New York; William Heath and John Thomas, of Massachusetts; John Sullivan, of New Hampshire; and Nathaniel Greene, of Rhode Island, were appointed brigadier-generals. Horatio Gates, formerly an officer in the British army, but then a resident of Virginia, was appointed adjutant general.

Having made provision for an army and its regulations, the next care of the Congress was to provide the "sinews of war"—money. The requisite amount could not be obtained in specie, so they acted upon the suggestion of the New York Provincial Congress, and on the 22d of June agreed to issue a sum not exceeding two millions of dollars in bills of credit. A month later another million was authorized; and emissions were made from time to time, as necessity demanded, until no less than two hundred millions of dollars, known as continental money, were issued. Much of this was never redeemed, and the bills were utterly worthless after the year 1781. They are now curious relics in the cabinets of collectors.

Washington left Philadelphia for Cambridge on the morning of the 21st of June, accompanied by Generals Lee and Schuyler, and chosen members of his military family. A brilliant civic and military cavalcade, composed of at least two thousand citizens, accompanied them several miles, and a corps of light-horse escorted them all the way to New York. When they approached Trenton they were met by a courier riding in hot haste for Philadelphia, to lay before Congress dispatches concerning the battle on Breed's Hill, and he relieved the mind of the commander-in-chief of a great burden of uncertainty when he informed him that the militia (on whom was to be his chief reliance,) behaved nobly in the conflict. "Then the liberties of the country are safe!" Washington exclaimed.

At New Brunswick General Schuyler addressed the following letter to the president of the New York Provincial Congress:

> "SIR: General Washington, with his retinue, is now here, and proposes to be at Newark by nine to-morrow morning. The situation of the men-of-war at New York (we are informed) is such as to make it necessary that some precaution should be taken in crossing Hudson's river, and he would take it as a favor if some gentlemen of your body would meet him to-morrow at Newark, as the advice you may then give him will determine whether he will continue his proposed route or not."

The Provincial Congress responded by appointing four of their number (one of whom was General Montgomery) to meet the commander-in-chief and suite at Newark. Peculiar circumstances produced perplexity. The Congress and the municipal authorities of New York city were placed in an awkward dilemma. Simultaneons with the approach of Washington, the republican general, came Tryon, the royal governor, on his return from England. He had just arrived at Sandy Hook. What must be done? To avoid offense honors must be given to both, and yet, as public officers, the functions of the two men were severely antagonistic, and their respective political friends were fiercely hostile. Only two days before, a small party of the Sons of Liberty, led by Marinus Willet, had confronted an Irish battalion, under Major Moncrief, as it evacuated Fort George and was marching, with some boxes of arms in wagons, to embark for Boston. The republicans seized the arms, conveyed them back to the fort, and took possession of that deserted post. On the same day the Congress had received official intelligence of the battle on Breed's Hill, and now the respective representatives of the King and of his rebellious subjects were approaching, with claims to the public courtesy. For a little while these legislators were at their wits' end, when it was agreed to honor each party and offend nobody by neglect. Colonel Lasher, commander of the militia, was accordingly ordered to parade his regiment, and be "ready to receive either the generals or Governor Tryon, whichever should first arrive, and wait on both as well as circumstances would allow."

Fortunately for all parties, the arrival of these public characters was not simultaneous. Washington and his party landed on the New York side of the Hudson, at Colonel Lispenard's seat, about a mile above the town, at four o'clock in the afternoon, and were "conducted into the city by nine companies of foot, in their uniforms, and a greater number of the inhabitants of that city than ever appeared on any occasion before."* They were there received by the civil authorities; and Mr. Livingston, the president of the Provincial Congress, pronounced a cautious and conservative address, to which Washington replied. Four hours afterward Governor Tryon arrived, and was conducted to the house of Hugh Wallace, Esq. The civic and military ceremonies of the afternoon were partially repeated in the evening, and all parties were well satisfied with the events of that Sabbath day, the 25th of June, 1775.

Washington and Schuyler spent the entire evening after their arrival, in earnest consultation concerning the present and prospective affairs of the Northern Department, to whose guardianship the latter was assigned. That de-

* *Pennsylvania Journal,* quoted by Frank Moore, *Diary of the Revolution,* i. 101.

partment included the whole of New York, a province then peculiarly situated both geographically and politically. It was an important link in the confederacy, uniting the New England provinces with those of the middle and southern; and upon its preservation from royal control depended the integrity of the union. On its northern border was Canada, with its inhabitants practically neutral in regard to the great question at issue, and likely to become hostile, because British power and influence were vastly predominant there. From that province might come speedy invasions. The central and western regions of New York were filled with the powerful tribes of the Six Confederated Nations of Indians, whose almost universal loyalty had already been secured by the agency of the Johnson family; while nearer the seaboard and in the metropolis, family compacts and commercial interests were powerfully swayed by traditional and natural attachments to the crown, and neutralized to a great extent the influence of the few sturdy patriots who, in the face of frowns and menaces, and fears of the timid, kept the fires of the Revolution burning with continually increasing brightness.

New York, in that crisis, thus presented three dangerous elements of weakness, namely, an exposed frontier, a wily and powerful internal foe, and a demoralizing loyalty. These visible signs of weakness in this important link of the confederacy gave much uneasiness to the commander-in-chief, and yet he felt a secret confidence that all would be well while a man like General Schuyler should be charged with the preservation of the strength and vitality of that link. To that officer, on the same Sabbath evening, the commander-in-chief gave the following instructions:

"You are to take upon you the command of all the troops destined for the New York Department, and see that the orders of the Continental Congress are carried into execution with as much precision and exactness as possible.

"For your better government therein you are hereby furnished with a copy of the instructions given to me by that honorable body. Such parts as are within the line of your duty you will please to pay particular attention to. Delay no time in occupying the several posts recommended by the Provincial Congress of this colony, and putting them in a fit posture to answer the end designed; nor delay any time in securing the stores which are, or ought to have been, removed from this city by order of the Continental Congress.

"Keep a watchful eye upon Governor Tryon, and if you find him directly or indirectly attempting any measures inimical to the common cause, use every means in your power to frustrate his designs. It is not in my power at this time to point out the mode by which this end is to be accomplished, but if forcible measures are judged necessary respecting the person of the governor, I should have no difficulty in ordering them if the Continental Congress were not sitting; but as this is the case, and the seizing of a governor quite a new thing, and of great importance, I must refer you to that body for direction should his Excellency make any motion towards increasing the strength of the Tory party or arming them against the cause in which we are embarked. In like manner watch the movements of the Indian agent, Colonel Guy Johnson, and prevent, as far as you can, the effect of his influence to our prejudice with the Indians. Obtain the best information you can of the temper and disposition of those people, and also of the Canadians, that a proper line may be marked out to conciliate their good opinion or facilitate any future operation.

"The posts on Lake Champlain you will please to have properly supplied with provisions and ammunition; and this I am persuaded you will aim at doing on the best terms, to prevent our good cause from sinking under a heavy load of expense. You will be pleased, also, to make regular returns to me, and to the Continental Congress, once a month, and oftener, as occurrences may require, of the forces under your command, and of your provisions and stores, and give me the earliest advices of every piece of intelligence which you shall judge of importance to be speedily known. Your own good sense must govern you in all matters not particularly pointed out, as I do not wish to circumscribe you within narrow limits."

On Monday morning Washington left New York for Cambridge. General Schuyler accompanied him as far as

New Rochelle, in Westchester county, where they met and conferred with General Wooster, who was in command of the troops raised by Connecticut, and which had been stationed on the shores of Long Island Sound to protect the southern frontier of that colony. A rumor having been spread, about ten days before Washington's arrival, that a regiment of British troops was soon to be landed in New York, the Provincial Congress sitting there invited General Wooster to march within five miles of the city for its defense, and while there to be under their command or of that of the Continental Congress. By permission of the government of Connecticut, Wooster complied with their request, and was on his way when met by Washington and his officers. He arrived in the neighborhood of the city on the 28th of June, with seven companies of his own regiment and that of Colonel Waterbury complete—in all about eighteen hundred men. They encamped in the vicinity of Murray Hill, then two miles from the city, where they remained for several weeks.

General Schuyler left Washington at New Rochelle, and returned to New York to enter upon the duties of his important command. He immediately addressed a letter to the Continental Congress, informing them of the scarcity of powder in New York; of efforts which he should make to cultivate a good understanding with the people of Canada; and of reports of hostile demonstrations on the part of the Six Nations. He also urged them to appoint a commissary-general and a quartermaster-general for his department; assured them that Governor Tryon had made professions of sorrow because of the unhappy controversy, and that he would not create any trouble in his government—professions which he believed to be sincere; and concluded by saying, "Be assured, honorable sirs, that I shall omit nothing in my power faithfully to discharge the important trust with which you have honored me. If, however, I should be unfortunate, I hope your candor will impute it to that want of abilities which I with much truth and sincerity avowed previous to my appointment, unless you should be convinced that any neglect of duty proceeded from wickedness of heart."*

Affairs on Lake Champlain demanded General Schuyler's first and most earnest attention, for the possession of Canada, either by an alliance in the cause or by conquest, was a consideration of the greatest importance. From the beginning of the contest that province, inhabited by French Roman Catholics, having no religious, social, or national sympathy with the Anglo-American colonies or the mother country, had been an object of great solicitude to both parties. The imperial government had made concessions by which they stimulated the loyalty of the clergy, and through them the laity; also made promises for the future, which caused the Canadians to be half forgetful of past animosities. The republican leaders of the colonies in arms had, meanwhile, made affectionate appeals to their brethren beyond the St. Lawrence to join in seeking a redress of grievances by the arguments of reason or the sword. In an address to the Canadians, put forth by the Continental Congress in 1774, the representatives of their sister colonists said:

"We are too well acquainted with the liberality of sentiment distinguishing your nation, to imagine that difference of religion will prejudice you against a hearty amity with us. You know that the transcendant nature of freedom elevates those who unite in her cause above all such low-minded infirmities. The Swiss Cantons furnish a memorable proof of this truth. Their union is composed of Roman Catholic and Protestant states, living in the utmost concord and peace with one another,

* MS. Letter Books, June 28, 1775.

and thereby enabled, ever since they bravely vindicated their freedom, to defy and defeat every tyrant that invaded them."

This address was translated into French and received the favorable notice of many leading Canadians. But, unfortunately, the Congress had practiced some duplicity which the ethics of diplomacy might excuse, but it completely neutralized the effects of this appeal. Only five days before the appeal was adopted, the Congress had said, in their address to the people of England, who delighted in shouting "No Popery!" and in burning the effigies of the Roman Pontiff and the devil together, as co-workers in iniquity:

"We think the Legislature is not authorized by the constitution to establish a religion [alluding to the Quebec Act] fraught with sanguinary tenets, in any part of the globe; nor can we suppress our astonishment that a British Parliament should ever consent to establish in that country [Canada] a religion that has deluged your island in blood, and dispersed impiety, bigotry, persecution, murder, and rebellion, through every part of the world."

This also was translated into French, and was read to a numerous audience of intelligent Canadians at Montreal. When the reader came to that part which treated of the "new modelling of the provinces," said a letter writer, "and drew a picture of the Catholic religion and Canadian manners, they could not contain their resentment, nor express it but in broken curses. 'Oh, the perfidious, double-faced Congress!' they exclaimed; 'Let us bless and obey our benevolent prince, whose humanity is consistent and extends to all religions; let us abhor all who would seduce us from our loyalty by acts that would dishonor a Jesuit, and whose addresses, like their resolves, are destructive of their own objects.'"

This was a most unfortunate occurrence, and the effect

of this duplicity was highly detrimental to the republican cause for a while. Sir Guy Carleton, the governor of Canada, took advantage of the feeling which it produced, and used every means in his power to conciliate the Canadians; but their resentment soon cooled, and the smouldering fires of national hatred of England, that had been burning for a thousand years, glowed too intensely to be quenched. When the address of the second Congress was sent to them at the close of May, 1775, in their own language and in printed form, many a Gallic bosom heaved with aspirations for freedom from English rule. Such was the prevailing feeling of the Canadians at the period immediately succeeding the capture of Ticonderoga and Crown Point; and had Congress then acted upon the earnest advice of Colonels Ethan Allen and Benedict Arnold, who were boldly asserting the supremacy of the republicans on Lake Champlain, the conquest of Canada might have been easily and completely accomplished. The former, with keen perception that proved to be almost prophetic in its suggestions, wrote a characteristic letter to the Provincial Congress of New York on the 2d of June. After speaking of the forts on Lake Champlain as the key "either of Canada or our own country," he said:

"The key is ours as yet, and provided the colonies would suddenly push an army of two or three thousand men into Canada, they might make a conquest of all that would oppose them in the extensive province of Quebec, unless reinforcements from England should prevent it. Such a diversion would weaken General Gage or insure us Canada. I would lay my life on it, that with fifteen hundred men I would take Montreal. Provided I could be thus furnished, and an army could take the field, it would be no insuperable difficulty to take Quebec.

"This object should be pursued, though it should take ten thousand men, for England can not spare but a certain number of her troops; nay, she has but a small number that is disciplined, and it is long as it is broad: the more that are sent to Quebec the less can she send to Boston, or any other part of the continent. And there will be this unspeakable advantage, in directing the war into Canada, that instead of turning the Canadians and Indians against us, as is wrongly suggested by many, it would unavoidably attach and connect them to our interest. Our friends in Canada can never help us until we first help them, except in a passive or inactive manner. There are now about seven hundred regular troops in Canada.

"It may be thought that to push an army into Canada would be too premature and imprudent. If so, I propose to make a stand at the *Isle aux Noix*, which the French fortified by intrenchments the last war, and greatly fatigued our large army to take it. It is about fifteen miles on this side of St. John's, and is an island in the river, on which a small artillery placed would command it. An establishment on a frontier so far north would not only better secure our own frontier, but put it into our power better to work our policy with Canadians and Indians, or, if need be, to make incursions into the territory of Canada, the same as they could into our country provided they had the sovereignty of Lake Champlain, and had erected headquarters at or near Skenesborough. Our only having it in our power thus to make incursions into Canada might probably be the very reason why it would be unnecessary so to do, even if the Canadians should prove more refractory than I think for.

"Lastly, I would propose to you to raise a small regiment of Rangers, which I could easily do, and that mostly in the counties of Albany and Charlotte, provided you should think it expedient to grant commissions, and thus regulate and put them under pay. Probably you may think this an impertinent proposal. It is truly the first I have ever asked of the government, and if granted, I shall be zealously ambitious to conduct for the best good of my country and the honor of the government."

No doubt the Provincial Congress did think it an "impertinent proposal," coming from a man who, by an assembly similar to their own, had, only the year before, been pronounced an outlaw, and placed under legal sentence of death as a traitor to the State. It was the first public proposition to invade Canada, and was made at a moment when timid prudence caused both the Provincial and the Continental Congress not only to hesitate, but to pointedly condemn any movement toward a forcible possession of the territory beyond the St. Lawrence. They considered the letter a bold and injudicious production of an ambitious and reckless man, intoxicated with momentary success, and who ought to be checked rather than encouraged. But in less than ninety days afterward, the Continental Congress authorized an invasion of Canada ; and the whole people who longed for freedom, from the far northeast to the extreme south, approved the measure. The battle on Breed's Hill and other circumstances had changed public opinion ; and the patriots had cause to regret that the voice of Colonel Allen had not sooner been heeded.

Allen and his confederates, who captured the lake fortresses, had counselled much together on the importance and feasibility of the conquest of Canada, and had made successful movements with that end in view. Immediately after the capture of those posts, a party of *Green Mountain Boys* had surprised Skenesborough, at the head of the lake, and made prisoners of Major Skene, a son of the proprietor,* and more than sixty other persons, and taken away with them a schooner and several bateaus. The former was immediately manned by Colonel Arnold, with some new recruits, and armed with a few guns from Ticonderoga. Thus equipped he sailed northward, followed by Colonel Allen and one hundred and fifty men in bateaus, to attack St. John's on the Sorel, the outlet of Lake Champlain.

Arnold's schooner outsailed Allen's bateaus. At the foot of the lake he left her, and with thirty-five men in two bateaux, he pushed down the Sorel to St. John's. At

* Philip Skene, father of the Major, arrived from England early in June, with a commission of Governor of Ticonderoga and Crown Point, and their dependencies, and was seized before he landed, by order of the Continental Congress, it having been rumored that he was authorized to raise a regiment in America. He was afterward released, and was living at Skenesborough when Burgoyne invaded the upper Hudson valley, in the summer of 1777.

six o'clock the following morning he surprised the garrison there, which consisted of a sergeant and twelve men ; captured a King's sloop, with seven men ; destroyed five bateaux ; seized four others ; put on board the sloop some valuable stores from the fort, and within two hours after his arrival, sailed with a favorable breeze for Ticonderoga, with his prisoners and booty. He met Allen and they held a council, the result of which was that Arnold and his prizes proceeded to Ticonderoga, and Allen went on to St. John's to garrison the fort with a hundred men, and act as circumstances should require.

Rumors reached Arnold, before he left St. John's, that a large reinforcement for the garrison there was hourly expected from Montreal and Chamblée. These rumors became certain information soon after the arrival of Allen, who, learning that the approaching party was more numerous than his own, crossed the river, and there, early on the following morning, was attacked by about two hundred men. He fled to his boats, and escaped to Ticonderoga without losing a man. Thus ended a series of exploits, bold in conception and gallant in execution. Within eight days two strong fortresses with their dependencies were wrested from the British by a handful of half-disciplined provincials, acting without special authority or specific aim ; and the little fleet of the enemy on the lake—his chief dependence there—was captured or destroyed in a day.

The British authorities in Canada were alarmed at these movements, and Governor Carleton sent a force of four hundred men—regulars, Canadians, and Indians—to St. John's, with the intention of recapturing Crown Point and Ticonderoga. Arnold, thirsting for opportunity to win by valor what he was deprived of by necessity, namely, the chief command on the lakes, was delighted when he heard of these preparations, and without waiting for orders from any source, he proceeded in fitting out the vessels in his possession to confront the enemy. Having armed and manned them, he appointed his subordinate officers, and, as self-constituted commodore of the first Continental Navy, he took post at Crown Point, with one hundred and fifty men in the vessels, to await the expected foe. He also assumed the command of the garrison at Crown Point, and became a sort of amphibious leader, ready to fight on land or water. He also busied himself in sending off the ordnance at Crown Point to the army at Cambridge, and in despatching emissaries to Montreal and the Caughnawaga Indians in that vicinity, to ascertain the feelings of the Canadians and savages toward the republicans in arms, and also to gain intelligence of the actual state of Carleton's preparations.

Arnold, like Allen, was anxious to invade Canada. He disliked the latter and his *Green Mountain Boys*, and avoided all coöperation with him as much as possible. Unmindful, and perhaps ignorant of the proposition of Allen to the Provincial Congress of New York concerning an invasion of Canada, Arnold wrote to the Continental Congress on the 13th of June, and laid before them a plan of operations whereby the conquest of that province might be secured. He asserted that persons in Montreal had agreed to open the gates of that city, when a continental army of sufficient force to maintain it should appear before it; assured the Congress that Carleton could not muster more than five hundred and fifty effective men; and offered to lead an expedition to the St. Lawrence and hold himself responsible for the consequences.

As no troops had been raised in New York at the time of the capture of the lake fortresses, the Congress of that province accepted the generous offer of Trumbull, the governor of Connecticut, to send a sufficient force, with supplies, to hold them until New York should be ready to perform that service. Connecticut had, from the beginning, acted in concert with Massachusetts in levying soldiers, making military preparations, and providing means for the support of an army ; and at this time the colony was alive with excitement on account of the result of the expedition to Lake Champlain.

Governor Trumbull, on the 30th of May, placed one thousand men in charge of Colonel Benjamin Hinman, with orders to march for Ticonderoga. These composed the fourth regiment raised by Connecticut. At about the same time, the general committee at Albany resolved to raise eight hundred men "for the defense of American liberty," and three companies were enlisted in the course of a few days, and marched for Lake Champlain. Aware of the approach of Hinman's regiment, and earnestly desiring the general command of a considerable force, Arnold, in a postscript to his letter to the Continental Congress, evinced that desire, and at the same time his aversion to Allen and the men under his immediate command.* He proposed, in order to give satisfaction to the different colonies, that Colonel Hinman's regiment should form part of the army ; that the remainder should be composed of five hundred New York troops, and five hundred of his own regiment,

* Arnold affected great contempt for Allen and his men. On the day after the surrender of Ticonderoga, he wrote to the Massachusetts Committee of Safety, saying: "Colonel Allen is a proper man to lead his own wild people, but entirely unacquainted with military service." And in a letter to the Committee of Safety at Albany, giving an account of his operations at St. John's, he speaks of meeting, on his return, "one Colonel Allen, with a party of near one hundred men, who were determined to proceed to St. John's and make a stand there," etc., and subscribed himself "Commander at Ticonderoga."

including the seamen and marines on the vessel under his command, "but no Green Mountain Boys."

At this time Colonel Allen and his lieutenant, Seth Warner, were in Philadelphia for the purpose of procuring pay for their soldiers from the Continental Congress, and to solicit authority to raise a new regiment for the public service in the New Hampshire Grants. The appearance of these heroes of the north produced a sensation in that city. They were introduced upon the floor of Congress, and permitted to make their communications to that body orally. Allen talked long and earnestly in his quaint style and slow-spoken sentences respecting affairs on the northern frontiers, and the dangers to which the confederacy and the cause of freedom in America would be exposed when the British regulars in Canada should be reinforced; and he again urged the great necessity of an immediate invasion of the province, while the arm of the imperial government was comparatively weak, and the friendship of the Canadians for the revolted colonies was strong. His words had a powerful effect, and on the very day when Congress received Arnold's letter, in which he expressed an ill-natured desire that "no Green Mountain Boys" should be employed in an invasion of Canada, the Continental Congress

"*Resolved*, That it be recommended to the convention of New York, that they, consulting with General Schuyler, employ in the army to be raised for the defense of America those called *Green Mountain Boys*, under such officers as the said *Green Mountain Boys* shall choose."*

The wishes of Allen and Warner in regard to pay were also complied with, and they departed for New York with cheerfulness, to present themselves before the Provincial Congress there. Their appearance on such an errand pro-

* Journals of Congress, June 17, 1775.

duced embarrassment in that body. They had been proscribed as outlaws but a few months before ; now no one doubted their patriotism. What should be done ? There were members of that Congress who had taken an active part against these very men. Could they give their old enemies a friendly greeting ? The prejudices of these members, and the scruples of others who could not perceive any propriety in holding public conference with men whom the laws of the land had declared to be rioters and felons, produced a strong opposition to their admission to the legislative hall. Debates on the subject ran high, until Captain Sears, the staunch leader of the Sons of Liberty, moved that "Ethan Allen be admitted to the floor of the House." The motion was carried by a large majority, as was a similar resolution in regard to Warner. The old feud was instantly healed. These men were received as heroes and patriots, and the New York Provincial Congress decreed that a regiment of *Green Mountain Boys*, five hundred strong, should be raised. The subject was referred to General Schuyler, who soon afterward proclaimed the resolution in the New Hampshire Grants. With grateful hearts Allen and his companion journeyed to Bennington, and the latter afterward wrote to the New York Congress, saying :

"When I reflect on the unhappy controversy which has many years subsisted between the government of New York and the settlers on the New Hampshire Grants, and also contemplate the friendship and union which has lately taken place, in making a united resistance against ministerial vengeance and slavery, I can not but indulge fond hopes of a reconciliation. To promote this salutary end I shall contribute my influence, assuring you that your respectful treatment, not only to Mr. Warner and myself, but to the *Green Mountain Boys* in general, in forming them into a battalion, is by them duly regarded ; and I will be responsible that they will reciprocate this favor by boldly hazarding their lives, if need be, in the common cause of America."

Colonel Hinman arrived at Ticonderoga, with four hundred Connecticut troops, at about the middle of June, assumed the general command, and held that position for a month, when he was formally superseded by General Schuyler. There were in the field, in the colony of New York during that time, less than three thousand men fit for duty, and yet, with this small force, preparations were made for the invasion of Canada.* The visit of Allen and Warner to the Continental Congress, and concurrent circumstances, had produced a great change in the views of that body, and on the day when General Schuyler parted with Washington at New Rochelle, and returned to New York to enter upon his duties as commander of the Northern department, the General Congress, by unanimous resolution, ordered General Schuyler, if he should "find it practicable, and not disagreeable to the Canadians, immediately to take possession of St. John's and Montreal, and pursue such other measures in Canada as might have a tendency to promote the peace and security of these provinces."†

These words were mild and cautious, but were understood as conveying an explicit order for the invasion of Canada. They reached General Schuyler on the 30th of the month, and on the same day he wrote as follows to the Continental Congress:

* According to General Schuyler's first returns, dated July 1, 1775, which he considered imperfect because of a want of entirely reliable material, the troops in the colony of New York mustered as follows: Of Brigadier General Wooster's regiment, at *New York*, 582; Colonel David Waterbury's regiment, at *New York*, 982; of Colonel Benjamin Hinman's regiment, at *Ticonderoga*, 495, at *Crown Point*, 302, at the *Landing*, foot of Lake George, 102, and at *Fort George*, head of Lake George, 104; of Massachusetts Bay forces, at *Ticonderoga*, 40, at *Crown Point*, 109, and at *Fort George*, 25; of the New York forces, at *Fort George*, 205.

† Journals of Congress, June 27, 1775.

"In obedience to the resolutions of Congress, I shall, without delay, repair to Ticonderoga. It will, however, be necessary, previous to my departure from hence, that I should take order to have the various articles necessary to carry into execution the views of the Congress, sent after me with all possible expedition.* These will probably detain me until Monday. The success of the intended operation will evidently depend so much on dispatch that I am sorry I do not think myself at liberty to move the troops now here to Albany without the immediate consent of Congress. At this place I do not apprehend they can be wanted; at Albany they would greatly facilitate and expedite the service, as well as save expense by their assistance in the transportation or stores and provisions, and by their aid in building boats, carriages, etc. And as they must ultimately go on this service, the forces at Ticonderoga being vastly inadequate to the enterprise, I wish the sense of the Congress with all possible dispatch, and therefore I send this by express.†

* On the 3d of July General Schuyler addressed a letter to the New York Provincial Congress, inclosing a list of necessary supplies for the army on the lakes. This first estimate for an army of between three and four thousand men is such a fair specimen of materials used in such service, that we give a copy of it for the gratification of the curious reader:

"50 swivel guns; 2 tuns musket balls or lead; what powder can be spared; 2 dozen bullet moulds; soldiers' tents for 3,500 men, 6 men to a tent; a proportionable number of bell tents; officers' tents; tents for two general officers and their suite; 15 casks of 24-penny nails; 10 casks of 20-penny; 15 casks of 10-penny; 1,000 weight of spike nails; 1 tun of oakum; 30 barrels of pitch; 300 felling axes, exclusive of those for the camp use of the soldiers; 200 bill-hooks; 200 spades; 200 shovels; 150 pick-axes; 20 crow-bars; 20 mason's trowels; 20 do. hammers; 2 tuns of bar iron; 500 weight of steel; 100 set of men's harness (believe there is some in Connecticut); 3 sets of gunsmith's tools, exclusive of those for the regimental armorer; 3 sets of blacksmith's tools; 50 broad axes; 20 whip saws; 20 cross-cut saws; 4 sets of blocks and tackles, strong; 50 lbs twine; 4 fishing nets, with ropes; 10 bolts of sail cloth; fifty oil-cloths, well painted; 1,500 oars, 12, 14, and 16 feet long; 500 fathoms of tarred rope, for painters for boats; half a ton of tarred rope, sorted; 4 chests of carpenter's tools; 28 mill saws, for Dutch mills; 7 do. for English mills; 5 dozen mill saw files; an assortment of articles in the artillery way; paper; shot cannisters; fusees; 1 dozen lime sieves; 50 small truck carriages, if they are ready made here; 10 do. for field pieces, if do.; necessaries for a hospital; 3 months provisions for 4,000 men. Much of the meat kind to be fresh, as it may be driven to the army, and save the expense of transportation; whatever arms can be spared; 20 grass scythes; flints."—*MS. Letter Books.*

† MS. Letter Books, June 30, 1775.

# CHAPTER XX.

General Schuyler left New York for Ticonderoga on Tuesday, the fourth of July, and was soon afterward followed by Richard Varick, as secretary, John Macpherson, as aid-de-camp, and Reverend John Peter Testard as French interpreter for the General, and chaplain to the New York troops. On the previous day he had reviewed Colonel Lasher's battalion of militia, accompanied by Generals Wooster and Montgomery, in the presence of quite a large concourse of ladies and gentlemen; and afterward received at his quarters the personal courtesies of most of the leading men of the city, who had espoused the republican cause.

General Schuyler had already addressed a letter to Colonel Hinman, apprising him of his (Schuyler's) appointment to the chief command in the North, and giving him some instructions concerning affairs on the Canadian frontier; and on the day before he left he addressed the following letter to General Wooster, in addition to particular instructions which he had given him five days before:*

* In these instructions he directed Wooster to keep up very exact discipline, to prevent jealousies between the troops and the citizens; not to allow any soldiers to go into town without a pass, and to discourage going altogether, because of the prevalence of the small-pox there; to call the rolls twice a-day; for all to pay the utmost attention to dress and cleanliness; to perfect the troops in military exercises; and drunkenness or disorderly conduct, and despoiling orchards, to be discountenanced and punished.

"America has recourse to arms merely for her safety and defense, and in resisting oppression she will not oppress. She wages no war of ambition, content if she can only retain the fair inheritance of English law and English liberty. Such being the purity of her intentions, no stain must be suffered to disgrace our arms. We are soldiers ambitious only to aid in restoring the violated rights of citizens, and these secured, we are to return instantly to the business and employments of civilized life. Let it be a truth deeply impressed on the minds of every one of us who bear arms, and let us evince to the world that in contending for liberty we abhor licentiousness; that in resisting the misrule of tyrants we shall support government honestly administered. *All unnecessary violence to the persons or property of his Majesty's subjects must therefore most strictly be forbidden and avoided.*

"The magistracy of the country are not only to be respected, but aided in all cases not incompatible with the great object of opposing that oppression which called us to defense.

"Let this be the magnet for directing the conduct of the army under my command. And if doubts arise on any particular occasion, and the emergency will permit, advise with the Congress of the colony in which you may act, and if time allows, apply to the Continental Congress and the general-in-chief. Only orders as general as these can be given respecting events not in immediate view.

"Close attention to the end of the service will direct to the means of attaining it. Let us act as becomes the virtuous citizen, who seeks for the aid of righteous Heaven and the just applause of an impartial world. Liberty, Safety, and Peace, are our objects—the establishment of the Constitution, and not the lust of Dominion.

"These are sentiments the goodness of your heart and your attachment to our righteous cause will inculcate. They are principles I wish deeply implanted in the heart of every soldier I have the honor to command. They will lead us to glory—they will merit for us the esteem of our countrymen."*

General Schuyler and suite reached Albany about one o'clock on Sunday, the 9th of July. He was received at the landing by the members of the general committee of the city and county, the City Troop of horse, under the command of Captain Tenbroeck, the Association Company, commanded by Captain Bleecker, and by the principal inhabitants of the city. They bestowed upon him the honors

* MS. Letter Books, July 3, 1775.

due to his rank, and escorted him to the City Hall, when the committee, through Dr. Samuel Stringer, the temporary chairman, presented to him the following address:

"Permit us, sir, to express our fullest approbation upon the appointment by which your country has raised you to the chief military command in this colony. While we deplore, as the greatest misfortune, the necessity of such an appointment, we have the utmost confidence that you have accepted of power for the glorious purpose of exercising it for the reëstablishment of the liberties of America, at present invaded by a deluded and despotic ministry.

"Born and educated amongst us, in a country which freedom has raised to a state of opulence and envy, you, whose principles are known, whose sentiments have been invariably opposed to power, afford us the pleasing prospect of the unremitted exertion of your knowledge, prudence, and experience, for the restoration of peace upon constitutional principles. When the sword is rendered useless, except against our natural enemies; when we shall see you restored to the peaceful state of a private citizen; when this happy period shall arrive, then, and not till then, will Americans enjoy the glorious blessings of freedom."

To this address the General replied as follows:

"I feel myself so sensibly affected by this public and friendly address, that whilst my heart overflows with sentiments of gratitude, I want words properly to convey my thanks.

"The honor you do me in the approbation which you are pleased to express of my appointment to a military command, confirms me in the pleasing reflection that I shall experience your assistance in a continuance of those generous exertions by which you have already so conspicuously manifested your love for your country, and your zeal for its cause.

"I most sincerely and unfeignedly deplore with you the unhappy occasion which has forced America to have recourse to arms for her safety and defense. Ambitious only to aid in restoring her violated rights, I shall most cheerfully return my sword to the scabbard, and, with alacrity, resume the employment of civil life, whenever my constituents shall direct, or whenever a happy reconciliation with the parent state shall take place.

"That indulgent Heaven may guide us through this tempestuous scene, and speedily restore peace, harmony, and mutual confidence to every part of the British empire, is the warmest wish of my heart."

General Schuyler was then escorted to his residence, half a mile south of the town, (now at the head of Schuyler street,) by the whole party that received him, and the city was illuminated in the evening. Beloved by his fellow-citizens as a man, and fully appreciated as a representative, his return to them clothed in such extraordinary honor and dignity excited their most ardent enthusiasm. This took the shape of violent indignation the next morning, when the following publication appeared anonymously, with the evident intention of casting ridicule upon the reception proceedings the previous day:

"*The mode of a late* VERY EXTRAORDINARY *and* VERY GRAND PROCESSION:

"I. The Congressional General.

"II. The *Deputy* Chairman, and who is only chairman *pro tempore.*

"III. Mr. Tenbroeck—through a mistake.

"IV. The Chairman.

"V. The Committee.

"VI. The troop of Horse, most beautiful and grand. Some horses long-tailed, some bob-tailed, and some without any tails, and attended with the melodious sound of an incomparably fine trumpet.

"VII. The Association."*

In consequence of this publication, the Committee of Safety, Protection, and Correspondence held an early meeting, and instituted a diligent inquiry after the author of the paper, which they pronounced a "scandalous reflection" on the reception proceedings. He was believed to be some concealed Tory, and for three days the public mind was greatly disturbed. Then, by his own confession, it was discovered that the author was Peter W. Yates, a member of the republican committee. In a moment of indiscreet playfulness he had cast that harmless missile among his fellow-townsmen. He made a most humble apology to his associates of the committee for his indiscretion, and sol-

* Minutes of the Albany Committee.

emnly disclaimed "any intention to injure the cause of liberty;" but the public mind would not be so readily appeased. The city was in an uproar, and at several public meetings Mr. Yates' expulsion from the committee was demanded. He resigned, but this did not satisfy the people. Nothing less than his public apology or his public disgrace would be accepted, and he accordingly appeared before his assembled fellow-citizens and made the required acknowledgment.* This event exhibits the extreme sensitiveness of the public mind at that period, when every man was suspicious of his neighbor, and two of a household often disagreed, and sometimes cherished the most bitter feud.

General Schuyler found the aspect of every thing connected with the republican cause in northern New York dark and unpromising. Rumor after rumor came that the Indians in the Mohawk valley and beyond were becoming extensively disaffected toward the republican cause through the influence of Guy Johnson, the Indian agent, with whom the New York Provincial Congress had recently held a somewhat spicy correspondence. Johnson professed peaceable intentions, but his movements for several months had been so suspicious, that Tryon county, which embraced the whole of the Mohawk region west of Schenectada, was filled with alarm. He had held a council with the Indians at Guy Park, (his residence, about a mile from the present village of Amsterdam, on the Mohawk,) in May, which was attended by delegates from the Albany and Tryon county republican committees. The result was unsatisfactory to all parties. The delegates, knowing that the Indians had been tampered with, mistrusted them; and Johnson, alarmed by the events at Lexington and Concord,

* *Life of Peter Van Schaack*, by his son, Henry C. Van Schaack, page 68.

and by intimations which he had received that the Provincial Congress contemplated the seizure of his person, broke up the council abruptly and called another at the German Flats, further up the Mohawk, whither himself and family immediately proceeded. But the council was not held there, and Johnson, with his family and the Indians, pushed on to Fort Stanwix (now Rome), and from there went into the wilderness far beyond the verge of civilization. He visited the different tribes in their habitations; sat with them at their council fires; estranged the Oneidas from the Reverend Mr. Kirkland, their beloved missionary; and weakened every bond by which the Six Nations had been held by the republican committees. And while he was thus stirring up the savages to an active alliance with the English authorities in Canada, Sir John Johnson was at Johnson Hall (which he had fortified), exerting a less public but equally powerful influence as brigadier general of the Tryon county militia, and having at his beck a large body of loyalists.

From the far north intelligence came to Schuyler that the Caughnawaga Indians had taken up the hatchet for the enemy, and Colonel Hinman reported that every thing was in the utmost confusion at Ticonderoga, owing to the quarrels of officers and the scarcity of supplies.

"The unhappy controversy" Schuyler wrote to the Continental Congress, "which has subsisted between the officers at Ticonderoga in relation to the command, has, I am informed, thrown every thing there into vast confusion. Troops have been dismissed; others refuse to serve if this or that man commands; the sloop is without either captain or pilot, both of which are dismissed or come away. I shall hurry up there much sooner than the necessary preparations here would otherwise permit, that I may attempt to introduce some kind of order and discipline among them."*

* MS. Letter Books.

The ambitious, unscrupulous, and quarrelsome Arnold was the cause of all the difficulty. We have already observed his assumptions of command and his offensive bearing toward other officers, especially toward Colonel Allen, who had been, by the committee in charge of the expedition against Ticonderoga, formally placed in supreme command there. When Colonel Hinman arrived, he too was subjected to like indignities. Arnold refused to give up to him the command of either Ticonderoga or Crown Point, claiming as before to be the chief by virtue of his commission from the Massachusetts authorities. Confusion ensued. Allen and Warner, and most of the Green Mountain Boys, returned home, and others became disgusted. Meanwhile, a statement of his conduct had been sent to the Legislatures of Massachusetts and Connecticut, and his character was portrayed in most unfavorable colors. No doubt his many faults were magnified, and his few virtues overlooked; yet a picture of his arrogance and ill-nature could not be over-drawn. The Massachusetts Provincial Congress believed their confidence in him had been misplaced, and appointed a committee to investigate all the charges against Arnold.

When that committee arrived Arnold was at Crown Point. Utterly ignorant of the nature of their errand, he received them courteously and talked to them enthusiastically of his plans for the future and his expected conquests. When the object of their visit was made known, his indignation was fearfully aroused. He felt conscious of having performed good and gallant service, and, almost doubting their allegations, he demanded a sight of their instructions. These increased his rage. He found that his inquisitors were commissioned to ascertain his "spirit, capacity, and conduct," and were clothed with authority to order his return to Massachusetts to give a full account of his transactions ; or if he remained, to direct him to be subservient to Colonel Hinman, whom Trumbull had appointed chief of the troops on service approved by the Congress of the province within whose domain the fortresses stood. Arnold was greatly enraged. He stamhed, swore, cursed congresses and kings, fate, and all committee-men, and declared, with terrible oaths, that he would be second to no man. Throwing up his commission he discharged his men on the spot, and these, becoming indignant in turn, some of them refused to serve under any other leader. Others, instigated by Arnold, threatened to sail for St. John's, independent of all authority ; while the majority, more thoughtful and patriotic, joined the corps of Colonel Easton. Arnold treated the committee with the greatest rudeness, but by judicious management they persuaded his men to acquiesce in their arrangements, while the indignant commander proceeded to Cambridge, to lay before Washington his complaint of ill-usage by the Provincial Congress of Massachusetts.

On the morning of the 13th of July, General Schuyler proceeded northward as far as his country seat at Saratoga, where his family were then residing, and made hasty preparations for his departure for Ticonderoga. Toward midnight he received a dispatch by express from the Albany Committee, giving him intelligence, which they had just received from Colonel Nicholas Herkimer, in the interior, that full eight hundred savages, under Joseph Brant and Walter Butler, had coalesced with the Scotch Highlanders and other Tories under Sir John Johnson, for the purpose of making forays upon the republican settlers in the Mohawk valley, and in cutting off supplies for the army on Lake Champlain. Brant, or *Thayendanegea*, was the Mohawk chief who became both famous and notorious as the leader of his people upon bloody scouts, and who, with Walter Butler, one of the most cruel of white savages, made Tryon county "a dark and bloody ground" for several years. His sister, Molly Brant, had been first the concubine and then the wife of Sir William Johnson.

This startling intelligence from the interior detained Schuyler at Saratoga for two or three days. He had ordered Captain Van Dyck of Schenectada to march with his company to Lake George. That order was countermanded at the suggestion of the Albany Committee, and he directed Van Dyck to march immediately up the Mohawk valley to the relief of the people of Tryon county. "On whatever duty you may be," Schuyler wrote, "I earnestly recommend vigilance and care, that you may not meet with the disgrace of a surprise. Be careful that your men do not commit any outrages on the inhabitants whom you are going to protect."*

The General's mind was relieved by a letter from the Albany Committee, written on the following day, informing him that the intelligence they had received from the interior was exaggerated. Yet the movements of Guy Johnson caused much uneasiness. He was evidently working upon the Indian mind unfavorably to the republican cause. With the pretext of an exercise of his duties as Indian agent, he had called a great council of the Six Nations at Ontario, in the heart of the country of the fierce Cayugas and Senecas. His family had gone with him into the wilderness, followed by a large train of Mohawk warriors. He was accompanied by Brant (whom Sir William Johnson had caused to be educated at Dr. Wheelock's school, in Connecticut,) as his secretary, and by Colonel John Butler and his son Walter. There he met almost fourteen

* Autograph draft of letter, July 14, 1775.

hundred savages, and held a conference, which, to him, was very satisfactory.

From that rude council chamber Johnson wrote the following letter to the president of the New York Provincial Congress:

ONTARIO, July 8, 1775.

"SIR: Though I received your letter from the Provincial Congress several days ago, I had not a good opportunity to answer it till now. I suppose, however, this will reach *you* safe, notwithstanding all the rest of my correspondence is interrupted by ignorant impertinents.

"As to the endeavor you speak of to reconcile the unhappy differences between the parent State and these colonies, be assured I ardently wish to see them. As yet, I am sorry to say, I have not been able to discover any attempt of that kind but that of the Assembly, the only true legal representatives of the people; and as to the individuals who you say officiously interrupt (in my quarter) the mode and measures you think necessary for these salutary purposes, I am really a stranger to them. If you mean myself you must have been grossly imposed on. I once, indeed, went with reluctance, at the request of several of the principal inhabitants, to one of the people's meetings, which I found had been called by an itinerant New England leather-dresser, and conducted by others, if possible, more contemptible. I had, therefore, little inclination to revisit such men, or attend to their absurdities. And although I did not incline to think that you, gentlemen, had formed any designs against me, yet it is most certain that such designs were formed. Of this I received a clear account by express from a friend near Albany, which was soon corroborated by letters from other quarters, particularly one from a gentleman of the Committee at Philadelphia, a captain in your levies, who was pretty circumstantial, and since I have had the like from many others. I have likewise found that mean instruments were obviously employed to disturb the minds of the Indians, to interrupt the ordinary discharge of my duties and prevent their receiving messages they had long since expected from me. To enter into a minute detail of all the falsehoods propagated and all the obstructions I met with, though it could not fail astonishing any gentlemen disposed to discountenance them, would far exceed the limits of a letter or the time I have to spare, as I am now finishing my congress, entirely to my satisfaction, with 1,348 warriors, who came hither to the only place where they could transact business or receive favors without interruptions, and who are much disatisfied at finding that the goods which I was necessitated to send for to Montreal were obliged to be ordered back by the merchant, to prevent his being insulted or his property invaded by the mistaken populace—that their ammunition was stopped at Albany—the persons on this communication employed in purchasing provisions for the Congress insulted, and all my letters, as well as even some trifling articles for the use of my own table stopped; and this moment the Mayor of Albany assured me that he was the other day aroused out of his bed, at a certain Mr. Thompson's, above the German Flats, by one Herkimer, and fifteen others, who pursued him to search for any things he might have for me.

"You may be assured, sir, that this is far from being agreeable to the Indians; that it might have produced very disagreeable consequences long since, had not compassion for a deluded people taken place of every other consideration. And that the impotent endeavors of a missionary (who has forfeited his honor pledged to me,) with part of one of the tribes, is a circumstance that, however trifling, increases their resentment.

I should be much obliged by your promises of discountenancing any attempts against myself, etc., did they not appear to be made on conditions of compliance with Continental or Provincial Congresses, or even committees formed, or to be formed, many of whose resolves may neither consist with my conscience, duty, or loyalty. I trust I shall always manifest more humanity than to promote the destruction of the innocent inhabitants of a colony to which I have been always warmly attached, a declaration that must appear perfectly suitable to the character of a man of honor and principle, who can on no account neglect those duties that are consistent therewith, however they may differ from sentiments now adopted in so many parts of America.

"I sincerely wish a speedy termination to the present troubles, and I am, sir, your most humble servant,

"G. JOHNSON.

"I shall have occasion to meet the Indians of my department in different quarters this season."

Johnson went from Ontario to Oswego, where he invited the Six Nations to another council, to "feast on a Bostonian and to drink his blood"—in other words, to eat a roasted ox and drink a pipe of wine. The council was held, and the Six Nations were further estranged from the republicans. Then Johnson, with a large number of the chiefs and warriors of the confederacy, who had been invited to an interview with Sir Guy Carleton and Sir

Frederick Haldimand at Montreal, crossed Lake Ontario and went down the St. Lawrence.

Meanwhile the Continental Congress, perceiving, from the frequent letters of General Schuyler and others in New York, the great importance of keeping a vigilant eye upon the Six Nations and other Indians, and of preserving their neutrality if not securing their alliance, established a Board of Commissioners for Indian Affairs, in three distinct departments, known as the Northern, Middle, and Southern. They appointed as such commissioners for the Northern department General Philip Schuyler, Major Joseph Hawley, Turbutt Francis, Oliver Wolcott, and Volckert P. Douw. They also adopted appropriate "talks" or addresses to the Indians, in which the nature of the quarrel between the colonists and the mother country was explained; and they were entreated to remain at home in peace:*

"We desire," they said, "you will hear and receive what we have now told you, and that you will open a good ear, and listen to what we are now going to say. This is a family quarrel between us and old England. You Indians are not concerned in it. We do not wish you to take up the hatchet against the King's troops. We desire you to remain at home, and not join on either side, but keep the hatchet buried deep. In the name and behalf of all our people we ask and desire you to love peace and maintain it, and to love and sympathize with us in our troubles, that the path may be kept open with all our people and yours to pass and repass without molestation. * * * What is it we have asked of you? Nothing but peace, notwithstanding our present disturbed situation; and if application should be made to you by any of the King's unwise and wicked ministers to join on their side, we only advise you to deliberate with great caution, and in your wisdom look forward to the consequences of a compliance. For if the King's troops take away our property, and destroy us who are of the same blood with themselves, what can you, who are Indians, expect from them afterward? Therefore, we say, brothers, take care! hold fast to your covenant chain."

* Journals of Congress, July 12, 13, 1775.

This was an honest effort to keep the savages from the field, and, had a like humane and discreet policy governed the councils of the British ministry and their agents, many a horrible deed, whose record stains the annals of that period, would never have been committed. But at that very time, when the Republicans were endeavoring to chain the bloodhounds, Johnson and his superiors in Canada were inciting them to engage in the contest, and carry on their hellish warfare side by side with the troops of enlightened England. British historians have asserted to the contrary; and the character of the really humane Carleton has been defended by assertions that he discountenanced all alliance with the Indians at the beginning of the war. But almost thirty years afterward, Brant, the most noted of the allied chiefs, bore explicit testimony to the contrary in the following extract from his speech, in which he recapitulated the services of the Mohawks during the contest:

"I exhort you," Carleton said to us, "to continue your adherence to the King, and not to break the solemn agreement made by your forefathers; for your own welfare is intimately connected with your continuing the allies of his Majesty. He also said a great deal more to the same purport. * * * A council was next convened at Montreal in July, 1775, at which the Seven Nations (or Caughnawagas) were present, as well as ourselves, the Six Nations. On this occasion General Haldimand told us what had befallen the King's subjects, and said, 'Now is the time for you to help the King. The war has commenced. Assist the King now, and you will find it to your advantage. Go, now, and fight for your possessions, and whatever you lose of your property during the war, the King will make up to you when peace returns.' This is the substance of what General Haldimand said. The Caughnawaga Indians then joined themselves to us. We immediately commenced in good earnest, and did our utmost during the war."*

* Stone's *Life of Brant*, i. 89. "The speech of Brant, from which the preceding extract is taken," says Mr. Stone, "was written in the Mohawk language, and never by him rendered into English." Mr. Stone procured its translation for his work.

General Schuyler reached Ticonderoga early on the morning of the 18th of July, and entered immediately into an examination of the condition of the fort and garrison. He found every thing in a wretched state. The army was comparatively but a handful, and the supplies were very meager. The troops under Colonel Hinman numbered only about twelve hundred. They consisted chiefly of Connecticut people, some New York volunteers, and a few Green Mountain Boys. Most of them were undisciplined, and those from Connecticut were extremely insubordinate. Unaccustomed to actual military service; having volunteered to perform the duty required of them; feeling a perfect equality with the officers set over them; and demoralized by the quarrels of their official superiors, of which they had been daily witnesses, they were in an unfit mood for yielding to the requirements of necessary discipline, especially such as General Schuyler felt it his duty to impose. He found Colonel Hinman only a nominal commander of the garrison, for very few of his men were disposed to obey him. This was a state of things which Schuyler could not endure for a moment. He was a thorough disciplinarian, naturally authoritative, and precise and systematic in all his arrangements. He was therefore much annoyed by all that he saw and heard after reaching the head of Lake George, and on the evening of the day of his arrival he wrote as follows to General Washington, at Cambridge:

"You will expect that I should say something about this place and the troops here. Not one earthly thing for offense or defense has been done. The commanding officer had no orders; he only came to reinforce the garrison, and he expected the general. (But this, my dear general, as well as what follows in this paragraph, I pray may be *entre nous*, for reasons which I need not suggest.) About ten last night I arrived at the landing-place, the north end of Lake George, a post oc cupied by a captain and one hundred men. A sentinel, on being informed that I was in the boat, quitted his post to go and awake the guard, consisting of three men, in which he had no success. I walked up and came to another, a sergeant's guard. Here the sentinel challenged, but suffered me to come up to him; the whole guard, like the first, in soundest sleep. With a pen-knife only I could have cut off both guards, and then have set fire to the blockhouse, destroyed the stores, and starved the people here. At this post I had pointedly recommended vigilance and care, as all stores for Fort George must necessarily be landed there. But I hope to get the better of this inattention. The officers and men are all good looking people, and decent in their deportment, and I really believe will make good soldiers, as soon as I can get the better of this *nonchalance* of theirs. Bravery, I believe, they are far from wanting."*

This letter brought a sympathetic response from Washington, written on the 28th of the month. The Commander-in-Chief had arrived at Cambridge on the 2d of July, where he was greeted by the shouts of a great multitude of soldiers and citizens, the clangor of bells, the strains of martial music, and the waving of banners, and escorted to the house in which he made his headquarters. On the following day, seated upon his large white horse of Arabian blood, he reviewed the troops and took formal command of the army. Like Schuyler, his first care was to make himself acquainted with the condition of the post and the character and position of the enemy's works. The inquiry revealed much to discourage a less trusting spirit than his. He found a disposition to insubordination the rule, and good discipline and cheerful obedience the exception; and with the hope of inspiring the troops with a due sense of the importance of the service and the necessity for perfect obedience, harmony, and good will, he issued a general order which may be regarded as a model of its class, in which, in a few words, he evoked harmony, order, the

* MS. Letter Books, July 18, 1775.

exercise of patriotism, morality, sobriety, and an humble reverence for and reliance upon Divine Providence.

Every day some new difficulty, some weakness unobserved before, some exhibition of an impatient if not an actually mutinous spirit in the troops caused Washington to feel that a fearful weight of responsibility was resting upon his shoulders ; and with a full appreciation of the situation of Schuyler, he wrote to him in reply to that officer's letter respecting affairs at Ticonderoga, saying :

> "I can easily judge of your difficulties in introducing order and discipline into troops who have from their infancy imbibed ideas of the most contrary kind. It would be far beyond the compass of a letter for me to describe the situation of things here on my arrival. Perhaps you will only be able to judge of it from my assuring you that mine must be a portraiture at full length of which you have had in miniature. Confusion and discord reigned in every department, which, in a little time, must have ended either in the separation of the army or fatal contests with one another. * * * However, we mend every day, and I flatter myself that in a little time we shall work up these raw materials into a good manufacture. I must recommend to you what I endeavor to practice myself—patience and perseverance."

To this Schuyler replied, after thanking him for his "very kind and polite letter :"

> "I foresaw, my dear sir, that you would have an herculean labor in order to introduce that proper spirit of discipline and subordination which is the very soul of an army, and I felt for you with the utmost sensibility, as I well knew the variety of difficulties you would have to encounter. * * * I can easily conceive that my difficulties are only a faint semblance of yours. Yes, my General, I will strive to copy your bright example, and patiently and steadily persevere in that line which alone can promise the wished for reformation."*

General Schuyler set about reforms with a will and energy that soon produced material changes. Yet there was so much tardiness in the service, in all directions, that he

* MS. Letter Books, August 6, 1775

could accomplish but little in preparations either for an invasion of Canada or a successful defense should a respectable force make its way up the lake from that province. It was very difficult to procure reliable intelligence from Montreal and Quebec. Every account concurred in representing the Canadians as being generally favorable to the republicans, while the elders of the Caughnawagas were hesitating whether to lift the hatchet for the King, as the young men desired to, or remain at home in peace. The moment seemed favorable for marching to the borders of, and perhaps into that province; and circumstances were occurring which made it probable that the golden moment was passing when an almost bloodless conquest might be won. Robert Benson, Chairman of the New York Committee of Safety, in a postscript to a letter, had said: "General Burgoyne has not been seen at Boston since the 17th ult. (June), and it is currently reported and believed that he is gone to Quebec;"* while a gentleman just arrived from Montreal stated that Governor Carleton was very sanguine that, through the influence of the Roman Catholic clergy, the Canadians might be kept neutral, if not be made friendly to the government, and that troops from England or Boston were expected at Quebec. Other accounts contradicted this.

These items of intelligence made Schuyler impatient, and he wrote to every person and public body from whom he had a right to expect aid, urging them to put forth all their energies in providing him with men, money, stores, and munitions of war. He was informed that the British were strengthening St. John's, at the foot of the lake, and were making preparations to construct vessels for a fleet.

* Autograph letter.

"But, unfortunately," he wrote to the Continental Congress, "not one earthly thing has been done here to enable me to move hence. I have neither boats sufficient, nor any materials prepared for building them. The stores I ordered from New York are not yet arrived. I have, therefore, not a nail, no pitch, no oakum, and want a variety of articles indispensably necessary, which I estimated and delivered into the New York Congress on the 3d instant. An almost equal scarcity of ammunition exists, no powder having yet come to hand. Not a gun carriage for the few proper guns we have, and as yet very little provision. There are now two hundred troops less than by my last return. These are badly, very badly armed, indeed; and only one poor armorer to repair their guns."*

The tardiness with which the troops for the service assembled gave Schuyler more uneasiness than any thing else. Those of Connecticut, under General Wooster, at New York and on Long Island, were very slow in their movements; and the preparations of the New York levies for the field seemed to have almost ceased after he left for the north. On this subject he wrote very urgent letters to the Provincial Congress. That body, utterly powerless, sent his letters to the New York delegates in the Continental Congress, with an earnest appeal.

"We have no arms, we have no powder, we have no blankets," they said. "For God's sake, send us money, send us arms, send us ammunition. Burgoyne, we learn, has gone to Quebec. If Ticonderoga is taken from us, fear, which made the savages our friends, will render them our enemies. Ravages on our frontiers will foster dissentions among us ruinous to our cause. Be prudent, be expeditious."

To General Schuyler they wrote at the same time in an equally despairing tone, saying:

"We have already ordered to Albany tents for one regiment. Our troops can be of no service to you. They have no arms, clothes, blankets, or ammunition; the officers no commissions; our treasury no money; ourselves in debt. It is in vain to complain. We will remove difficulties as fast as we can, and send you soldiers whenever the men we have

* MS. Letter Books, July 21, 1775.

raised are entitled to that name. * * * Use, we pray you, the bad troops at Ticonderoga as well as you can."*

Yet Schuyler was not discouraged. "I hope," he wrote to Governor Trumbull, "in a little while to make all obstacles vanish. Much may be done when people set down to business with hand and heart." A few days afterward he was cheered by the announcement that his wishes had been complied with, in the appointment of necessary officers for his department. Walter Livingston (already employed by Schuyler) was appointed deputy commissary-general of stores and provisions, Donald Campbell was made deputy quarter-master general, and Gunning Bedford deputy muster-master general.†

Feuds had caused delay in the organization of the regiment of Green Mountain Boys. Schuyler had no confidence in their professions of strength in numbers and zeal in patriotism. Under their title he had known, for several years, a set of rioters and lawless men, who had defied the authorities of his province, and he was not at all pleased with the idea of having those train-bands as a part of his army. He was, therefore, extremely cautious, and took pains to know whom he was to call to the field before he issued his proclamation of the resolves of the two congresses. He accordingly wrote to Stephen Fay, a leading man of Bennington, saying:

"Who the people are that are designated by the appellation of Green Mountain Boys, I am at a loss particularly to determine. Perhaps such of the inhabitants of this colony as reside on what are commonly called the New Hampshire Grants are intended. In this doubt I find myself under the necessity of applying to you for information, which I entreat, and make no doubt but you will give me with all that candor which, as a friend to your country, is your indispensable duty to do."‡

* Journals of the New York Committee of Safety, July 15, 1775.

† Journals of Congress, July 17, 1775.

‡ MS. Letter Books, July 10, 1775.

He then urged Mr. Fay to take such necessary steps "as that the Green Mountain Boys, whoever they may be," might immediately proceed to the election of their officers, and fill the regiment without delay. Mr. Fay assured him that the inhabitants of the Grants were the Green Mountain Boys alluded to, and that they would "esteem it a favor to be incorporated into an independent battalion," subject to the required regulations. "As to the nomination of the officers," he said, "I am advised to mention none to your honor except the field officers, which are universally approved of, namely, Mr. Ethan Allen and Mr. Seth Warner."*

Meanwhile, Allen and Warner had become impatient of the delay. In a letter to Governor Trumbull, the latter said:

> "Were it not that the grand Continental Congress had totally incorporated the Green Mountain Boys into a battalion, under certain regulations and command, I would forthwith advance them into Canada and invest Montreal, exclusive of any help from the colonies; though, under present circumstances, I would not, for my right arm, act without or contrary to order. If my fond zeal for reducing the King's fortresses, or destroying or imprisoning his troops in Canada, be the result of enthusiasm, I hope and expect the wisdom of the continent will treat it as such; and on the other hand, if it proceed from sound policy, that the plan will be adopted."†

Allen and Warner visited Ticonderoga, and laid before General Schuyler the state of affairs in the Grants. They spoke of the feuds that delayed the organization of the regiment, and acknowledged, what Schuyler had suspected, that the number of Green Mountain Boys was so small that they would be compelled to recruit in New England to make up the complement of five hundred men. Not

* Autograph letter, July 13, 1775.

† American Archives, ii. 1,649, July 12, 1775.

doubting their own election to the highest posts, they urged him to empower them to appoint all the subordinate officers. He referred them to the resolutions of both congresses, which left the choice of all the officers to the people ; and they departed, not well pleased with the results of their visit, nor with each other.

Soon after this Allen and Warner quarreled. Their respective friends became antagonistic partisans and the feud was intensified. Others felt disposed to drop them both, and give the field offices to less objectionable men. Mr. Fay's letter, in which he had recommended them, offended some of the leading persons in the Grants, and they wrote to Schuyler on the subject, urging him not to issue any commissions until the voice of the people, expressed in a convention about to be held, could be heard, when he should "be favored with an authentic answer to his letter." Schuyler paid very little attention to these communications. He had no love for the Green Mountain Boys as a body, and these feuds, standing in the way of the public service, disgusted him. He was willing to dispense with the services of Colonel Allen altogether, for, prejudiced perhaps by past occurrences, he regarded him as selfish in his ambition, naturally insubordinate, and too indiscreet to be a safe leader.

The more thoughtful men of the Grants, looking at the past, and contemplating the aspect of the future, also felt a doubt of the policy of placing Allen at the head of the regiment ; and when, at last, toward the close of July, the election was held, he was passed by. They omitted to choose a colonel, and Warner was nominated for lieutenant-colonel.

Allen, who had not the least doubt of his election, was much mortified. "Notwithstanding my zeal and success in my country's cause," he wrote to Governor Trumbull, "the old farmers in the New Hampshire Grants, who do not incline to go to war, have met in a committee meeting, and in their nomination of officers for the regiment of Green Mountain Boys have wholly omitted me." Many were pleased; and General Montgomery, when he heard of it, wrote to Schuyler, saying: "It is a change which will be very acceptable to our convention."

Allen, who was undoubtedly a true patriot, and did not really deserve the suspicions and dislike of Schuyler, did not suffer this severe disappointment to chill his zeal in the cause, and he immediately repaired to Ticonderoga and offered his services to the General as a volunteer. Even these were at first refused, for Schuyler doubted whether he could keep the restless republican within due bounds. He finally accepted his services, and employed him in pioneer duties on the frontier, in which he was energetic and faithful.

Another volunteer for similar service appeared. Major John Brown, an American resident on the banks of the Sorel or Richelieu river, who was well acquainted with the character of the Canadians, the impressions to which they were most susceptible, and the topography and resources of their country, offered to use his influence in persuading the inhabitants to join the republican standard. He came well recommended, and General Schuyler at once commissioned him for the service, and furnished him with the following general letter to such persons as, in his judgment, would give information and efficient aid:

"TICONDEROGA, July 21, 1775.

"SIR:—Reports prevail that General Carleton intends an excursion into these parts; that for that purpose he is raising a body of Canadians and Indians; that he is preparing to build as well armed vessels as other craft to transport troops across the lake; that he is strongly fortifying St. John's; that Colonel Guy Johnson is to join him with a body of In-

Indians; that vast magazines of arms and ammunition are collected at Montreal; that the Canadians are averse to take part in the unhappy contest; that they nevertheless wish we would enter Canada and attack the regular troops. On every one of these articles I wish the fullest information, together with such other as you may be enabled to give me. The regular troops at Boston have been severely handled by the provincials; a list of the killed and wounded officers you will see in the newspapers which I send you. Many of the wounded are since dead.

"General Washington commands an army before Boston of twenty-three thousand men, which is continually increasing.

"Pennsylvania has raised five thousand; these, with three thousand from Jersey, are encamped in different towns in the Jerseys, as near New York as they conveniently can. Brigadier General Richard Montgomery, of New York, and Brigadier General Wooster, of Connecticut, who command under me, are on their way up to join me. The latter, with two thousand Connecticut people, join me to-day. The former, with three thousand New Yorkers, is following—the front reach Fort Edward to-day. Five hundred Green Mountain Boys are to join me in ten days, as also Colonel Ross, with six hundred riflemen from the back parts of Pennsylvania. When these all meet, my force will consist of near 8,000 men.

"We have just received information that the accounts of the Lexington affair had got home. It threw the nation into the greatest ferment; the ministry were loaded with curses, the Guards at St. James' doubled, the city of London in the greatest confusion, and, to add to all this, they just then received the most alarming accounts of the intentions of the Spaniards. If the ministry would but suffer his Majesty to see the injury they are doing to the empire, oh! they would give us an opportunity to fight the royal foes of his royal house; to spend our blood and treasure in supporting his dignity and resenting the insults the nation is threatened with by the haughty Spaniards, who are preparing to take the advantage of a divided empire.

"PHILIP SCHUYLER.

"Please to settle a mode of correspondence with the bearer. I do not direct this, lest the consequences should prove detrimental to you, should they fall into some hands."*

In his instructions to Major Brown, the General said: "Try to get the Caughnawagas to come and speak to me here. I will give them presents, and renew that friendship which subsisted between them and my ancestors. Wild-

* Schuyler's Order Book.

man knows me, and so does Mr. Williams'* sister. I gave her some things the winter before last, having sent for her to my house at Saratoga."

General Schuyler gave Major Brown a letter to Mr. Price, a merchant of Montreal, who was well-disposed toward the republican cause; and on Monday morning, the 23d of July, he set out with Captain Cochrane and a sergeant, and two Frenchmen.

"I am determined," he wrote to Schuyler, on his departure, "to touch at Caughnawaga the first place after hauling our boat out of the lake into some thicket near the river La Colle. Shall endeavor to see John Station, an English Indian and good old friend, by whose assistance I hope to get access to my friends at Montreal, by which means I shall find it in my power to execute your orders in every particular. Hope to return as soon as may be; but if, through misfortune, I am detained and ill-treated, I pray you to advance with force sufficient to effect with power that which I ought to have done with policy."†

* The reputed father of Eleazer Williams, the "Lost Prince,"—the alleged Dauphin of France, son of Louis the Sixteenth. The "Prince" died at Hogansburg, New York, in 1859.

† Autograph letter, July 23, 1775.

# CHAPTER XXI.

After the exercise of the greatest diligence and energy, General Schuyler found himself, at the beginning of August, as little prepared for offensive or defensive operations as at the beginning of July. Every thing appeared to work unfavorably. The country had been parched during a drought, which rendered food for draught cattle so scarce that the transportation of timber for boats and of provisions for the garrison had been much delayed.

"It gave me pain," he wrote to Governor Trumbull, "to learn that not less than fifty milch cows were on their way here for the use of Colonel Hinman's regiment. Our working cattle are in a starving condition, the country being parched up by the excessive drought. Such an additional number of cattle would destroy the little feed we have left, and be of very little use to the troops."*

Because of the scarcity of provisions, Schuyler ordered General Montgomery, who had arrived at Albany on the 17th of July, to encamp there all the troops that he might receive, until the commissariat at Ticonderoga should be in better condition. A few days later he wrote to General Washington, saying: "Provisions of the bread kind are scarce with me, and therefore I have not dared to order up a thousand men that are at Albany, lest we should starve here."†

Schuyler endeavored to create some supplies near at

* MS. Letter Books, July 21, 1775. † Ibid, July 31, 1775.

hand. The property of Colonel Skene, which the republicans had seized, was put to profitable use. His schooner, as we have observed, had already done good service on the lake. Now his saw-mill was used in preparing lumber, and his small iron works were put in operation under the direction of Samuel Keep, who employed negroes to dig ore near Crown Point, and transport it in scows to Skenesborough. At the same time orders were given that nothing should be done detrimental to the private interests of Colonel Skene. All lawless use of his property had been restrained by General Schuyler; and in a letter to Patrick Langan (who had the supervision of the Colonel's affairs), directing the saw-mill to be put in operation, he expressed a hope that order might be restored, "as" he said, "the view of my constituents is, not to distress any person or injure private property."

August was passing away, and Schuyler was still unsupplied with men and means.

"Not a man from this colony has yet joined me," he wrote to Washington, "except those I returned to you [July 15th], and who were raised and paid by the Committee of Albany; nor have I yet received those necessary supplies which I begged the New York Provincial Congress to send me as long ago as the third of last month, which the Continental Congress had desired them to do. The troops here are destitute of tents, and they are crowded into vile barracks, which, with the natural inattention of the soldiery to cleanliness, has already been productive of disease, and numbers are daily rendered unfit for duty."*

Jealousies arising out of the clashing authorities of the Continental Congress and the provincial legislatures were now beginning to bear their legitimate fruit, in the form of assumptions by inferiors which were detrimental to harmony and efficiency in the military service.

We have already observed the insubordination of the

* MS. Letter Books, August 6, 1775.

Connecticut troops, owing chiefly to their idea of perfect equality with their officers, forgetting that in their agreement to follow a leader some of their rights as citizens were surrendered. The private soldier, who felt at liberty to obey or not to obey his captain, also claimed the right to be fed and sheltered by whomsoever he might choose to administer the comfort, and not by another. This feeling of individual independence was shared by most of the Connecticut officers and men as a body ; and when the Continental Congress placed them in service on Lake Champlain, under the general command of a New York officer, they felt shorn of their dignity as citizens of another province, seemingly forgetful that in the great struggle before them the united colonies composed their country, and not the single commonwealth in which they happened to reside. This feeling had manifested itself in many ways, much to the annoyance of General Schuyler, whose views of patriotic sympathy, zeal, and service were broader than the domains of his own province. It at length found expression so offensive that he felt it his duty to rebuke it.

When troops were raised in Connecticut, Elisha Phelps was appointed by the Assembly of that province a general commissary to supply them, and Jedediah Strong, a representative in that assembly from Litchfield, was made a deputy commissary to supply the troops under Colonel Hinman. Strong was engaged in that service when those soldiers where placed under the command of General Schuyler, and Phelps made his residence at Albany, from which place he might more readily forward supplies to the army at Ticonderoga. Both he and Strong appear to have been energetic and faithful men, and had reason to expect promotion if any should be given.

Unfortunately for the harmony and best interests of the

service, Walter Livingston, a nephew of General Schuyler, and quite a young man, was, on the recommendation of his uncle, appointed by the Continental Congress, as we have seen, deputy commissary-general for the Northern department. He was every way competent to perform the duties of that office, and his numerous family connections gave him valuable advantages in the work of his department. But he superseded those already in the service, and aroused a feeling of jealousy on the part of the New England officers and troops which was productive of evil to the common cause.

Mr. Strong, under the direction of Mr. Phelps, had visited General Schuyler at Ticonderoga on business connected with the supply of the Connecticut troops, and was returning to Albany in company with Mr. Livingston, when they met, on Lake George, a gentleman from Philadelphia, bearing from the Congress the latter's commission as deputy commissary-general. The question immediately arose as to the extent of his powers. Livingston properly contended that his commission gave him official superiority to both Phelps and Strong. They denied it. High words ensued. Phelps and Strong contended that Livingston was only a deputy to the former; that it was his business to purchase provisions, etc., and deliver them to Phelps at Albany; and that the Continental Congress did not intend to turn the latter out of office while he behaved himself.

"I told him," wrote Phelps to Schuyler, "that there need be no difficulty between us; that he would have business enough, so should I. However, it did not satisfy the young gentleman, who said if he could not have all the business he would not have any, and added that your Honor had procured him his commission; that he was a nephew of yours, and that he would write to you and let you know that I would not resign. I think I can not answer it to the honorable Continental Congress, or the colony of Connecticut or the Massachusetts Bay [the latter concurred with Connecticut in the appointment of Mr. Phelps,] if I did, for I think him not a faithful and good soldier who gives up his commission before he is superseded or regularly dismissed."*

The three contestants wrote to General Schuyler on the same day. Phelps' letter, in courteous words, submitted the simple facts in the case, and begged General Schuyler to "interpose and direct," that the business might be so managed by them as not "to interfere with or disoblige the common cause." Strong, less discreet, wrote an offensive letter. He spoke of his own ill-requited services ; the unfulfilled promises of supplies for the Connecticut troops made by the Provincial Congress of New York ; and of his recent purchases of provisions and live cattle for those troops. He inquired what should be done with his purchases ; referred to the appointment of Livingston by saying : "I find employed some people never recommended to that department by the colony [Connecticut], to purchase our cattle with our own money at an advanced price ;" reminded Schuyler of an alleged promise on his part to recommend Strong to the commissary-general, whomsoever he might be ; and expressed a hope that Commissary Phelps might be retained in office, because he had conducted the business with fidelity and dispatch. After some remarks complimentary of General Schuyler, Strong said :

"'T is, therefore, from your well known acquaintance with human nature, your candor, justice, and generosity, that I entertain the highest expectations and strongest assurance that your influence will be successfully used in removing every jealousy and every cause of it which might tend to alienate the affections of any colony or any part of the army towards so worthy a general and so noble an enterprise. God forbid that any *overgrown colony* or *overbearing man* should at this critical juncture use such pernicious partiality as to *attempt to monopolize every emolument*

* Autograph letter, July 28, 1775.

and exclude every instrument of public service, for no other accusation or complaint than that he belongs to the most patriotic, free, and generous colony on earth."*

General Schuyler took fire at the perusal of Strong's letter, and wrote an indignant reply. That letter had im-impeached his honor, and, by implication, arraigned his integrity. After reminding Strong that it was the duty of all to acquiesce in the determinations of the Continental Congress, and "to obey their orders without entering into the reasons upon which they were founded;" that Mr. Livingston, by virtue of his commission, had the control of all other commissaries in the department, because he was responsible for their conduct; that none but incompetent or useless men would be discharged, and that Captain Phelps would be retained, he informed him that Mr. Livingston would receive the provisions and cattle whenever they should be delivered to him. He then said:

"I should have closed my letter here, but that I think myself under a necessity to put you right in some matters. You say 'When I find employed some people never recommended to that department by the colony, to purchase our cattle with our own money.' Remember, sir, that the appointment was not made by me; that it was made by the Continental Congress, in which the colony of Connecticut is represented. That neither the cattle nor any other stores are to be bought at the expense of the colony of Connecticut; they are to be purchased at the joint expense of the associated colonies, agreeable to the quota fixed or to be fixed by the Continental Congress; and I believe it will be no great hardship, in that case, for the people of Connecticut to have their cattle purchased by whomsoever it may be done, or with any current money whatever.

"I really do not know what you mean by 'monopolizing every emolument.' I do not know who has done it. I have not. If the Continental Congress has done it, I am not the person you should complain to. I am their servant, and not their superior. A copy of your letter I shall transmit to that respectable body.

"I readily, sir, agree with the encomium you have bestowed on the

* Autograph letter, July 28, 1775.

colony of Connecticut, having ever entertained the highest opinion of their virtue and patriotism, in which I am not singular.

"What you intend by using the epithet 'overgrown' is best known to yourself; my construction of it is not very favorable to you.

"I shall always consider it an indispensable part of my duty to try to remove every cause of jealousy in the army which I have the honor to command, and I sincerely wish none may prevail between any colonies, *overgrown* or not. I am not conscious that I have given the least cause for any. If I have, I wish you would complain of me to the Congress. If not, you might have spared the observation."*

To Mr. Phelps the General wrote:

"Mr. Livingston's appointment is made by the Continental Congress, who are my constituents, and whose orders I am implicitly to obey, and so, indeed, is every person that has any concern with the army, in whatever station he may be. You seem to be little acquainted with military distinctions, not to know that a deputy commissary-*general's* commission supersedes a mere *commissary's*. Such an appointment is absolutely necessary, that every general who commands an army may have only one person to apply to to furnish him with what may be wanted, and that person must then be accountable."†

General Schuyler also wrote to the Continental Congress on the same day, and inclosed copies of the letters of Phelps and Strong. He acquainted that body of the refusal of Strong to yield to Livingston, and added: "I should not have troubled you with these letters, but that you may from them see the necessity of some general resolution of the Congress to cure all this jarring."

Before this letter reached Philadelphia, the Continental Congress had adjourned until the fifth of September, after having appropriated "a sum not exceeding one hundred and seventy-five thousand dollars to be applied toward the discharge of monies advanced and the debts contracted for the public service," by the convention of New York and the Albany Committee; and a further sum of one hundred

* MS. Letter Books, July 31, 1775. † Ibid.

thousand dollars for the use of the northern army, "in such manner as General Schuyler, by his warrant, shall limit and appoint."*

The correspondence between Schuyler and the Connecticut commissaries produced much ill-feeling at the time, nd was one of the causes of discord and contention, distrust and heart-burning, which prevailed in the Northern army during the remainder of the campaign. The sectional feeling of both the New York and Connecticut troops was strong, and General Schuyler was not the person to allay it by concessions. He was eminently just and generous as a man; as a soldier he was inflexible in his demands for obedience and the respect due to his rank and position. He was naturally quick-tempered, but placable; impatient of disobedience; punctilious in his requirements of attention to every form of etiquette pertaining to the service; never deigning to argue with an inferior, and seldom explaining his motives for a command. In his manner he was dignified, but not haughty; as a disciplinarian he was exacting and uncompromising. He made labor a rule—an absolute necessity—for each soldier reported fit for duty. Work, work, work, whenever needed and in whatever form, was required of the troops; and the idleness that prevailed in the camp previous to his arrival entirely disappeared. The exigencies of the service required such industry, and the health of the soldiers demanded it. Laborers outside of the army were few, and money for wages was scarce. He therefore converted the garrison into a hive of industry, and had every soldier thoroughly drilled for the service before him. This discipline, and labor, and authoritative exactions, so essential to the success of the expedition, were novelties in the expérience of the troops. They were en-

* Journals of Congress, August 1, 1775.

dured as a scourge by those who imagined that a soldier had little else to do while in camp but to keep his weapons clean and practice the military art; and Schuyler was regarded by many as an imperious taskmaster. But those who knew him intimately, shared his confidence, and appreciated the value of his discipline to the service, loved and honored him as a wise, kind-hearted, noble, and generous man.

While Major Brown was absent on his mission, Schuyler received intelligence from Canada that made him more impatient than ever to move down the lake and take possession of St. John's. He was informed that a force of four or five hundred Canadians were assembled at that place, and were supplied with provisions from Montreal and Quebec; that two fortifications were in process of erection there, and that one was nearly completed, mounting eight field-pieces and some small mortars; that thirty or forty heavy guns, with carriages, had been brought up to Chamblée, twelve miles distant; that the enemy were building large vessels at St. John's, to carry sixteen to eighteen guns each; that four regiments of regulars were expected at Quebec; that Colonel John Johnson, and his brother-in-law, Colonel Daniel Claus, were in the neighborhood of Montreal, with about five hundred Tories and Indians; and that the clergy and seigniors of Canada were endeavoring to stimulate the inhabitants to take up arms against the republicans. He was also informed that the Canadians were generally disposed to be neutral; that in a recent attempt, by officers sent for the purpose, to compel them to take up arms, in which several who refused were killed, they had assembled to the number of three thousand, disarmed some of the officers, and obliged others to desist; and that the inhabitants were so well disposed toward the republicans, that if an army sufficient to protect them should be immediately marched into the province, they would certainly not take up arms for the King, and would probably be active in the liberal cause.*

But Schuyler's efforts toward adequate preparations for advancing upon St. John's were, as yet, almost unavailing. He had constructed some boats, was building others, and had procured officers to command them; but men, and supplies of every kind, were wanting. He appealed to the Continental Congress for powder, for money, and for hospital stores.

> "I shall not have quite a ton of powder when the troops are completed to a pound a man," he wrote. "Out of about five hundred men who are here, near one hundred are sick, and I have not any kind of hospital stores. The little wine I had for my own table I have delivered to the regimental surgeon. That being expended, I can no longer bear the distress of the sick, and, impelled by the feelings of humanity, I shall take the liberty immediately to order a physician from Albany (if one can be got there, as I believe there may,) to join us with such stores as are indispensably necessary."†

The Continental Congress had adjourned and gone home, and Schuyler's letters remained unanswered by them for a month. Dr. Franklin, the president of the Philadelphia Committee of Safety, opened them and sent them to President Hancock, but that officer had no delegated power to give orders in the premises, and Schuyler was left to "act," as he said, upon his "own ideas of things in a critical situation." He appealed to the Provincial Congress of New York, but almost in vain. At that moment they could do absolutely nothing. Their inability was called indifference by some, and disaffection by others.

* MS. Depositions of John Duguid and John Shatforth, taken before General Schuyler, at Ticonderoga, August 2, 1775.

† MS. Letter Books, August 6, 1775.

"By all the appearances of the conduct of the province of New York," wrote Samuel Mott from Ticonderoga to Governor Trumbull, "they still are unsound at heart. They make a great noise, and send forward a few officers to command, etc., and all the carpenters and artificers who are to have extra pay; but I believe as to soldiers in the service, they are not more than one hundred and fifty strong at all the posts this side of Albany; and it is feared by many discerning men that even their Provincial Congress have scarcely a majority who are sound friends to the cause. * * * The General drives things on as fast as he can, considering what hinderance he has for want of nails, etc., and I believe him to be a very resolute, good officer."* "The New Yorkers," wrote Major Brown to the same gentleman, "have acted a droll part, and are determined to defeat us if in their power. They have failed in men and supplies."

The omission of New York to raise *men* at that time, ought not to have been a cause for unqualified censure, for it had been mutually stipulated that Connecticut should furnish troops, and New York supplies. But the latter was a difficult task.

"You can't conceive," wrote Livingston, president of the New York Congress, to General Schuyler, in a private postcript to a public letter announcing the forwarding of supplies by Peter Curtenius, the contractor; "you can't conceive the trouble we have with our troops for the want of money. To this hour we have not received a shilling of the public money. Two of our members have been at Philadelphia almost a fortnight waiting for the cash. Our men insist on being paid before they march, not their subsistence only, but also their billeting money. Perhaps no men have been more embarrassed than we."†

"The corporation arms," wrote Alexander McDougall, the ardent Son of Liberty, who had been appointed colonel of the first regiment of New York troops, "were so scattered in the hands of the people, that it was with infinite trouble we were able, out of 530, to collect 470, notwithstanding a severe resolution of Congress issued to call them in; and when they were sent to the gunsmith's, for want of money to discharge their bills they gave the preference to other work."‡

Major Brown returned to Ticonderoga on the 15th of

* August 4, 1775, American Archives, iii. 22.
† Autograph letter, August 21, 1775.
‡ Autograph letter, August 9, 1775.

August, and reported that there were seven hundred regular troops in Canada, three hundred of whom were at St. John's; others formed a small garrison at Quebec; and the remainder were at Montreal, Chamblée, and posts at the Cedars and Oswegatchie (now Ogdensburgh), further up the St. Lawrence. He had learned that Sir John Johnson was at Montreal, with a band of almost three hundred Tories and some Indians, trying to persuade the Caughnawagas to take up the hatchet for the King. He confirmed the previous report of fortifications, vessels, and cannon at St. John's, and gave it as his opinion that the Canadians (who believed that the old French laws, which would impose heavy taxes upon them, were about to be revived) were anxious to see a strong army enter their province and relieve them from British rule, but were unwilling to take up arms. He was assured that the Indians would go with the Canadians; and he closed his report by an expression of his belief that the conquest of Canada, if undertaken at at once, might be easily achieved.

Major Brown did not accomplish all that Schuyler had expected, but his information was sufficiently reliable and complete to induce the General to push forward to St. John's even with his small force, inadequately supplied, as soon as he should receive positive orders from Washington to do so. "I am prepared," he wrote to the commander-in-chief, "to move against the enemy, unless your Excellency and Congress should direct otherwise."*

Troops and supplies were then going forward. The Provincial Congress of New York were using every effort to furnish the quota of one thousand men required of them by the Continental Congress. They had organized four regiments of infantry, under the respective commands of

* MS. Letter Books, August 6, 1775.

Colonels McDougall, Van Schaick, Clinton, and Holmes; and some of them were on the point of departure for the North at this time. Captain John Lamb, who had received valuable instructions on engineering and gunnery from Christopher Colles, had been, at his own request, commissioned to raise an artillery company of one hundred men. These were attached to Colonel McDougall's regiment, but on a footing superior to that of the infantry, and were ordered to join General Schuyler as speedily as possible. General Wooster, who had been ordered to Ticonderoga with one thousand troops, had despatched "the whole of Colonel Waterbury's regiment, except the sick," and "Captain Douglas' company."* Waterbury arrived at Albany at about the time when Schuyler wrote to Montgomery to detain the troops there on account of scarcity of provision at Ticonderoga; and at his own request, he had advanced as far as Half-Moon Point (now Waterford), to avoid "the small-pox and debauchery" in Albany. His men were employed in repairing the roads between his camp and Forts Edward and George. These now marched toward Ticonderoga.

The New Hampshire Committee of Safety offered to send to Schuyler three companies of sixty men each, "rangers, hunters, and men accustomed to the woods," under Colonel Bedell, whom they recommended as "a person of great experience in war, and well acquainted in Canada."† These had been raised as a guard on the western frontiers of Connecticut. Their services were not needed there, and they had been offered to General Washington. His army was sufficiently strong, and he recommended them to the army of the North. They were accepted gladly, for the

* Wooster to Schuyler, autograph letter, July 29, 1775.

† Matthew Thornton to Schuyler, autograph letter, August 7, 1775.

tardiness of the Green Mountain Boys in forming their regiment, gave indication that they might not fulfill the bright promises made by Allen and Warner at the beginning.

Governor Trumbull sent Schuyler cheering words of encouragement; and Silas Deane, one of the most active of the Connecticut delegates in Congress, and who had been among the earliest promoters of the scheme for capturing the lake fortresses and invading Canada, advised him to rely upon the Connecticut people for provisions, for, he said, "I fear you will find New York but a broken reed, and if you should depend too far I fear the consequences. Cattle, and sheep, as well as pork, can best be procured in this colony."*

Dr. Franklin, who had been touched by Schuyler's appeals to the Continental Congress in the letters he had opened, wrote to him, as president of the Philadelphia Committee of Safety, saying:

"I did myself the honor of writing to you by the return of your express on the 8th instant. Immediately after dispatching him, it occurred to me to endeavor the obtaining from our Committee of Safety a permission to send you what powder remained in our hands, which, though it was thought scarcely safe for ourselves to part with it, they, upon my application, and representing the importance of the service you are engaged in, and the necessity you are under for that article, cheerfully agreed to. Accordingly, I this day dispatch a wagon with twenty-four hundred pounds weight, which actually empties our magazine. I wish it safe to your hands, and to yourself every kind of prosperity.†

The cautious Chase, deputy from Maryland, who had not favored the invasion of Canada, wrote from Annapolis on the same day, saying:

"I am sensible of the many difficulties you have to encounter, and of the anxiety of mind naturally attendant on your very important, and

* Autograph letter, August 15, 1775.
† Autograph letter, August 10, 1775.

I am afraid, very dangerous command. I sincerely wish you may be enabled to render any effectual service to America. Powder you will receive; provisions, I hope, will be better supplied, and a sufficient body of troops furnished to render the event favorable to your most sanguine expectations.

"I can not but interest myself in your success. The expediency, the prudence of the expedition is left to your judgment. A provident condition, a *sine qua non* of marching into Quebec, is the friendship of the Canadians; without their consent and approbation it is not to be undertaken. So I understand the resolution of the Congress. The generality, the bulk of mankind judge only from the success. I think you, therefore, in a very critical situation, and that an exertion of all your faculties of mind and body are necessary. May I be permitted to wish that a military ardor, a soldier's honor, or a compliance with the temper and inclinations of others, may not prevail over your better judgment. There may be some, from want of discretion, and others from envy, who may be urging you to undertake what your prudence may condemn. I hope I have not said too much, and that my anxiety will be imputed to no other cause than my zeal for America and my regard for you. God grant you success."*

Toward the middle of August, Jonathan Trumbull, son of the Connecticut governor, was appointed paymaster-general for the Northern Department, and at about the same time Judge William Duer, residing at Fort Miller, in Charlotte county, received from the New York Provincial Congress the commission of deputy adjutant-general of the New York forces. Sometime before, Schuyler had contemplated nominating Colonel Arnold for that office. Notwithstanding Arnold's infirmities of temper and haughtiness of spirit, Schuyler admired his daring courage, his energetic industry, and his skill and judgment as a military commander; and no one doubted his patriotism. Before Arnold left Crown Point for Cambridge in partial disgrace, Schuyler wrote to Silas Deane on the subject, and upon that hint, which was communicated to Arnold, the indignant Colonel asserted, in support of his character, that the

* Autograph letter, August 10, 1775.

office of adjutant-general of the Northern department had been offered to him. This report produced some uneasiness in the public mind.

"I am informed," wrote Mr. Duer, "that Colonel Arnold reports that you have offered him the commission of adjutant-general to the New York forces. If this is the case (though I must confess that I think it is not), his late conduct at Ticonderoga must have been grossly misrepresented to you; for I am very sensible you would not think of showing any mark of favor to any one whose unaccountable pride should lead him to sacrifice the true interests of the country. From this motive, and from the consideration of my being engaged in his controversy with the Boston Committee, I am led to request that you will make an inquiry into the matter; and I am sensible that if you ever had such an intention as he reports, the result of a mature investigation into his conduct will induce you to abandon it. If you never had such a design, I shall be glad to have permission to contradict it, because a public belief of your intentions in his favor is a tacit reproach of my conduct, who exerted myself to the utmost in defeating his designs."*

Schuyler saw the impropriety of his nomination at that time, although he had not lost his confidence in the real value of the services of Arnold. He afterward offered to nominate Judge Duer to the same office, who hesitated in agreeing to accept it, because his business connections with his brothers in the island of Dominica might cause them to lose their fortunes on account of his political conduct. He received the appointment, however, but when his commission arrived he went immediately to New York to submit his case to a confidential committee of the Congress. "Be assured," he wrote to Schuyler, "that nothing less than the critical situation in which I am could prevent me from joining you at this time."† He felt compelled to refuse the appointment, and Schuyler undertook the invasion of Canada without an adjutant-general.

Mr. Deane, meanwhile, had conferred with Arnold at

* Autograph letter, July 19, 1775.

† Autograph letter, August 10, 1775.

Cambridge, who yet had hopes, it appears, of receiving that appointment, or some other of equal importance, under Schuyler.

"Colonel Arnold has been hardly treated, in my opinion, by this colony, through some mistake or other," Deane wrote to Schuyler. "You once wrote to me in his favor for the office of adjutant-general in your department. If the post is not filled I wish you to remember him, as I think he has deserved much and received little, or less than nothing, and it would be a very unhappy state of things if every gentleman concerned in the first adventure that way should be neglected. If you design for Montreal, Colonel Arnold will, I trust, have the command of a body of men capable of making a powerful diversion in your favor; but, at any rate, he ought to be made use of, not to provide for him merely, but to make use of those abilities and activity of which I am sure he is possessed."*

* Autograph letter, August 10, 1775.

## CHAPTER XXII.

WHILE waiting for orders from General Washington to proceed to St. John's, General Schuyler went to Albany to confer with the Committee of Safety there, and with the Indian Commissioners. He had written urgent letters to both concerning the importance of an immediate conference with the heads of the Six Nations ; and also with the Caughnawagas, if they could be induced to attend. There had been delay in the action of the Committee and the commissioners, in consequence of the absence of Douw and Francis, two of the most active members of the board. Of this tardiness Schuyler had complained to the Committee, who, in reply, assured him that it had not been for want of zeal on their part, and that they should heartily coöperate with the commissioners.

Schuyler left Brigadier-General Montgomery in chief command at Ticonderoga during his absence, and departed for Albany on the 17th of August, with the intention of returning in the course of a few days. On his arrival at Saratoga, he was informed that quite a large body of Indians, of the Six Nations, were to be in Albany the following week, and that his presence at the conference to be held with them, by the commissioners, would be indispensable. As preliminary to this conference, Douw and Francis had held a council with some of the chiefs at the German Flats, on the 15th and 16th of the month, and explained to them the importance of immediate action. But the attendance of Indians at Albany was not large. The great body of the Mohawk warriors had left the country with Brant; and the most influential of the Onondagas, Cayugas, and Senecas, had accompanied Guy Johnson and Brant to Montreal. The larger number of those present were Oneidas, and leading men of the Schoharie canton of the Mohawks, the latter headed by Little Abraham, the sachem of the Lower Mohawk Castle, and next to Brant in influence over the minds of the Nation.

The Indians first held a conference with the Albany Committee concerning some local matters, and then, on the 24th, received a complimentary visit from the Indian Commissioners, and a deputation of the leading men of Albany. Schuyler was at the head of the commissioners, and the chiefs were all rejoiced to see him. He had, long before, been adopted as a child of the Mohawks, and made a chief, with the name of *Tho-rah Than-yea-da-kayer.* All the other commissioners appointed by the General Congress were present, except the venerable Major Joseph Hawley, of Watertown, Massachusetts, one of the soundest and purest patriots of the day. His old age and ill-health compelled him to decline the office. In his letter to Schuyler, acquainting him with his determination, Major Hawley said:

"From your known character as a most trusty and able friend to the liberties and rights of America, but more especially from the character given you by the delegates for this colony, I greatly rejoice at the honorable and most important offices which you sustain, and am ready to anticipate the happiness of hearing, in a very few days, of your success in the all-important expedition which you are upon, and that you shall have safely penetrated into Canada, at least as far as Montreal, and thereby secure the Canadians and all the Indians in the American interest. But I ask your pardon, sir, for so much as seeming to suggest to you the infinite importance of your enterprise to the American colonies. May Heaven protect, direct, and animate you and honor you with glorious success, which will rejoice the hearts of all good men in Britain and America."*

The conference was commenced on the 25th of August. It was opened by a speech from an Oneida sachem, after which, all sat down and smoked the pipe of peace together. When this ceremony was ended, General Schuyler read to them an appropriate and effective speech in behalf of the commissioners, reminding them of former covenants of friendship with the English, and exhorting them to cherish union among themselves, and peace and friendship with the colonists. This pleased the Indians, for they had expected to be called upon to take up arms against the king. With this anticipation the Oneida orator had explicitly declared that they considered the great dispute a family quarrel, in which they would not interfere, but would remain neutral, and hoped the commissioners would not require more of them. The Rev. Mr. Kirkland was the interpreter.

On the following day, the address, prepared by the Continental Congress (considerably modified by the commissioners), was presented to the Indians, the delivery and interpretation of which occupied the sittings of two days. The Indians then required a whole day to deliberate among themselves upon the subject; and their final answer, made by Little Abraham, was not delivered until the 31st of August.

Little Abraham's speech was pacific. Deceived by Sir Guy Johnson, they assured the commissioners that he had advised them, at the recent council at Oswego, to assume and preserve a neutral position. He must have spoken to

* Autograph letter, August 23, 1775.

these friends of the colonies with a "forked tongue"—in dissimulation—for he immediately led others, as we have seen, to Canada, to become allies of Sir Guy Carleton and Sir Frederick Haldimand. In the course of his speech Little Abraham professed a great attachment on the part of himself and his people to Sir John Johnson, who had been born among them, and they desired that he should be unmolested. They also preferred the same request in behalf of their missionary, the Rev. Mr. Stuart, a Scottish minister, who had been sent among them by the king. They also requested that the Indian trade might be re-opened with them, both at Albany and Schenectady, and that somebody might be appointed to guard the tree of peace at Albany, and keep the council-fire burning.

On the first of September, the commissioners, in their reply to Little Abraham's speech, acceded to the principal requests of the Indians, exhibited toward them the most conciliatory feelings, and informed them that General Schuyler and Mr. Douw had been appointed to keep the council-fire burning, and to guard the tree of peace at Albany. On the following day another council was held by the Indians with the Albany Committee; and that afternoon many of the savages turned their faces homeward, and went over the sand hills toward the setting sun. This was the last Indian council ever held in Albany, notwithstanding Schuyler and Douw were appointed to keep the fire burning. The result was satisfactory to all parties. The people of Tryon county were relieved of fears of any immediate danger from the Indians, and the labors of the Albany Committee of Safety were directed to other important matters.

The final effect of the conference was not important. Unfortunately a malignant fever broke out among the

Indians soon after their return home, and many were swept away by it. The Schoharie delegates suffered most severely. They had never experienced sickness like it; and believing it to be a scourge used for their punishment by the Great Spirit because they had not taken sides with the King, the survivors followed their brethren who went to Canada with Guy Johnson; and in subsequent invasions of Tyron county these were among the most relentless and cruel.

The fact that Sir John Johnson yet lingered in Johnson Hall, at Johnstown, with a large body of loyalists around him ready to act at any moment as he might dictate, gave the republicans at Albany and in the Mohawk Valley much uneasiness. They were well assured that he was in secret communication with Governor Tryon at New York, and they felt the necessity of keeping constant watch over his movements. Already the Tories had committed acts of violence under the shadow of his protection; and between the Whigs and Tories of the Mohawk Valley there was great exasperation of feeling. One of the most obnoxious of the latter was Alexander White, sheriff of the county. When the first liberty-pole set up in the Mohawk Valley was raised, at the German Flats, White, at the head of a band of Loyalists, cut it down. The Dutch and German population in that vicinity were mostly Whigs, and a decided majority of the population. After this outrage, the inhabitants were regularly enrolled by the Tryon County Committee, and organized as militia. Sheriff White was deposed, and Joshua Frey was appointed in his place; and the General Committee took into their hands all civil and military jurisdiction over a large section of the county.

Further obnoxious acts of White caused increased irritation. On some flimsy pretext, he committed an active Whig, named Fonda, to the jail near Johnson Hall. About fifty Whigs proceeded to the jail at night, released Fonda by force, and then proceeded to the residence of White and demanded his legal release. White fired upon the Whigs from an upper window. The latter broke open his doors, and he would doubtless have been captured by them, had not the report of a gun, fired at Johnson Hall, warned them that Sir John had signalled his partisans and retainers, five hundred strong, to come to the rescue. The Whigs withdrew, assembled at Caughnawaga, and sent a deputation to Sir John to demand a surrender of White to them. It was refused; and White, who had been dismissed from office by the people, was re-commissioned by Governor Tryon. The County Committee would not let him enter upon his duties; and the tide of popular indignation soon ran so high against him that White deemed it prudent to fly toward Canada. He was captured at Jessup's Landing, on the Upper Hudson, and conveyed to Ticonderoga, where, on the 12th of August, he wrote a most humble note to General Schuyler, saying:

> "With the greatest submission I humbly make bold to trouble you with this, hoping that you'll take my case into your tender consideration. If you doubt anything that I have said, I would be proud if you would leave it to the Committee of Albany to inquire into the whole affair, and to send up for evidences. I will make oath before you that I came away with no intention to act against the liberties of the country."*

General Schuyler sent White under a guard to the Committee of Albany, with a request that they should forward him to the Provincial Congress of New York. The Committee were about to do so, when, at the suit of

* Autograph letter.

Abraham C. Cuyler, the Mayor of Albany, White was retained. The mayor was a moderate loyalist, and for this interference he received a severe rebuke from Schuyler. White was imprisoned in Albany for a while, and was then released on parole.

Having thus disposed of one of the most active of Johnson's partisans, the Tryon County Committee resolved to probe the intentions of the baronet to the core. Every day evidence of his malign influences became more and more visible, yet he had adroitly avoided any outward show of hostility to the republican cause. His retainers, chiefly Scotch Highlanders, had become very offensive in their conduct. They cast every obstacle in the way of the Tryon County Committee, slandered its members, spoke openly for the crown and against the Whigs, and at the same time were sharing the confidence and the bounty of Sir John. On this account, the Committee, early in September, denounced him to the Provincial Congress of New York, saying—"We have great suspicions, and are almost assured, that Sir John has a continued correspondence with Colonel Guy Johnson and his party." These suspicions were well founded, for it was afterward ascertained that letters had passed between them, carried by Indians in the heads of their tomahawks and the ornaments about their persons. The Tryon County Committee, of whom Nicholas Herkimer* was chairman, took some action in the matter, a little later; but the Provincial Congress, governed by a wise policy, advised them not to molest Sir John as long as he should continue inactive.

On the 26th of August, General Schuyler received information from the North that caused his immediate de-

* His autograph, before me, shows the orthography of his name, from his own pen, to have been *Herkheimer*

parture for Ticonderoga. A dispatch from Major Brown to General Montgomery contained alarming intelligence of the activity of the enemy at St. John's. That gentleman urged an immediate forward movement of the army, as Carleton was almost ready to proceed up the lake to attack Ticonderoga.

"I am so much of Brown's opinion," wrote Montgomery, "that I think it absolutely necessary to move down the lake with the utmost dispatch. Should the enemy get their vessels into the lake, 'tis over with us for this summer, for which reason I have ordered two twelve pounders to be gotten ready to-morrow, if possible, and iron-work to make logs fast together for a boom, and hope to be able, if we can get down in time, to prevent their entrance into the lake, by taking post at Isle aux Noix. This intelligence has involved me in a great dilemma —the moving without your orders I don't like ; but, on the other hand, the prevention of the enemy is of the utmost consequence. If I must err I wish to be on the right side. The express will go night and day, and I hope you will join us with all expedition. Let me entreat you (if you can possibly) to follow us in a whale-boat, leaving somebody to bring forward the troops and artillery. It will give the men great confidence in your spirit and activity. How necessary this confidence is to a general, I need not tell you. * * * I most heartily wish this may meet with your approbation; and be assured I have your honor and reputation highly at heart, as of the greatest consequence to the public service; that all my ambition is to do my duty in a subordinate capacity, without the least ungenerous intention of lessening that merit so justly your due, and which I omit no opportunity of setting in its fullest light."*

This letter, so decisive, frank, and generous, is a fair index to the character of Montgomery, whom Schuyler dearly loved as a brother. He was a handsome Irish gentleman, and had been a soldier in service since the fifteenth year of his age. He was now in his fortieth year. He was near the gallant Wolfe when he fell upon the Plains of Abraham, in 1759 ; and he afterward followed General Lyman to the siege of Havanna. Disappointed in his expectations of promotion, he sold his commission in the army, emigrated to America, and settled on

* Autograph Letter, Aug. 25, 1775.

the banks of the Hudson, in Duchess county, where, in 1773, he married a daughter of Robert Livingston, and sister of the eminent Chancellor Livingston. He had just commenced building a pleasant mansion near Rhinebeck village* when he was honored with the commission of a brigadier in the Continental army, and called to the field. It was a hard trial for him to leave his young wife, and the pleasures and repose of domestic life in the country, where he was surrounded with everything to make him happy; but he sacrificed all cheerfully for the public good, saying, "It is an event which must put an end, for a while, perhaps forever, to the quiet scheme of life I had prescribed for myself; for, though entirely unexpected and undesired by me, the will of an oppressed people, compelled to choose between liberty and slavery, must be obeyed."

With such sentiments glowing in his bosom, Montgomery hastened to join Schuyler at Ticonderoga, leaving in the ears of his sorrowing wife, when he had imprinted upon her lips the parting kiss, at Saratoga, the delightful words—"You shall never blush for your Montgomery." She remembered with pride this noble assurance and its more noble vindication, during a widowhood of more than half a century.

Schuyler highly approved of Montgomery's proposed course in moving down the lake, and he made immediate preparations to return to Ticonderoga, and follow him, notwithstanding the extreme illness of his wife, his own tortures by a rhuematism almost as severe as his hereditary gout, and menaces of a bilious fever.

It was on Saturday evening when Montgomery's letter came; and almost at the same moment a dispatch was received from General Washington at Cambridge, informing

* Now (1860), the residence of Lewis Livingston, Esq.

him that several of the St. Francis tribe of Indians had just visited the camp and confirmed previous accounts of "the good disposition of the Indian nations and Canadians to the interest of America;" that British troops had *not* left Boston for Quebec; and that he had considered the plan of an expedition "to penetrate into Canada by way of Kennebec River, and so to Quebec by a route ninety miles below Montreal," to coöperate with the expedition under Schuyler, the final determination concerning it being deferred until he should hear from that officer. He desired Schuyler, if he meant to proceed toward Canada, to acquaint him speedily and particularly with all information that might be "material in the consideration of a step of so much importance." "Not a moment's time," he said, "is to be lost in the preparation for this enterprise, if the advices received from you favor it. With the utmost expedition, the season will be considerably advanced, so that you will dismiss the express as soon as possible."

Schuyler detained the express over night, and dispatched him with a reply to Washington early on Sunday morning. After saying that he was under the necessity of leaving the Indian business at Albany in the hands of his colleagues, and repairing immediately to Ticonderoga, and giving his views about the Canadians and the Indians, he said:

"I thank your Excellency for the honor you have done me in communicating to me your plan for an expedition into Canada. The inclosed information of Fèrès, which corroborates not only the information of Major Brown [that contained in the two affidavits of Duguid and Shatford], but every other we have had, leaves not a trace of doubt on my mind as to the propriety of going into Canada, and to do it has been my determined resolution (unless prevented by my superiors) for some time; and I have, accordingly, since my arrival here, requested General Montgomery to get every thing in the best readiness he could, for that I would move immediately, weak and ill-appointed as we were; and I learn with pleasure that he has, since the receipt of Griffin's information, ordered the cannon to be embarked, and he will probably be off from Ticonderoga so soon that I shall only be able to join him at Crown Point. Such being my intentions, and such the ideas I have formed of the necessity of penetrating into Canada without delay, your Excellency will easily believe that I felt happy to learn your intentions, and only wished that the thought had struck you sooner. The force I shall carry is far short of what I would wish. I believe it will not exceed seventeen hundred men, and this will be a body insufficient to attempt Quebec with, (after leaving the necessary detachments at St. John's, Chamblée, and Montreal, should we succeed and carry those places), which must be respectable, to keep an open and free communication with Crown Point, etc.

"Having now given your Excellency the time, force, and latest intelligence I have had, together with my opinion of the sentiments of the Canadians, I proceed to inform you of the enemy's strength. As far as I have been able to learn, it is from three hundred and fifty to four hundred at St. John's; one hundred and fifty or two hundred at Chamblée; about fifty at Montreal; and one company at Quebec. These are regular troops, besides between three hundred and five hundred Indians, Scotchmen, and some few Canadians, with Colonel Johnson at La Chine. Of this party the Indians that are at St. John's are a part. Whether any ships of war are at Quebec I can not say. As none have been mentioned to me, I am rather inclined to believe there are none. Should the detachment of your body penetrate into Canada, and we meet with success, Quebec must inevitably fall into our hands. Should we meet with a repulse, which can only happen from foul play in the Canadians, I shall have an opportunity to inform your party of it, that they may carry into execution any orders you may give, in case such an unfortunate event should arise.

"Your Excellency will be pleased to be particular in your orders to the officers that may command the detachment, that there may be no clashing should we join."*

General Schuyler arrived at Ticonderoga on the evening of the 30th of August, very sick with a bilious fever that had seized him on the way. He was too ill to proceed in a whale-boat, as suggested by Montgomery; indeed, he was too ill to proceed at all, with any comfort or safety.

* MS. Letter Books, Sunday morning, 6 o'clock, Aug. 27, 1775.

Montgomery, who had been detained at Crown Point, began to feel impatient. "A barbarous north wind," he wrote on the 30th, "has kept me here. To-morrow morning I expect to go away. I begin to be uneasy about you, as my express must have reached you on Saturday night, and it is now Wednesday night." As he expected, the wind was favorable the next morning, and the eager brigadier sailed down the lake with portions of the regiments of Waterbury, McDougall, Parsons, and Wooster, in all about twelve hundred men. These were as many as his small supply of boats could carry.

Feeling better after a night's rest, Schuyler gave orders the next morning for five hundred of Hinman's regiment and three hundred of Van Schaick's, with some artillery, to move forward as quickly as possible; also for sending forward the artillery from New York, under Lamb, then daily expected at Albany, with other troops, if they should arrive, and a supply of provisions and stores. Having made these arrangements, he embarked in a whale-boat, and overtook Montgomery and his troops at Isle la Motte, toward the foot of Lake Champlain, on the morning of the 4th of September.

On his arrival at Ticonderoga, Schuyler was informed of an occurrence which gave him much uneasiness, and strengthened his prejudices against the eastern troops, especially the Green Mountain Boys. It was one of those cases of disobedience and independent action, with which he was exceedingly annoyed during the whole campaign, and which, more than any other cause, contributed to the final disasters of the expedition. Captain Remember Baker, who had figured largely in the troubles between New York and the people of the New Hampshire Grants, and was a leader among the Green Mountain Boys, had been for a while, on his own solicitation, employed as a scout by General Schuyler, with strict orders not to molest either Canadians or Indians. These orders he violated, and fatal consequences ensued. The circumstances of the case were thus related by Schuyler in a letter from Ticonderoga to Messrs. Douw and Francis :

> "Captain Baker, of the unenlisted Green Mountain Boys, lately went into Canada, without my leave, with a party of five men, and discovering a boat manned by an equal number of Indians (which, from authentic intelligence sent me from Canada, I learn were of the Caughnawaga tribe), attempted to fire on them, but his gun missing, and he, putting his head from behind the tree where he stood in order to hammer his flint, received a shot in his forehead, and instantly expired, upon which his party returned the fire and unfortunately killed two of the Indians. This event, my Canadian correspondent informs me, has induced some of the Indians of that tribe to join the regular forces at St. John's. What the consequence of Baker's imprudence will be, is hard to forsee. It behoves us, however, to attempt to eradicate from the minds of the Indians any evil impressions they may have imbibed from this mortifying circumstance; but what measures to take to gain so desirable an end I am utterly at a loss to determine. Perhaps a few Indians of the Six Nations might be willing to join the army under my command on a peaceable message to those of Canada; and as this account will most certainly reach the Six Nations, I believe it will be most prudent to prepare them for it in such a manner as you, who can be assisted with the best advice at Albany, shall determine."*

The commissioners, viewing the event as one of great importance, as it might seriously affect the temper of the Caughnawaga and other Indians toward the republicans, acted promptly on the suggestions in Schuyler's letter. They immediately communicated the whole matter to Little Abraham and his associates, who had not yet left Albany. They listened with patience, and believed the words of the commissioners, who assured them that Baker's conduct was unauthorized, and was condemned by Schuy-

* Schuyler's MS. Letter Books.

ler and all true republicans. They also agreed to send a deputation to their brethren in Canada, to explain the matter. "Mr. Fulmer goes with them as interpreter, and to help them forward," wrote the commissioners to General Schuyler, "and we have given special directions that they should be accommodated at the several stages. You will, sir, observe by their reply, that they received the news with candor, and we do not perceive that it has made any ill impressions upon them. They considered the fact, if true (for they seemed much inclined to disbelieve it), was merely an unfortunate accident."*

The anxiety manifested by Schuyler and the commissioners, because of the acts of Baker and his men, shows how sensible they were of the real weakness of the invading army, and the necessity of preserving every element of strength, positive and negative, in the perilous campaign before them. They could not afford to lose the friendship or even the advantages of the neutrality of a single man of the forest or inhabitant of Canada; and every possible measure was employed to conciliate both.

The friendship of the Canadians (or at least their neuterality), as we have seen, was considered of vast importance to the republican cause, at that juncture, by the Continental Congress and the military leaders; and every art of kindness and conciliation was employed to make them active or passive friends. The Canadians were dis posed to be friendly to "the Bostonians," as the republicans were called in that province, and many suffered imprisonment and other punishments because they would not take up arms for the king. But most of them were cautious, and refrained from openly espousing the cause of the colonists so long as there remained a doubt of the

* Autograph letter, September 4, 1775.

ability of the republican army to maintain a successful invasion of their province. Emissaries were accordingly sent among them to speak words of encouragement and explain the delays; and on the 5th of September General Schuyler sent out from Isle aux Noix, which his troops had just taken possession of, the following manifesto, in the French language, to be distributed among the Canadians:*

---

* It seems proper here to notice some erroneous statements made in Hollister's *History of Connecticut* (published in two volumes, in 1855), in which the writer, in defending the character of General Wooster, considered it necessary to defame that of General Schuyler—a very illogical as well as unfair method of defense. After speaking of the march of Arnold through the wilderness to Quebec, he says: "Generals Montgomery and Wooster, in the meantime, had been joined by General Schuyler at Isle la Motte, where they moved on together to Isle aux Noix. Here Montgomery drew up a Declaration, which he sent among the Canadians by Colonel Allen and Major Brown, assuring them that the army was designed only against the English garrisons, and was not intended to interfere with the rights, liberties, or religion of the people."

This declaration was drawn up by General Schuyler (see his letter to Washington, Correspondence of the Revolution, i. 40), and was translated into French by his interpreter, the Rev. Mr. Tetard. Two copies of the manifesto, before me, are in the latter named gentleman's hand-writing.

As to General Wooster, he did not join the army under Schuyler and Montgomery, until full six weeks afterward. He lingered about Harlem until late in September, when he received a peremptory command from the Continental Congress, to proceed to Albany, and there await the orders of General Schuyler. (See Journals of Congress, Sept. 20, 1775.) His reply, on the 23d, is dated at Harlem. He embarked for Albany on the 28th, and did not leave that city until the 8th of October. On the 5th of that month he wrote a brief note to Schuyler, from Albany, inclosing a return roll of "six companies of the First Regiment of the Connecticut forces." On the 8th Walter Livingston, in a letter to Schuyler, from Albany, said: "Brigadier-General Wooster leaves this morning for Ticonderoga." He held a court-martial at Fort George, on the 13th of October, wrote to General Schuyler from Ticonderoga on the 19th, and joined the army under Montgomery, then investing St. John's, only a few days before the capitulation of that place—in time to share in the honors of the victory, and the praises of Congress. (See Journals of Congress, Nov. 30, 1775.)

I should not have taken this special notice of the errors here corrected, had not the writer of the history alluded to made them a part of a series of

"*Friends and Countrymen:* The various causes that have driven the ancient British colonies in America to arms have been so fully set forth in the several petitions, papers, letters, and declarations, published by the grand Congress, that our Canadian brethren, at the extirpation of whose liberty, as well as ours, the various schemes of a cruel ministry are directly tending, can not fail of being informed. And we can not doubt that you are pleased that the grand Congress have ordered an army into Canada to expel from thence, if possible, those British troops who, now acting under the orders of a despotic ministry, would wish to enslave their countrymen. This measure, necessary as it is, the Congress would not have entered on but in the fullest confidence that it would be perfectly agreeable to you, for, judging of your feelings by their own, they could not conceive that any thing but the force of necessity would induce you tamely to bear the insult and ignominy that are daily imposed on you, or that you could calmly sit by and see those chains forging which are intended to bind you, your posterity and ours, in one common and eternal slavery. To secure you and ourselves from such a dreadful bondage; to prevent the effects that might follow from the ministerial troops remaining in Canada; to restore to you those rights which every subject of the British empire, from the highest to the very lowest order, whatever his religious sentiments may be, is entitled to, are the only views of the Congress. You will readily believe me, when I say that the Congress have given me the most positive orders to cherish every Canadian and every friend to the cause of liberty, and sacredly to guard their property; and such is the confidence I have in the good disposition of my army that I do not believe I shall have occasion to punish a single offense committed against you.

"A treaty of friendship has just been concluded with the Six Nations at Albany, and I am furnished with an ample present for their Caughnawaga brethren and other Canadian tribes. If any of them have lost their lives it was done contrary to my orders, and by scoundrels ill-affected to our glorious cause. I shall take great pleasure in burying the dead and wiping away the tears of their surviving relations, which you will communicate to them."*

Well supplied with copies of this manifesto, Colonel Ethan Allen and Major Brown, with interpreters, started

charges against General Schuyler in succeeding pages of his work, which are not only ungenerous in the extreme, but utterly unjust, as I shall attempt to show in future pages, when considering the difficulties that occurred between Schuyler and Wooster, both patriots of purest stamp but different in temper, views, and position. Wooster at that time was old and infirm.

* This was in allusion to those killed by Captain Baker's men.

for Canada the next morning, to confer with Colonel James Livingston, then residing near Chamblée, to reconnoiter the country between the Sorel and the St. Lawrence, to present the friendly address to the people, and to ascertain their sentiments. This was a delicate and somewhat perilous mission, for the British troops, alarmed by the presence of the invaders, were extremely vigilant, and the Canadians, who were timid and fickle, were sometimes treacherous.

## CHAPTER XXIII.

The army under Schuyler took possession of the Isle aux Noix, twelve miles south of St John's, on the evening of the 4th of September, the day of the arrival of the General at Isle la Motte. On the following day he drew up the declaration already mentioned, and sent Allen and Brown among the Canadians with it, and then prepared to push on to St. John's, notwithstanding his effective force did not exceed one thousand men. With these he embarked early on the morning of the 6th, leaving the baggage and provisions, except a supply for four days, at the Isle aux Noix. They proceeded to within two miles of St. John's without molestation, when the garrison opened a harmless cannonade upon them from the fort. They pushed forward half a mile nearer the post, and landed in a deep, close swamp, which extended very nearly to the fort. There they landed and marched in the best order possible in such a tangled way, with a detachment from Waterbury's Connecticut troops, under Major Hobby, as a flank for the left wing, that moved a little in advance of the main body. Hobby was attacked when crossing a deep, muddy brook, by a party of Indians and some Tories, who delivered a heavy fire ; but the loss on both sides was trifling. The republicans lost only a sergeant, corporal, and three privates killed, and one missing, and eight privates wounded, of whom three died the ensuing night. Hobby was shot through the thigh, Captain Mead through the shoulder, and Lieutenant Brown in the hand, but all soon recovered of their wounds. This was the first blood shed in the actual invasion of Canada. The assailants were driven back, and the Americans, taught by the event to be more cautious, concentrated their forces on the approach of night, and cast up an intrenchment for their defense, in the event of a sudden attack.

In the evening, a gentleman living in the neighborhood entered General Schuyler's tent very cautiously, and gave him information that caused him to fall back to the Isle aux Noix. He informed Schuyler that there were no regular troops in Canada, except the twenty-sixth regiment, under the command of General Richard Prescott, most of whom were at St. John's and Chamblée, the latter a fort, twelve miles further down the Sorel than the former. He said there were one hundred Indians at St. John's, and quite a large body of savages were with Colonel Guy Johnson at Montreal; that the works at St. John's were complete and strong, and plentifully furnished with cannon and stores; that one armed vessel, pierced for sixteen guns, was launched, and nearly ready to sail; and that he believed not one Canadian would join the republicans, while all would remain strictly neutral. He assured the general that they would be pleased to have a republi can army penetrate their province, provided the safety of their persons and property might be insured, and they were paid in gold and silver for all they might furnish ,the troops; that he thought it imprudent to attack St. John's at that time, and advised Schuyler to send some parties among the inhabitants, while the remainder of the army should draw back to the Isle aux Noix, from whence he might have intercourse with Laprairie and Montreal.

Much of this information proved to be deceptive, but it so impressed Schuyler as truth that he called a Council of War early on the morning of the 7th, to whom he communicated it.* The result was, that considering the forward state of the armed vessel at St. John's, it was "unanimously agreed to be indispensably necessary to take measures for preventing her entrance into the lake. It was the opinion of the council that this could only be effected at the Isle aux Noix. The weak state of the artillery affording no prospect of silencing the enemy's guns under the protection of which they were rigging her, it was therefore resolved to return, without delay, to the Isle aux Noix, throw a boom across the channel, erect the proper works for its defense, then wait for certain intelligence touching the intentions of the Canadians, and when reinforced, send a strong detachment into the country by land, should the Canadians favor such a design."†

When this course was determined on, Schuyler gave immediate orders for the embarkation of the troops "without hurry and without noise;" and they returned to the Isle aux Noix in the same order as they left it—the New York troops in front, the Connecticut troops next, and the row-galleys in the rear of all.

On arriving at the Isle aux Noix, General Schuyler sent a detailed account of operations in that quarter to the President of Congress, in which he observed:

"I can not estimate the obligations I lie under to General Montgomery for the many important services he has done, and daily does, in which he has had little assistance from me, as I have not enjoyed a moment's health since I left Fort George. I am now so low as not to be able to hold the pen. Should we not be able to do any thing de-

* The council was composed of Generals Schuyler and Montgomery, Colonel Waterbury and Lieutenant-Colonel Whiting of the Fifth Connecticut Regiment, and Lieutenant-Colonel Ritzema of the First New York Regiment.

† Schuyler's Orderly Book.

cisively in Canada I shall judge it best to move from this, which is a very wet and unhealthy part of the country, unless I receive your orders to the contrary."*

This letter, which reached Philadelphia on the 18th, occasioned much uneasiness in Congress, for it was apparent that the success of the expedition into Canada was most to be desired of all the operations of the campaign. All other business was suspended for the purpose of discussing its contents, and after an animated debate, Messrs. Deane, Rutledge, Chase, and Jay, were appointed a committee to draft a letter to General Schuyler on the subject. On the 20th it was addressed to him by the President of Congress, who said:

"I am directed by the Congress to express their approbation of your conduct, as stated in your letter. Your taking possession of the Isle aux Noix, and the proposed measures for preventing the enemy's vessels from entering the lake, appear to them highly expedient and necessary. The Congress have such a sense of the importance of that post as to wish it may not be abandoned without the most mature consideration, or the most pressing necessity. They view the expedition intrusted to your care as of the greatest consequence to the general cause; and as they clearly forsee that its influence, whether successful or otherwise, will be great and extensive, they are desirous that nothing necessary to give it a fortunate issue, may be omitted. They have ordered all the forces raised in New York immediately to join you; and those under General Wooster to march immediately to Albany; from whence, if you should think such reinforcement necessary, you will be pleased to order them. Should you stand in need of further reinforcements, the Congress desire you will apply to General Washington.

"The Congress repose the highest confidence in the abilities, the zeal, and the alacrity of the officers and forces employed on this expedition. They are determined to spare neither men nor money; and should the Canadians remain neuter, flatter themselves that the enterprise will be crowned with success, notwithstanding the great and various difficulties to which it has been and still is exposed.

"It is with great concern that the Congress hear of your indisposi-

* Schuyler's MS. Letter Books.

tion. They desire me to assure you of their warmest wishes for your recovery, and to request that, in discharging the duties of your station, you will not omit the attention due to the reëstablishment of your health."

Several members of the Congress wrote to Schuyler privately, urging him to be careful of his health, for they felt assured that the success of the campaign depended chiefly upon him.

"It gives me great concern," wrote Thomas Lynch, of South Carolina, "to find your health so much injured. Don't you know that it is the duty of a general to take the utmost care to bring the army into the field in good health? If so, how much care is to be taken of the head? You must spare your body, and not expect it can possibly keep pace with such a spirit. If you push it too far, it will leave you and us in the lurch; in short, you will kill our general.

"I see the difficulties with which you are surrounded. These can can only add glory to the success of your enterprise. The Congress is awake at last, and feel the importance of your expedition—that every thing depends on its success—and I think you may depend on every support that is consistent with the delay that attends popular assemblies."

After returning to the Isle aux Noix, General Schuyler made strenuous efforts to hasten forward reënforcements. He commenced some fortifications there preparatory to the reception of his artillery, then hourly expected, and also the construction of a boom to obstruct the channel. In the course of a few days his little army was swelled to more than seventeen hundred men.

But there was a foe at work in the camp more insidious and more to be dreaded than the enemy in the field. Malaria commenced its destructive ravages. The Isle aux Noix is situated in the midst of a low, marshy country; and before the troops had been there a week more than six hundred of them were on the sick list. And the unwholsomeness of the air so greatly aggravated General

Schuyler's disorders that he was soon brought to the borders of the grave. Bilious fever and severe rheumatism attacked him alternately, and he was confined to his bed most of the time, with great suffering of mind and body. Yet he persevered in duty, and did not yield until menaced with speedy death.

From Livingston, Allen, and Brown, Schuyler received such intelligence concerning affairs in Canada, and the temper of the people, that on the 10th he detached eight hundred men, under General Montgomery, in the direction of St. John's. These consisted of portions of Hinman's, Waterbury's, McDougall's ,and Van Schaick's regiments. They landed about three miles from St. John's, at nine o'clock in the evening, near the place where the republicans had thrown up breast-works on the afternoon of the 6th. From that point Montgomery sent Lieutenant-Colonel Ritzema of the New Yorkers, with five hundred men, to take post on the road leading from St. John's to Laprairie, in order to cut off the communication between St. John's and the country, according to General Schuyler's orders to that officer, issued before his departure from the Isle aux Noix. They had not proceeded far when a false alarm created a panic, and the troops fled back in confusion, some of them turning into the woods to avoid the officers at the breast-work, who, they apprehended, would again command them to move forward. When mustered, in order to advance again, Ritzema had only about fifty men. These were soon increased to two hundred, but the day was so far spent that it was determined to delay further attempts until morning.

Early the next morning, at the request of several officers, Montgomery called a Council of War, composed of himself, Colonel Waterbury, Lieutenant-Colonel Ritzema, Majors Elmore, Zedwitz, and Dimon, and Captains Starr, Smith, Bearsley, Reed, Brown, Weissenfeldts, Willett, Mott, Lyon, Yates, McCracken, and Livingston. It was unanimously determined to proceed, and the consent of the troops was obtained by a vote—a mode of proceeding so unmilitary and detrimental to all authority, that Montgomery consented to it only on the compulsion imposed by the exigencies of the case. Just as the detachment was about to march, intelligence came that the enemy's armed vessel was lying only half a mile from them, and it was thought prudent to reëmbark, and return to the Isle aux Noix. While this matter was under consideration, half the detachments from the New England regiments embarked without orders.

On the way back to the Isle aux Noix, the general ordered the boats to stop at a point eight miles from St. John's, to try the temper of the troops by asking them to march from that point against the fort. The proposition was voted down. "When the halt was made at the point," says the narrator from whose notes these facts have been drawn, "the general and captains, with a few guards, disembarked; and on a cry by one of the men that *boats were coming!* the troops were with difficulty restrained from pushing off without their officers!"*

Montgomery was mortified by this bad conduct of the soldiers, and foresaw nothing but disaster before him, if such were the men on whom he was to depend for support in the invasion of Canada. Some persons at the time had strong suspicions that Ritzema was either a coward or a traitor. He deserted to the enemy within a year from that time; and Major Zedwitz was

* MS. Narrative by General Montgomery.

cashiered for an alleged attempt at a treasonable correspondence with Governor Tryon.

Schuyler and Montgomery now arranged a plan for an immediate attack upon St. John's. The troops under Ritzema, who had returned to duty, seemed heartily ashamed of their "unbecoming behavior," and Montgomery considered their sensibility to ridicule as a promise of better conduct in the future. Schuyler accordingly issued orders on the 13th for an embarkation on the following day of the artillery that had arrived, and of the whole army on the 15th. He was then too ill to leave his bed, but on the 14th he felt so much better that he had hopes of moving with the troops. "But by ten o'clock at night," he said, in a letter to Washington, "my disorder re-attacked me with redoubled violence, and every fair prospect of a speedy recovery vanished." Yet he lingered in that unhealthy spot a day or two longer, still hoping to move with the army. At last he was compelled to transfer the general command to Montgomery, and take passage in a covered boat for Ticonderoga, where he arrived at three o'clock in the afternoon of the 18th, feeling somewhat invigorated. "I find myself much better," he wrote to Washington, on the 20th, "as the fever has left me, and hope soon to return where I ought and wish to be, unless a barbarous relapse should dash the cup of hope from my lips."

An hour after Schuyler left the Isle aux Noix, he met Colonel Seth Warner, with one hundred and seventy Green Mountain Boys, in boats, on their way to the camp, "being the first," the general said, "that appeared of that boasted corps." Part of the corps had already mutinied and deserted, and some had been left at Crown Point. Captain Allen's company of the same corps, "every man of which was raised in Connecticut," arrived at Ticonderoga on the 19th ; Colonel Bedell's New Hampshire troops had arrived on the 16th ; Captain Henry B. Livingston's corps had already passed down the lake ; and Captain Lamb, with his artillery, was expected to join Montgomery on the 20th. The last-mentioned corps was of great importance, for there were none in the invading army that knew any thing about the proper management of cannon. Some troops yet remained at Ticonderoga, and others had just arrived. Schuyler at once issued orders for the most of these to embark immediately for Montgomery's army, and by this means a reënforcement of several hundred men was given to it.

Schuyler found the promises of convalescence fallacious. Fever and rheumatism had reduced him to a skeleton, and he found no relief at Ticonderoga. He was also constantly annoyed by the bad conduct of troops, and in his vexation of mind and body, he wrote as follows to the Continental Congress, on the 25th of September :

> "The vexation of spirit under which I labor, that a barbarous complication of disorders should prevent me from reaping those laurels for which I have so unweariedly wrought, since I was honored with this command; the anxiety of mind I have suffered since my arrival here lest the army should starve, occasioned by a scandalous want of subordination and inattention to my orders in some of the officers that I left to command at the different posts; the vast variety of disagreeable and vexatious incidents that almost every hour arise, in some department or other, not only retard my cure, but have put me considerably back for some days past. If Job had been a general, in my situation, his memory had not been so famous for patience. But the glorious end we have in view, and which I have a confident hope will be attained, will atone for all."*

Two days after writing this letter he received the one from the President of Congress, already given, approving

* Schuyler's MS. Letter Books.

of his conduct, and urging him to take good care of his health. This, and the private letters sent from Philadelphia, soothed his spirit.

"The honorable Congress have my warmest acknowledgments," he said in reply, "and they may rest assured that nothing on my part shall be wanting to insure that success they so earnestly wish; and I hope soon to congratulate them on it. Whilst I deprecate the untimely misfortune which prevents me from sharing in the immediate glory, it was perhaps inflicted in such a critical hour to serve the common cause, for if I had not arrived here on the very day I did, as sure as God lives the army would have starved."

It was, indeed, fortunate for the army that Schuyler returned to Ticonderoga at that time. He found every thing connected with the forwarding of provisions in the greatest disorder. Neglect, dishonesty, peculation—every thing calculated to rob the army of necessary stores were rife, and provisions on the way were detained by neglect or indolence, in a most shameful manner. "The letters I have been obliged to write to several officers," he said to the Congress, "I have been under the necessity of couching in terms that I should be ashamed of, did not necessity apologise for me." He then gave in detail illustrations of the neglect, and added, "the horrid anxiety I suffered from this dreadful situation of the army is now abated, and I hope for so sufficient a restoration as to enable me to join soon."

Less cautious than Schuyler, Montgomery left the Isle aux Noix on the day when the invalid commanding general departed for Ticonderoga, and advanced upon St. John's with about one thousand men. Major Brown had been sent with one hundred and fifty continental troops and thirty Canadian recruits to reconnoiter the vicinity of Chamblée and make friends of the inhabitants; Major James Livingston had gone farther down the river and was collecting the inhabitants under his standard; and Colonel Ethan Allen was near the St. Lawrence again, "preaching politics" and beating up for recruits. Alarmed by the temper shown by the inhabitants, and the menaces of the invading republicans, Sir Guy Carleton had issued a proclamation in French, setting forth the disloyalty of the king's subjects, and offering pardon to all who should, within a given time, return to their allegiance and join the standard of the crown. But his proclamation, and the efforts of the French clergy and nobility, were of little avail. Hardly one hundred Canadians were induced to join the garrison at St. John's, and few Indians had taken up the hatchet for the king. Carleton, in despair, wrote to General Gage at Boston, "I had hopes of holding out for this year, had the savages remained firm; but now we are on the eve of being overrun and subdued."

Montgomery arrived at his old encampment near St. John's on the evening of the 17th of September, and made a forward movement early the next morning.

"I take the opportunity of Fulmer's return with the Oneidas," Montgomery wrote to Schuyler, "to acquaint you of our arrival here on the 17th, in the evening. Yesterday morning I marched, with five hundred men, to the north side of St. John's, where we found a party of the king's troops, with field-pieces. This party had beaten off Major Brown a few hours before, who had imprudently thrown himself in their way, depending on our more early arrival, which, through the dilatoriness of our young troops, could not be sooner effected. The enemy, after an ill-directed fire for some minutes, retired with precipitation, and lucky for them they did, for had we known their situation (which the thickness of the woods prevented our finding out till it was too late) there would not a man of them have returned. The old story of *treachery* spread among the men as soon as we saw the enemy. We were trepanned—drawn under the guns of the fort, and what not. The *Woodsmen** were not so expert at firing as I expected, and too many

* The Green Mountain Boys and New Hampshire troops.

of them hung back. Had we kept silence at first, before we were discovered, we should have gotten a field-piece or two."*

The insubordination which had annoyed Schuyler and Montgomery so continually had performed its disastrous work, and prevented a small but very important victory. Caution, secresy, and concert of action were out of the question; and the leader, utterly powerless to command them, yielded with as much patience as his fiery spirit could maintain. He pushed on a little further to the northwest, and at the junction of the roads leading respectively from St. John's to Longeuil and Chamblée, he formed an entrenched camp of three hundred men to cut off the supplies for the enemy sent from the interior. Having accomplished this important work, he hastened back to the camp to bring his artillery up to bear upon the walls of the fort. These were too light to perform very essential service. Captain Lamb, with the heavier cannon had not yet arrived.

Montgomery now commenced the investment of Fort St. John. His preparations were meager, for his artillery was light, his mortars defective, his ammunition scarce, and his gunners unpracticed in their duties. Yet he worked on cheerfully. Schuyler, tireless in his efforts, was sending on additions to his forces and supplies of food, as full and as fast as circumstances would allow; and Montgomery was soon constrained, in gratitude, to exclaim, in a letter to his chief, "What does not this army owe to your patriotism and indefatigable labors!"

A battery was completed on the 21st, on a point of land that commanded the fort and the vessels in the river, and another was cast up on the east side of the stream, some distance below the fort. For a week the seige went

* Autograph Letter, Sept. 19, 1775.

slowly on. Disease, frightful in its effects, broke out among the soldiers. The ground was low and swampy, and the trees, small and thickly planted, completely shut out the sun. Deadly malaria arose from the dank soil, and Montgomery perceived that the decimation of his army would speedily take place, if he should remain there.

At this juncture Captain Lamb arrived with his heavy ordnance, and on the 26th of September, he bedded a thirteen inch mortar near the battery, on the east side of the river, and hurled many shot and shell against the enemy. But the distance from the fort was too great to allow much execution from the bombardment, and Montgomery resolved to abandon the batteries and take a new position nearer the fort, where the ground was firm and the water wholesome. But the troops, thoroughly imbued with the spirit of independence, and judging for themselves that an attack would be unsuccessful, refused to acquiesce in the plan of their leader. Insubordination was at once rampant, and the general was informed that most of the troops would leave him should he attempt coercion by virtue of his authority.

Unable either to punish them for their mutiny, or to convince them of their error, Montgomery yielded so far as to call a Council of War. It resulted, as was expected, in a decision against his plan. This triumph of insubordination made the recusants more bold. They set all law at defiance, and alarming disorder pervaded the American camp. At length a better spirit prevailed. Montgomery controlled his feelings, and kept his impulses under the restraints of his judgment. He was eloquent in speech and possessed most winning ways. The mutinous knew him to be brave and firm; and these faculties and attributes, working in harmony, accomplished what official power had failed to achieve. His plans were finally adopted; and on the 7th of October the camp was moved to higher ground, northwest of the fort, where intrenchments were thrown up, and the investment was made complete. But for want of siege guns the republicans were unable to breach the walls of the fort, or do much damage to the out-works of the enemy.*

* Autograph letter, Sept. 24, 1775.

## CHAPTER XXIV.

While the siege of St. John's was very slowly progressing, because of a want of proper supplies, a defiant, meddling spirit of insubordination, general inefficiency in the service, and the ambition of inferior leaders who had been sent among the Canadians to acquire personal renown by some bold stroke for the common cause, cast serious obstacles in the way, and lost to the republicans not only precious time, but the most cordial, active, and general support of the Canadians.

Colonel Ethan Allen and Major Brown were both obnoxious to this charge. The former, as we have seen, was regarded by Schuyler as a dangerous man, not because of any lack of patriotism, or for evil intentions, but because he could not be kept within subordinate bounds. Events partially justified the opinion. His boldness, zeal, peculiar personal bearing, and extravagant promises, captivated the simple Canadians, and he had been a very successful political preacher among them. Within a week after he left the camp at the Isle aux Noix he was at St. Ours, twelve miles southeast of the Sorel, with two hundred and fifty Canadians under arms, and he wrote to General Montgomery that within three days he should join him in the siege of St. John's. His letter was characteristic—sanguine, boastful, and indicative of the elation of success. "I could raise," he wrote, "one or two thousand in a week's time; but I will first visit the army with a less number, and, if necessary, go again recruiting. Those that used to be enemies to our cause come cap in hand to me; and I swear by the Lord I can raise three times the number of our army in Canada, provided you continue the siege."*

On the morning of the 24th of September, while Allen was on his way to Montgomery's camp, he fell in with Major Brown, on the road between Longueuil and Laprairie, who was at the head of a party of two hundred Americans and Canadians. Allen had with him a guard of eighty men, chiefly Canadians. He and Brown, and their confidants, held a private interview in a house near by, when the latter told the former, that the garrison at Montreal, where no danger was apprehended, did not exceed thirty men, and the town might easily be taken. He proposed that they should, with their respective forces, cross the St. Lawrence at separate points above and below Montreal, make a simultaneous attack upon it, and secure a joint and very important victory. Allen eagerly approved of the proposition. He doubtless remembered the pleasures of success at Ticonderoga a few months before, and the applause that followed, and also the indignity cast upon him in the Grants, in omitting to choose him the leader of the Green Mountain Boys; and he saw a fair prospect of enjoying a repetition of the glory and honor achieved on Lake Champlain, and a vindication of his character as a brave and successful leader. His partisan spirit was thoroughly aroused; and no doubt visions of victory and the plaudits of posterity suddenly assumed the shape of reality in his mind, and made him impatient for action.

The plan was soon arranged between the partisans.

* Autograph letter, Sept. 22, 1775.

Allen was to return to Longueuil, on the southern shore of the St. Lawrence, a little below Montreal, and cross there, while Brown and his two hundred followers were to cross at Laprairie, just above the city. The passage was to be accomplished in the night, and early the next morning the exchange of three huzzas, by the two parties, was to be the signal of attack upon the town. These arrangements were made by the parties without the consent of Montgomery, who was anxiously waiting for the reënforcements expected from these men, to push the siege of St. John's to completion.

Allen hastened back to Longueuil, added about thirty "English-Americans" to his party, collected a few canoes, and crossed the river during the night of the 24th. The night was dark and windy, the current and eddies of St. Mary's rapids strong and dangerous, and the canoes few and frail. The passage was protracted and tedious. Three times the canoes crossed and recrossed before all were landed on the opposite shore; and when the last canoe-load had touched the bank, day had dawned.

Allen placed guards in such a way that intelligence of his presence should not reach Montreal; and then he anxiously awaited the promised huzzas from Brown's party. The sun arose, and yet no signal was heard. It mounted higher and higher toward the meridian, and still all was silent above. The gallant Vermonter, conscious of being alone, and too weak to carry out the enterprise, would have retreated, but it was too late. Already an escaped captive had alarmed the garrison and the city, and all but the first canoe-loads must become prisoners if an attempt should be made to recross the river. Allen would not leave any of his men. "This," he said, "I could not reconcile to my feelings as a man, much less as an officer, and I therefore concluded to maintain the ground, if possible, and all to fare alike."

On the appearance of this band, the people of Montreal were greatly excited. Allen took a defensive position, and resolved to sell his life dearly. The morning wore away, and it was afternoon before any opponents appeared. At three o'clock, Major Campbell, with a "mixed multitude," composed of forty regular troops, over two hundred Canadians, and some of the Indians then in Montreal, came down upon the invaders. A very sharp conflict ensued, which lasted almost two hours. Allen commanded skillfully and fought bravely, until only thirty or forty of his men remained. Some of them were wounded, and some had been killed. The Canadians, almost to a man, had deserted him at the beginning of the engagement.

"Being almost entirely surrounded with such vast unequal numbers," says Allen, in his *Narrative*, "I ordered a retreat, but found that those of the enemy who were of the country, and their Indians, would run as fast as my men, though the regulars could not. Thus I retreated more than a mile, and some of the enemy, with the savages, kept flanking me, and others crowded hard in the rear. In fine, I expected in a very short time, to try the world of spirits; for I was apprehensive that no quarter would be given to me, and, therefore, had determined to sell my life as dear as I could. One of the enemy's officers, boldly pressing in the rear, discharged his fusee at me; the ball whistled near me as did many others that day. I returned the salute and missed him, as running had put us both out of breath (for I conclude we were not frightened); I then saluted him with my tongue in a harsh manner and told him that inasmuch as his numbers were so far superior to mine, I would surrender, provided I could be treated with honor, and be assured of good quarter for myself and the men who were with me. He answered I should. Another officer coming up directly after, confirmed the treaty, upon which I agreed to surrender with my party, which then consisted of thirty-one effective men, and seven wounded. I ordered them to ground their arms which they did."*

* *A Narrative of Colonel Ethan Allen's captivity, written by himself:* Walpole, 1807.

The prisoners were conducted in triumph into Montreal, and delivered to General Prescott, a narrow-minded, petty tyrant, who, as his subsequent conduct on Rhode Island showed, seldom exercised the common courtesies of life toward the unfortunate who fell into his hands. Toward a man like Allen, he was disposed to be specially cruel; and his anger was made hot by the first sight of his prisoner, who was rough in manner and personal appearance. He exhibited none of the common characteristics of a soldier or a gentleman. His jacket was made of deer-skin; his undervest and breeches of Sagathy; his shoes of cow-skin, the soles well fortified by hob-nails; and on his head was a red woolen cap. Most of his followers were equally rough in appearance; and to the eye of Prescott they seemed more like free-booters than soldiers.

"Who are you? What is your name?" inquired Prescott in a loud and angry tone, when Allen was brought to him in the barrack-yard at Montreal, closely guarded by the regular troops. He was answered by the prisoner, when Prescott roared out, "Are you the scoundrel who took Ticonderoga?" "I am the very man," Allen replied fiercely. Prescott then stormed, called him hard names, denounced him as a rebel, in bitter terms, and shook his cane over Allen's head, threatening to beat him. "I told him," says Allen, "he would do well not to cane me, for I was not accustomed to it; and I shook my fist at him, telling him that was the beetle of mortality for him, if he offered to strike." A British officer standing by, whispered to Prescott that it would be dishonorable to strike a prisoner, and the brigadier contented himself with bestowing a few curses upon the "rebel," and assuring him that he should "grace the halter at Tyburn." He then ordered the prisoners to be taken by a guard on board the *Gaspé* war-schooner, Captain Ryall, lying at Montreal, placed them in irons, and thrust them into the hold of the vessel. This barbarous order was rigidly executed. A bar of iron eight feet long, was rivited to the shackles of Allen, and his fellow-prisoners were fastened together in pairs, with hand-cuffs.*

Allen's shackles were so tight that he could not lie down except on his back. He obtained permission to write to Prescott, and in his respectful letter reminded that officer that he was receiving treatment undeserving his own humane conduct toward British prisoners who had been in his power. "When I had the command, and took Captain De Laplace and Lieutenant Fulton, with the garrison of Ticonderoga," he said, "I treated them with every mark of friendship and generosity, the evidence of which is notorious even in Canada. I have only to add that I

* Allen in his *Narrative* says his "handcuffs were of the ordinary size, but his leg irons, which were very tight, would weigh, he imagined, thirty pounds; the bar was eight feet long and very substantial." When, a few weeks later, General Wooster was in command at Montreal, he instituted inquiries concerning the harsh treatment of Colonel Allen, by order of General Schuyler. From a number of depositions, in manuscript before me, I copy only one, the others being substantially the same:

"I, the subscriber, being of lawful age, do testify and say, that a gentleman known as Colonel Allen, was brought on board the *Gaspé* man-of-war, then lying before the town of Montreal, some time in the month of September, 1775, and pursuant to the orders of Captain Ryall, who then commanded said ship, I put a pair of irons on said Allen's legs, which he wore for seven or eight days, during which he was kept by the boatswain's cabin. Afterwards the irons were taken off his legs and handcuffs were put on his hands, which was the practice for some considerable time; then only one leg was ironed in the night, and handcuffs in the day." Further saith not

WM. BRADLEY, midshipman on board the *Gaspé*.

This deposition is given, because the statements of Colonel Allen that he was put in irons, or otherwise treated than as a prisoner of war, have been denied. Of the midshipman who made this deposition, Allen in his *Narrative* says: "One of the officers, by the name of Bradley, was very generous to me; he would often send me victuals from his own table; nor did a day fail but he sent me a good drink of grog."

expect an honorable and humane treatment, as an officer of my rank and merit should have." The brutal Prescott gave the prisoner no response. He remained in irons on board the *Gaspé* between five and six weeks, when he was sent to Quebec, and from thence to England to be tried for treason.

The treatment which Colonel Allen received during a captivity of two years and six months, at different times, was disgraceful to the British authorities, and it was only because of the fear of unpleasant consequences to the British officers in the hands of the Americans, that he was released from confinement in Pendennis Castle, and sent to America as a prisoner of war. He was exchanged for Colonel Campbell, in May, 1778.

Allen's raid increased Montgomery's difficulties, prolonged the seige, and produced a disastrous effect upon the campaign. It discouraged the Canadians, and caused for the moment a great change in their feelings toward the republican cause. Brooke Watson, an English merchant, who was in Montreal two or three weeks after the affair, and who went to England in the same ship with Allen, writing to Benjamin Faneuil, of Boston, said:

"Surely the kingdom of Great Britain can not much longer be governed by such weak councils and feeble efforts. She has scarcely got a secure province in America. As to this, it has long been on the brink of falling into the hands of the most despicable wretches. Had not the inhabitants of this town gone out to meet *Colonel* Allen on Monday, the 25th ultimo, the town and the principal part of the province, would now have been in their hands, and that fellow would probably have been governor of Montreal. Thank God, that day's action turned the minds of the Canadians, and I have reason to hope the province out of danger, at least, for this year."*

To John Butler he wrote three days later:

"*Colonel* Allen, who commanded this despicable party of plun-

* Autograph letter, October 16, 1775.

derers (they were promised the plunder of the town) was, with most of his wretches, taken. He is now in irons on board the *Gaspé*. This action gave a sudden turn to the Canadians, who before, were nine-tenths for the Bostonians. There are great numbers now in arms for the King, but the enemy have possession of the South side of the river as low as Verchere, except the garrison of St. John's, which they still invest with little hopes on their side, and little fear on ours of its being taken."*

Montgomery was much annoyed by Allen's affair, yet it appears from his letters that he was not wholly ignorant of the project of the partisans before its attempted execution. On the morning of the 28th of September, he wrote to Schuyler, saying:

"Allen, Warner, and Brown, are at Laprairie and Longueuil, with a party of our troops and some Canadians—how many I can't tell. They all speak well of the good disposition of the Canadians. They have a project of making an attempt on Montreal; I fear the troops are not fit for it."†

In the afternoon of the same day he wrote:

"Since mine of this morning, I have received a letter from Mr. Livingston,‡ and another from Colonel Warner, who is at Laprairie, acquainting me that Colonel Allen had passed the river at Montreal, or below it rather, with thirty of ours and fifty Canadians; that he had been attacked by a superior party from the garrison; that he was taken prisoner, two or three killed and as many more wounded, and that the rest took to their heels. I have to lament Mr. Allen's imprudence and ambition, which urged him to this affair single-handed, when he might have had a considerable reinforcement."

Not fully comprehending the circumstances, nor aware of the greater blame that attached to Major Brown, General

* Autograph Letter, Oct. 19, 1775.

† Autograph Letter.

‡ Mr. James Livingston, who had for some time resided near Chamblée, was a favorite among the Canadians in that parish. He was then encamped with quite a large number of them, at Point Olina, not far from Fort Chamblée. In his letter he said: "Mr. Allen should never have attempted to attack the town, without my knowledge, or acquainting me of his design, as I had it in my power to furnish him a number of men."

Schuyler, who clearly foresaw the evil effects of Allen's expedition, upon the Canadians, wrote to the Continental Congress, saying—"I am apprehensive of disagreeable consequences arising from Mr. Allen's imprudence. I always dreaded his impatience of subordination, and it was not until after a solemn promise made me, in the presence of several officers, that he would demean himself properly, that I would permit him to attend the army. Nor would I have consented then, had not his solicitations been backed by several officers."

Three weeks afterward, Washington said in a letter to Schuyler: "Colonel Allen's misfortune will, I hope, teach a lesson of prudence and subordination to others, who may be too ambitious to outshine their general officers, and regardless of order and duty, rush into enterprises which have unfavorable effects upon the public, and are destructive to themselves." But the lesson was not heeded.

October was wearing away, and the inclement season was fast approaching, and yet the successful termination of the siege of St. John's appeared as remote as when first begun. Very little had been accomplished. Montgomery was surrounded by a host of difficulties. He had no officers of military experience and proper military spirit, to whom he might turn in his perplexity for sound advice; and while he was thus left to rely wholly upon his own judgment, he was continually annoyed and his plans thwarted by the interference of those whose ability and position gave them no right to counsel or decide.

The garrison appeared to be too well supplied with provisions to allow a hope on the part of Montgomery that they might be conquered by starvation. The ground on which he was encamped was low and very wet, for the autumn rains had begun, and the troops were suffering severely from sickness. General discontent prevailed, and the Canadians who had joined the Americans, or received them as friends, became very uneasy at the prospect of failure, notwithstanding the general assured them that if his army should be compelled to retire without a victory, he would take care of all those who dared not remain in the country.

The discontent in the army culminated in open opposition to the general, when he proposed to change the position of the camp to higher and dryer ground, and to plant a battery within four hundred yards of the north side of the fort. He was preparing for this movement, when Major Brown informed him that unless attention was immediately directed to the east side of the river, from which the troops thought they could more effectually damage the enemy, and sooner win a victory, and give them the privilege of returning home, a meeting would be called to devise measures in accordance with their views. Notwithstanding he was used to insubordination, Montgomery was astonished at this information. "I did not consider," he said, in a letter to Schuyler, "I was at the head of troops, who carry the spirit of freedom into the field, and think for themselves. . . . . I can not help observing to how little purpose I am here. Were I not afraid the example would be too generally followed, and that the public service might suffer, I would not stay an hour at the head of troops whose operations I can not direct."*

Notwithstanding his patience was tried to the utmost, Montgomery's sense of obligation to his adopted country, at that critical moment, overcame his disgust. He yielded so far as to call a council of war. "Upon considering the fatal consequences which might flow from the want of sub-

* Autograph Letter, Oct. 13, 1775.

ordination and discipline should this ill-humor continue," he wrote to Schuyler; "my unstable authority over troops of different colonies, the insufficiency of the military law and my own want of powers to enforce it, weak as it is, I thought it expedient to call the field officers together." The council was held, they decided against Montgomery's plan, and he was compelled to acquiesce, not, however, without unburdening his mind freely to Schuyler, who was suffering annoyances of every kind at Ticonderoga, arising from similar causes.

"The New England troops," he wrote, "are the worst stuff imaginable, for soldiers. They are home-sick; their regiments have melted away, and yet not a man dead of any distemper. There is such an equality among them, that the officers have no authority, and there are very few among them in whose spirit I have confidence. The privates are all generals but not soldiers; and so jealous, that it is impossible, though a man risk his person, to escape the imputation of jealousy."*

Such feelings and such imputations, as we shall have occasion to observe, were afterwards freely bestowed upon Schuyler.

Of the first regiment of New Yorkers (McDougall's) Montgomery gave a still worse account, and laid before Schuyler instances of great unworthiness both in the officers and men. Of the latter he particularly complained, and regretted much that McDougall had not yet joined the army.

"I think it will be much aid to the service to give Ritzema a regiment," he wrote to Schuyler. "He has the talent for making a regiment as much as any man I have known. Out of the sweepings of New York streets, he has made something more like regular troops, than I have seen in the Continental service. Should not McDougall resign? We can't afford sinecures. Much have I missed him, as you will easily judge, when you consider our talents in this part of the world."†

* Autograph letter, October 31, 1775. In the same letter speaking of appointments and changes that he had made in the army, he said—"Dimon's brigade-majorship I bestowed on Weisenfels, a man of exceeding good character, and more acquainted with the service than most of us."

† Ibid.

To his father-in-law, Robert Livingston, Montgomery wrote:

"The difficulties I have labored under from want of discipline in the troops (being all generals and few soldiers), want of provisions, ammunition, and men, have made me most heartily sick of this business; and I do think that no consideration can ever induce me again to step out of the path of private life. As a volunteer, I shall ever be ready when necessity requires, to take my part of the burden."* In deep bitterness of spirit he again wrote—"The Master of Hindostan could not recompense me for this summer's work. I have envied every wounded man who has had so good an apology for retiring from a scene where no credit can be obtained. O fortunate husbandmen; would I were at my plow again!"

As, from time to time, Montgomery unbosomed himself to Schuyler, that officer responded with sympathetic feeling, caused by his daily experience of the effects of wrong-doing. "Such scenes of rascality," he wrote, "are daily opening to me, as will surprise you to learn. But you must not be troubled by any from hence, having doubtless enough where you are to try your temper. The difficulties you labor under are extremely distressing to me, but patience and perseverance, my friend, I hope will carry you through."

It is an unpleasant duty to report these complaints concerning the troops who were engaged in the important campaign against Canada, in the autumn of 1775. That they were just, impartial history, enlightened by facts, fully concedes. Washington suffered more severely from similar causes, while in command of the army engaged in the siege of Boston at that time. His letters to the Continental Congress and to others, are full of complaints of a similar character to those uttered by Schuyler and Montgomery. Those we have already recorded, and shall hereafter record, are not given in a caviling or narrow spirit,

* Autograph letter, October 20, 1775.

with a view to disparage any man or body of men, but as unquestioned facts, necessary to be used as rebutting testimony in vindication of General Schuyler's character from foul aspersions at that time, and the ungenerous attacks of partisan writers at the present day.

Surely no American can ask for better evidence in the case, than the word of that early martyr to Liberty in America, Richard Montgomery. He and Schuyler—á noble pair of brothers—at the sacrifice of every comfort to be derived from exalted social position, wealth, and happy domestic relations (and one of them suffering from most distressing illness), devoted their talents, energies, influence, fortune and health, to the cause of their country in a most critical hour, with beautiful disinterestedness; honored then and now by the wise and good; loved by all who could appreciate genius, genuine patriotism, and the value of generous sacrifices; and regarded by the infant nation, then in its first struggles for independent existence, as the conservators of their most precious interests at that moment. "The more I reflect on your expedition," Washington wrote to Schuyler, "the greater is my concern lest it should sink under insuperable difficulties. I look upon the interests and salvation of our bleeding country, in a great degree, as depending upon your success."

Amidst the gloom that gathered around the northern expedition as the season advanced, there were occasional gleams of hope. At one time there seemed a prospect of a speedy closing of the campaign by peaceful arrangements, propositions for which were made to Montgomery through the Caughnawagas, by "the formidable Le Corne St. Luc" and other principal inhabitants of Montreal. A conference at Laprairie was proposed and held, the republicans being represented by Majors Livingston, Brown, and

Macpherson, the latter Schuyler's accomplished aid-de-camp, and now the favorite in Montgomery's military family. The general doubted Le Corne's sincerity, and was cautious. He committed to him a letter to Sir Guy Carleton, and bade his commissioners to be exceedingly circumspect in their negotiations. The conference, as Montgomery feared it would be, was a failure. "It has ended in smoke," he wrote to Schuyler. "St. Luke made the Indian deliver my letter to Mr. Carleton, who had it burned without reading it. The Indian told the Governor very honestly that he was sent to me by St. Luke and others. The Indians at Caughnawaga attended at Laprairie, according to appointment, and are much displeased at the tricks put upon them by these gentlemen. They seemed to think St. Luke was discovered in his plan, and dared not venture to carry it through. I hope we shall have more powder!" He had just written, "Your diligence and foresight have saved us from the difficulty that threatened us. We are no longer afraid of starving;" and now he added, "Your residence at Ticonderoga has probably enabled us to keep our ground. How much do the public owe you for your attention and authority."*

A victory now cheered the commanders and their troops. After Allen's raid, Carleton felt a great anxiety to relieve St. John's, and succeeded in assembling about nine hundred Canadians at Montreal. But mutual distrust was such a strong element of dissolution, that it was difficult to keep them together.

It was well-known that the inhabitants south of the St. Lawrence, generally favored the Americans; and the Canadians who joined Carleton, timid and dispirited, deserted him by scores, until few were left. He could not depend

* Autograph letter, October 9, 1775.

upon the Indians. Indeed, he probably did not wish to, for his nature revolted at the idea of letting such bloody savages loose upon the colonists.

With a foolish confidence that the fort at Chamblée could not be reached by the invaders, while St. John's held out, Carleton had neglected to arm it. Only a feeble garrison was there, and they had been kept in a state of alarm by Livingston. These facts were communicated to Montgomery, and he directed Livingston, with the assistance of Major Brown and Colonel Bedel, to make a night attack upon the fort. The inhabitants of the parish of Chamblée, three hundred strong, cheerfully ranged themselves under the banner of Major Livingston for the purpose, and these were joined by about fifty from Montgomery's camp, under Brown and Bedel. The plan of attack was arranged by the Canadians, who were acquainted with the place. Under the cover of an intensely dark night, some cannon were conveyed by them from the camp, on batteaux, past the fort at St. John's to the head of the Chamblée rapids, where they were landed, mounted on carriages, and dragged to the place of attack. The garrison, under Major Stopford, a well-educated and polished gentleman, surprised and overpowered, made a feeble and brief resistance, and surrendered.*

This victory occurred on the 18th of October, and was a most important event to the beseigers of St. John's, whose ammunition was almost exhausted. Among the articles that fell into the hands of the republicans were six tons of gunpowder, between five and six thousand musket cartridges, five hundred hand-grenades, three hundred swivel shot, and a large quantity of provisions and

* The inhabitants of the garrison, surrendered by the capitulation, were ten officers, seventy-eight private soldiers, thirty women, and fifty-one children. The prisoners were sent to Connecticut.

stores. As a trophy, the Americans secured the colors of the 7th regiment of British regulars, which Montgomery sent to General Schuyler, at Ticonderoga. This, the first military trophy of the kind captured by the republicans, was sent by Schuyler to the Continental Congress at Philadelphia, and for a while, graced the walls of the residence of John Hancock, the president of that body.*

* Christopher Marshall, of Philadelphia, in his Diary, made the following record:

Nov. 3, 1775. Account just brought by express, of the surrender of Fort Chamblée to Major Brown, on the 14th [18th], of October, in which was a great quantity of amunition, provisions, and warlike stores, with the colors of the Seventh Regiment, or Royal Scotch Fusileers, which were brought to the Congress. . . .

Nov. 6. Near five, son Benjamin accompanied me to Colonel Hancock's lodgings, in order to see the ensigns or colors taken at Fort Chamblée, &c.

## CHAPTER XXV.

The easy reduction of Chamblée gave Montgomery assurances of success ; and having thereby secured an ample provision of powder, he prepared to prosecute the seige of St. John's with greater vigor. His troops were inspirited, a better feeling prevailed among them, and he had the most satisfactory declarations that the Caughnawaga Indians would remain strictly neutral. He had succeeded in sinking the enemy's armed schooner and possessing himself of every avenue to the country from the fort ; and he at once proceeded to the erection of a battery within two hundred and fifty yards of the enemy's strongest works, upon which he mounted four heavy guns and six mortars. He also erected a block-house on the opposite side of the river, and there mounted one gun and two mortars, and then commenced the assault with great earnestness. The gallant Major Preston, who commanded the fort, held out manfully, for he was in daily expectation of relief from Governor Carleton.

At this time General Schuyler had some unpleasant experiences in connection with General Wooster and his troops, who had arrived at Ticonderoga. He had received assurances from time to time that Wooster was prepared to act as independently as possible, and to be governed by the regulations of the Continental Congress and the mandates of the commander-in-chief of the army of the North, no further than was absolutely necessary to comply with the strict letter of his obligations. He also heard rumors that Wooster was provided with ample provisions for his troops, independent of the Continental commissariat; that he regarded his commission as major-general in the Connecticut service as giving him rank superior to that of brigadier-general in the Continental service; and that he would claim to outrank Montgomery.

Schuyler foresaw in this disposition much trouble for himself and great danger to the expedition, and desired to avoid it if possible. He had, from the beginning, been much annoyed by letters from Wooster, who, naturally presuming upon his age and past services, made suggestions concerning military operations at the North, that at times were quite censorious in tone. Schuyler was not a man to receive such letters with complacency, and at length, being irritated by Wooster's impracticable suggestions too much for further forbearance, he wrote a spicy letter to the veteran that made him more sparing of his advice about matters of which he knew very little.

"You speak," wrote Schuyler, "with as much ease of marching into Canada as if there were no greater obstacles in getting there than marching from Greenwich to New York. Taking possession of Montreal and Quebec is more easily said than done, for as our troops have not yet learnt to swim across a lake of an hundred miles extent, we who are upon the spot find some difficulty to 'march directly into Canada, and take possession of Montreal and Quebec!' The building of boats when not one material was on the spot; when even the saw-mills were to be erected or repaired to cut the plank; when after the 18th of July, on which I arrived here [Ticonderoga], I had to send down the country for carpenters, and to bring up every individual article for the very existence of the troops, was found a matter that required a little more time than you seem to be aware of, although I flatter myself that as much has been done since my arrival as could have been completed by any man in my situation."*

* Schuyler's MS. Orderly Book, August 14, 1775.

When, a month later, the Continental Congress directed Wooster to proceed to Albany with his troops, in order to join the expedition against Canada, and Thomas Lynch, a delegate in Congress, wrote on the same day, "There will arise a difficulty (and God knows you need no additional ones) about the old Connecticut general," Schuyler felt a strong desire not to risk the interests of his expedition by the collisions of authority that might occur. Tender of his brother officer's reputation, he was unwilling to lay before the Congress his real reasons for not desiring the presence of Wooster and his troops, and he simply remarked, as if incidentally, in a letter to that body, on the 28th of September:

"I do not think I shall have occasion for General Wooster's regiment, as I only wait for batteaux to send on five hundred New Yorkers that I now have here, and which I suppose will soon embark, as the wind is now favorable for craft to come from St. John's, and which I expect with impatience."*

But the Congress was already aware of the assumptions of Wooster, and the independent feeling, of his troops; and on the receipt of Schuyler's letter they wrote to the Connecticut general informing him that it was thought his services would not be needed in the North, and ordering him to march with his troops "to the batteries erecting on the Highlands, on the North River," there to leave as many of them as the officer in charge of the works might desire, and to proceed with the rest to New York, and remain there until further orders from the Congress. They added:

"But in case you should have any orders from General Schuyler previous to the receipt of this, to join the army under his command, or in any way to be aiding to his ex-

* Schuyler's Letter Books.

pedition, you are wholly to conform yourself to his directions, the above orders of Congress notwithstanding."*

Long before this order was issued Wooster and his troops had made their way northward; and the day before its date, they had left Fort George at the head of Lake George, and arrived at Ticonderoga, where the veteran was courteously received by Schuyler. But the latter had resolved that Wooster should not proceed any further, because information which had just been communicated to him by Gunning Bedford, the deputy muster-master-general, then at Fort George, made him fearful that on his arrival at the camp the Connecticut general would assume rank and authority superior to Montgomery, and cause disturbances that would be fatal to the expedition.

"Suffer me to condole with you," wrote Bedford, one of the most active, truthful, and reliable men in the army—"suffer me to condole with you at the approach of troubles I see ready to be heaped upon you. General Wooster and his regiment will be with you in a few days. They are making great preparations, as if all the execution of the army was to be done by them alone. He brings provisions of his own, they tell me, to serve his regiment for the campaign. They will not touch Continental stores, nor eat Continental provisions! They boast of having nothing to do with the Continent. Indeed, to me they appear rather to come with a determination to abuse the Continental troops and their commanders, and to make the most profit by the campaign they can, than to serve the cause.

"Officers and all seem to be concerned in *sutling;* but your calling some of them to account at Ticonderoga has frightened them from carrying their stores across, at least under appearance of their sutling. General Wooster has bought up the stores of Majors Lockwood and Colt, the former of whom is secretary to the General, and the latter, commissary to the regiment! So that he means to carry them down as necessary stores for his regiment! He told me himself he had a large quantity of pork he had brought with him, with molasses, sugar, peas, rice, chocolate, and soap enough, to last his troops; and they would not go forward without them, nor indeed till they saw them go before. The general told Dr. Stringer that he was *Major General of the Connecticut forces*, and that no man on this side Connecticut had a right to discharge one of his soldiers, but himself.

* October 19th, 1775.

"Mr. Cobb, the commissary here, is a Connecticut man (but who despises them thoroughly in his heart), and was let into his counsels. He was present when General Wooster was about calling a court-martial. He had not officers enough of his own to form it, and how to get others he did not know, without signiug himself brigadier-general. He mentioned the difficulty to his officers, 'Why,' one of them replied, you have two strings to your bow;' another, 'take ca:e you don't pull on the weakest;' and a third, 'you may pull on both, on occasion.' Cobb says he believes he signed brigadier-general, but would not be certain; however, it might be found out by getting the orders.

"So I foresee the difficulties you will be involved in by the jealousy Wooster's regiment must create among the other troops, when they see them so much better provided with everything than they are or can be, and more especially, should Wooster oppose your superior command over the Connecticut forces. It is almost incredible, but their conduct is really astonishing. I am very apprehensive lest they may more disserve the cause, than if they had not come at all.

"As the most virtuous character is never secure from the envious, malignant tongue of slander, so the disaffected to you, in your army, have delighted your enemies by poisoning your fame therewith. They would wish the contagion to spread, but their tools are too insignificant, and your upright conduct must ever check its progress; and I assure you, dear sir, I feel particularly happy in having it in my power to do your character that justice it really merits."*

Walter Livingston, the deputy commissary-general, writing from Albany at about the same time, confirmed Bedford's statement of the independent provision made by Wooster for his troops. "The general himself told me," he wrote, "that he had twenty day's provisions with him, and that he had ordered his own commissary to furnish him from time to time, and that he would not trouble me on that score. Provisions have arrived for him since he left this."

These accounts confirmed Schuyler's worst anticipations of difficulty with Wooster. And the conduct of some of his troops who preceded him a few days, made him resolve not to allow Wooster to join Montgomery. They evinced

* Autograph Letter, Oct. 15, 1775.

a disposition to recognize no authority except that of their own commander.

"Two hundred and fifty-three of General Wooster's regiment came across Lake George on Sunday," wrote Schuyler to the Continental Congress on the 18th of October, "but the general is not yet arrived, and they do not choose to move until he does. Do not choose to move! Strange language in an army; but the irresistible force of necessity obliges me to put up with it. This morning I gave an order to Lieutenant-Colonel Ward, to send a subaltern, a sergeant, corporal, and twenty privates, in two batteaux, to carry powder, artillery, stores, and men. The colonel, who is a good man, called upon me to know if he would not be blamed by General Wooster for obeying my orders. I begged him to send the men, and urged the necessity. The men, I believe will condescend to go. I could give many instances of a similar nature, but General Montgomery has most justly and emphatically given the reasons: 'Troops who carry the spirit of freedom into the field, and think for themselves, will not bear either subordination or discipline.'"*

Schuyler, as we have observed, received Wooster courteously. He was agreeably disappointed in his apparent disposition. He found him courteous, conciliatory, yielding, and self-sacrificing. "My intentions," he wrote to the Continental Congress, on the 18th, "were to have him remain at this post, but assuring me that his regiment would not move without him, and that although he thought hard of being superseded,† yet he would most readily put himself under the command of General Montgomery; that his only views were the public service, and that no obstructions of any kind would be given by him; this spir-

* Schuyler's MS. Letter Books.

† When, in June, 1775, the Continental Congress made their appointments of general officers for the army, Wooster was major-general and commander-in-chief of the Connecticut troops. He was raised only to the rank of brigadier in the Continental service, while Israel Putnam, his inferior in rank in the Colonial service, was promoted to major-general. He felt the slight keenly, yet, with the spirit of true patriotism, he consented to serve in the subordinate capacity, and took the field among the earliest of the Continental officers.

ited and sensible declaration I received with inexpressible satisfaction, and he moves to-morrow with the first division of his regiment."*

On the following morning Schuyler received official notice that Wooster had held a general court-martial at Fort George (hinted at in Bedford's letter of the 15th) without apprising him of the fact. He could not, in justice to his position, and the good of the service, overlook the indignity; and he felt specially aggrieved that Wooster had not, by either a written or oral communication, mentioned the subject to him. He naturally regarded Wooster's professions as insincere, and he immediately addressed to him the following letter:

"The Continental Congress having taken the first six regiments raised this year, in the Colony of Connecticut (of which yours is one), into the pay and service of the associated colonies, at the earnest request of the honorable delegates representing the colony of Connecticut, and you having, in a variety of instances, obeyed the orders of Congress, who have conferred on you the rank of brigadier-general in the army of the associated colonies, I was taught to believe that you considered yourself as such, both from what I have above observed, and from your declarations to me yesterday. But I am just now informed that you have called a general court-martial at Fort George, on your way up here; a conduct which I can not account for, unless you consider yourself my superior, and that can not be in virtue of your appointment by Congress, by which you are a younger brigadier-general than Mr. Montgomery; and unless you consider yourself as such, I can not, consistently with the duty I owe the public, permit you to join that part of the army now under Brigadier-General Montgomery's command, lest a confusion and disagreement should arise that might prove fatal to our operations in Canada. You will, therefore, Sir, please to give me your explicit answer to this question: Whether you consider yourself and your regiment in the service of the associated colonies, and yourself a younger brigadier-general than Mr. Montgomery or not? that no misapprehensions or misrepresentations may hereafter arise."†

* Schuyler's MS. Letter Books.

† Schuyler's MS. Letter Books.

To this letter General Wooster immediately replied, as follows:

"In answer to your favor of this day, give me leave to acquaint you that, immediately upon my receiving the Continental articles of war I gave them out to the different captains and commanders of companies in my regiment, but they universally declined signing them; of consequence in the discipline of the troops under my command I was obliged to continue in the use of the law martial of Connecticut, under which they were raised, which I certainly had a right to do, by virtue of my commission from that colony. Upon the same principle I ordered a general court-martial at Fort George, which, whether right or not, was never designed in the least to contradict or counteract your authority as commander-in-chief of the troops within this department.

"With regard to the other question, my appointment in the Continental army, you are sensible, could not be very agreeable to me, notwithstanding which, I never should have continued in the service, had I not determined to observe the rules of the army. No, Sir! I have the cause of my country too much at heart to attempt to make any difficulty or uneasiness in the army, upon whom the success of an enterprise of almost infinite benefit to the country is now depending. I shall consider my rank in the army what my commision from the Continental Congress makes it, and shall not attempt to dispute the command with General Montgomery at St. John's. As to my regiment, I consider them as what they really are, according to the tenor of their enlistments and compact with the colony of Connecticut by whom they were raised, and now acting in conjunction with the troops of the other colonies in the service and for the defense of the associated colonies in general. You may depend, Sir, that I shall exert myself as much as possible to promote the strictest union and harmony among both officers and soldiers in the army, and use every means in my power to give success to the expedition."*

This letter, and the following official notice of the action of the General Assembly of Connecticut, which both Schuyler and Wooster received at about that time, were satisfactory. Complaints had been made to Governor Trumbull, from time to time, of the insubordination of the Connecticut troops; and finally, on the second Thursday of October the Assembly took action, as follows:

* Autograph Letter, October 19, 1775.

"This Assembly being informed that certain questions and disputes have arisen among the troops lately raised by this colony, and sent into the colony of New York, and such as are now employed against the ministerial forces in Canada, which disputes, unless prevented, may be attended with unhappy consequences: Therefore, it is hereby *Resolved*, by this Assembly, that all the troops which have been lately raised by this colony, for the special defense thereof, and sent into the colony of New York, and all such as are now employed against the ministerial troops in Canada, are, and shall be subject to the rules, orders, regulations, and discipline of the Congress of the twelve united colonies, during the time of their enlistment."*

General Wooster sailed with his troops for St. John's, on the 21st of October, and arrived at the camp on the morning of the 23d. The soldiers departed with great reluctance on account of the lateness of the season and the possibility of their not being able to return. They numbered three hundred and thirty-five men, including the officers.

On the day after Wooster left, Schuyler suffered a severe attack of rheumatism, and on the following day the fever returned with great violence. Mrs. Schuyler had been with him for a while, and when she left for home, on the 12th, he was so much better that he wrote to General Montgomery, saying, "I am gaining strength so fast that I propose to join you as soon as I have sent on Wooster's corps, who are now at Fort George."

He was now tortured by both disease and disappointment, and while in that state of mind and body, he was informed, by some injudicious person, of remarks made by Wooster, at different times, since his arrival at Fort George, disparaging to the skill and bravery of both Schuyler and Montgomery. Under the lashes of keen irritation, he wrote to Wooster, as follows, on the 23d:

* Schuyler's papers.

19*

"SIR:—Being well informed that you have declared on your way to this place, that if you were at St. John's, you would march into the fort at the head of your regiment, and as it is just that you should have an opportunity of showing your prowess, and that of your regiment, I have desired General Montgomery to give you leave to make the attempt if you choose. I do not wish, however, that you should be too lavish of your men's lives, unless you have a prospect of gaining the fortress."

Schuyler inclosed this in his letter to Montgomery, alluded to, saying, "You may seal and deliver, or destroy as you choose." Montgomery should have destroyed it, for he well knew that only under the influence of extraordinary irritation would Schuyler have written it. Wooster made no reply to it, but in a letter written to Schuyler some months afterward, he referred to it with indignation, as having been a false accusation.

Montgomery, wearied and worn, was glad when the arrival of Wooster gave him a prospect of release.

"I am exceedingly well pleased," he wrote to Schuyler, "to see Mr. Wooster here, both for the advantage of the service, and upon my own account, for I most earnestly request to be suffered to retire, should matters stand on such a footing this winter as to permit me to go off with honor. I have not talents nor temper for such a command. I am under the disagreeable necessity of acting eternally out of character—to wheedle, flatter, and lie. I stand in a constrained attitude. I will bear with it for a short time, but I can not support it long. The Canadians, too, distress me by their clashing interests and private piques."*

Montgomery and Wooster acted in concert, and upon the most friendly footing. Montgomery asked the veteran soldier to live with him, and he showed him every attention in his power. Together they pressed the seige of St. John's with vigor.

Carleton made great efforts to relieve the garrison at St. John's. He sent to Quebec for aid, and Colonel McLean,

* Autograph letter, October 31, 1775.

a gallant Scotch officer, who had served the British King in the famous rebellion in 1745, and was now at the head of three hundred Highlanders at Quebec, called *The Royal Highland Emigrants*, agreed to ascend the St. Lawrence to the mouth of the Sorel, march along its bank, and join Carleton at St. John's. With this assurance, Carleton with a motley force of one hundred regulars, several hundred Canadians from the northward of the St. Lawrence, and a few Indians, accompanied by Le Corne St. Luc, embarked in thirty-four batteaux, and attempted to land at Longueuil, a mile and a half below the city. Colonel Seth Warner, with a detachment of three hundred Green Mountain Boys, and a part of the second (Van Schaick's) New York Regiment, was on the alert in the neighborhood, and lay in covert near the spot where Carleton was about to land. Warner allowed the batteaux to approach very near the shore, when he opened upon them a severe storm of grape-shot from a four pound cannon, and volleys of musketry. The enemy were driven back in great confusion, and Carleton, utterly disconcerted, retired to Montreal, leaving behind him a few killed and wounded, and four prisoners. The latter were sent immediately to Montgomery's camp.

McLean, meanwhile, had landed at the mouth of the Sorel, and had increased his force by pressing many Canadians into his service. With full expectation of success against a band of undisciplined rebels whom he affected to despise, he was marching toward St. John's when he was met by Majors Brown, Livingston, and Easton, flushed by their recent victory at Chamblée, and their little force strengthened by some Green Mountain Boys. McLean was driven back to his landing place, where his Canadian recruits by compulsion, deserted him. There intelligence of the repulse of Carleton met him. A panic seized his troops, and before the republicans reached the mouth of the Sorel, the gallant McLean and his followers had embarked, and were on their way to Quebec. Brown and Livingston took post there, erected batteries, and prepared to oppose the passage of vessels up or down the St. Lawrence.

Warner's prisoners arrived at Montgomery's camp toward the evening of the day on which they were captured, and while the great guns of the assailants were playing briskly upon the British works. The cannonade was immediately silenced, and a flag with a letter, was sent in to Major Preston, by one of the captives, to inform him of the repulse of Carleton and to demand an instantaneous surrender of the fort. Major Preston affected to doubt the story of the prisoner, and asked for a delay of four days. The request was denied, and the demand was instantly renewed. The garrison had then been on half allowance for some time. Menaced with starvation, and perceiving no hope of relief, the gallant Preston was compelled to yield. On Friday, the 3d of November, Montgomery wrote to Schuyler, saying:

"I have the pleasure to acquaint you, the garrison surrendered last night. This morning we took possession. To-morrow I hope the prisoners will set off. Inclosed you have the capitulation, which I hope will meet with your approbation, and that of Congress. I have ventured to permit an officer or two to go to their families, which are in some distress at Montreal, on their parole. They can't do us any harm, and there would have been a degree of inhumanity in refusing them. . . Several men of rank in Canada are among the prisoners. I have permitted them to remain at Crown Point till the return of two gentlemen they sent to their friends for money, etc. They pleaded hard to return home, but they are too dangerous to let loose again. . . I am making the necessary preparations to press immediately to Montreal, by way of Laprairie, as the enemy have armed vessels in the Sorel."*

* Autograph Letter.

The siege had continued fifty-five days, and Preston was honored by all for his gallant defense in the midst of every discouragement. When he with the other prisoners were about to depart for Connecticut (that great receptacle of captives during the earlier years of the war), under the charge of Captain Mott, General Schuyler wrote as follows to Governor Trumbull:

> "From Major Preston and the officers of the 26th Regiment, I have experienced the most polite and friendly attention when I was a stranger, a traveler in Ireland. A return of good offices is the duty of every honest man, and I therefore beg leave to recommend them to your Honor's notice, and would wish if there is any choice in the quarters which you shall destine to them, that theirs were the best, which I shall consider as a particular favor done me."*

Honorable terms were granted to the garrison at St. John's. They marched out of the fort with the honors of war, and the troops grounded their arms on the plain near by. The officers were allowed to retain their side-arms; and the baggage of both officers and men was secured to them. The generous Montgomery went still further—even beyond what, perhaps, courtesy or the usages of war, under the circumstances, required. He allowed to each of the privates a new suit of clothes from the captured stores. Of this the scantily clad (and some half-naked) republicans made complaint. The rigors of a Canadian winter were about to set in, and they needed thick and ample clothing, while the captives were to be sent to a milder climate. Both officers and men murmured loudly, and finally they boldly demanded a reconsideration of the capitulation. But Montgomery refused even while the harsh sounds of mutinous discourse were ringing in his ears. "The officers of the first regiment of Yorkers and artillery

* Schuyler's MS. Letter Books, Nov. 10, 1775.

company," he wrote to Schuyler, "were very near a mutiny the other day, because I would not stop the clothing of the garrison of St. John's. I would not have sullied my own reputation, nor disgraced the continental arms, by a breach of capitulation, for the universe. There was no driving it into their noddles that clothing was really the property of the soldier—that he had paid for it, and that every regiment (in this country especially), saved a year's clothing to have decent clothes to wear on particular occasions."*

The garrison that surrendered to the republicans, consisted of five hundred regular troops and about one hundred Canadian volunteers, many of them of the rank of *noblesse*, or gentry. Among the officers were Major (then Captain) Andrè, the unfortunate spy in after years. Also Captain Anbery and Lieutenant Anstruther, who were exchanged, and again made prisoners with Burgoyne, in the autumn of 1777. Anbury published, in two volumes, an interesting account of his sojourn in America, while a prisoner the second time.

The spoils of victory were seventeen brass ordnance, from two to twenty-four pounders ; two eight-inch howitzers ; twenty-two iron cannon, from three to nine pounders ; a considerable quantity of shot and small shells ; eight hundred stand of arms, and a small quantity of naval stores. The ammunition and provisions were inconsiderable, for the stock of each was nearly exhausted.

The Congress voted thanks to both Montgomery and Wooster, for their services in securing the victory ; and the president of Congress, in his long letter to the former, fully approved of his course in the capitulation.

"Nor are the humanity and politeness with which you have treated those in your power," he said, "less illustrious instances of magnanimity

* Autograph Letter, Nov. 13, 1775.

than the valor by which you reduced them to it. The Congress, utterly abhorrent from every species of cruelty towards prisoners, and determined to adhere to this benevolent maxim till the conduct of their enemies renders a deviation from it indispensably necessary, will ever applaud their officers for beautifully blending the Christian with the conqueror, and never, in endeavoring to acquire the character of a hero, lose that of a man."

## CHAPTER XXVI.

On the day when General Montgomery achieved his victory at St. John's, Colonel Benedict Arnold, who, with with a few troops, had passed the great wilderness of the Kennebec and Chaudiére, and achieved a more wonderful triumph, were gathering at the first of settlements that stretched from the forests to the St. Lawrence, preparatory to a march to the high banks of that river, opposite Quebec.

That expedition, which formed a part of the campaign against Canada, of which Schuyler held the chief command, considered in all its features and circumstances, was one of the most wonderful on record.

We have already observed Arnold leaving Crown Point in a towering passion, to lay complaints of ill-usage before Washington at Cambridge. The commander-in-chief, as usual, considered the whole matter dispassionately. He appreciated the services of Arnold, and received him in a most friendly manner at head-quarters. His story, straightforward and well corroborated, soon changed the tide of popular feeling that had been rising strongly against him. His exploits on Lake Champlain, so chivalric and useful, created the greatest enthusiasm, and he soon found himself borne upon a flood of popular sympathy, in which Washington himself was a participant. Adventurous, a good tactician and disciplinarian, and possessed of the faculty of inspiring his troops with his own enthusiasm, Arnold appeared to Washington as precisely the right man to lead a coöperating expedition to Quebec by way of the wilderness, which he had contemplated, and concerning which, as we have seen, he consulted General Schuyler. When his plans were matured, Washington, with his usual wise discrimination, gave the command of the expedition to Arnold, and commissioned him as colonel in the Continental army. Arnold, in past years, had carried on a trade in horses between Quebec and the West Indies, and had often visited the Canadian capital in the pursuit of his vocation. He was familiar with the town and understood the people, and Washington expected to see him successful.

Arnold's ambition was now fully gratified, and he entered upon the duties of his office, in organizing the expedition, with the greatest zeal. Very soon eleven hundred men were enrolled for the perilous service, consisting of ten companies of New England infantry (part of them from General Greene's Rhode Island brigade), two rifle companies from Pennsylvania, and one from Virginia, and a number of volunteers. These formed a battalion. Roger Enos of Connecticut (whose courage was not sufficient to carry him through the wilderness), and the brave Christopher Green of Rhode Island, were Arnold's lieutenants. The majors were Meigs of Connecticut, and Bigelow of Worcester, Mass. Morgan, afterward the famous leader in the southern campaigns, with Heth, who behaved bravely at Germantown two years later, and Humphreys, led the Virginia riflemen. Hendricks commanded a Pennsylvania company. Thayer, who behaved so gallantly at Fort Mifflin, in the autumn of 1777, led a company of Rhode Islanders, and Dearborn another of the Massachusetts infantry. Among the volunteers was Aaron Burr, a wayward grandson of the renowned theologian, Jonathan Edwards, then a youth of nineteen, who arose from a sick bed on hearing of the expedition, joined it, and behaved nobly to the end. Samuel Spring of Massachusetts was the chaplain.

Arnold was invested with ample, and even extraordinary powers, yet these were subservient to very explicit instructions, prepared by Washington with great care. In these, Arnold was charged to push forward with all possible expedition, and to endeavor to discover the real sentiments of the Canadians toward the republican cause, particularly as to the undertaking in which he was engaged. He was instructed not to prosecute the enterprise, if the Canadians should be decidedly opposed to it. He was furnished with a quantity of friendly addresses in the French language, which he was to distribute among the Canadians when he should emerge from the wilderness on the St. Lawrence slope. He was also instructed to enforce rigid discipline and good order, that his troops might not commit the least outrage upon the inhabitants, either in person or property; to "check every idea, and crush, in its earliest stage, every attempt to plunder even those who were known to be enemies to the cause." He was directed to pay full value for every thing the Canadians should provide for him on his march; by no means to press the people or their cattle into his service; and not only to pay perfect respect to the religious feelings and observances of the country, but to do every thing in his power to protect and support the free exercise of those observances on the part of the inhabitants.

Acting upon the hint given him by the commanding-general of the Northern department, Washington added: "In case of a union with General Schuyler, or if he should be in Canada upon your arrival there, you are by no means to consider yourself as upon a separate and independent command, but are to put yourself under him, and follow his instructions. Upon this occasion, and all others, I recommend most earnestly to avoid all contention about rank. In such a case, every post is honorable in which a man can serve his country."

Lord Pitt, a younger son of the Earl of Chatham, and aid-de-camp to Sir Guy Carleton, it was supposed was still in Canada, and Washington instructed Arnold, that in the event of that young gentleman falling into his hands, he should treat him with the greatest consideration. "You can not err," he said, "in paying too much honor to the son of so illustrious a character, and so true a friend to the Americans."

In his address to the Canadians, Washington, after exhorting them to espouse the cause of the colonists, said: "The cause of America, and of liberty, is the cause of every virtuous American citizen; whatever may be his religion or descent, the united colonies know no distinction but such as slavery, corruption, and arbitrary dominion may create. Come, then, ye generous citizens, range yourselves under the standard of general liberty, against which all the forces and artifices of tyranny will never be able to prevail."

With ample appointments for the expedition, the troops sailed from Medford to Newburyport on the evening of the 13th of September, and on the morning of the 20th, after a night of tempest—wind, lightning, and rain—they reached Gardiner, on the Kennebec, in safety, and in two hundred batteaux, already prepared for them, ascended the river to Fort Western, at the present city of Augusta, then on the verge of the great wilderness. That was the designated place of general rendezvous. Beyond it, toward Norridgewock Falls, only a log house appeared here and there, and above that cascade no white man's dwelling was known. An exploring party was immediately dispatched toward the Dead River, a considerable tributary of the Kennebec, and another toward Lake Megantic or Chaudiére Pond, the head waters of the Chaudière, each pursuing the paths of the moose-hunters, and directed by the maps of Colonel Montressor, who, fifteen years before, had come from Quebec, ascended the Chaudière, crossed the Highlands near the head waters of the Penobscot, passed through Moosehead Lake, and entered the east branch of the Kennebec.

The whole detachment followed in four divisions, one day apart. Morgan and his riflemen formed the van; Green and Bigelow, with their musketeers, followed next; then Meigs, with four other companies. The rear was composed of three companies, under Enos. Arnold left Fort Western last, and at Norridgewock Falls overtook Morgan and his riflemen.

At the Falls the greater fatigues of the journey commenced. Before them lay an uninhabited and almost trackless wilderness, yet they were not wholly unprovided with guides, for Arnold procured an imperfect copy of Montressor's journal, and also a journal and plans of Samuel Goodwin, of Pownalborough, in Maine, who had been in that country as a surveyor for twenty-five years.

Along the swift Kennebec the expedition moved, carrying provisions, baggage, boats—every thing—around the rapids, up steep, rocky banks, through tangled woods, and across deep morasses, sometimes rowing, sometimes poleing, sometimes wading and dragging their batteau. On the tenth of October they reached the dividing ridge between the Kennebec and Dead Rivers.

Already the weak and timid had faltered, and sickness and desertion had reduced the battalion to about nine hundred and fifty effective men. These were in fine spirits and full of enthusiasm. The lovely Indian summer had commenced, and the forests were arrayed in their robes of autumnal splendor. The future appeared encouraging, and on the 12th of October two subalterns were sent forward with a party to explore and clear the portages. On the following day, Arnold dispatched a Canadian, named Jakins, to Sertigan, the nearest French settlement, to ascertain the political sentiments of the people. He also sent forward with Jakins two Indians, Sabatis and Eneas, each with a letter, one to General Schuyler and the other to friends in Quebec, announcing to the former his plan of coöperation, and asking information of the latter concerning the number of troops in the Canadian capital, what ships were there, and what were the dispositions of the merchants. One of the Indians (Eneas) proved faithless. He delivered Arnold's letter into the hands of the lieutenant-governor of the province,* and Schuyler never received the communication directed to him.

The main body of the army were now on the Dead River, a deep and sluggish stream, as its name imports. They followed it eighty miles, making seventeen portages

* These letters brought the friends to whom they were addressed into trouble. One of them, John Dyer Mercier, a merchant, was arrested and imprisoned on suspicions of treason. A gentleman in Quebec, writing to a friend on the 9th of November, said, in relation to Mr. Mercier: "On Saturday, the 28th of October, while he was going into the Upper Town, he was laid hold of by the Town Sergeant, and conducted to the main-guard, and there confined, and his papers were seized and examined merely by the order of the lieutenant-governor, without any crime or accusation alleged against him, and at day-break the next morning he was put on board the *Hunter*

at falls, until they reached the timber-clogged ponds at its sources. Up to this time the salmon-trout had been caught in such abundance that there had been no lack of food ; but now a scarcity began. They made their way through these ponds with the greatest difficulty, toward the great carrying place to the Chaudière, which they reached on the 26th. There, in the neighborhood of Lake Megantic, is the summit of the water-shed between Canada and New England.

The fatigue and privation suffered during this portion of the journey, which occupied ten or twelve days, were terrible. The records of them have no parallel in history. "The company," says a private soldier in his journal, "were ten miles wading knee deep, among alders the greatest part of the way, and came to a river which had overflowed the land. We stopped some time, not knowing what to do, and at last were obliged to wade through it, the ground giving way under us at every step. We got on a little knoll of land and went ten miles, where we were obliged to stay, night coming on ; and we were all cold and wet. One man fainted in the water with cold and fatigue, but was helped along. We had to wade into the water and chop down trees, and fetch the wood out of the water, after dark, to make a fire to dry ourselves. However, at last we got a fire, and after eating a mouthful of fish, laid ourselves down to sleep around the fire, the water surround-

sloop-of-war. This was very alarming to the citizens of Quebec, who thereupon had a meeting, and appointed three of their number to wait on the lieutenant-governor to know the cause of so remarkable a step. He made answer that he had sufficient reasons for what he had done, which he would communicate when and to whom he should think proper. But he soon thought better of it; for the next morning he called together the six captains of the British militia, and communicated to them one or more intercepted letters, directed to Mr. Mercier, of a nature that was sufficient to warrant his being secured for the safety of the town."—*American Archives*, *Fourth Series*, iii., 1419.

ing us close to our heads. If it had rained hard it would have overflowed the place we were on."*

While on this dreadful journey, intelligence came to Arnold that Lieutenant-Colonel Enos had deserted the expedition, and with three companies had returned to Cambridge. By rare good fortune Enos escaped punishment, the friendly court-martial that tried him having found an excuse for his return because his provisions had given out. But the remainder of the battalion, notwithstanding this material diminution of their strength, pressed forward in the midst of privations, of which Enos and his troops had no conceptions. The winter was coming rapidly on. The mountains were covered with snow, and yet their course, for many a weary league, lay northward. Over those bleak Highlands they wandered, exposed days and nights to drenching rains, sometimes mixed with snow, their clothes torn and their flesh lacerated by shrubs and thorns ; some walking whole hours barefooted, and sleeping with no other covering but the wet branches of the evergreens. Worse than all, their provisions failed, and dogs' meat became a luxury. Some of the poor sufferers carefully washed their moose-skin moccasins and boiled them, with

* SENTER'S JOURNAL.—Judge Joseph Henry, of Pennsylvania, was in this expedition, and wrote a narrative of it. He speaks of two women who had followed their husbands, and who exhibited the most remarkable fortitude and endurance in this portion of the march. "One was the wife of Sergeant Grier," says Henry, "a large, virtuous, and respectable woman." The other was the wife of a common soldier, named Warner. "Entering the ponds," says Henry, "and breaking the ice here and there with the butts of our guns and feet, we were soon waist-deep in mud and water. As is generally the case with youths, it came to my mind that a better path might be found than that of the more elderly guide. Attempting this, the water in a trice cooling my arm-pits, made me gladly return in the file. Now Mrs. Grier had got before me. My mind was humbled, yet astonished, at the exertions of this good woman. Her clothes were then waist high. She waded on before me, to firm ground. Not one, so long as she was known to us, dared to intimate a disrespectful idea of her."

the hope of procuring a little mucilage to appease the demands of consuming hunger. To such straits were some of Arnold's party reduced, after having hauled up their boats, with baggage and provisions, one hundred and eighty miles, and carried them on their shoulders nearly forty miles.

On the borders of Lake Megantic, the chief source of the Chaudière, Arnold and a large portion of the expedition found Jakins, who brought back intelligence of the friendly disposition of the inhabitants in the Chaudière Valley. Inspirited by this information, he prepared to descend the river immediately. It was a fearful voyage. The water rushed toward the St. Lawrence with rapid current, sometimes foaming over rough rocky bottoms, and sometimes leaping, in cascades, beautiful to the eye but perilous to the voyager. Boats were overturned, and ammunition and precious stores were lost. Perils quite as formidable as those they had passed were again gathering around them, when the lowing of cattle fell upon their ears as sweetly as the most ravishing music, for it assured them of life. Two Canadians, on horses, had come up from the settlement with five oxen. These were timely relief; and the republicans, in their joy, fired a salute. In the course of a few days every fragment of the broken battalion that survived the horrors of the wilderness, emerged from the forests, and gazed with delight upon the roofs of the dwellings and the spire of the parish church at Sertigan, a settlement twenty-five leagues from Quebec. There the troops rendezvoused and rested; and from there Arnold sent young Burr with a verbal message to Montgomery, who, on the 29th of October, had written to him from St. John's. All the letters that Arnold had sent to Schuyler, while on his march, had miscarried—been intercepted or betrayed into the hands of the enemy. But young Burr, disguised as a priest, and speaking both French and Latin pretty well, passed through the country unsuspected, and conveyed all necessary information to Montgomery. Before the youthful ambassador's arrival the general was a victor at Montreal.

Montgomery had already been apprised, through intercepted letters, of Arnold's approach, and was very anxiously waiting for a dispatch from his own hand. It came on the 17th, a few days after Burr's arrival, accompanied by a letter for General Washington. Montgomery was charmed by the manners, intelligence, and enthusiasm of young Burr, and invited him to remain at head-quarters. He did so, and was with the general at Quebec, as his aide-de-camp.

Arnold was joined at Sertigan by about forty Norridgewock Indians, and, in the face of a severe snow storm, set out for Point Levi, opposite Quebec. The fertile valley of the Chaudière was filled with friendly inhabitants, and abundant provisions might be obtained. The troops were in excellent spirits, for they believed they would speedily share in the glory of taking possession of Quebec. They were perfectly orderly, and Arnold was enabled to carry out the most strict provisions of Washington's instructions, in regulating the conduct of his troops toward the Canadians. His approach to Quebec was known two or three days before his appearance; and when, on the 9th, he reached Point Levi, the snow yet falling, and several inches deep, every boat had been removed from that side of the river or destroyed. Here was the termination of the toils of travel. They had journeyed over three hundred miles, most of the way through a gloomy wilderness. For thirty-two days they did not meet a human being; and their preservation in the midst of fearful and multifarious dangers seemed like a miracle.

Until within two days nobody at Quebec believed that the little band whom they had heard of as struggling with the storms in the wilderness, would ever reach the St. Lawrence. Cramahé, the lieutenant-governor, laughed at the idea of such an invasion; and, when early in the morning of the 9th, the little army stood behind the vail of falling snow, upon the heights above Point Levi, they appeared like specters to the startled inhabitants of the capital. The drums immediately beat to arms, for some who had crossed the river to Point Levi with the intelligence, taking counsel of their fears, greatly magnified the number of the republicans. And by a mistake in a single word the alarm of the people was greatly increased, for the news spread that the mysterious army which had descended from the wilderness or had fallen from a cloud, were clad in sheet-iron! Morgan's riflemen, with their linen frocks, had been first seen. "They are *vêtu en toile*" (clothed in linen cloth), exclaimed the Canadian messengers of alarm. The last word was mistaken for *tôle* (iron plate), and thus occurred the mistake that created a fearful panic in Quebec.

While waiting for the rear of his troops to come up, Arnold employed Canadian carpenters in making ladders, and his men in collecting canoes, and on the 14th he wrote to Montgomery, saying:

"The wind has been so high these three nights that I have not been able to cross the river. I have nearly forty canoes ready, and, as the wind has moderated, I design crossing this evening. The *Hunter* (sloop) and *Lizard* (frigate), lie opposite to prevent us, but make no doubt I shall be able to avoid them. I this moment received the agreeable intelligence, *via* Sorel, that you are in possession of St. John's, and have invested Montreal. I can give no intelligence, save that the merchant ships are busy, day and night, in loading, and four have already sailed."*

Here we will leave Arnold, while considering the position of Montgomery and his army, whom we left victors at St. John's.

Inclement weather and insubordination among the troops retarded Montgomery's march upon Montreal, and he did not arrive before it until the 12th of November. Major Henry B. Livingston had been sent forward toward Caughnawaga, with one hundred men of Colonel James Clinton's regiment, to protect the friendly Indians, but found them under no apprehensions.

"I sent for them," he says, "as soon as I came in town [Laprairie], to know whether they wanted us at their castle or not. The chiefs told me that General Montgomery had been imposed upon by some of their meaner people, who had been frightened at nothing—that they feared no invasion from Mr. Carleton at all, and if he did attack them, they thought themselves able, without assistance from abroad, to defeat him."†

It was with much difficulty that Montgomery persuaded many of the troops to advance with him. "I was obliged, at St. John's," he wrote to Schuyler, "to promise all such their dismission as choose it, to coax them to Montreal. Indeed, Wooster's regiment showed the greatest uneasiness."‡ Most of his troops finally agreed to accompany him, and he moved toward Laprairie on the 6th.§ The inhabitants of Montreal, informed of this, be-

* Livingston's MS. Journal.

† Autograph Letter, Nov. 14, 1775. ‡ Autograph Letter, Nov. 13, 1775.

§ Major Livingston made the following entry in his Diary, at Laprairie:

"Nov. 6.—General Montgomery arrived in town at two o'clock, and at different times of the day, the first of our battalion.

"7.—General Wooster and Colonel Waterbury, with their regiments and part of the fourth battalion, came in town this afternoon, and encamped in the fields about a quarter of a mile from town.

came greatly alarmed, and on the 7th the merchants of that city held a council, and then waited upon Governor Carleton to ascertain his views concerning a defense of the town. Deeply chagrined because of the evident disloyalty of the French inhabitants, Carleton told them that he should quit the place in a day or two, and that they might take care of themselves. They instantly determined to apply to General Montgomery for protection, and for that purpose a deputation was appointed to meet him at Laprairie. This was prevented by Carleton, who had resolved to force the inhabitants into resistance. But when the governor saw Montgomery approaching in force, he fled in alarm, with the garrison, on board a flotilla of ten or eleven small vessels lying in the river, with the intention of escaping to Quebec. He took with him the powder and other important stores. Perceiving this movement, Montgomery dispatched Colonel Easton, with Continental troops, cannon, and armed gondolas, to the mouth of the Sorel, to intercept the flotilla in its passage down the river. At the same time he crossed the St. Lawrence, sat down before the town, and sent in the following letter, addressed to those citizens who had been appointed by the merchants to negotiate with him :

"9.—Captain Lamb and his company came in with six field pieces (brass), taken from the enemy at St. John's.

"10.—Thirteen batteaux were conveyed from Chamblée, almost all the way by land, to a stream of water two miles east of Laprairie, and from thence brought to the landing by the town.

"11.—At nine this morning, the General, Colonel Waterbury's regiment, some of the first battalion, and a few of the fourth battalion, and General Wooster's regiment, in all about five hundred men, with six field pieces, crossed the river St. Lawrence, and landed on Isle St. Paul, directly opposite Laprairie, and one and a half miles from Montreal. As soon as Governor Carleton saw our people embark, he ordered all his regulars on board the vessels he had lying at Montreal, and fled down the river."—*Livingston's MS. Journal.*

*Gentlemen*:—My anxiety for the fate of Montreal induces me to request that you will exert yourselves among the inhabitants to prevail on them to enter into such measures as will prevent the necessity of opening my batteries on the town. When I consider the dreadful consequences of a bombardment, the distress that must attend a fire (at this season especially), when it is too late to repair the damage which must ensue, how many innocent people must suffer, and that the firm friends of liberty must be involved in one common ruin with the wicked tools of despotism, my heart bleeds at the dire necessity which compels me to distress that unfortunate city. I conjure you, by all the ties of humanity, to take every possible step to soften the heart of the governor; for he, if he be sincere in his professions to the people committed to his charge, must commiserate their condition. In vain will he persist in a resistance, which can only be attended with misery to the inhabitants, and with lasting disgrace to his own humanity."

To this he added, in a postscript:

"I have just heard that it has been falsely and scandalously reported that our intentions are to plunder the inhabitants. I have only to appeal to your own observation, whether such a proceeding be consistent with our conduct since we have entered this province."

The governor and the garrison had fled, and Montgomery encountered no resistance. He marched into the city cheered by many greetings, and won the esteem and affection of the inhabitants by his kindness, toleration, and humanity. He found there a great quantity of woolen goods with which he prepared his troops for the rigors of a Canadian winter, and at the same time shocked the Puritan prejudices of the New England soldiers by his courtesy to the functionaries of the Roman Catholic Church—a proceeding which the highest policy as well as the best feelings of human nature sanctioned.

"I have had," Montgomery wrote to Schuyler, "some conversation with Père Flaquet, a Jesuit, at the head of the society here, and esteemed a very sensible fellow. He complained of some little indignities shown their order, particularly in making part of their house the common prison, by his majesty's governors. I promised redress, and hinted, at the same time, the great probability of that society enjoying their estates (notwithstanding Sir Jeffrey Amherst's pretensions) should this province accede to the general union. I hope this hint may be of service, the priests hitherto having done us all the mischief in their power in many parishes. They will not give the people absolution. However, I have shown all the respect in my power to religion, and have winked at the behavior in the priests for fear of giving malice a handle."*

Montgomery also assured the inhabitants that the Continental Congress would be mindful of their political rights, and that as soon as he had effected the complete conquest of the province, by taking Quebec, he should return and call a convention of the people.

Contrary winds had detained Carleton's flotilla, and gave Easton an opportunity to well prepare for opposing him. He posted his troops so advantageously, with six cannon in battery, and two armed row-galleys in the river, that the enemy were easily kept at bay.

Montgomery meanwhile prepared to attack them with field artillery, mounted in batteaux, but before he could effect that object Easton captured the little fleet. General Prescott, the commander of Montreal, and several officers, some members of the Canadian council, and one hundred and twenty private soldiers, with all the vessels and stores, were surrendered by capitulation. But Carleton, disguised as a Canadian *voyageur*, and under cover of darkness, had escaped the previous night, in a boat rowed by himself and others, with muffled oars, and soon reached Quebec in safety, to the great joy of the loyal inhabitants there, who had been trembling in the presence of Arnold.

The spoils of this little victory were, quite a large quantity of provisions, three barrels of powder, four cannon, artillery ammunition, a quantity of small arms, balls, musket-cartridges, two hundred pairs of shoes, and some

* Autograph letter, Nov. 19, 1775.

intrenching tools. Among the vessels captured was the *Gaspé*, Colonel Allen's prison ship, which was placed under the command of Captain Cheeseman, of McDougall's regiment, who fell at Quebec a few weeks later.

Montgomery now placed a garrison at St. John's, under Captain Marinus Willett; another in the fort at Chamblée; gave Wooster the command at Montreal, and prepared to push forward to Quebec; for he said, without that city, "Canada remains unconquered." "By intercepted letters," he wrote to Schuyler, "I am informed that the king's troops are exceedingly alarmed by the presence of Arnold, and expect to be besieged, which, by the blessing of God, they shall be, if the severe season holds off, and I can prevail on the troops to accompany me."*

"The inhabitants," he wrote a little later, "are our friends on both sides of the river, to Quebec. Our expresses go without interruption, backward and forward. A young man who has got out of Quebec, informs me that the lieutenant-governor, the chief justice, and several others, have put their baggage on board ship, and that no ship is permitted to sail. This looks as if they despaired of making a defense."†

Having formed his plans, Montgomery issued the following proclamation, on the 15th of November, signed by his aid-de-camp, James Van Rensselaer:

"The general embraces this happy occasion of making his acknowledgment to the troops for their patience and perseverance during the course of a fatiguing campaign. They merit the applause of their grateful countrymen. He is now ready to fulfill the engagements of the public. Passes, together with boats and provisions, shall be furnished upon application from the commanding officers of regiments, for such as choose to return home; yet he entreats the troops not to lay him under the necessity of abandoning Canada; of undoing in one day what has been the work of months; of restoring to an enraged, and hitherto disappointed enemy, the means of carrying on a cruel war into the very

* Autograph letter, Nov. 13, 1775. † Autograph letter, Nov. 19, 1775.

bowels of their country. Impressed with a just sense of the spirit of the troops; their attachment to the interests of the united colonies, and of their regard to their own honor, he flatters himself that none will leave him at this critical juncture, but such whose affairs or health absolutely require their return home.

"He has still hope, notwithstanding the advanced season of the year, should he be seconded by the generous valor of the troops, hitherto highly favored by Providence, to reduce Quebec, in conjunction with the troops which have penetrated by the Kennebec River, and hereby deprive the ministerial army of all their footing in this important province.

"Those who engage in this honorable cause shall be furnished completely with every article of clothing requisite for the rigor of the climate—blanket-coats, coats, waistcoat, and breeches, one pair of stockings, two shirts, leggings, sacks, shoes, mittens, and a cap, at the Continental charge, and one dollar bounty. The troops are only requested to engage to the 15th of April. They shall be discharged sooner if the expected reënforcement arrives before that time."

# CHAPTER XXVII.

General Montgomery found a large proportion of the troops indisposed to comply with his invitation to accompany him to Quebec; and many precious days—days composed of those golden moments of opportunity that might have secured victory—passed by, while he was engaged in futile endeavors to persuade the New Englanders, whose terms of service had expired, to reënlist. Even those who had yet a short time to serve became turbulent, and some absolutely refused to go another step forward. Home-sickness, a most natural malady under the circumstances, took possession of whole companies; and day after day they left the camp in groups, and made their way up Lake Champlain to Ticonderoga, to receive their discharge from General Schuyler. "I believe," wrote that officer to Montgomery, on the 18th of November, "that you have few of the New England troops left, as near three hundred have passed here within these few days, and so very impatient to get home that many have gone from here by land."

To the Continental Congress Schuyler wrote, on the 20th, saying:

"Our army in Canada is daily reducing—about three hundred of the troops raised in Connecticut having passed here within a few days—so that I believe not more than six hundred and fifty or seven hundred from that colony are left. From the different New York regiments about forty are also lately come away. An unhappy home-sickness prevails. Those mentioned above all came down as invalids, not one willing to reëngage for the winter service. Unable to get any work done by them, I discharged them in groups. Of all the specifics ever invented for *any*, there is none so efficacious as a discharge for *this* prevailing disorder. No sooner was it administered but it perfected the cure of nine out of ten, who, refusing to wait for boats to go by the way of Lake George, slung their heavy packs, crossed the lake at this place, and undertook a march of two hundred miles, with the greatest good will and alacrity." He added: "The most scandalous inattention to the public stores prevails in every part of the army. The tents are left lying in the boats; axes, kettles, etc., lost, and every thing running into confusion. The only attention that engrosses the minds of the soldiery is, how to get home the soonest possible. Nothing, sir, will ever put a stop to this shameful negligence but obliging the officers to pay for what is not accounted for, and let them deduct it out of the men's wages. They can not think this a hardship, as they were informed by me that every article that was issued to them should be returned into store, or properly accounted for. If they were suffered to do it with impunity this year, it will be the same next."*

Washington was also experiencing trouble at this time with the New England troops.

"Such a dearth of public spirit, and such a want of virtue—such a stock-jobbing and fertility in all the low arts to obtain advantages of one kind or another in this great change of military arrangement—I never saw before," he wrote to the Continental Congress, "and pray God's mercy that I may never be witness to again. What will be the end of these maneuvers is beyond my scan. I tremble at the prospect. * * * * The Connecticut troops will not be prevailed upon to stay longer than their term, saving those who have enlisted for the next campaign and are mostly on furlough; and such a mercenary spirit pervades the whole, that I should not be at all surprised at any disaster that may happen."†

Having complained of their conduct to Governor Trumbull, informing him of their leaving in great numbers, and carrying with them, in many instances, the arms and ammunition belonging to the public, that functionary, whose views of patriotic duty were not bounded by the outlines of his own province, wrote:

* Schuyler's MS. Letter Books.

† Sparks's *Life and Writings of Washington*, iii., 178.

"The late extraordinary and reprehensible conduct of some of the troops of this colony impresses me, and the minds of many of our people, with grief, surprise, and indignation, since the treatment they met with, and the order and request made to them [to remain until the arrival of other troops, already engaged], were so reasonable, and apparently necessary, for the defense of our common cause and safety of our rights and privileges for which they freely engaged; the term they voluntarily enlisted to serve not expired, and probably would not end much before the time when they would be relieved, provided their circumstances and inclination should prevent their undertaking further." He added, apologetically: "Indeed there is great difficulty to support liberty, to exercise government, to maintain subordination, and at the same time to prevent the operation of licentious and levelling principles which many very easily imbibe. The pulse of a New England man beats high for liberty; his engagement in the service he thinks purely voluntary; therefore when his term of enlistment is out he thinks himself not holden without further engagement."*

At about this time a circumstance occurred at Ticonderoga, which increased the ill-feeling of some of the Connecticut troops toward General Schuyler. The prisoners taken at Chamblée and St. John's, as we have seen, were sent to Schuyler for his final disposition of them. A schooner and row-galley, with more than one hundred persons, many of them prisoners, and quite a number of women and children, from Canada, arrived at Crown Point late in November. The ice prevented their reaching Ticonderoga, and they became destitute of provisions. In that perilous hour they sent an express to General Schuyler imploring relief. He immediately ordered three captains of Wooster's regiment who were at that post with a considerable body of men, to attempt the relief of the sufferers. They manifested much unwillingness to go, and made many frivolous excuses. This display of selfish inhumanity disgusted and irritated the benevolent and high-minded Schuyler, and in a public order, on the following day (November 29th), he

* Spark's *Life and Writings of Washington*, iii., 183. Note.

mentioned the circumstances, and named the three captains (Porter, Arnold, and Peck), and said: "The general, therefore, not daring to trust a matter of so much importance to men of so little feeling, has ordered Lieutenant Riker, of Colonel Holmes's regiment, to make the attempt. He received the order with the alacrity becoming a gentleman, an officer, and a Christian."*

This was a severe but merited rebuke; and these officers were loud in their denunciations of Schuyler in the willing ears of their superiors.

November was passing away, and Montgomery was yet at Montreal. "I am ashamed," he wrote to Schuyler, on the 24th, "of dating my letter from hence. You will no doubt be surprised at my long stay here, but day after day have I been delayed, without a possibility of getting to Arnold's assistance. To-morrow, I believe, I shall sail with two or three hundred men, some mortars, and other artillery."

Montgomery had just heard that Lieutenant Halsey, of Waterbury's regiment, whom he had left as assistant engineer, to put up barracks at St. John's, had not only been chiefly instrumental in urging the Connecticut troops to leave for home, but had "run away without leave," taking with him the artificers Montgomery had left to carry on the work. While greatly annoyed by this information, he was subjected to the indignity of remonstrances from several of his officers because he had shown certain humane indulgences to British prisoners in his possession. "Such an insult," he wrote, "I could not bear, and immediately resigned. However, they have to-day qualified it, by such an apology as puts it in my power to resume the command with some propriety, and I have promised

* Schuyler's MS. Orderly Book.

to bury it in oblivion. Captain Lamb, who is a restless genius, and of a bad temper, was at the head of it. He has been used to haranguing his fellow-citizens in New York, and can not restrain his talent here. He is brave, active, and intelligent, but very turbulent and troublesome, and not to be satisfied."*

General Schuyler communicated these facts to the Continental Congress, saying:

"This turbulent and mutinous spirit will tend to the ruin of our cause; and the necessity of checking it immediately, and taking measures to prevent it in future, strikes me so forcibly, that I take the liberty to observe that it is worthy of the immediate attention of Congress. I speak the more freely on this subject, as I would not wish that General Montgomery's and my successors, whoever they may be, should lead the disagreeable lives that we have."†

Day after day Montgomery's little army dwindled, when it should have increased, and even the Green Mountain Boys, who were among the latest to join the expedition as an organized corps, and on whose promises he had relied, left him "in the lurch," he said, at the moment of his greatest need.

"It may be asked," wrote Schuyler to the Continental Congress, on the 27th of November, "why Warner's regiment was suffered to come away, and some other of the troops raised in this colony, as the term for which they were engaged would not expire until the last day of next month? The unhappy cause is this: At St. John's the Con-

* Autograph letter, Nov. 24, 1775. Montgomery fully appreciated the value of Captain Lamb to the service. Four days before, he had written to Schuyler concerning him, saying: "I have had some difficulty in persuading him to stay. He says the pay is such a trifle that he is consuming his own property to maintain himself, and that by and by his family must starve at home. He is absolutely necessary with this army, if we are to have artillery. He is active, spirited, and industrious; and I do think he should have an appointment adequate to the services he has rendered. I have entreated him to stay, with the assurance that I would represent his circumstances to Congress. I hear of your bad health with the most real concern."

† Schuyler's MS. Letter Books.

necticut troops were so very importunate to return home that General Montgomery was under the necessity of promising that all those that would follow him to Montreal should have leave to return. This declaration he could not confine to the Connecticut troops, as such a discrimination would have been odious. It might have been expected that men, influenced by a love of liberty, would not have required such a promise, and that others to whom it was not immediately intended would not have taken the advantage of it."*

While the army was thus melting, the Continental Congress were very dilatory in furnishing men to fill the vacancies, notwithstanding their eagerness to possess Canada; and Montgomery found himself, at the close of November, when on the point of marching to Quebec, in command of less than two thousand men in all Canada, including those under Arnold, and the garrisons to be left at St. John's, Chamblée, and Montreal. He yearned for relief, yet his duty to his adopted country would not permit him to leave the chief command of the army in the field with General Wooster, who, Gates wrote, it was "on all hands agreed, was too infirm for that service." "Will not your health," he wrote to Schuyler, "permit you to reside at Montreal this winter? I must go home, if I walk by the side of the lake. I am weary of power, and totally want that patience and temper requisite for such a command. I wish exceedingly for a respectable committee of Congress. I really have not weight enough to carry on business by myself. I wish Lee could set off immediately for the command here."†

* Schuyler's MS. Letter Books.

† Autograph letters, Nov. 13–24. Schuyler and Montgomery had both urged the Congress to send a committee of their body to act in concert with the military commander in the northern department, in the management of the campaign, and in the formation of civil government, in the event of the reduction of Canada, or in the arrangement of a new army for that service, if the campaign should not prove successful.

On account of the continued ill health of General Schuyler it had been proposed to make General Charles Lee commander-in-chief of the northern department.

Schuyler's health would not permit him to go to Montreal, nor even to remain at Ticonderoga; and for the purpose of rest as a means of recovery, he was compelled to leave for his home at Albany, early in December. He deeply regretted the stern necessity that deprived him of participation in the toils, dangers, and glory of the conquest of Canada, for the consummation of which he had so earnestly labored. He had daily and hourly afforded Montgomery all the aid in his power; and before leaving Ticonderoga he had disposed of all the prisoners sent to him, put the entire service on as good footing as the means at his command would allow, and arranged every thing that might facilitate the labors of Colonel Knox in removing the cannon, mortars, and artillery stores from Ticonderoga to Boston, on which service he had been sent by General Washington. Leaving the post of Ticonderoga in charge of Colonel Holmes, with very particular instructions for his conduct, he proceeded southward by the way of Lake George (at the head of which he met Colonel Knox), and arrived at Albany on Thursday, the 7th of December. On Saturday, the 9th, he addressed the following note to the pastor of the church in Albany which he and his family attended:

"General Schuyler's respectful compliments: He begs the Rev. Mr. Westerlo publicly to acknowledge the manifold favors he, and the army under his command, have experienced from the Fountain of all Grace and Mercy; and while he approaches the throne of Heaven with a grateful heart for mercies past, humbly to supplicate a continuance of the Divine protection, and to pray for a speedy and a happy reconciliation with the mother country."*

On his arrival at Albany, Schuyler found about sixty of the Six Nations of Indians waiting for him. Mr. Douw was the only other commissioner present, yet the

* Autograph draft of letter.

exigency of the case demanded action, and Schuyler and Douw opened business with them. The savages had come to testify their friendship, and the communications which they made were important.

"The Indians," said Schuyler, in a letter to the Continental Congress, on the 14th of December, "delivered us a speech on the 12th, in which they related the substance of all the conferences Colonel Johnson had with them the last summer, concluding with that at Montreal, where he delivered to each of the Canadian tribes a war-belt and a hatchet, who accepted it; after which, they were invited to feast on a Bostonian and to drink his blood, an ox being roasted alive for the purpose and a pipe of red wine given to drink. The war-song was also sung. One of the chiefs of the Six Nations that attended at that conference accepted of a very large, black war-belt, with a hatchet depicted in it, but would neither eat nor drink nor sing the war-song. The famous belt they have delivered up, and we have full proof that the ministerial servants have attempted to engage the savages against us." To Washington he wrote: "The Mohawks have received a severe and public reprimand from the other Nations, because they did not immediately send for the few of that tribe that were in Canada [under Brant], some of whom were killed by our people." And to Montgomery he wrote: "The Indians have delivered to us Colonel Johnson's war-belt, which he gave them at Montreal. Your conquests have convinced them that they cannot do without us, and they are all humiliation."*

At about this time the Congress received such information concerning the conduct of Sir John Johnson and the Tories of the Mohawk Valley, indicative of their speedy activity in the royal cause, such as collecting arms, ammunition, and military stores, that they resolved to take countervailing measures. When the committee appointed to inquire into the matter reported, it was—

"*Resolved*, That the said committee be directed to communicate this intelligence to General Schuyler, and, in the name of the Congress, desire him to take the most speedy and effectual measures for securing the said arms and military stores, and for disarming the said Tories, and apprehending their chiefs."*

* Schuyler's MS. Letter Books. † Journal of Congress, Dec. 30, 1775.

Although further removed from the most important events transpiring in the northern department, than when he was at Ticonderoga, General Schuyler was equally useful and efficient, with his head-quarters at Albany, (while Montgomery and Arnold were prosecuting the campaign on the St. Lawrence,) in the general management of the details of the service, and the paramount duty of furnishing the troops with supplies, urging forward reënforcements, and keeping the civil authorities and the commander-in-chief of the armies so constantly and clearly advised of all matters pertaining to his department, that nothing to promote the success of the expedition was left undone because of a lack of information.

No officer was ever more vigilant and active than Schuyler. Nothing escaped his observation ; and nothing of the least value to the service was too insignificant to engage his earnest attention. Instead of leaving the entire management of separate departments—commissary, quarter-master, muster-master, and hospital-superintendent—to those whom Congress had appointed for that service, he exercised a direct personal supervision of all. He made out careful estimates of provisions and stores for the commissary ; directed many of the details of the quarter-master's department ; made lists of materials used in the construction of vessels, and took great interest in the hospital provisions for the sick. He attended with zeal and courtesy to the wants and comfort of prisoners, and listened with complacency to the petitions of private soldiers who could obtain no redress for alleged wrongs through their immediate superiors. Some of the letters of these humble men (carefully filed among his papers), in which they laid their grievances before him, are most touching examples of that unhesitating faith in his justice which was felt by all who knew him, and the love and reverence of every man whose worthiness made him an object of General Schuyler's kind regard. It was only to the assuming, the disobedient, the insubordinate, the idle, and the vicious, that he appeared as a stern master.

General Schuyler was as tender and tenacious of the rights of others as of his own; and in all his intercourse with the officers of his army his conduct was so inflexibly and irreproachably honorable that no man, not even his bitter enemies, ever complained that General Schuyler had claimed for himself that which he was not willing to allow to others, or by his just authority invaded any right belonging to a fellow-soldier, high or low in rank or merit. He was scrupulously just to all; and in exacting from others that loyalty to his official power which he was ever quick to give to his own superiors in rank, he was always governed by the highest sense of right. Therefore, when we see him rebuking insubordination, peculation, and waste, in the army, sternly, and sometimes passionately, in clear Saxon language, which all might understand; speaking out his sentiments without circumlocution, or using soft and submissive words as a cover to a dissimulating spirit, we behold a man, fearless in the performance of duty, regardless of reputation, except that which rests upon the solid basis of useful actions, and so fortified by the consciousness of rectitude against the shafts of "envy, hatred, and malice," that he could afford to be dutiful at the expense of present unpopularity. A careful guardian of the public welfare, economical in his management, and an exact disciplinarian, it is no wonder that the disorderly spirit manifested by the troops, the peculations of commissaries and others in offices of trust, wastefulness in every department, and the selfishness and sectional jealousy that continually appeared, that vexed and annoyed him every hour, made him weary of the service, and caused him at last to ask Congress to allow him to retire.

From the beginning, Schuyler's illness had given Washington and the General Congress much uneasiness, for upon him hung the best hopes of the northern campaign. The commander-in-chief had been specially concerned when he found that Wooster was about to join the army of the North, and might claim to be next in rank and command to Schuyler. "General Wooster," he wrote to Schuyler, "I am informed, is not of such activity as to press through difficulties with which that service is environed. I am therefore much alarmed for Arnold, whose expedition was built upon yours, and who will infallibly perish, if the invasion and entry into Canada are abandoned by your successors."* But when Schuyler, as we have seen, by prompt action, settled the point concerning Wooster's rank, Washington's mind was relieved, and he wrote to him saying: "I much approve your conduct in regard to Wooster. My fears are at an end, as he acts in a subordinate character."†

Washington's mind was again disturbed, when Schuyler, tortured by disease and vexed beyond all forbearance by the conduct of the troops around him, gave notice to the commander-in-chief of his intention to resign. "Gentlemen," he said in his letter to Washington, "find

* Sparks's *Life and Writings of Washington*, iii., 119.

† Ibid, iii., 143. Gunning Bedford, writing to Schuyler from Philadelphia, said: "I find that the majority of the members are by no means pleased with the Connecticut troops, and are glad to hear you managed General Wooster as you did. I own, for myself, I had great fears of this dangerous tendency of his and their prevailing spirit, and it gives me particular pleasure that your most prudent conduct has relieved you of so much trouble and anxiety. The gentlemen here all feel for your disagreeable situation; but put that confidence in your conduct, that when restored to health, and aided by some new regulations for the government of the soldiery, you will find yourself more comfortable, at the head of a more obedient army.—*Autograph Letter.*

it very disagreeable to coax, to wheedle, and even to *lie*, to carry on the service. Habituated to order, I can not, without the most extreme pain, see that disregard of discipline, confusion, and inattention which reigns so generally n this quarter, and I am, therefore, determined to retire."

The Congress entreated Schuyler to remain at his post, because, they said, his retirement "would deprive America of the benefits of his zeal and abilities, and rob him of the honor of completing the work he had so happily begun."

Washington, regarding Schuyler as one of the main supports of the Continental army, was much concerned, and immediately wrote to him an expostulatory letter.

"I know your complaints are too well founded," he said; "but I would willingly hope that nothing will induce you to quit the service, and that, in time, order and subordination will take the place of confusion, and command be rendered more agreeable. I have met with difficulties of the same sort, and such as I never expected; but they must be borne with. * * * The cause we are engaged in is so just and righteous that we must try to rise superior to every obstacle in its support; and, therefore, I beg that you will not think of resigning, unless you have carried your application to Congress too far to recede." Three weeks later, Washington wrote to him, saying: "I am very sorry to find, by several paragraphs [in Schuyler's letter to Congress], that both you and General Montgomery incline to quit the service. Let me ask you, sir, when is the time for brave men to exert themselves in the cause of liberty and their country, if this is not? Should any difficulties that they have to encounter, at this important crisis, deter them? God knows there is not a difficulty that you both very justly complain of, which I have not, in an eminent degree, experienced, that I am not every day experiencing; but we must bear up against them, and make the best of mankind as they are, since we can not have them as we wish. Let me, therefore, conjure you and Mr. Montgomery to lay aside such thoughts—thoughts injurious to yourselves, and extremely so to your country, which calls aloud for gentlemen of your abilities."*

General Schuyler felt the force of this appeal, and replied as follows:

* Sparks's *Life and Writings of Washington*, iii., 209.

"I do not hesitate a moment to answer my dear general's question, in the affirmative, by declaring, that now or never is the time for every virtuous American to exert himself in the cause of liberty and his country, and that it becomes a duty cheerfully to sacrifice the sweets of domestic felicity to attain the honest and glorious end America has in view; and I can, with a good conscience, declare that I have devoted myself to the service of my country, in the firmest resolution, to sink or swim with it, without anxiety how I quit the stage of life, provided I leave to my posterity the happy reflection that their ancestor was an honest American." Then anticipating the question, "Why, then, do you wish to retire from public office?" General Schuyler unburdened his full heart in the confidence of brother with brother, and said: "I think I should prejudice my country by continuing any longer in this command. The favorable opinion you are pleased to entertain of me, obliges me to an explanation which I shall give you in confidence. I have already informed you of the disagreeable situation I have been in during the campaign, but I would waive that, were it not that it has chiefly arisen from prejudice and jealousy, for I could point out particular persons of rank in the army who have frequently declared that the general commanding in this quarter ought to be of the colony whence the majority of the troops come. But it is not from the opinion or principles of individuals that I have drawn the following conclusion: *That troops from the colony of Connecticut will not bear with a general from another colony.* It is from the daily and common conversation of all ranks of people from that colony, both in and out of the army; and I assure you, that I sincerely lament that a people of so much public virtue should be actuated by such an unbecoming jealousy, founded on such a narrow principle—a principle extremely unfriendly to our righteous cause—as it tends to alienate the affections of numbers in this colony, in spite of the most favorable constructions that prudent men and real Americans among us attempt to put upon it. And although I frankly avow that I feel a resentment, yet I shall continue to sacrifice it to a nobler object—the welfare of that country in which I have drawn the breath of life."*

Entreated by leading men of all classes, who knew his worth, to remain in command of his department, Schuyler yielded; and in the events of 1776, in that quarter, his services were of incalculable value to the cause which he had so heartily espoused.

* Schuyler's MS. Letter Books.

## CHAPTER XXVIII.

The successes of Montgomery, and especially his triumph at Montreal, had given great joy to the whole country. This was heightened by the intelligence of Arnold's arrival before Quebec, with his troops in good spirits. "We receive, with very great satisfaction, your congratulations on the glorious success of the Continental army in Canada," wrote Nathaniel Woodhull on behalf of the New York Provincial Congress, to General Schuyler, "and we can assure you that it is much heightened by the consideration that we recommended the generals who have, with so much activity and success, conducted an expedition which was attended with difficulties, thought to be insuperable by those who were acquainted with them."* And the Continental Congress, in testimony of their appreciation of his services, promoted Montgomery to the rank of major-general on the 9th of December.

The thoughtless many believed the conquest of all Canada to be an easy task after these victories, but there were a wise few, in and out of legislative halls, who shared in the anxieties of the leaders in the northern army, and condemned, without stint, the conduct of the troops, who, at the moment of greatest need, had practically abandoned the cause and returned home. The Continental Congress received its share of blame because of its tardiness in

* Autograph letter, Dec. 9, 1775.

affording needed coöperation. Time after time, both Schuyler and Montgomery had besought them to send re-enforcements and supplies, and also an advisory committee like the one dispatched to Cambridge to confer with Washington, but it was not until too late to be of service in the current campaign that such committee were appointed,* and made their way toward Montreal. Montgomery was therefore compelled, by circumstances, to make unauthorized arrangements with the troops to induce them to go forward; and he left Montreal for Quebec without seeing the committee.

"Be so good," he wrote to Schuyler from near Quebec, "as to show Congress the necessity I was under of clothing the troops to induce them to stay and undertake this service at such an inclement season. I think, had the committee been with me, they would have seen the propriety of grasping at every circumstance in my power, to induce them to engage again. I was not without my apprehensions of not only being unable to make my appearance here, but even being obliged to relinquish the ground I had gained. However, I hope the clothing and dollar bounty will not greatly exceed the bounty offered by Congress * * * Upon another occasion I have also ventured to go beyond the letter of the law. Colonel Easton's detachment at the mouth of the Sorel was employed on the important service of stopping the fleet. They were half naked, and the weather was very severe. I was afraid that not only they might grow impatient and relinquish the business in hand, but I also saw the reluctance the troops at Montreal showed to quit it. By way of stimulant, I offered as a reward all public stores taken in the vessels, to the troops who went forward, except ammunition and provisions. Warner's corps refused to march, or at least declined it. Bedel's went on, and came in for a share of the labor and honor. I hope the Congress will not think this money ill laid out."†

Arnold, as we have seen, was baffled in his attempts to cross the St. Lawrence at Quebec, by a tempest of wind and sleet that continued for several days and nights Meanwhile the garrison in the city was strengthened by

* Robert R. Livingston, Robert Treat Paine, and John Langdon.

† Autograph letter, Dec. 5, 1775.

the Highlanders under McLean, that fled from the Sorel. At length the wind ceased, and at nine o'clock in the evening of the 13th of November, Arnold began the embarcation of his troops in birch canoes. Before dawn the next morning over five hundred of them had crossed, unperceived until the last moment by the British vessels lying in the river, and rendezvoused at Wolfe's Cove, where the lamented hero of the old war prepared to scale the heights of Abraham. One hundred and fifty men were yet at Point Levi, but it was too late to return for them; so Arnold, emulating the daring of Wolfe, placed himself at the head of his little band of heroes, and before sunrise on the 14th, scaled the acclivity at the exact point where his predecessor ascended, sixteen years before.

That little band presented a sublime spectacle. There they stood, only five hundred and fifty strong, upon a bleak eminence, in the dim light of a keen, wintry morning, thinly clad, scantily fed, more than half their muskets made useless by the storms of the wilderness, with a dark castle and massive stone walls, that inclosed an alert garrison and five thousand inhabitants, frowning upon them, yet with the expectation of seeing the proud city bow to them as its conquerors!

Yet all were not enemies within those walls, nor even within that garrison. In fact, Lieutenant-Governor Cramahé, in command there, could not certainly rely upon any one except the Royal Scotch regiment—McLean's Banditti, as Montgomery called them. Most of the Canadians in the city were friendly to the invaders; and many who bore arms, pressed unwillingly into the service, would do but feeble execution against the republicans. Indeed, they would have joined them at the first opportunity. It was upon these friends and their disaffected soldiers that

Arnold relied more for success than upon the arms of the men under his command. He believed that a shout from his troops, under the walls of Quebec, would be the signal for an insurrection in his favor within; and he accordingly drew up his men within eight hundred yards of the gates of St. Louis and St. John, and ordered them to give three cheers. He expected, at least, to see the regulars sally out to attack him, when, he hoped, by the assistance of friends in the city, to be able to rush in through the open gates, and seize the town. But Cramahé and McLean were too wary to open the gates without perceiving a sure prospect of success; and the people within, awed by the presence of troops, were comparatively passive and silent. The parapets of the walls were, however, soon covered with people, and many of them responded to the huzzas of the republican troops. The Americans also discharged several guns at the British soldiery, but without effect, while the shot of a thirty-two pound cannon, brought to bear upon the republicans, proved equally harmless.

The whole affair now began to assume the character of a solemn farce. It was soon rendered completely so by Arnold, who sent to Lieutenant-Governor Cramahé, by a flag, a pompous proclamation and demand for a surrender. After a preface, in which he set forth that he had been sent by General Washington to coöperate with General Schuyler by taking possession of the city of Quebec, he said:

"I do, therefore, in the name of the united Colonies, demand immediate surrender of the town, fortifications, etc., of Quebec to the forces of the united colonies under my command, forbidding you to injure any of the inhabitants of the town in their persons or property, as you will answer the same at your peril. On surrendering the town, the property of every individual shall be secured to him; but if I am obliged to carry the town by storm, you may expect every severity practised on such occasion; and the merchants, who may now save their property, will probably be involved in the general ruin."

The bearer of this summons was fired upon; but on the following day Arnold found means to convey it to Cramahé, with a letter, in which he assured him that he had several British prisoners in his hands, who should receive the same treatment that the lieutenant-governor had given, as he understood, an American prisoner, then in irons within the town.* But the letter and the proclamation were treated with contempt. There were no signs of insurrection in the city, and the invaders were considered harmless.†

Colonel Arnold thought it not prudent to attempt to storm the town with a force so feeble. He accordingly proceeded to invest it, so as to cut off all communication with the country, with the hope of reducing the garrison by starvation, he having been informed that provisions were scarce in the city. He made the large mansion of Major Caldwell, "half a league from the city," his head-quarters, and his extensive out-buildings were converted into barracks for the troops. He also took possession of a nunnery for the same purpose, and made provision for the sick and wounded. The detachment left at Point Levi had made its way to the camp meanwhile, and his force numbered a little less than seven hundred men.

But Arnold was soon compelled to raise the siege.

* This was a young Virginian, named George Merchant, who had been suddenly seized by a party of British, while on duty as a sentinel near the walls.

† "This ridiculous affair," wrote an eye-witness, "gave me a contemptible opinion of Arnold. Morgan, Febiger, and other officers did not hesitate to speak of it in that point of view. However, Arnold had a vain desire to gratify. He was well known at Quebec. Because he had traded in horses there he was despised by the principal people. The epithet of *horse-jockey* was freely and universally bestowed upon him by the British. Having now obtained power, he became anxious to display it in the faces of those who had formerly despised and contemned him."—Judge Henry's *Campaign against Quebec.*

Friends from above informed him that Carleton was approaching Quebec in an armed vessel, with two hundred men; and other friends in the city assured him, on the 18th, that McLean would sally out with several field-pieces, the next day, and attack him. He at once perceived the danger of his situation; and on a strict examination of his ammunition, he found that he had not more than five rounds of powder to each man, so much had been spoiled in the march across the wilderness. Under these circumstances he deemed it prudent to withdraw. On the morning of the 19th he broke up his camp, and retired to Point aux Trembles (Aspen-Tree Point), eight leagues above Quebec, and there awaited the orders of Montgomery. On his way he saw the vessel that was conveying Carleton and his friends to Quebec. It had touched at Point aux Trembles, but proceeded immediately on hearing of the approach of the republicans. Soon afterward, Arnold heard the booming of the cannon that welcomed the governor back to the capital.

In full view of the difficulties before him, Montgomery left Montreal for Quebec, on the 26th of November, thoroughly imbued with the spirit of a soldier and a lawgiver commissioned to redeem and remodel a state. He confidently expected success in his military enterprise; and he wrote to Schuyler: "I shall lose no time in calling a convention when my intended expedition is finished." He proceeded in three armed schooners, with artillery and provisions, and only three hundred troops. On the 1st of December he arrived at Point aux Trembles, and on the 3d made a formal junction between his own and Arnold's troops, and took the chief command.

The fearful rigors of a Canadian winter were at hand, and yet, feeble as were his preparations for the perilous service before him, the valiant Montgomery was hopeful. "I need not tell you," he wrote to his father-in-law, "that until Quebec is taken, Canada is unconquered; and that, to accomplish this, we must resort to siege, investment, or storm." The first was out of the question, because he had no battering train; and from the impossibility of making trenches in a rocky soil and in winter, the second could not be successfully accomplished without ample reënforcements, for the city had provisions for eight months; but the third he thought feasible.

"To the storming plan," he said, "there are fewer objections; and to this we must come at last. If my force be small, Carleton's is not great. The extensiveness of his works, which, in case of investment, would favor him, will, in the other case, favor us. Masters of our secret, we may select a particular time and place for attack, and to repel this the garrison must be prepared at all times and places; a circumstance which will impose upon it incessant watching and labor, by day and by night, which, in its undisciplined state, must breed discontents that may compel Carleton to capitulate, or perhaps to make an attempt to drive us off. In this last idea there is a glimmering of hope. Wolfe's success was a lucky hit, or rather a series of such hits; all sober and scientific calculation was against him, until Montcalm, permitting his courage to get the better of discretion, gave up the advantage of his fortress, and came out to try his strength on the plain. Carleton, who was Wolfe's quarter-master-general, understands this well, and, it is to be feared, will not follow the Frenchman's example."*

With these views Montgomery prepared to march upon Quebec. He was much pleased with Arnold's troops, and spoke of them in high terms in a letter to Schuyler:

"I find Colonel Arnold's corps," he said, "an exceedingly fine one. Inured to fatigue, and well accustomed to cannon shot (at Cambridge), there is a style of discipline among them much superior to what I have been used to see this campaign. He, himself, is active, intelligent, and enterprising. Fortune often baffles the sanguine expectations of poor

* American Archives, Fourth Series, iii., 1638.

mortals. I am not intoxicated with the favors I have received at her hands, but I do think there is a fair prospect of success. The governor has been so kind as to send out of town many of our friends, who refused to do military duty;* among them several very intelligent men, capable of doing me considerable service—one of them, a Mr. Antill, I have appointed chief engineer."†

Montgomery clothed Arnold's corps with thick suits from the public stores; and while they were paraded in front of the parish church at Point aux Trembles, he addressed them in words of just praise and patriotic exhortation. "A few huzzas," says Henry, "from our freezing bodies were returned to this address of the gallant hero. New life was infused into the whole corps;" and the little army of republicans, less than a thousand strong, with two hundred Canadians under Colonel James Livingston, pressed on toward the capital in the face of a severe snow-storm.

Montgomery arrived before Quebec on the 5th of December, made his head-quarters at Holland House, in the parish of St. Foi, between two and three miles from the town, and from there, on the same day, wrote a long and interesting letter to Schuyler.

"Mr. Carleton," he said, "who is, I suppose, ashamed to show his face in England, is now in town, and puts on the show of defense. The works of Quebec are extremely extensive, and very incapable of being defended. His garrison consists of McLane's banditti, the sailors from the frigates and other vessels laid up, together with the citizens obliged

* Carleton was unpopular with the great mass of the people, toward which he had shown much reserve, confining his intimacy to the military and the Canadian gentry. He was well aware of his unpopularity, and looked with distrust on all around him. Perceiving many malcontents in Quebec, he issued a proclamation on the 22d of November, ordering all persons who should refuse to take up arms for the king, to leave the town within four days from the date of the proclamation, and, with their wives and children, to leave the district of Quebec before the first day of December, under the penalty of being treated as rebels or spies.

† Autograph Letter, December 5, 1775.

to take up arms, most of whom are impatient of the fatigues of a siege, and wish to see matters accommodated amicably. I propose amusing Mr. Carleton with a formal attack, erecting batteries, etc.; but mean to assault the works of the Lower Town, which is the weakest part. I have this day written to Mr. Carleton, and also to the inhabitants, which, I hope, will have some effect. I shall be very sorry to be reduced to this mode of attack, because I know the melancholy consequences, but the approaching severe season, and the weakness of the garrison, together with the nature of the works, point it out too strongly to be passed by."*

Montgomery's letter to Carleton, above-mentioned, was a demand for the instant surrender of the city. This was his first act after disposing his troops before Quebec. In violation of the rules of honorable warfare, the governor ordered McLean to fire upon the flag, and not allow it to approach the walls. Montgomery was made very indignant by this treatment, and on the following morning he addressed a very menacing letter to Carleton, in which he exaggerated the strength and appointments of his army, and made a demand for an instant surrender. This letter, and one of like tenor to the inhabitants, were carried into the town by a woman from the country, and a copy of the letter was afterward shot over the walls upon an arrow. But Carleton, innately brave, and relying upon his known resources, refused to hold any communication with the "rebel general," nor would he permit the least intercourse between the citizens and the people outside the walls. He was well informed of the real strength of Montgomery's forces, felt confident that the garrison would keep the disloyal citizens quiet, and expected to see the rigors of the winter soon drive the besiegers away.

Montgomery now prepared for an assault. His quarters, as we have observed, were at Holland House. Those of Arnold were near Scott's Bridge on the St. Charles River,

* Autograph Letter, Dec. 5, 1775.

and the greater portion of the republican troops were encamped near the Intendant's Palace in the suburb St. Roque, of the Lower Town, not far from Palace Gate. His prospects were certainly very unpromising. With a feeble, ill-clad, ill-fed army, exposed to the most severe frosts and storms in the open fields; with no other ordnance than a field-train of artillery and a few mortars; with few intrenching tools, and the ground frozen to a great depth and covered with snow-drifts, how could the republican commander hope for success? Yet his brave heart and generous spirit would not yield to these formidable obstacles, and he resolved to force the garrison and people to surrender by a series of annoyances, hinted at in his letter just quoted. He accordingly planted four or five mortars in the suburb St. Roque, of the Lower Town, and from these cast about two hundred shells into the city, in the course of thirty hours, but without other serious effect than setting a few buildings on fire. He had already commenced the construction of a six-gun battery and other works under the direction of Captain Antill, on the plains of Abraham, about seven hundred yards from the walls. It was a difficult task, for the ground was deeply frozen, and the snow lay in immense drifts. Indeed, the earth could not be penetrated, and gabions and fascines were set up and filled with snow, upon which water was poured, and instantly congealed. Thus, an ice mound was soon formed, and upon this glittering embankment Captain Lamb placed six twelve-pound cannon and two howitzers, in battery.

When these works were completed, Montgomery sent Colonel Arnold, and Captain Macpherson (his favorite aid-de-camp), with a flag of truce, to bear letters to the governor. They reached the walls without molestation, when they were ordered off immediately. To their question, whether the governor would receive any letters from them, they were answered with an emphatic No, and ordered to leave. Carleton utterly refused to hold any kind of parley with the besiegers. Montgomery was exceedingly indignant, and on the following morning he contrived to send in to Carleton a letter, in which, after charging him with personal ill-treatment, and cruelty to American prisoners, and informing him that he well knew the governor's situation, and that only motives of humanity caused him to make another overture for a surrender, he said:

"I am at the head of troops accustomed to success, confident of the righteousness of the cause they are engaged in, inured to danger and fatigue, and so highly incensed at your inhumanity, illiberal abuse, and the ungenerous means employed to prejudice them in the minds of the Canadians, that it is with difficulty I restrain them till my batteries are ready, from assaulting your works, which would afford them a fair opportunity of ample vengeance and just retaliation. Firing upon a flag of truce, hitherto unprecedented, even among savages, prevents my following the ordinary mode of conveying my sentiments; however, I will, at any rate, acquit my conscience. Should you persist in an unwarrantable defense, the consequence be upon your own head. Beware of destroying stores of any sort, as you did at Montreal or in the river. If you do, by Heaven, there will be no mercy shown."*

Carleton paid no attention to this letter; and Montgomery ordered Lamb to open his battery upon the enemy's works. Bombs were sent from the Lower Town at the same time, and did some damage, but the cannon made no serious impression upon the walls. At length heavy balls, hurled from the citadel, shivered Lamb's ice-battery and the brittle breast-work near, and very soon silenced his cannon, and compelled him to withdraw.

It was toward the close of the day, when this destructive gun was brought to bear upon the ice battery. Mont-

* American Archives, Fourth Series, iii., 289.

gomery, accompanied by his youthful aid-de-camp, Aaron Burr, paid a visit to the trenches, and at the moment when he approached the spot where Lamb was plying his guns, a shot from the enemy dismounted one of them and wounded several of the men. A second, and almost equally destructive shot, immediately followed. "This is warm work, sir," said Montgomery, addressing Captain Lamb. "It is, indeed," replied the gallant soldier, "and certainly no place for you, sir." "Why so, captain?" asked Montgomery. "Because," he answered, "there are enough of us here to be killed, without the loss of you, which would be irreparable." The general quickly perceived the insufficiency of the batteries, and, on retiring, gave Captain Lamb permission to withdraw his men whenever he might think proper; immediately if he chose to do it. But Lamb decided to remain until dark, when, securing all the guns, he abandoned the ruined redoubt. Lamb, who had never seen Burr before, wondered that the general should encumber his military family with a boy. But on observing his perfect coolness in the midst of the greatest danger, and the fire in his keen, black eye, and perceiving no trace of the disturbances of fear in his singularly striking countenance, he was convinced that the young volunteer was no ordinary youth, and not out of place by the side of the brave Montgomery.*

The commander had not expected much breaching service from his cannon. They were intended more to lull the enemy into security at other points than as means of much destructive execution. He had other and more effective plans in view; and on the evening of his first cannonade, he wrote to General Wooster, saying:

* Leake's *Life of Lamb*, p. 125.

"The enemy have very heavy metal, and I think will dismount our guns very shortly; some they have already rendered almost useless. This gives very little uneasiness; I never expected any other advantage from our artillery than to amuse the enemy and blind them as to my real intention. I propose the first strong northwester, to make two attacks by night: one with about a third of the troops, on the Lower Town, having first set fire to some houses, which will, in all probability, communicate their flames to the stockade lately erected on the rock near St. Roque; the other upon Cape Diamond Bastion, by escalade. I have not time to point out my reasons for this particular attack; let it suffice that it is founded on the nature of the grounds, works, and the best intelligence I have been able to procure. However, I am not sure whether the troops relish this mode of proceeding."*

That evening (16th of December) Montgomery called a council of all the commissioned officers of Arnold's detachment, to determine upon future proceedings. A large majority voted for making an assault as soon as reënforcements should arrive, and the men should be furnished with bayonets, hatchets, and hand-grenades. But in these contingencies lay all the difficulty.

"I have been near a fortnight before Quebec, at the head of upward of eight hundred troops," Montgomery wrote to Schuyler, "a force, you'll say, not very adequate to the business in hand. But we must make the best of it. It is all I could get. I have been so used to struggle with difficulties, that I expect them of course." He anxiously desired the reënforcements, that he might act promptly and efficiently. "I hope the troops will be sent down," he said, "as soon as possible, for should we fail in our first attempt, a second or a third may do the business before relief can arrive to the garrison. Possession of the town, and that speedily, I hold of the highest consequence. The enemy are expending their ammunition most liberally, and I fear the Canadians will not relish a union with the colonies till they see the whole country in our hands, and defended by such a force as may relieve them from the apprehensions of again falling under the ministerial lash. Were it not for these reasons, I should have been inclined to a blockade till toward the 1st of April, by which time the garrison would probably be much distressed for provisions and wood."*

* American Archives, Fourth Series, iii., 289.

† Autograph letter, Dec. 18, 1775.

Schuyler was utterly powerless. He had tried recruiting, but failed in the attempt. He had already written to Montgomery—"I am much afraid that we shall not have a man left at either Fort George or Ticonderoga by the first day of January. The recruiting parties that have been sent out meet with little or no success."* He had earnestly importuned the Congress for reënforcements, and in a special manner for hard money, for the soldiers were averse to receiving the Continental bills, and but few of the Canadians would touch them. "I am amazed no money is yet arrived," Montgomery wrote to Schuyler. "The troops are uneasy, and I shall by and by be at my wits' end to furnish the army with provisions. I have almost exhausted Price, having had upward of £5000, York, from him."†

In the lack of hard money may be found the secret of many of the discontents in the army, and the failure in the recruiting service. The Congress was even dilatory in replying to Schuyler's letters; and now, when Montgomery was appealing to him for more troops and supplies, he again wrote an urgent, at the same time a quietly sarcastic letter, to the president of the supreme legislature, saying:

* MS. Letter Book, Dec. 17, 1775.

† Autograph letter, December 26, 1775. Mr. James Price was a wealthy merchant of Montreal, and from the beginning had been an active friend of the republicans. "I must take this opportunity," wrote Montgomery to Schuyler, "of acknowledging Price's services. He has been a faithful friend to the cause indeed! His advice and assistance upon every occasion I have been much benefited by; and when I consider that he has been the first mover of those measures which have been attended with so many and great advantages to the united colonies, I can't help wishing the Congress to give him an ample testimony of their sense of his generous and spirited exertions in the cause of freedom." In a letter to Schuyler, from Montreal, on the 5th of January, 1775, Mr. Price wrote: "I fear the army here will be in great want of cash. Our house has advanced them, since their arrival here, £20,000. We are now almost out of that article; and I am sorry to say I don't find any of the merchants here willing to lend."

"I cannot procure any gold or silver here to send to Canada. I am afraid it is not to be had at Philadelphia, as a considerable time has already elapsed since Congress gave me reason to hope that a supply would be sent. I can not help, sir, repeating my wish, that a considerable force should be immediately sent into Canada. The necessity appears to me indispensable, for I do most sincerely believe that unless such a measure be adopted we shall severely repent of it, perhaps when too late to afford a remedy. I beg a thousand pardons of Congress for my importunity on this occasion, and I hope they will have charity enough to impute it to my zeal for the American cause. From what I can learn, the troops that are at Ticonderoga will leave it to-morrow, and I have none to send there. The few that are here [Albany] refuse to remain until Tuesday, to escort the prisoners, before which I can not move them for want of carriages. I have been so very long without hearing from Congress, that I am exceedingly anxious to have the honor of a line from you."*

* MS. Letter Books, Dec. 31, 1775.

# CHAPTER XXIX.

ALMOST three weeks were consumed by Montgomery in ineffectual efforts to compel Carleton to surrender, or to make an attempt to enter the town. Mutinous murmurs became audible in the camp. The term of enlistment of many of the men was nearly expired, and the small-pox made its appearance among the soldiers. The commander perceived that something effectual must be done immediately, or the attempt to reduce Quebec must be abandoned.

A fearful web of difficulties was gathering around Montgomery, and he called a Council of War. Price and Antill had expressed a belief that if he could get possession of the Lower Town, the merchants and other citizens would induce Carleton to surrender rather than expose all their property to destruction. He laid before the council the plan he had hinted at in his letter to General Wooster on the 16th, and it was approved. But when he proceeded to make the final arrangements for the assault, he found some of Arnold's battalion indisposed to join in the measure, on account of difficulties among the officers.

"When last I had the honor to write to you," wrote Montgomery to Schuyler, "I hoped before now to have had it in my power to give you some good news. I then had reason to believe the troops well inclined for a *coup-de-main.* I have since discovered, to my great mortification, that three companies of Colonel Arnold's detachment are very averse from the measure. There is strong reason to believe their difference of sentiment from the rest of the troops arises from the influence of their officers. Captain Hanchett, who has incurred Colonel Arnold's displeasure by some misconduct, and thereby given room for harsh language, is at the bottom of it, and has made some declarations which, I think, must draw upon him the censure of his country, if brought to trial. Captains Goodrich and Hubbard seem to espouse his quarrel. A field officer is concerned in it, who wishes, I suppose, to have the separate command of those companies, as the above-mentioned captains have made application for that purpose. This dangerous party threatens the ruin of our affairs. I shall, at any rate, be obliged to change my plan of attack, being too weak to put that in execution I had formerly determined on. I am much afraid my friend, Major Brown, is deeply concerned in this business. I will hereafter acquaint you more particularly with this matter."*

That after communication was never made. This was the last letter that Montgomery ever wrote to Schuyler. His suspicions concerning Major Brown's complicity in the affair, was justified by facts. That officer and Arnold had quarreled on Lake Champlain, and there was a deadly feud between them. Forgetful of his duty to the cause, Brown made the dispute with Captain Hanchett an occasion to annoy Arnold, from the time they left Point aux Trembles, by widening the breach, and endeavoring to seduce the three captains named, from the command of their leader to that of his own. He was so far successful that the commanders and their companies threatened to leave the army unless they should be detached from Arnold's corps. "I must try every means to prevent their departure," wrote Montgomery to Schuyler. "In this matter I am much embarrassed. Their officers have offered to stay, provided they may join some other corps. This is resentment against Arnold, and will hurt him so much that I don't think I can consent to it."

Montgomery's wisdom and firmness finally healed the dissensions and restored order. At sunset on Christmas day, he reviewed Arnold's battalion at Morgan's quarters, and addressed them with warmth of sentiment and eloquence of expression. He then called a council of war, and it was agreed to make a night attack upon the Lower

* Autograph letter, December 26, 1775.

Town, much after the manner he had already proposed. One third of his men were to set fire to houses in St. Roque, so as to consume the stockade in that quarter of the British works, while the main body should attempt to take Cape Diamond bastion, by escalade, and thus gain command of the fortress and the Upper Town.

Preparations for the assault were carried on actively. Young Burr, now holding the rank of captain in Montgomery's military family, was eager for renown. He sought and obtained permission to lead a forlorn hope in scaling Cape Diamond bastion. He prepared his ladders and drilled his men with care. Every evening, while waiting for the dark and stormy night on which Montgomery had determined to make the attempt, he reconnoitered the proposed point of attack, and made himself thoroughly acquainted with every foot of the locality.

It was with impatience that Montgomery waited for the serene cold days and nights to pass away, and a stormy hour to begin. Favorable omens at length appeared. On the 30th, only the day before the expiration of the term of service of his troops, the air thickened, and early in the evening a snow storm from the northeast set in. His troops were now reduced by desertion and the small-pox to seven hundred and fifty men. But the brave General was not to be deterred from attempting the capture of the Canadian capital. No doubt he would have succeeded, had not false Canadians, who deserted, apprised the garrison of his plans. Carleton and McLean, and the loyal inhabitants and the garrison, were consequently on the alert. Two-thirds of the men lay on their arms, to be prepared for a surprise, and Carleton and other civilians slept in their clothes. Aware of all this, Montgomery again changed his plan of attack.

Colonel Livingston, with his corps, was directed to

make a feigned attack on St. Louis Gate, and set it on fire, and at the same time Major Brown was to menace Cape Diamond bastion. Arnold, with three hundred and fifty of his men, and forty of Lamb's artillery company, was to assail the works in the suburb St. Roque, while Montgomery with the remainder was to pass below Cape Diamond bastion, carry the defenses at the base of the declivity, and endeavor to press forward and form a junction with Arnold. Being thus in possession of the Lower Town, the combined forces were to carry Prescott gate, at the lower end of Mountain street, and rush into the city.

Montgomery gave orders for the troops to be ready at two o'clock on the morning of the 31st; and that they might recognize each other, each soldier was directed to fasten a piece of white paper to the front of his cap. Some of them wrote upon the paper the thrilling words of Patrick Henry, "LIBERTY OR DEATH."

At the appointed hour the troops were put in motion. The New Yorkers, commanded by Lieutenant-Colonel Campbell, and a party of Easton's corps, paraded at Holland House, and were led by Montgomery, in single file, down the ravine to Wolfe's cove, and thence along the St. Lawrence shore (now Champlain street), about two miles toward the barrier under Cape Diamond. Meanwhile Arnold, who had paraded with his division at Morgan's quarters, advanced from the General Hospital, on the banks of the St. Charles, through the suburb St. Roque, to attack the barrier below Palace Gate, and Brown and Livingston proceeded to their respective points of action.

The path along the St. Lawrence was exceedingly rough, being blocked with rocks, snow, and ice. The wind had increased almost to a gale. It came from the northeast, freighted with snow, sleet, and cutting hail, and blew furiously in their faces. The progress of the troops on both sides of the town was very slow, and Montgomery was yet some distance from his expected point of attack, when Brown's signal of assault on Cape Diamond bastion was given. He pushed forward with his aid-de-camp, Macpherson, and the companies of Captains Cheesman and Mott, and arrived at the first barrier before daylight. It was undefended, and Montgomery and the brave young Cheesman were the first to enter it after the carpenters who accompanied them, had sawed away some pickets. He sent messengers back to hurry on the remainder of the troops, and at the same time he pressed eagerly forward along the narrow shelf between the foot of the Cape Diamond cliff and the river, to observe the character of the way and the nature of the obstructions. He found a log building across the path, with loop-holes for musketry, and a battery of two small field-pieces. Perceiving no signs of life, he believed the garrison not to be on the alert. Burning with impatience and certain of success, about sixty of his men had passed the first picket barrier. Montgomery shouted, "Men of New York, you will not fear to follow where your General leads; push on, my boys, and Quebec is ours!" and rushed forward to surprise and take the battery.

But there had been vigilant eyes and ears within that log-house all this while. It was occupied by thirty Canadians and eight British militia-men, under Captain John Coffin, with nine seamen, under Captain Barnsfare (master of a transport), who acted as cannoniers. The noise on Cape Diamond had given them the alarm, and through the vail of snow, in the dim light of a winter's dawn, they had seen the republicans approaching. They waited until Montgomery and his men had gained a slight eminence within fifty yards of the mouths of their cannon, which were loaded with grape-shot, when Barnsfare gave the word, and they were discharged with deadly effect. Montgomery, Macpherson, Cheesman, and ten others in the narrow pass were slain. The remainder of the troops, appalled by the death of their general, fled in confusion toward Wolfe's Cove, when Lieutenant-Colonel Campbell, the quarter-master-general, being the senior officer, took the command.

Captain Samuel Mott was eager to go forward, but he was almost alone in sentiment. The other officers counseled a withdrawal. The deadly battery of cannon and musketry was pouring forth volley after volley, and Campbell, after brief consultation, ordered a retreat.

In the death of Macpherson and Cheesman, the cause of liberty lost two noble and gallant young champions. Only three weeks before, the former wrote to General Schuyler, saying:

> "Will you give me leave to mention to you my inclination to serve in some regiment in the new levies? The happiness I experienced while in yours, and since I have been of General Montgomery's family, is lessened when I reflect that I am but half a soldier, as being at head-quarters exempts me from many fatigues which others undergo. This, and a natural desire of rising, which is, I believe, common to every one, lead me to request the favor of your recommendation for such a commission as you think I deserve. If this takes place, I should not desire, on that account, to quit the present service till the reduction of Quebec (an event, I imagine, at no great distance), till when I think the service of all here indispensably necessary. After that, many of us may be spared."*

On the very day of the death of these gallant soldiers, Schuyler wrote to Montgomery—"I have warmly recommended Macpherson to Congress for a majority, happy if I can, at any time, serve so worthy a young gentleman."†

* Autograph letter, Dec. 6, 1775. † MS. Letter Books, Dec. 31, 1775.

Only a week before, young Cheesman wrote to his father, saying:

"I am now within one mile of Quebec, waiting for an opportunity, or rather a convenient time, to enter the city, which must be taken by storm. . . . Our army is dwindled away to almost nothing, officers as well as men. Every trifling disorder that overtakes them renders them unfit to remain longer with their company or in the service of their country. My company, only, keeps their officers, all of whom are in health, for which I thank that God who has hitherto preserved and given us victory. . . . I can't tell when I shall return home, for I can't do like many of my fellow-citizens—after putting my hand to the plow, look back; especially now, when my country calls loudly for assistance. I hope those who come to reinforce us will press forward, and not shrink, like numbers who came about the time I did in the service, both Yorkers and New England men. My love to brothers and sisters; my respects to Messrs. Franklin and inquiring friends, and duty to you and mamma."*

While these sad events were occurring on the St. Lawrence side of the town, Arnold was making his way through St. Roque to barriers on the St. Charles. The snow lay in huge drifts, and as he approached the Sault au Matelot the pathway was narrowed by heavy masses of ice, which the wind and tide had cast upon the shore.

It was before daybreak when Arnold, at the head of a forlorn hope of twenty-five men, passed the foot of the declivity below Palace Gate. The town was in an uproar. The bells of the city were ringing, the drums were beating a general alarm, the cannon were beginning to roar, and musketeers were mounting the walls. Arnold was accompanied by his secretary, Captain Oswald, and followed by Captain Lamb and his artillery, with a single field-piece upon a sled. Next to these were a party with ladders and other scaling implements, followed by Morgan and his riflemen; and in the rear of all was the main body, in number twice that of Montgomery's division. They were compelled

* Autograph letter, December 23, 1775.

to march in single file, and the drifts of snow became so deep, as the pathway narrowed, that Lamb and his company abandoned their cannon, and joined in the assault with small arms.

The first barricade was a two gun battery at the Sault au Matelot, a narrow place below a projecting crag of the promontory. Just as Arnold, with the advance, entered the narrow space leading to this battery, he was observed by the sentinels upon the walls, and the whole detachment were immediately exposed to an enfilading fire of musketry. Livingston, by some mistake, had failed to make the attack upon St. Louis Gate, and hence the attention of the enemy was not drawn off from Arnold's movements.

Arnold, with his forlorn hope, now rushed forward to attack the barrier, when he was severely wounded in the right leg, near the knee, by a musket ball that passed through it. He was completely disabled, and was borne away to the general hospital. Morgan's men immediately rushed forward and fired into the port-holes, while their leader, with Porterfield and others, mounted the redoubt by ladders, made prisoners of the captain and guard, and took possession of the battery with a shout that struck terror into the ranks of the enemy.

The command of Arnold's division now devolved on Morgan. The storm was beating furiously, and the cold was intense. Joined by Greene, Meigs, and Bigelow, the assailing party numbered about two hundred. Day was just dawning, and without guides or any knowledge of the way before them, they pressed forward in the morning twilight to the second barricade, at the eastern extremity of Sault au Matelot street. There the defenses extended from the rocky declivity to the river, and the present [1860] custom-house, then a private dwelling, had cannon projecting from the wings of the gable. A fierce contest ensued. For three hours the contestants fought desperately, and many were killed on both sides. Above the din of battle and the roar of the tempest, the voice of Morgan was heard encouraging his men, and at last the republicans gained the victory. They drove the British from their guns, captured the battery, and took refuge in the stone houses near. Captain Lamb was severely wounded in the cheek by a grape shot, and was borne off senseless; and other officers were more or less injured.

Inspirited by success, Morgan was preparing to push forward and force his way into the town, when news of sad disaster reached him. Captain Dearborn had been stationed near Palace Gate, in the rear, and was discovered by the sentinels at day-break. By that time Carleton was aware of the repulse at Cape Diamond and that Brown's attack was only a feint; he therefore directed all his energies against Arnold's division. He immediately dispatched a considerable force toward the suburb St. Roque, to gain the rear of the Americans. As they sallied out of Palace Gate, they surprised and captured Dearborn's corps, pressed onward to the Sault au Matelot, and cut off the retreat of the republicans from the lower town. Intelligence of this movement and of the retreat of Campbell, reached Morgan at the same time. He perceived that further efforts to penetrate the walled city would be vain without coöperation, and he proposed to his soldiers to cut their way through their enemies in the rear. This was impossible, and at ten o'clock, the brave leader of riflemen and the whole surviving party under him, four hundred and twenty-six in number, were surrendered prisoners of war. More than one hundred, it was estimated, had been killed and wounded. The remainder of Arnold's division, who were in the rear as a reserve, retreated, leaving the brass six pound field-piece imbedded in the snow.

Carleton, still fearing the disloyalty of the inhabitants of

Quebec, was afraid to send out troops in pursuit of the fugitive Americans; and their camp, formed by order of Arnold a short distance from the town, remained undisturbed. Although badly wounded and suffering severely, that intrepid officer was not for a moment forgetful of his duty. He had been borne through the snow to the general hospital on the St. Charles, exposed to the enfilading fire of the musketeers upon the walls of Quebec; and, while tortured with pain, he wrote a dispatch to General Wooster, giving an account of the disaster as far as he was informed (his detachment was yet fighting), and asking for immediate reinforcements; for, he declared in another letter, "I have no thoughts of leaving this proud town until I enter it in triumph. I am in the way of my duty, and I know no fear." Well would it have been for his memory, had he perished like Montgomery on that tempestuous morning, and been wrapped in the winding-sheet of deep snow-drifts.

When the contest was ended and the prisoners were secured, Carleton sent out a detachment to search for the body of Montgomery, his old companion-in-arms, whom he remembered as a noble young man, and beloved by Wolfe's army for his vivacity, generous spirit, and manly virtues. He was also well-known and fondly remembered by Lieutenant Governor Cramahé, Major Caldwell, and other officers in Quebec, who were with him at its conquest by the English in 1759. His body was found with those of Macpherson, Cheesman and others, at a point now called Pres-de-Ville, where he fell, shrouded in the snow-drifts. The bodies were conveyed into the city; and when that of Montgomery was identified, it is said Carleton pronounced over it a brief and touching eulogy, while his eyes were streaming with the tears of real sorrow. Cramahé took charge of the remains and buried them, with those of

Macpherson, within the fortifications of the city, where they reposed forty-two years, and were then conveyed to New York and deposited beneath a beautiful mural monument erected by order of Congress, on the exterior of the front wall of St. Paul's Church, in that city.

Intelligence of Montgomery's death went over the country, like the tolling of a funeral bell. His victories had awakened the voices of loudest praise in all parts of the land, and his death was felt as a personal bereavement by thousands who admired and loved him for his bravery and goodness. "Never was a city so universally struck with grief," wrote Thomas Lynch, in Philadelphia, to Schuyler, in Albany, "as this was, on hearing of the loss of Montgomery. Every lady's eye was filled with tears. I happened to have company at dinner, but none had inclination for any other food than sorrow or resentment. Poor, gallant fellow! If a martyr's sufferings merit a martyr's reward, his claim is indisputable. I am sure from the time he left Ticonderoga to the moment of his release by death, his sufferings had no interval. He now rests from his labor, and his works can't but follow him."*

The sad intelligence fell with blighting force upon the heart of Schuyler, who loved Montgomery as a brother. In his last letter to him, he had said, in conclusion—"Adieu, my dear sir; may I have the pleasure soon to announce another of your victories, and afterward, that of embracing you." Five days afterward in a brief letter to Washington, Schuyler wrote, "I wish I had no occasion to send my dear General the inclosed melancholy accounts. My amiable friend, the gallant Montgomery, is no more! The brave Arnold is wounded, and we have met with a very severe check in an unsuccessful attempt on Quebec. May heaven

* Autograph Letter, January 20th, 1776.

be graciously pleased to terminate the misfortune here! I tremble for our people in Canada."*

Schuyler sent an express to the Continental Congress with the sad intelligence of Montgomery's death; and that body, by resolution, decreed to "transmit to future ages, as examples truly worthy of imitation, his patriotism, conduct, boldness of enterprise, insuperable perseverance, and contempt of danger and death," by erecting a monument to be procured "from Paris or any other part of France," by Dr. Franklin, "with an inscription, sacred to his memory, and expressive of his amiable character and heroic achievements." They also requested the Rev. Dr. Smith, of Philadelphia, "to prepare and deliver a funeral oration in his honor."†

The opposition members of the British Parliament, with eloquent words spoke his praise. Chatham and Burke displayed some of their happiest specimens of eulogy, mixed with the keenest reproof of ministers; and Colonel Barre, who was a fellow-soldier with Montgomery in the last war, shed tears of real grief, as, upon the floor of the House of Commons, he expatiated upon the virtues of the slain hero. But the premier, Lord North, whose unwise measures had kindled the war, said, "I can not join in lamenting the death of Montgomery, as a public loss. He was undoubtedly brave, humane, and generous; but still he was only a brave, humane, and generous rebel. Curse on his virtues, they 've undone his country." Fox retorted—"The term rebel is no certain mark of disgrace. All the great assertors of liberty, the saviors of their country, the benefactors of mankind in all ages, have been called rebels. We owe the Constitution which enables us to sit in this House to a rebellion."

* MS. Letter Books, January 13th, 1776.

† Journals of Congress, January 25, 1776.

END OF VOL. I.

www.ingramcontent.com/pod-product-compliance
Lightning Source LLC
LaVergne TN
LVHW021322110826
845150LV00003B/644